# Rules of Engagement

Dedicated to the soldiers of Ireland who left their native land
to fight for the Crown so that small nations might be free.

# CONTENTS

# ACKNOWLEDGEMENTS

This book would not have been possible but for the dedication of the men of the 1st Battalion the Royal Irish Regiment and their dedication to duty. I also wish to acknowledge the accurate and balanced reporting of Sarah Oliver of the *Mail on Sunday* whose dispatches allowed me the opportunity to have my words heard by the world, as well as for taking many of the photographs which illustrate this book. I am indebted to the British and Irish public for their support during dark times with their numerous letters and cards of support, and particularly the Royal Ulster Rifles Association, the Kent Constabulary and the Police Service of Northern Ireland who had seen it all before.

Special thanks must go to Phil Ballard, my interpreter who did more than most men to ensure the success of our endeavours with his superb language skills, understanding and natural diplomacy. Many owe their very lives to him. I will forever be grateful to Lewis Cherry, sharp solicitor, defender of truth and champion of the innocent, for ensuring that the allegations against me were swiftly dispatched. My thanks, as always, to the men of the US Marines ANGLICOS, ably led by Stan Coeur who gave unstintingly in combat and was equally vigorous in my defence when the British Army turned on me.

In writing this book, the patience and guidance of Mark Lucas in helping me refine my ideas was invaluable. I owe a debt of thanks to Alex Gardiner, a friend and mentor, who also took many of the superb photographs. I am grateful for the friendship of Lieutenant Colonel Tim

Spicer OBE, Ronnie Patterson and all of the staff at Aegis Defence Services who gave me things to do when I was bored with writing, and who encouraged me to get on with it when the time came.

Additionally, I must thank the staff at Headline, especially Val Hudson who encouraged me in the writing of the book and Jo Roberts-Miller for her patient editing. I must, of course, acknowledge the support and love of my wife Caroline, my mother and my whole family in all my endeavours. Finally, I am indebted to the people of Iraq, who we went to liberate and not to conquer, and who made 1 R Irish and myself so welcome. I pray for happier times for them all.

# PROLOGUE

*25 May 2003*

The tip-off came from a Fleet Street contact that Saturday evening: something serious was brewing in the media, something 'pretty big'. I'd been under the cosh for the last week after being accused of war crimes, so I wondered how much bigger it could get.

But I was the Army's man through and through. I still believed I would quietly clear my name, safe within a system where, at the very least, my proven loyalty, rank and long service in the Field Army and Special Forces would stand me in good stead.

I called the Director of the Army's Corporate Communications and asked if he had heard of an impending attack. He said that he had heard something, but he dismissed it lightly; it was, after all, the weekend. I was reassured by his tone. Despite the rumours, the Army wouldn't let me down.

The next morning was my daughter Olivia's fifth birthday. We set off for church as usual and I bought the Sunday papers on the way home. I didn't open them immediately.

When I did so, I couldn't believe my eyes.

COLONEL TIM: NEW SHOCK ALLEGATIONS

Under a blazing banner headline, I was charged with setting on fire and executing a Ba'athist captive, while my fellow men of the Royal Irish were charged with massacring prisoners in cold blood.

My wife wept quietly and my older sons sat silently by. Olivia, in her innocence, skipped about in delight with her birthday presents and Henry, aged one, played happily on the floor, oblivious to the blow that had struck our family.

How, I wondered, could this have been allowed to happen? It was preposterous. I called the Army's press chief again, to reassure myself that my defences were in place. What was to be done? Who was planning to challenge this?

The answer chilled me. Nothing. No one. I was on my own.

# — 1 —

# SIERRA LEONE

*August 2000*

It was time for morning coffee and I was standing at the open window of my office, smoking a cigar. My room, on the top floor of the Duke of York's building in London's King's Road, was spacious, with a tour-brochure view. The structure had once been home to the Duke of York's Military School but was now occupied by various TA regiments as well as my place of work, the Headquarters of the Director of Special Forces, hidden away and accessible only by a side staircase. As I stood there contemplating my recent holiday in France and watching the well-heeled children in a private school play on the green in front of this grey building, I could see the first signs of autumn on the leaves of the mighty London plane trees below.

I was in the final months of my tour of duty on the staff before taking command of my regiment, the 1st Battalion the Royal Irish Regiment[1] (1 R Irish in the Army's nomenclature). As the lieutenant colonel responsible for the operations of the United Kingdom's Special Forces, arguably the world's most elite force, I was well used to surprises and fastballs. But nothing could have prepared me for the shock that awaited me that morning.

---

[1] The 1st Battalion the Royal Irish Regiment (27th Inniskillings, 83rd and 87th and Ulster Defence Regiment) is Ireland's only remaining line infantry battalion in the Field Army.

A clerk knocked and entered my office, waving a telegraph message marked Secret. 'You'll need to see this, sir,' he said, handing it to me and then watching me as I read the message. In stark army language it stated that eleven men of the 1 R Irish were missing in Sierra Leone. My blood ran cold. I threw away my cigar and walked down to the intelligence branch. I needed to establish the facts, as I knew that a call to the Director's office to brief him was minutes away. Further investigations revealed that some members of C Company had gone missing during a routine liaison visit. They were in all likelihood hostages of the self-styled 'West Side Boys', an armed faction with a history of reckless violence.

I was well aware, of course, that my future battalion was serving in the war-ravaged west African state of Sierra Leone, in the aftermath of the most recent British intervention against a rebel insurgency in that unhappy land. Having stabilised the country and driven off the rebels, the British Army were now engaged in an operation to support the democratic government and to train a new Sierra Leonean Army (SLA) on behalf of the President, Ahmed Tejan Kabbah.

As part of this effort, 1 R Irish had a contingent of 200 in the country. This consisted of a training team based on C Company and in addition a defence force, which accounted for the large size of the deployment, some eighty men above the usual company strength of around 120. It was the aim of the training team to turn the frightened conscripts of the SLA into a cohesive force with a clear command structure and the confidence to stand up to the rebels of the Revolutionary United Front (RUF), a Liberian-backed insurgency who threatened to take control of this chaotic but diamond- and mineral-rich country.

There had not always been chaos in Sierra Leone. When it was granted independence in 1961 under Prime Minister Sir Milton Margai, Sierra Leone had been one of the most well-ordered and affluent countries in west Africa. The future looked bright. Then in 1964 Sir Milton died, leaving no clear successor, and 'the Atlantic Switzerland' soon deteriorated under the weight of corruption, food shortages, tribal tensions and violence. The disintegration continued with a cycle of military coups and one-party states until it reached the point where, despite being extremely fertile, the country was unable to feed itself. In the 2000 United Nations index of Quality of Life it was ranked 174th out of 174. The local currency was worth 1/2000th of what it had been on independence. The once-prosperous streets of Freetown were now a jumble of ruins and shanty buildings.

I had barely heard of the place when I took over as Operations Officer at Stirling Lines, the SAS base in Herefordshire, back in December 1994, shortly after two British Voluntary Service Overseas workers had been taken hostage by the notoriously bloodthirsty RUF, led by an enigmatic figure called Foday Sankoh. The dialogue between Sankoh and Metropolitan Police negotiators was conducted by long-wave radio and featured Sankoh's bemoaning the state of Sierra Leone since independence and the endemic corruption. At this point what he was demanding in exchange for the hostages was for the UK to return as the colonial power. The negotiators persuaded him there would never be British troops there again, at least in any numbers. The hostages, who had been moved from jungle camp to jungle camp and had often had close access to Sankoh, were eventually returned a little slimmer but otherwise in good health.

The United Kingdom's Special Forces interest in Sierra Leone had been awakened. Over subsequent years we watched this almost casual insurgency gather pace, bringing that sad nation to its knees. As so often in Africa, the conflict was fuelled by greed (diamonds) and the ambitions of a neighbouring tyrant (Charles Taylor of Liberia, backed by Libya's Colonel Qaddafi) disputing the borders drawn by long-forgotten colonists.

By early 1995 the RUF had rediscovered their enthusiasm for hostage taking. They began with a large group of westerners, mainly missionaries, but the affable relations and good will of the previous occasion had disappeared and it wasn't long before one of them, Irish priest Father Edward Kerrigan, was murdered, allegedly for trying to escape. (The RUF blamed a botched Nigerian Army rescue attempt and said he had died in 'crossfire'.)

By February it looked as if the RUF had a serious chance of capturing the capital and taking power. A number of the larger civilian companies began hiring security guards. As his ragged, under-age and poorly paid military crumbled, Captain Valentine Strasser[2], who had taken power in a 1992 coup, followed suit. He engaged the services of the Gurkha Security Guards, led by a Canadian, Captain Robert MacKenzie. A veteran of Vietnam with the US Airborne and the Rhodesian SAS, Mackenzie brought a force of around fifty retired Gurkhas, with the aim of training and then leading the Sierra Leonean Army against the rebels.

---

[2] Strasser was deposed by his deputy, Captain Julius Bio, in 1996. He now works as a doorman in a club in south London.

During one of his first forays into the jungle, he and a small team found themselves deserted by the men they had come to protect and surrounded by the RUF. MacKenzie was killed in action, along with his British second in command and one of his Gurkha officers. The rebels cooked and ate the dead mercenaries, savouring their livers in particular in the belief that they would absorb their fighting power by doing so. Not surprisingly this sent a shockwave through Sierra Leonean society, and the remaining Gurkhas withdrew.

Desperate for help, Strasser turned to the South Africa-based Executive Outcomes (EO), which had enjoyed significant success in Angola and could call on ex-members of the South African Defence Force and their considerable experience of such conflicts. Within a month of arriving, they had stopped the RUF in its tracks.

EO built on these successes with further raids into the RUF heartland while conducting a hearts-and-minds operation among the local population. In particular they forged an alliance with the Kamajor, warrior hunters of the indigenous Mende tribe. The Kamajor, brought up in the jungle, were at one with the forest. Deeply immersed in the animist beliefs of the region and black magic, they relied on wood spirits and magic charms to guide them and protect them from harm. Operating deep in the forest, they struck fear into the hearts of their sworn enemies, the RUF, who would often awake to find a sentry with his neck broken or discover that whole patrols had fallen silent quarry to these jungle predators.

As the threat from the RUF receded and confidence was restored, the UN dared to venture back into the country and arrange democratic elections. With the return of stability in March 1996, and perhaps forgetting how that stability was achieved, a number of governments brought pressure on the newly elected President Kabbah to terminate the EO contract and rid Sierra Leone of private military firms. He complied, and the last elements of Executive Outcomes had withdrawn by March of 1997. Kabbah was overthrown and living in exile within three months.

His successor as President, an ex-convict called Johnny Paul Koroma, set up the Armed Forces Revolutionary Council, which included the RUF and the group from which Koroma himself had sprung, the infamous West Side Boys. Once more the country collapsed into anarchy and the UK and US mounted an evacuation. Only a hard core of Lebanese and the odd British national opted to stay.

The crisis deepened. Sandline International, led by Lieutenant Colonel

Tim Spicer OBE, restored Kabbah to power. The Nigerian-led ECOMOG[3] along with the Sandline-backed Kamajors secured the capital and restored a form of democracy. The UN stepped in, sending seventy observers as part of the United Nations Mission, UNAMSIL, who quickly became targets for the RUF. In August 1999 the Lome Peace Accord, signed by Kabbah and Foday Sankoh, gave the rebels a blanket amnesty and offered power sharing. The sprit of this amnesty was to add to the confusion of later events, especially the question of who were and who were not friendly forces in the eyes of the British troops who were sent there. Easter 2000 saw the shattering of the fragile peace. Sankoh and the RUF were now bitterly anti-British, corrupted by greed and furious at the British support for the democratically elected government.

In the face of a crumbling UNAMSIL force, now over 11,000 strong, the RUF drove for the capital, aiming to cut off the airport at Lungi, where previous evacuations had been mounted, killing, abusing and raping all before them. Those they spared were asked if they wished for 'long sleeves' or 'short sleeves'; they had their arms cut off to order in accordance with their response. The UK, concerned that the capture of Lungi Airport would remove any hope of intervention from the outside world, went into crisis mode.

The only resistance within Sierra Leone came from the truculent West Side Boys and the Kamajor tribesmen. The WSB, volatile and mercurial, took on the RUF as they advanced on Freetown, but in doing so bought time for the UK's intervention. Without it, the RUF would have seized Freetown and driven the UN into the sea. By the time UK forces arrived, there was a complex situation of a war: the RUF versus the WSB versus the Kamajors versus the RUF, with the ECOMOG and UN running for their lives.

As the RUF advanced, Major Andy Harrison of the Parachute Regiment was among those captured. He escaped to find refuge with the 500 men of the 8th Simoor Gurkha Rifles, Indian Army Gurkhas, who were themselves surrounded near the town of Kailahun in the east of the country. The Kenyan contingent, seventy-two strong, was also under siege. It was clearly time for action. The Indian general, Vijay Kumar Jetley, head of the UN contingent, was under severe pressure from the UN and his national government.

---

[3] Economic Community of West African States Ceasefire Monitoring Group, a peacekeeping force of local states, but led by the Nigerians.

I was on leave, golfing in southern Ireland, when the call came to mobilise. By the time I was back at my desk a sizable force was being assembled. Operation Palliser was coordinated from the Ministry of Defence's Crisis Management Centre (CMC), five storeys beneath the MOD in Whitehall and connected to the outstations – Headquarters Land at Wilton, RAF Strike Command and the Joint Headquarters in Northwood – by fibre-optic links. This subterranean village comprised sleeping accommodation, mess halls, briefing rooms and a large conference room where the service chiefs could talk to the key headquarters by video link from high-backed swivel chairs. It was accessible only with a special pass via a guarded airlock.

As the Special Forces representative, I watched the action unfold from both the CMC and COBRA, the Cabinet Office Briefing Room on the other side of Whitehall. COBRA was the executive forum. In contrast to CMC, it was an open-plan room with soundproof booths around the walls, where departmental staff could consult with the outside world as meetings progressed. While CMC was the preserve of senior military men, COBRA attracted cabinet ministers.

For the first few days of the crisis, the tenor was calm and the Government's approach was to attempt to re-implement the Lome Peace Accord of August 1999 through diplomatic channels. By 6 May 2000, however, little hope of a diplomatic solution remained. Only intervention could prevent a humanitarian crisis that threatened to rival the excesses of Rwanda in terms of horror. Only the UK had the forces and political will to act. There was, quite simply, no choice but to strike and no time to lose.

CH-47 Chinook helicopters flew an epic journey from the UK via Gibraltar and Senegal, and the Commando carrier HMS *Ocean* made best speed from the Mediterranean. The 1st Battalion of the Parachute Regiment (1 Para) were flown into theatre by heavy transport aircraft, along with a significant deployment of SAS.

By this time over 1,000 UN personnel had been surrounded, captured or killed by the rebels. On arrival in Sierra Leone, the UK forces surprised the warring factions and quickly secured Freetown, and more importantly the airport. Foday Sankoh, convinced that the British foothold was a tenuous one, went to the capital to whip up support for his insurgency, believing that a personal appearance would spark a popular rising, but he had badly miscalculated his appeal to the masses and was mobbed by locals and captured on the outskirts of Freetown.

He was dragged off to prison in his pink underpants, where he was to die some years later, awaiting trial.

With Freetown secure, we settled down to see if the RUF would back off. It soon became clear that despite Sankoh's arrest, the influence of nearby Liberia was stiffening their resolve, and the Indian Government's patience was running out. Having provided the commander and one of the more effective contingents to the force, the situation was seen as a major humiliation for them. I briefed the Chief of the Defence Staff, Sir Charles Guthrie, on a joint UK/Indian plan to relieve the besieged force. We then walked across the hall to put Geoff Hoon, the Secretary of State for Defence, and Dr Lewis Mooney, Minister for Armed Forces, in the picture.

The morning of Saturday 10 July 2000 was sunny in London, but there was low cloud and heavy rain in Sierra Leone. UK CH-47s landed Indian Special Forces at the approaches to Kailahun and then lifted out around sixty noncombatant personnel, the UN observers and Major Harrison from the besieged Gurkha camp. Many of the RUF fighters, their senses dulled by the night's drinking and drug-taking, were to see their last dawn through bloodshot eyes as the Gurkhas moved silently among them.

Indian Special Forces secured the exit points before joining the Gurkhas in their uncompromising progress towards the town of Daru, sixty miles to the south, while the Indian Army Grenadiers made their way towards the besieged Indian Gurkhas in Kailahun, supported by artillery. They lost one sergeant and suffered a small number of wounded. Six hundred men were recovered, along with all of the 8th Gurkhas' regimental property and silver. The RUF were smashed to pieces.

Having stabilised the country and driven off the rebels, the British Army launched an operation to support the democratic government and train a new Sierra Leonean Army on behalf of President Kabbah. By August the men of 1 R Irish were working with their new and enthusiastic recruits at a camp in Benguema, south-east of the capital. Many believed that even the West Side Boys were on the brink of leaving the jungle to join the training.

Their capture of eleven of our men came without warning.

The Royal Irish was my parent regiment. I had served with them for six years, until I was volunteered for SAS selection in 1988. I was now on my third Special Forces tour and had only been back with the Royal Irish for a two-year tour as a company commander before being summoned back to Special Forces and my current job in London. My command for those two years with the Royal Irish had been C Company – the very men who were in captivity. I knew them extremely well. One of the two officers captured, a captain, was an old boy of my school and his father had taught me Maths. The sergeant major who had been captured had been in my platoon as a soldier when I was a young officer and I'd known both him and his brother since they were teenagers. This was brought home to me when I went into the intelligence cell one morning and was confronted by a line of photographs. A shiver ran down my spine. I would move heaven and earth to get the boys out.

As I briefed the Director of Special Forces on the latest situation in Africa, he listened intently, his face a mask of concentration. We were sitting in deep leather armchairs in his corner office, surrounded by oil paintings from the National Army Museum collection. Dominating the room was a tapestry from Egypt that showed the vulture god, his wings outspread. It is said that this tapestry inspired the founder of the SAS, David Stirling, in the design of the distinctive SAS wings. When I had finished, we sat in contemplative silence. The Director lit a cheroot. Finally, he looked up and asked my staff major to get over to Main Building[4] and find out what he could.

As we prepared to leave, he said, 'I see they're your boys. How do you feel?'

I was aware that he was watching my face closely. 'Embarrassed. Worried too. I know them all – it was my last command before I came here.'

'You won't let that bother you, will you?'

'Luckily I'm schizophrenic,' I said. 'I've got my SAS trousers on today.'

The small group led by the commander of C Company had been captured when they had gone to see the West Side Boys on a routine liaison visit after lunch with the Jordanian contingent of the UN. Inspired perhaps by the part apparently played by the West Side Boys in delaying the RUF advance five months earlier, or perhaps by the protestations of loyalty to Kabbah's regime by Johnny Paul Koroma, former head of the West Side Boys and now a colleague of the President, the small patrol seemed to expect at least a courteous if not a warm welcome from this enigmatic group[5]. That, after all, was the spirit of the

---

[4] MOD in Whitehall.

[5] At the time there was a widespread acceptance that the excesses in Sierra Leone were such that an amnesty of sorts would have to be given, if only to bring the large numbers of armed men at large, as well as child soldiers, back into the fold. There was a general optimism that the West Side Boys would be among the first to come out of the cold.

Lome Accord. No one knew at the time that these erstwhile allies of the local government, led by the deranged scavenger 'Brigadier' Kallay, were in the throes of a drink and drugs party of epic proportions.

Kallay, a defector from the RUF, had taken command of the West Side Boys after Johnny Paul Koroma had left. With about 300 West Side Boys, Kallay had set up base in a haphazard collection of huts by Rokel Creek, a fast-flowing river fed from the nearby Occra Hills, from which they terrorised the immediate area.

The eleven-man C Company patrol was in three Land-Rovers, two fitted with radios and one a stripped-down reconnaissance version with an American Browning .5 inch heavy machine gun. The first sign of things going wrong was when they were confronted by 100 armed men at a roadblock outside Magbeni, a small village about fifteen miles from Freetown, on the bank of the creek that marked the border of the West Side Boys' territory.

The West Side Boys acted swiftly. A flatbed Bedford lorry mounted with an anti-aircraft gun slid across the road to the rear of our patrol to cut off the escape. This, and the aggressive reaction of the WSB commander, the self-styled 'Colonel Savage', told the British company commander all he needed to know. He sensibly decided to lay down their weapons, but not before one of his soldiers had the presence of mind to switch the powerful heavy machine gun from fully automatic to single shot. In the days that followed, the rebels never figured out how to switch it back.

Once the West Side Boys had gathered the patrol together, our men were beaten and robbed. The Company Commander, Regimental Signals Officer, Company Sergeant Major, an intelligence sergeant, three corporals and four rangers[6] had become hostages to one of the most depraved and volatile groups in Africa. Also captured with them was Mousa, the SLA guide, a young corporal. Much of the anger and excessive behaviour of the captors was to be directed towards him.

Thankfully the beating ended when the West Side Boys' attitude suddenly changed, presumably on direction from higher command, and the captives were taken across the river to the heavily guarded village. This swing between subjecting the captives to atrocious behaviour and treating them in a friendly manner was to be a feature of their captivity. In the sixteen days that followed, they were frequently beaten and

---

[6] A 'ranger' is the term used in 1 R Irish for a private soldier.

11

threatened with death. They were also to witness the rape, murder and torture of innocent African captives, conducted against a backdrop of drink- and drug-fuelled debauchery.

The West Side Boys, in keeping with many armed groups in Africa, obtained a lot of their recruits as abducted children. These would be brutalised by beatings and sexual abuse while being fed a constant cocktail of drink and drugs before eventually being turned into killers themselves. The West Side Boys would also take young girls as sex slaves and older women as cooks and manual labourers. These African 'warriors' would spend their day drunk or high on drugs, indulging in whatever abuse they fancied, including the random murder of captives. From time to time they would sally forth to attack villages and take recruits, who would then be led back to the camp to have their heads shaved before being indoctrinated and eventually initiated into the West Side Boys' group in a voodoo ceremony that was also supposed to bring protection from gun shots. On other occasions they would capture children as they played on the fringes of villages, using ruses such as the 'Monkey Jump Game', in which they would don monkey skins and masks to leap out of the bush, howling like apes. The children, frozen by terror at the sight of these creatures, would then be dragged back to their base. In captivity the British soldiers could only watch helplessly as these captives led their lives of misery.

The Royal Irish Commanding Officer undertook most of the negotiations for the release of his men. He was an able and clever man, who with the help of Metropolitan Police negotiators was able to effect a rapport with the terrorists. We in London knew that the hostage takers were impressed by his seniority and enjoyed talking to him as 'equals', and I'm in no doubt that he kept them as calm as possible and so bought time for a potential rescue operation. I say 'potential' operation with some care. Within COBRA there was a smaller group called the Cabinet Office Group, which was chaired by a senior civil servant. The attitude of this group was clear throughout the crisis: if possible, the hostage situation should be resolved by negotiation. There was no malicious intent to use this opportunity to attack the West Side Boys or anyone else. There was to be no military option until all other lines of communication had broken down. While this was understandable, it didn't make the military man's job any easier.

The highlight of the negotiations was the release of five hostages in exchange for a satellite telephone, an event which was celebrated in the

West Side Boys' camp by another drink and drugs party, and for a while the captives were feted and well treated by their jailers.

Initially the married men were selected to be released. At the last moment, however, the hostage takers decided to keep the Regimental Signals Officer, along with his signals corporal, which allowed two other men to go free. It was agreed that they would draw lots to decide who would have the two tickets to freedom from their living hell. The major counted himself out, so of the six men left, the sergeant and four rangers, two would be going free. The Signals Officer was about to make the draw when the Intelligence Sergeant, a lanky taciturn Belfast man, stepped forward and said, 'Take my name out. I'll stay. We'll let a youngster go.' The impact of that selfless act on the morale of those who had to stay was incalculable. Two soldiers, one a talented footballer from Belfast, the other from the Curragh, HQ of the Republic of Ireland's Army, went to freedom. Two rangers stayed behind with the Major, the Captain, the Sergeant and a Corporal. I cannot imagine how difficult it must have been for them to wave off their comrades as they went to freedom.

We met in COBRA every day for the duration of the crisis. The release of the five soldiers gave us some reason for optimism, but it was short-lived. The West Side Boys allowed their small triumph to go to their heads, and their approach thereafter swung between the hostile and the ridiculous. One minute they demanded to leave Sierra Leone on safe passes to the UK to attend college; the next they outlined their plans to take over the country.

When COBRA gathered on Thursday 7 September, the atmosphere was sombre. The Director of Special Forces had deployed forward to Sierra Leone and was controlling events on the ground. We had had men with 'eyes on' the target area for the last two days. A close reconnaissance team had deployed across the treacherous mangrove swamps by boat and foot and even swimming right up to the fringe of the terrorist camp, but they hadn't seen the hostages for twenty hours.

From what could be seen by the patrol, what was gleaned from Human Intelligence reports (HUMINT), and the observations of the hostage negotiators, we had put together a reasonably detailed intelligence picture. It was believed that the hostages, if they were alive, were being held in huts beside a football pitch, covered by a Russian-made DShK 12.7mm heavy machine gun. Our captured vehicles, complete with .5 inch machine gun, were on the far side of the river and if crewed could also bring fire to bear on the planned landing zone. Firing bullets that could breeze through the most resilient body armour, destroy an engine at a single hit and even smash their way from one end of a Chinook to the other, both of these guns would have to be dealt with in the opening seconds of the rescue or the consequences could be disastrous.

There had been a worrying hostility at the most recent meeting between the hostage negotiators and the West Side Boys. It was clear that the rebels were making preparations to move off and we had no idea where to. If they did so, future rescue attempts would be considerably more complicated. With drafts passing between HQ DSF and the Task Force Headquarters on the ground, we refined our strategy.

Initially there had been a 'deliberate plan', a technical term for an operation mounted at a time and place of our choosing, and a back-up 'emergency action plan' in case things went wrong. This would be cruder and less certain, but available at short notice in response to actions by the hostage takers. The deliberate plan had been to forward-mount troops to the fringes of the camp and, using the still of early morning and surprise, stalk up to the hostages and spirit them away before the West Side Boys even became alerted to their presence. Then, using a distraction to catch the terrorists' attention, the troops would overpower them and release the African men, women and children who were also held as captives. But it had become clear that the going in the jungle would make the approach too difficult. Stealthy movement through the mangroves was impossible – it was slow and noisy – and, taken with the deteriorating situation, it meant that we would have to be bold.

The fact that we had not had 'proof of life' for the hostages for twenty-four hours clinched the matter. We would go with an enhanced emergency action plan. (Enhanced in that we would be choosing the timing of the assault.) This involved a daring helicopter assault at first light right on top of the hostage takers' base. As we considered the plan, my eyes wandered to an SAS badge on the wall outside my office. The symbol of the SAS is a winged dagger – the instrument of destruction borne on the wings of opportunity, fledged with the feathers of death. The motto 'Who Dares Wins' seemed particularly apt for our latest plan. Only daring would succeed. Our instrument of destruction was in place in the form of the assault force, and we would choose the opportunity. That evening we had to consider those feathers and assess the potential cost in lives.

Finally we produced the plans in graphic form, ready for a briefing that would decide the fate of many lives and potentially our nation's reputation.

I set off for our house in Wandsworth to snatch some sleep. As I travelled in the taxi I carried an added burden. Once I was away from the infectious optimism of the HQ, the cool evening air made me consider again the terrible thought that the men I knew so well, who would have known I would be involved in planning their rescue, were possibly already beyond human help. As the taxi drove along one road I would be thinking, 'They've probably decided to lie low to rest. They'll be run down by the environment. That's why we haven't seen them.' In the next street I would be gazing out of the window, thinking, 'I hope it was quick. I hope they didn't suffer.'

When I got home, the kitchen was lined with birthday cards. Only then did I remember it had been my son's eighth birthday. He had carefully arranged his presents on the kitchen table so that I would see them on my return. I left the next morning before anyone else had got up.

There was a briefing scheduled with the Secretary of State and Chief of the Defence Staff (CDS) before the main COBRA session. I met Geoff Hoon in the loos just before we went in. As we washed our hands, he asked, 'Have we met before?'

'Yes, sir,' I replied. 'I briefed you on an operation in July.'

'Oh yes – that was a brilliant stroke.'

'Let's hope this is too,' I said.

The DSF's Chief of Staff briefed the plan. It fell into two parts: Operation Barras, the rescue, and Operation Amble, which aimed to involve the local SLA on the periphery, in order to give them some apparent credit for the outcome and to demonstrate the effectiveness of the British training to any other not-so-innocent bystanders.

We would strike at dawn. The Chinooks would suppress known enemy billets on their approach, and their door gunners would take down the 12.7mm heavy machine gun as they landed on the football pitch. SAS teams already in place would provide covering fire. Simultaneously, Lynx helicopters from the Special Forces detachment would strafe the area to the south of the river, preventing use of the captured vehicles and more importantly the captured machine gun, keeping reinforcements at bay and creating an opportunity for the Para distraction force to land and assault the rebel village of Gberi Bana to the south.

The main assault troops, guided from the football pitch by the observation teams already in place, would close in on the hostages and take them to safety. A four-man team would go after Kallay. We wanted him alive. A sixteen-strong troop would cover the rescue force and dispatch any West Side Boys who tried to interfere.

Finally, the Chief of Staff detailed the possible butcher's bill. We might not get the hostages. We might lose a Chinook, up to sixty SAS and, in all likelihood, the 1 R Irish hostages as well. We probably wouldn't get all the African hostages out alive, and we were most unlikely to nail Kallay.

He glanced at me with a 'mission accomplished' look and stepped out from behind his lectern. Everyone seemed satisfied with the plan but then, to my astonishment (because it had been agreed in principle in his office the previous day), CDS announced that he wasn't happy about the SLA taking a role. Despite protestations from the representative from the Prime Minister's office, that part of the plan was dropped.

We adjourned to the main conference room and a sanitised version of the plan was briefed by CDS himself. I stood at the back in the Special Forces booth, with the DSF on the secure telephone. 'It's on,' I said, 'but we've lost the SLA bit.'

'Good. Great. Bugger,' was his reply.

We went back to our offices. It was game on. By now, within my heart I didn't expect to see any of the captives again. But we had to try, and there was a lesson to be delivered. As the conclusion of the 1980 Iranian Embassy siege rang a big alarm bell for a whole generation of would-be terrorists, so this mission had to discourage the RUF and their kind from interfering with British servicemen when they come calling with their hands extended. I put it more succinctly. Make it Biblical.

The final meeting between the hostage takers and the negotiating team was due to take place on the afternoon of Friday 8 September, but as the delegation arrived it was clear that there was an unusual amount of tension. They turned and left before the West Side Boys decided to take them too. As they did so, one of the major WSB players, who called himself 'Colonel General Staff' or GS, collared one of the soldiers escorting the negotiating team. 'You tell your friends that if I see you again I will cut off your head and eat you. Tell them!'

The guard remained impassive. 'I'll bear that in mind,' he said.

'No,' GS insisted, 'if we meet again, one of us must die!'

Little did he know the man he was talking to was an SAS sergeant.

*

The mission went ahead early on Sunday 10 September. Far beyond hope or expectation, we extricated all of our men, and all but one of the African hostages. We also got Kallay alive. But it was not without cost. 1 Para suffered casualties in the diversionary attack that secured the south bank of the river, and an SAS trooper, former airborne gunner Brad Tinnion, was shot in the chest in the first seconds of the assault, when a Special Forces helicopter landed and the SAS stormed forward in the face of fierce opposition from the terrorists. Brad was evacuated on the helicopter, along with several other wounded. Every effort was made to keep him alive. A needle was inserted through his ribs and connected to a two-pint drain to control the flow of blood into his chest and sustain his breathing, but he died on the operating table of the hospital ship in Freetown harbour.

The West Side Boys did less well. Dozens of bodies were brought back to Freetown on helicopters. Quite a few had tried to escape into the jungle, or by leaping into the fast-flowing, crocodile-infested river at Rokel Creek. I held out little hope for their survival. 'Colonel General Staff' did get to meet his SAS friend again. But he didn't get to eat anybody.

As a souvenir of the rescue, a blood-spattered Heckler and Koch G3[7] was presented to me by the CO of the battalion. I had it mounted on the wall of my office. Sadly for the brave men of 1 R Irish, while the media and the British military hierarchy celebrated the success of the rescue, they virtually ignored the men who had been held in captivity. The only people who showed any interest in them were Brigadier Peter Wall, Commander 16 Air Assault Brigade, and the Colonel-in-Chief, His Royal Highness the Duke of York. Not for the first time, the men and their families had reason to thank this frequent visitor.

The battalion was delighted to receive warm messages of congratulation from the President of Ireland, Mary McAleese. From the British Government there wasn't a word.

---

[7] The 1st Battalion Parachute Regiment recovered two rifles to be deactivated as souvenirs of their part. The rifles were old British Army self-loading rifles. It was only when they were back in the UK that it was discovered from the serial numbers that one of the rifles was actually an old 1 Para rifle. It was used on 'Bloody Sunday' in Londonderry in 1972 when thirteen protesters had been shot – and it had been declared destroyed when the Saville inquiry into the shootings had asked for it.

# —2—

# TAKING CHARGE

*January 2001*

1 R Irish was a 690-strong battalion in the UK's elite rapid intervention 16 Air Assault Brigade, working alongside the 1st, 2nd and 3rd Battalions of the Parachute Regiment. It was trained to move light and fight, if necessary, behind enemy lines. When I moved with my family into the Commanding Officer's residence in Howe Barracks, Canterbury, I was forty years old.

Howe Barracks is part of what had once been a large garrison. The camp that we lived in had been the Regimental Training Depot of 'The Buffs' (East Kents). The guardroom there had the dubious distinction of once holding the Kray twins when they were doing their National Service. It was an attractive place built of rustic red brick, on a site that had been a barracks since Roman times. It had received the attentions of the Luftwaffe in 1941 and there was a memorial to the nineteen men who had lost their lives in the attacks. Set on the edge of the city and covering a square mile, it was surrounded by sports pitches and parkland.

It was a picturesque place to be stationed, but the Royal Irish battalion had been on operations for each of the previous years since 1994 and had barely become acquainted with it since moving there in 2000 from its former base in Catterick. The married officers and soldiers lived in Army houses near the barracks. Quebec House, my residence, was one of three large houses on camp. The single men lived in accommodation blocks. Sergeants lived in the warrant officers' and sergeants' mess. Single officers lived in the officers' mess. This was a mixture of smart country house hotel and museum, decked out with objects, silver and paintings acquired over the last 300 years. Generations of officers had donated these pieces during their service. Some, like our grandfather clock, were bought as a memento of a campaign, and not a small amount would have been booty. Generally the rule was that captured silver would be melted down and made into something else. I have no doubt that the silver candelabras with a Dublin hallmark of 1818 were once the silver ornaments and cutlery of some French regiment's mess. The only exception was Empress Josephine's mirror, captured at Waterloo, which was now a base for an elaborate silver fruit bowl. The oil paintings showed scenes from our history, the storming of the Indian Mutineer citadel at Jhansi in 1857 when we won three VCs, the capture of a French imperial eagle at Barossa in 1812 or the Inniskillings storming ashore at Gallipoli, in 1915. Some had poignant personal touches. The picture of Captain Gerry O'Sullivan winning his VC on the heights above Achi Baba was commissioned as a memorial (he was killed three days later and his body was never found). Because the artist had not shown his face, it was sent back and amended. Now, on some nights, in the candlelight of a mess dinner, an observant eye could see the outline of a ghostly figure, albeit painted out, leaning forward to throw a grenade behind the new image of Gerry, his face now clearly shown. A great deal of it had become very valuable too; some watercolours (twenty-two of them) that Field Marshal Gerry Templar had bought as Colonel of the Regiment in 1965 for £400 were now worth in excess of £4,000 each.

Arriving back in the battalion was like coming home for my family and myself. I knew the vast majority of the men, with the exception of those who had joined over the previous two years, and even they were often from places I knew or were related to old comrades. Some, like my next-door neighbour and Battalion second in command, John Douglas, I had known since we were at school together. Mike, commanding B Company, lived in the house on the other side with his wife Georgie and two little boys. I had known him since he was a 'potential officer', studying at Trinity College Dublin. Mike was also from Belfast but an old boy of St Malachy's College, the leading Catholic boys' school in the city.

The senior soldier at the time was Jim Pritchard, the Regimental Sergeant Major, solid and dependable and deeply immersed in the life of the regiment. His brother was in the mortar platoon and his wife's father had been the quartermaster and a legendary figure in the regiment, until his untimely death of a heart attack on the very evening of his retirement.

A commanding officer needs a strong administrator at his side and I had Sean, a County Sligo man as my adjutant. He was responsible for keeping the young officers in line and had their healthy respect. The senior officer who had been commissioned from the ranks was Paddy, the Quartermaster. He hailed from Catholic west Belfast and was both respected and feared for his high standards and incredible eye for detail. Known as the 'Dark Lord', he was always a reliable source of advice for me.

Despite thirty years of violence in Northern Ireland, and the fact that Eire was a separate sovereign state, large numbers of men from both communities, and from both sides of the border, served in 1 R Irish. Our history long predated the civil strife in Northern Ireland, and the men who volunteered today were little different from those who had manned the British Army for the last three hundred years. The Duke of Wellington, Montgomery, Alexander, Auchinleck and Dill, to name but a few, were all Irish, as were up to a third of British soldiers in all regiments during the 19th century.

The number of Irishmen who volunteered for the First and Second World Wars is a testament to a tradition of service that has been forgotten all too often. My father, who grew up in Dublin, was a small boy when the 1916 Easter Rising swept through the city. When his mother took him to see the Sinn Fein rebels being led through the streets to be shipped to jail in England, he vividly remembered the violent hostility of the crowd. Women whose husbands, brothers and sons were in the trenches in Flanders spat at, abused and stuck hatpins into the prisoners as they passed. But their loyal abhorrence of *any* traitors to the Crown was turned at a stroke when General Maxwell took the decision to shoot twelve of the rebel leaders. That single, thoughtless act turned the machinations of a group of fanatics into the will of a people. It was a lesson I was determined never to forget.

Within the Army, though, more deep-seated loyalties prevailed. The willingness of Irishmen from both sides of the border to volunteer in times of crisis remained undimmed. The spirit of the men who had defended the Brussels crossroads against the French Imperial Guard at Waterloo, who had swept through the supposedly impregnable Schwaben Redoubt on the first day of the Battle of the Somme, and who had landed by air and sea on D-Day, still animated the young men who filled our ranks. Many of them, even today, were leaving Ireland for the first time. Kipling once said that 'the Irish move to the sound of the guns like salmon to the sea'. Perhaps he was right.

A total of nineteen nationalities served within our ranks. 'Jimmy the Shark' hailed from Trinidad; we had twenty-two Fijians; there was even an Iranian. People's backgrounds did not matter and the old Irish Argument was left in Ireland, as were all other potentially divisive grudges. We had a Muslim and a Jewish officer serving in the same company, and one of my South African lads, brought up in the Orange Free State and speaking English as his second language, shared a room with three Fijians. We even had two Gypsies from families at daggers drawn, and that rivalry too was left at home.

Prejudice of any sort was unforgivable in such an environment. A single culture – that of the Royal Irish Regiment and Ireland as a whole – was what defined them. Our traditions were worn with pride, within the Army and beyond. From our distinctive green caubeens[8] to our pipers' saffron kilts, our appearance – not to mention our accents – had always marked out the men of 1 R Irish as something special.

Our origins in 1 R Irish stretched back to 1689. Since then, Irish regiments have served across the world and in most of the wars the British have fought. 1 R Irish has 147 battle honours that we carried with pride on our regimental flags: 'The Colours'. A selection of world war battle honours was displayed on the union flag or 'Queen's Colour'. A selection of our numerous campaigns in the wars of empire was carried on the 'Regimental Colour', a green flag with a harp and crown surrounded by a sheaf of shamrock (our badge).

My family had served in this regiment as far back as anyone could remember. My father's great-uncle had fought with the regiment in the Indian Mutiny of 1857. My father would tell me how, as a little boy, he had sat on his knee and heard stories of that terrible war. We still had his pistol, a black powder Colt revolver supplied by Thos Weekes & Sons, Essex Quay, Dublin. The case had been made in India in happier times, from a strange but beautiful wood with a chestnut-like grain shot through with black flecks. My granny had numerous brothers who had served in India and her son, my uncle, had served in Burma with the Chindits[9] and commanded a battalion in the regiment decades before

---

[8] Irish Gaelic for headdress.
[9] A commando force operating behind Japanese lines, led by the charismatic maverick Orde Wingate.

me. My mother's father had settled his affairs on the day the First World War broke out and signed on with the regiment exactly one week after the declaration of war, only to be gassed on the Somme and discharged as a broken invalid. He died, horribly, of his injuries years later. I have his medals framed, and his documents in a chest, along with an Imperial five-pfennig piece given to him by a German prisoner he had looked after during the March 1916 offensive.

I was not the only one with family connections. Many men in the battalion had relatives who had served together in previous wars. One major had a great-uncle who had commanded the platoon in which my grandfather served and had been killed in action leading it in France. We had a total of five sets of fathers and sons serving in the battalion and numerous sets of brothers and countless cousins or in-laws. For us, family was crucial.

Getting to grips with the job of leading an organisation like this was a matter of delegating responsibility and making your intentions clear. I could not have had a more effective team. In my early days in command I tried to get around the companies to get to know them better. Accompanied by the RSM and sometimes the Quartermaster (QM), I would drop into departments or observe training, before being dragged back to the office for the inevitable paperwork Sean would pile neatly in my in-tray. I had a quiet corner office in Battalion HQ with pictures on the walls charting my personal history as well as regimental oil paintings. Across from my desk was an oil portrait of one of my predecessors, Bala Bredin. He commanded the regiment in the Second World War and was later seconded to command a parachute battalion at Suez, retiring as a general. Looking down on me with the ribbons of his three Distinguished Service Orders and two Military Crosses, he was a legend still spoken of with awe in the messes and canteens. But now in his ninetieth year he sat at home, with no memory of those times and little idea of those around him. But Bala was no peacetime soldier and would have scorned some of the modern direction of the British Army. One glance at his stony face reminded me, if I needed it, of the fleeting nature of our existence and to get out and address the things that mattered.

The dark spectre of Sierra Leone still hung over the battalion. The reminders were there. In the motor transport hangars sat the vehicles in which the patrol had been captured, awaiting repair. The ragged bullet holes and gouged metal spoke silently of the near miss our battalion and the rescue force had experienced. There were, we knew, some individuals with dark thoughts haunting them, but like any close-knit family we did our counselling in-house and closed ranks on the hurt that incident had caused.

I asked the RSM how he thought the healing process was going one day as I walked with him and the QM. He shrugged his shoulders.

'People are embarrassed. Getting men captured, even when it's not their fault, hurts their pride. They'd like to get out and do somethin' to recover their name. They're also conscious that you, coming from the SAS, will blame them for the lad that got killed.'

I was slightly taken aback. 'It was just another mission for the SAS. They're all volunteers. They accept that. I am proud of the way the boys behaved. I want them to know that. Should I speak to them?'

Paddy, the QM, spoke up. 'Best leave it for now, sir. When the boys are ready they'll talk about it, but it's still a raw nerve.'

The lack of self-confidence was becoming apparent in the manner in which the battalion was struggling to come to terms with its new role in 16 Air Assault Brigade. Within the airborne and Special Forces, readiness for action is very much a state of mind. While my new battalion was very effective and had recent operational experience – it had taken part in the invasion of Kosovo shortly before going to Sierra Leone – it was clear to me that their ethos was not quite yet of the 'Can do, go immediately if necessary, with whatever is in your pockets' variety that defines the 'airborne spirit'. I knew this from the rather cautious approach in which new projects were tackled and the lack of initiative I frequently encountered.

The Royal Irish Regiment had been formed in 1992 with the amalgamation of the Royal Irish Rangers and the Ulster Defence Regiment (UDR). This had been a political move to try to make the UDR more acceptable to the Nationalist population in Northern Ireland. It did not change the fact that the battalions that had been the old UDR and were now known as 'Home Service' Royal Irish still served only in Northern Ireland. We rarely saw them or had much to do with them. But for the Irish Rangers it meant losing a battalion and a name change.

Previously there had been the 1st and 2nd Battalions Royal Irish Rangers. Each had its own character and style. The 1st Battalion was based on the former Inniskilling Fusiliers (the 27th Foot) and was the senior of the three regiments that had been merged to form the Irish Rangers.[10] In that battalion the ethos was very strict, everyone knew his

---

[10] Royal Inniskilling Fusiliers, Royal Ulster Rifles and Royal Irish Fusiliers amalgamated in 1968 into the Royal Irish Rangers.

place and was conscious of the Inniskilling's long history and tradition. The 2nd Battalion was based on the Royal Ulster Rifles and, in keeping with the tradition of rifle regiments, things were done at a faster pace and much more on the hoof. The relationship between officers and men was a much closer one.

Not surprisingly, this translated across to the rifle companies in the new Royal Irish Regiment. Ed, the commander of A Company, was from the old 2nd Battalion and he led from the front and was often found among the men. Mike, who led B Company, was from the 1st Battalion and so for him the lines of distinction were clearly drawn and firm discipline was the way. Both styles were equally successful, but as I hailed from the 2nd Battalion and had spent half my career in the SAS, I leaned towards the more informal style.

C Company, the company involved in the Sierra Leone incident, had gone into virtual suspended animation on return. The major in charge at the time had been transferred, at his request, to another regiment and what was left of the company were spread out across the battalion to fill holes. As a temporary replacement we had an entire company of 110 Gurkhas, led by Marcus Reedman, an excellent young English major.

Life in camp with my own battalion was always a pleasure and I often wondered if anybody had a better job in the world. Soldiers getting ready for field training or cleaning weapons would pepper their activities with chat that would range from the humorous to touching insights into their lives. One soldier related to me how his parents had worried when he had joined up, as they had sent him to private school and his brother was a solicitor. He explained he just wanted action and, even though qualified to apply for an officer's commission, he had no interest in anything but being a member of an eight-man section with his mates. Another soldier, one of a family of ten brought up in a tenement in Dublin, one day told me, in a matter-of-fact way, that the first new clothes he had ever had were his British Army uniform. Not a few of the soldiers from Northern Ireland had flirted with or had brushes with the paramilitaries on both sides. I once heard a man describing to the lads he was working with on the engine of a vehicle how he had carried out an armed robbery on a pub for the outlawed Ulster Volunteer Force (UVF) when he was sixteen.

'I got lifted, like,' he explained. 'Didn't take the peelers long but I'd handed over the dough and the pistol to the man in charge already.'

'Who was that?' I asked.

He paused, spanner in hand, and straightened up. 'Oh, he was this bloke, used to go round in a long leather coat with all the jewellery and that. We all thought he was top man, like. To be honest, I was thrilled when he asked me and me mate to do the job. See when we was lifted, didn't want to know us – except to say if we squealed we were dead.' He bent under the bonnet once more and continued, 'So the peeler who interviewed me takes me dad to one side. Next thing I'm in a police car goin' down the recruiting office.'

'What about the robbery?' someone enquired.

'That was it.' He shrugged. 'I joined the Army, me mate stayed on – I reckon working as a tout[11] for the police till he moved to Scotland, and yer man in the coat got shot a year later in a feud with the Wombles[12] over drugs.'

A corporal who was a real hard case had beaten up a two-man IRA punishment squad who had come to discipline his brother, an IRA associate. He had to get out of Belfast or be shot and so joined the Army. 'These fellas turn up at our door, right. Me ma opens it an' they walks into the parlour an' says to our Jim, "Provisional IRA. You're under arrest." 'Ra[13], arrest? I focken ask ye? I came runnin' outs the kitchen and battered these two fockers roun' our house. They scampered pretty quick. So did I. I never stopped till I got on the boat to Liverpool and joined the Army. Next thing I'm in Ballymena surrounded by youse. That's me, though, I can't go back. The 'Ra put it around I was an Urb[14] and an RUC[15] tout.'

Just as I had a Regimental Sergeant Major as a wise old head to interface with the men, each company commander had a Company Sergeant Major (CSM). For A Company it was Dougie, formerly an instructor at the Royal Military Academy Sandhurst. He had a calm but effective style. In B Company the CSM was Eddie, known to the boys as 'Big Eddie'. He was a tough, tall Dubliner who enjoyed a reputation as a disciplinarian. His catchphrase – 'Oi'll get focken mediaeval wid ye' – was much quoted by the men, but only out of his earshot.

---

[11] Informer.

[12] Slang for Ulster Defence Association (UDA), a rival loyalist gang.

[13] 'Ra is slang for IRA

[14] Member of the Irish National Liberation Army (Republican paramilitary faction and rivals to the IRA).

[15] Royal Ulster Constabulary.

Below them the young officers who commanded the platoons would learn their trade from the company commanders and their manners from the CSM. Each company had three platoons, twenty-five to thirty strong, and every one of these had three sections of six to eight men. The corporals led the sections and the sergeants were the second in command of the platoons (although in practice some commanded the platoons with an eager young officer as an apprentice).

Of the men who had been in captivity, some fared better than others. I was sad to find that two had left. The lad from the Republic of Ireland went home. He had a brother in the mortar platoon who I knew well from when he first joined my company in 1997 and I went to see him. He assured me his brother was fine but agreed that he would have been better off staying with his mates to ride out any demons he had. (He rejoined a year later.) Another lad transferred to the Home Service. Of the corporals who had been captured, one went home to Northern Ireland on a posting, another transferred to the Home Service and the remaining corporal became my signaller in Battalion Tactical Headquarters. I went running a couple of times with the Intelligence Sergeant. Despite being out of breath I once asked why he gave up his chance of freedom when it could have sealed his death warrant. He shrugged and said, 'It was the right thing to do.'

When I took command there was a non-commissioned officers' (NCOs) cadre running. This was where we selected the men who would be promoted from ranger to lance corporal, the first management rank in the Army, where the man would be expected to become a leader. These are necessarily tough courses and have a high wastage rate as much from soldiers opting out from the daunting prospect of embracing leadership for the first time in their lives as the actual hardship of the course.

At this time I was delighted to see that Ranger G, one of the rangers who had been a hostage in Sierra Leone, was a volunteer and from what I heard was doing very well indeed. He had been an inspiration to the men around him in captivity and his indomitable optimism and black Belfast humour had kept spirits up in even the darkest moments. I had not actually met this remarkable little red-headed character and I felt I needed to. The cadre, which had moved to the Sennybridge training area in Wales, was completed on the morning of Saturday 27 January 2001. They were due in camp in the evening. I had a call at 0730 that morning. It was John Douglas, my second in command.

'Sir, some bad news, there's been a road traffic incident in Wales.

The lorry with the NCO cadre on board has crashed on black ice. There've been quite a few casualties.'

'How many and how bad?' I asked.

'Pretty bad. Nine men injured, some seriously – and Ranger G has been rushed to intensive care. He has a broken neck[16].'

Command of a battalion is as much about setting a standard as delegating and giving orders. You have to be seen as the man in charge. Soldiers must have confidence in their leader's professional abilities and standing. Above all they must trust and respect them as a person. Now, setting a standard is interpreted by some as slavish adherence to a code or doctrine that is written in a manual. I came to 1 R Irish having spent the majority of the previous eight years either on or directing operations. To me what mattered was being always ready to react and with enough understanding of the task in hand to deliver results as quickly and economically as possible. I was not overly given to formal marching and I should think that for some the standard of saluting in 1 R Irish was below par. That did not worry me in the least. I sought perfection in the field. I wanted to forge a battalion that could react to my will at an instant and interpret my intent with such flare that they could conceive solutions and methods that would both delight me and add to the momentum of our collective efforts. I knew that when this caught on it would grow naturally and, once instilled across the command structure, would make the battalion an unstoppable force which could move like a flock of birds and press home an attack with the ferocity of a hurricane finding ways through adversity.

I was fortunate that I already knew many of the men well, but I made certain to get to know the others. I knew that men who were content in themselves served better and were an asset. Men with problems were a burden, and it was in all our interests to solve their problems if we could. I knew that they were also wary of me as a new leader, and by getting around them and sharing tea, even going to eat in the cookhouse with them, I could listen to the things they enjoyed and hear about the things they disliked. This was vital.

I also took every opportunity to educate my officers and pass on my experience of life and the Army and what I had learned from some great soldiers. I urged them to rehearse, experiment and discuss any and all

---

[16] He was to be convalescing for the next nine months but was well enough to return in time for our deployment to the Gulf.

situations we might find ourselves in, to seek to understand them and through innovation and application and teamwork, overcome any and all difficulties. We needed the chance to turn the theory into practice and to have space to grow and develop. We also needed to have fun doing it.

An opportunity to start to instil self-confidence and the airborne spirit, both of which I had noticed were lacking, came fairly swiftly. We were invited to take part in an RAF Tactical Leadership Training exercise (TLT), involving up to 100 aircraft, based in an airfield near St Andrews in Scotland. Initially we had a fairly benign role. Foot-and-mouth crisis restrictions on army training prevented us from bringing our allotted company, and only the headquarters elements went forward. During the evening before the exercise started, however, and inevitably in the pub, the Brigade Commander told me the exercise was to be conducted within a sealed area on an abandoned USAF base at Machrihanish, on the Mull of Kintyre, which was free of foot-and-mouth restrictions, and wasn't it a pity that we hadn't brought our rifle company?

I responded by promising him a company – or even two – as quickly as he wanted.

The Brigade Commander seemed enthusiastic. 'But how can you get them up?' he asked. 'Canterbury's a good 400 miles away.'

At this point, Simon Footer, an RAF wing commander, a former Special Forces colleague and commander of LXX Squadron RAF, offered to fly them up from Kent's Manston Airport in two Hercules C-130s. The deal was sealed over a few more pints of Guinness. As I made my way back to the officers' mess in the early hours of the morning, I realised that I had made a substantial and rather risky bet. But it was just the sort of opportunity I was looking for. I got on the phone to John Douglas back in Canterbury.

'You realise,' he warned me, 'that some of the more traditionally minded members of the battalion won't take this well. They reckon it can't be done in the time you've given us. You know who I mean.'

'Ah, the trade unions,' I replied. 'Sod 'em; they're the source of the problem.'

Two rifle companies, A Company under Ed and the Gurkhas were assembled in twelve hours and driven to Manston. As the heavy-lift aircraft landed in St Andrews after an hour's flight north, the fast jets were already taxiing to scream off into the evening sky in close formation.

After the briefest set of orders and a quick bite to eat the men re-embarked. It was clear that the adrenaline rush of this no-notice move had infected even the newest recruits. I could see the eagerness in their faces, and I knew they were wearing their uniforms with a little more pride than they would have when reporting for duty that morning, expecting another day in camp.

The helicopters that would take some of them on the last leg of their journey into action were warming their rotors. The tailgates of the C-130s closed on our vehicles and the remaining troops. I was to command the exercise from a Lynx helicopter with my RAF coordinator beside me. I adjusted my night-vision goggles. As we awaited clearance for take-off, I could see the fighters rally overhead before streaking off to find the enemy interceptors.

Our aircraft hovered its way onto the departure point and lifted into the night sky. As I looked around I could see other units joining us. I listened as they announced their arrival on the net and my RAF assistant ticked off each stage. The afterburners of our guardian angels from the fast jet screen flashed purple above us. Above them, far from harm's way, an E-3D Sentry early-warning aircraft (a converted passenger aircraft with a massive saucer radar) watched our progress and relayed the 'Recognised Air Picture' (RAP) back to HQ.

As we flew to the attack, I could see the weird phosphorescent disc light ahead of me caused by the speed of the rotors driving the Puma force and Royal Navy Sea Kings in front of me. I confirmed that the ground-attack aircraft softening the target for us had completed their strike on the target, then ordered the C-130 heavy lifters to begin finals for the ground attack. Ahead of me I could see the infrared tail lights of the massive Chinooks bringing my companies against the target at low level. The lumbering Hercules aircraft swung in from left and right, joining the stream of aircraft now bearing down on the target.

I knew what it would feel like for those on board as they waited to deploy. They would be enduring the claustrophobic sensations of the movement of the aircraft and the coming certainty of action. How well I knew the excitement and terror of parachuting out of an aircraft at night with a container, often weighing over 100 pounds, attached to you with your equipment. One could scarcely believe a mere parachute could hold such weight, much less withstand the impact of snapping it to a drifting speed from the terminal velocity of your fall to earth. There would be tension and not a few queasy stomachs as the men sat in their glowing red capsule, waiting for the bump of the landing gear and the release of the cargo door.

Theory was about to turn into practice in the first free-play ground manoeuvre that I had led the men on and with seconds to go my heart raced as we bore down on the target. Then my world blurred. Our helicopter banked steeply to the right, the straps of my seat harness digging into me as we turned away, the G-force pressing me into my seat. Just before this happened I had been transfixed in disbelief as I heard on the radio the code word 'abort mission'. That was *my* call; I was the commander forward and in charge of the mission. In the green-tinted world of my night-vision goggles I could see the whole scene shattering as aircraft scattered in every direction, beyond recall, evading the enemy interceptors as they headed back to base. On the return flight I busied myself accounting for our aircraft as they flew low and at best speed to avoid detection back to our home airstrip. How could this be happening?

It wasn't until we got back to base that I discovered the assault had been cancelled because of bad weather, by a faceless controller back at HQ acting on weather reports, even though every pilot in the stream of aircraft had been content to press on. We had been so close to the target that we could certainly have got away with the landing, turning the fog to our advantage. We could have succeeded by seizing the moment and acting boldly. But the judgement had been made and there was no going back. That is why commanders need to go forward, instead of reading the battle from an operations room. That's where daring and estimation combines with experience to deliver informed decisions.

Despite this, the exercise had served as a psychological fillip to all involved. The men of 1 R Irish took away a lesson on preparedness, and I had learned that to influence events and avoid such misunderstandings on real operations I would need to be well forward, in a position where I could control events.

One of our most pressing requirements en route to being fully operational as an air assault battalion[17] was to increase the size of our sniper section. Our new role required us to have more snipers, whose job it was to probe forward and to report, identify and direct aerial attacks as much as to shoot opportunity targets. Snipers work in pairs, one observing the scene while one concentrates on seeking prey or examining

---

[17] In this role the battalion was air-delivered either by helicopter or Hercules C-130 aircraft. Its job was to rapidly exploit fractures in the enemy's force and to move swiftly on light scales to achieve effect.

a target or disposition for weaknesses and vulnerabilities. I had attached my sniper instructors to B Company, who were in Botswana selecting and training new snipers against the backdrop of the unfamiliar terrain of Africa even as we were sweeping across the skies of Scotland.

We already had a small but effective group of snipers, combat-proven in the Balkans. One of our lads – known as 'Red Ball' because of his flame-red hair – had his first experience as a newly qualified sniper in Bosnia when the Irish Rangers had been serving on the first-ever deployment there by the British Army in 1992. During that sectarian war a sniper in Gornji Vakuf had been terrorising the town and killing many. He had been meticulous in his preparations and had always shot, killed, then moved. But he had built up a pattern and one evening, as he slid into position to take a bead on his prey, Red Ball was waiting for the shadow to emerge stealthily from exactly where he had deduced it would. The Serbs recovered the enemy sniper's body the next day shot clean through the head.

We now needed ten more snipers. The gruelling selection progress had begun in Canterbury with runs, gym work – snipers needed to be resilient, fit and self reliant – map-reading lessons and instruction on the sniper's equipment. The volunteers then progressed through advanced radio communicating skills and observation tests. The physical and technical aspects of the course intensified until the group was whittled down to leave only those for whom the complex and expensive full training would be a cost-effective investment. When they moved to Africa they had to confirm their abilities in the final phase of the course, the 'badge test', while coping with the strains and stresses of the extremes of the Kalahari Desert.

I visited B Company in Botswana to watch their progress. They were based under canvas in Belfast Camp, in an open stretch of bush near the town of Shoshong, 100km north of the capital, Gaborone. The tents were laid out in neat rows, overlooking the ranges. There was an administration area, an ablutions block served by a water tower, and a single-storey cookhouse.

Routine was fairly brisk, with reveille at first light, 0600 hours. As the sun rose, a bugler would sound off from the top of the huge rock behind the camp, and a piper walked through the lines playing an Irish march. Everyone was definitely awake at this stage. The men would don boots and combat trousers for a platoon run into the desert. It was the only time to do it; once the sun was up, temperatures could reach 50°C. In the rose-tinted light, only a low curtain of dust would mark their progress. By the time they returned forty-five minutes later it would invariably have become a race. The fastest soldiers, faces straining crimson, veins standing out, would sprint for the camp gates. After the final stragglers had returned, they would gather once more in platoon groups to get a quick brief for the day, then set off to get washed and shaved before breakfast.

I joined Mike and his CSM, Eddie, for my morning run. They set quite a pace. The unforgiving environment reminded me of the Australian desert, across which I had trained with the Australian SAS: flat red sand, sparse thorn trees and clusters of small hills, dotted with enormous rocks, perched like dinosaurs among the desert scrub.

I went to watch the snipers at Baboon Rock, a striking outcrop in the middle of the bush. By now they had proved their map reading and observation capabilities and were completing the stalk, where they had to crawl, sometimes for as much as a day, heavily camouflaged, to take a shot at a target. Observers would search for them through binoculars and send those they spotted back to the starting point. Anyone seen twice would fail the whole course. It was always a difficult phase and now in the heat and dust of the desert scrub, crawling across the flint-sharp rocks and with only the scrub for cover, it was quite a test. The gillie suits they wore originated in the Boer War and were based on those worn by the gamekeepers on Highland estates, who sewed green and brown rags to their clothes to conceal them in the heather as they closed on their ever-vigilant prey. In the African heat they added to the burden and the men were glad of the CamelBak drinking systems they wore on their backs, from which a straw allowed them to drink without making any obvious movements that might alert the watchers to their position.

I joined them for the marksmanship test. The targets were virtually impossible to see through the heat haze without the aid of our Tasco sights, which magnify the target eight times and have coated lens to reduce the glare of the desert sun. I had a go myself as one of the newer rangers monitored my shots through a high-powered telescope. Paul Cochrane was a lad of nineteen, from the same part of Belfast as me, and had been selected as my spotter because the company commander had tipped him as a potential NCO. He was already a promising soldier – he'd been to Canada on exercise and to Norway with the battalion skiing team before Christmas – and was now a trainee sniper. At over six foot, he was also clearly going to be a force to be reckoned with when he filled out. He had an easy manner and was full of self-confidence.

I focused my eye on the distant target. 'How do you like Botswana?' I said as I scanned the bush for my mark.

'Brilliant . . .' He swatted one of the thousands of bluebottles that swarmed over the rock. 'But I hate these focken flies.' His accent was pure east Belfast. 'It's them monkeys,' he said, referring to the species after whom the rock was named. 'They've crapped all over the place, so they have.'

I squeezed the trigger.

'Hit.' Cochrane lowered the telescope and marked the record keeper's scorebook he had clipped to a plastic board in front of him. 'See, when we go to Northern Ireland, sir, is it true we're off to Belfast?'

I shook my head. 'East Tyrone. Where did you hear Belfast?'

'Och, one of the lads says we're bein' sent there and it's a big secret.'

'Too big for anybody to have told me.' I gave him a grin. 'Tell your mate, if we do go to Belfast, I'll eat my hat.'

I squeezed off another shot. Cochrane squinted into the 'scope. 'Miss.'

'What?' I rolled over, incredulous, holding the rifle in my left hand.

'Only kiddin' ye, sir,' he chuckled. 'Hit.'

While the snipers were doing their tests, Mike and the training officer put the rest of the company through its paces. The training was progressive and sought to take full advantage of the terrain. We had our stripped-down Land-Rovers with a .5 inch heavy machine gun at the rear, on a Weapons Mount Installation Kit (WMIK). At the front was a medium belt-fed 7.62mm General Purpose Machine Gun (GPMG), known to the boys as the 'gimpy'. These vehicles would be employed spitting lead and tracer rounds at targets up to six hundred metres away as the platoons, loaded with their battle stores, would run and crawl to the area of the target they were to assault and then call on the vehicles to switch fire to the flanks while they assaulted the 'enemy' positions with a hail of grenades and handheld rockets and finally, close in, with rifle fire and bayonets. It was hot, dusty, physical and exhausting work in the scorching desert glare.

My trip ended with a barbecue for the soldiers, at which we were joined by Adrian Naughten, who had been my first CO when I had arrived with the Royal Irish in Berlin twenty years before and who now lived in Africa. He had led us in the days of the Cold War when the battlefield we had envisaged was armour versus armour with infantry dug in waiting for the Soviet hordes. He was impressed with our new fast, aggressive tactics and agile manoeuvres. While he loved his new African home, he was delighted to be immersed in the Irish once again, especially as there were some lads from his native County Tipperary.

Faced with dire manpower shortages when I took command, I had reacted by forming my own teams to recruit exclusively in Ireland, rather than waiting for the faceless national recruiting organisation, whose efforts had resulted in no more than a trickle of recruits. In any case, as an Irish Regiment we wanted Irishmen. We weren't able to recruit in the Republic of Ireland, but we sent a team with some of our signature air assault equipment to Northern Ireland on a recruiting drive and made an effort to have our displays seen in as wide an area as possible, and especially in the towns and villages around the border. It was a huge success and the reaction across the province and from both communities was heartening.

I was particularly delighted when, as a result, we were invited to take part in the Derry Airshow at Eglinton airfield in County Derry. We were asked to provide a display of a tactical landing operation or 'TALO'. This would entail landing two Hercules C-130s and simulating the storming of a target for the entertainment of the crowd. It was to be the centrepiece of the show and it was always going to be controversial for a number of reasons. First, the attitude of the military establishment in Northern Ireland was that such interfaces with the public were generally not a good idea. The second reason was that while both the predominantly Nationalist local council, who had extended the invitation, and the local Unionists were all for our display, the local Republicans, from Sinn Fein, were potentially hostile. To our relief, however, aware of the large number of Southern Irish soldiers in our ranks and our popularity in the Irish Republic, they declared themselves ambivalent.

We had decided to use some of our Gurkhas to act out the role of enemy and they were extremely keen to visit the province as it was normally off limits to them. Two heavy-lift aircraft and two Chinook helicopters were duly provided. As the day drew close, a crew from Ireland's national broadcaster RTE approached us to film the display and I agreed. We flew to the province with the assault troops and Gurkhas, arriving at RAF Aldergrove, the main airbase in Northern Ireland, around forty miles away from the airshow, where we divided ourselves into air assault and enemy forces.

The Gurkhas arrived at the airshow first, to the applause of an enthusiastic audience, where they met the RTE TV team. As the time for the display approached, the commentator began to describe the TALO and the role of 1 R Irish. Just then the operations warrant officer who was manning the recruiting caravan received a phone call from an irate staff officer from HQ Northern Ireland asking if it was true that we were mounting a TALO display. He complained that he had not been briefed and ordered it to be cancelled immediately. The warrant officer tried to explain, but the staff officer was having none of it.

'What I demand,' he barked, 'is an immediate briefing on the status of this enterprise.'

The warrant officer, mobile telephone pressed to his ear, looked up to the sky and said, 'Well, sir, I can give you an immediate update as you requested. Five, four, three, two, one . . . too late!'

The two C-130s had roared in across the Atlantic coast at ultra low level and then steeply climbed before dropping nose first onto the runway and pulling up to land right at the last moment, to the gasps of the crowd. Almost immediately they flared their huge engines as 120 troops and stripped-down Land-Rovers raced from the back of the aircraft, guns blazing away with blank rounds. To hoots of delight, the thirty Gurkhas fired off blank rounds and threw combat noise simulators. Coloured smoke was flung in every direction as the display gathered pace. The RTE camera crew sped around recording the event.

Just at that point, the other wild card was played. The hardline Republican camp, having initially said that they didn't care, had clearly changed their minds. Stuck for ideas, they had resuscitated a protest they had prepared for a visit by ex-President Clinton but had decided not to use entitled 'Stop the US Arms Trade'. Suddenly a group of about four protesters, mysteriously carrying a Palestinian flag, marched into the arena and unfurled their enigmatic banner, with the coloured smoke swirling around them. The Gurkhas and the crowd, equally baffled, assumed they were part of the display. What is more, the Gurkhas assumed from their odd dress and flag and banner that that they were on their side and went over to join them, only for a startled local policeman to try to arrest them all – Gurkhas included.

Confusion reigned as the vehicles raced around in the smoke firing blanks, to the cheers of the enthusiastic crowd. I stood to one side, enjoying the show. At the time I didn't know for certain who the interlopers were – though I had a shrewd idea – and I only intervened, with tears of laughter rolling down my cheeks, when the Gurkhas tried to take the protesters and the policemen to the safety of their helicopters and back off to Canterbury.

The crowd loved it and were completely unaware that there had been a protest as the troops boarded the aircraft once again and the Gurkhas ran back to their helicopters, leaving only the protesters and the confused peeler in the arena. The protesters were inundated with requests for more information on 1 R Irish, with some youths even enquiring where to join. They rather sportingly directed them to our overwhelmed recruiting caravan, where we had the best response of our whole campaign.

# —3—

# EAST TYRONE

The surge in recruiting came not a moment too soon. The battalion was off once more on operations, this time to East Tyrone. We had served there before in '97 and knew the place well. We also had more than a few soldiers from the area. In the league table of Northern Ireland's most lawless places, East Tyrone was only just behind South Armagh's 'Bandit Country'. Some of the most spectacular confrontations between the Army and the IRA had taken place in this area and roadside shrines testified to these encounters. Behind the Army/IRA clash was a bitter sectarian war between the Loyalists and the Republicans that set neighbour against neighbour. The area had spawned one of the most active PIRA groupings and its activities included several high-profile attacks on mainland Britain and in Europe. The main difference between Armagh and Tyrone, in my view, as someone who had served in both, was that attacks in South Armagh came out of nowhere and one never saw actual terrorists in the commission of their acts. In East Tyrone they would come out and fight. For my money they were the most volatile and dangerous terrorists in Ireland.

Set on the edges of Lough Neagh, the largest inland body of water in Europe, the area known as East Tyrone is split between the hills on the edge of the Sperrin Mountains dominated by Slieve Gallion at 528m and the lough itself. The land and the people are inextricably intertwined and share characteristics and personality. The rural villages have their tribal allegiance, with Coagh and Newmills, small towns in the central valley with broad high streets, being Unionist, the hamlet of Ardboe on the shore and the larger town of Coalisland to the east and the hamlets of Cappagh and Dunnamore in the hills to the west being Republican. To those who knew the area well the very names of these hamlets and villages had the resonance of battle honours. Locals and the police could recite the murder and mayhem that was associated with each place. Our job was to ensure the litany of violence was never added to again.

I recall visiting Tyrone only once when I was growing up in Northern Ireland and my lasting impression was of a pearl-grey sky, damp fields and grey villages with a sullen, hungry look about them. My return in 1997, in command of C Company 1 R Irish, found the place transformed. It was brighter in every respect, the shops were busy and well stocked and the villages light and confident. Even the all-pervading sectarian tension, once a feature of the place, was barely noticeable.

With the border with the Republic of Ireland marking the southern boundary, the area we would operate in was 30km at its widest and 50km deep. My main base was in the central town of Dungannon, collocated with the local police commander. The town is a sharply divided place. Built on a hill, it dominates the area around for miles. When one approaches Dungannon the first sight is indeed the dreary spires of the Catholic parish church and St Ann's Church of Ireland or Anglican church. The buildings in the town are solid constructions reminiscent of the town's Georgian boom years, although there are much older parts around the castle, which is approached through an impressive square that also serves as a market.

Tyrone had been one of the counties settled in what became known as the Plantation of Ulster during the reign of James I in the early 17th century. The Planters, Anglican colonists from England and lowland Scotland, had settled the most fertile lands and built stronghouses, bringing indentured farmhands who themselves eventually acquired land. The native Irish, ill organised, feudal and badly led, were marginalised to the unproductive swampy enclaves on the shores of the lough or into the subsistence farms on the hills. In 1641 the native Irish rebelled and, indulging in excesses that would be recognisable in modern Rwanda, provoked a reaction from General Munro, who avenged the slaughter of 400 Scots at Dungannon with some slaughter of his own, which was to settle the matter for centuries to follow. The legacy of the Plantation remains to this day in East Tyrone and bitterness handed down through generations remained undimmed until recent times.

The bitter split in the province's paramilitary grouping between those dedicated to full-scale violence and those who supported the nominal ceasefire produced dangerous splinter groups determined to carry the fight on. They were extremely active and militant in Tyrone. Republicans in East Tyrone were largely well disciplined and mostly under strong IRA leadership. The campaign in Europe and attacks on the British mainland had won them recognition and influence within Sinn Fein. But it also spawned terrorists who would not stop fighting for any reason. These were the Dissident Republicans, who brought with them a significant quantity of weapons and ammunition and had no shortage of cash from their supporters in the United States, from where the thirty years of misery and suffering at the hands of the terrorists had been handsomely funded.

A former IRA assassin led the Dissidents in the field. His second in command was one of a set of brothers who were all extremely active in both terrorism and smuggling. The grouping had recently attracted a close relative of the leader, making the whole grouping some ten men in total. In my view, the newest addition, a young guy, was potentially the most dangerous, as he was dedicated to carrying out a murder of a policeman, soldier or any Protestant before a lasting peace overtook him. He was quite prepared to walk up to a policeman and shoot him in the back. Intelligence at the time suggested that they had acquired a sophisticated Yugoslavian rocket called an RPG-22[18], which could cause our armoured vehicles problems if fired at the right place.

By now, however, they were also masters of the smuggling trade. They exploited the border between the Republic of Ireland and Northern Ireland to take advantage of export duties and European Union subsidies and made a fortune. The trade in cigarettes, diesel, illicit drink and pornography netted millions of pounds, sometimes with ridiculous ease. I recall one occasion when a smuggler was stopped as he drove a lorryload of pigs back and forth across the border, clocking up subsidies on each crossing. However, the reason they eventually stopped him was nothing to do with Customs and Excise – that was too difficult and discouraged by the peace lobby – but because the pigs were clearly becoming exhausted and needed a break.

During this tour of duty, we assisted the police in smashing a number of major smuggling operations, one raid netting a warehouse with £600,000 worth of counterfeit cigarettes and booze. The booze was in concentrated sachets and would be decanted into bottles marked with

---

[18] A group of men were later caught red-handed with the weapon and arrested. They walked free after the judge accepted that they had actually only found it on the way to a burglary.

well-known brands. I would not wish to be on the receiving end of it. Progress was being made in disrupting the trade in smuggled diesel, though it was so widespread it was difficult to control (so much so that some well-known car manufacturers will not honour the warranty on their diesel engines in Northern Ireland). The scam concerns subsidised diesel that is supplied for the agricultural industry as part of the EU Common Agricultural Policy at a cost of around 30p per litre. To control its use, it is dyed red in Northern Ireland and green in the Republic of Ireland. The smugglers buy it up in bulk and put the diesel through large filter tanks filled with Fuller's Earth, which removes the dye. In many cases now, however, they don't even bother. In theory the Customs and Excise have the power to stop lorries and check the colour of the diesel. But large transport fleets and haulage contractors linked to Republican terrorist families still make huge profits by running their fleets on illegal fuel with a saving of the order of 50p per litre. In addition they openly sell the illegal fuel. Our local Dissidents even opened their own outlet from a wooden garden shed set at the side of the road. The money from these fuel sales is not only used to fund the campaign of terror but also increasingly to fund gangster lifestyles. Whole families, proud of the fact that they have never openly worked in their lives, live in palatial mansions and drive expensive cars on the profit of this trade. They would also have no hesitation in killing anyone who tried to interfere with it.

This was the Tactical Area of Responsibility (TAOR) I took over on 16 June 2001. Our arrival in Northern Ireland followed another Dissident Republican attack. The 2001 general election had seen a determined attempt by the East Tyrone Dissidents to carry out a 'spectacular' murder. Their efforts had been much frustrated by the activity of security forces and had culminated in a hasty, opportunistic attack on a polling station in Draperstown. The novice terrorist, his face barely disguised by a scarf, walked into the school where the polling station was set up. The two policemen on duty were standing with their backs to him, chatting to voters. He pulled out a pistol. Both policemen fell, shot in the back, and a woman who was talking to them was injured in the arm. Outside the unit commander was waiting in a car and he and the gunman drove off, hooting with delight. While the identity of the gunman was well known, witnesses were unwilling to testify. When it was revealed that neither policemen had died the terrorists resolved to redouble their efforts to get a kill.

1 R Irish deployed with a strength on the ground of 510 men, grouped

into four rifle companies. (The remainder were guarding our base in Canterbury, with the Gurkhas attached to 1 R Irish going to the Falklands.) I commanded the area of operations from the base in Dungannon with two rifle companies, one under my direct command and one on call to the 3rd Infantry Brigade. In addition I had a Home Service Royal Irish (part-time) company under command, some fifty to eighty strong. I had one of my companies in a mortar-proof base on the border with the Republic of Ireland in Aughnacloy. This massive purpose-built fortification, entered by airlocks with bank vault doors, overlooked a notorious crossing point. A further company was detached and based with 3 Infantry Brigade in Armagh, a thirty-minute drive away, in addition to the company allocated to them and co-located with me in Dungannon.

Our base in Dungannon was a large 18th-century house on the edge of the old town called Killymeal House. With several bedrooms and large reception rooms it was covered in ivy and from the outside could have been a country house hotel. Around the house, in the once well-kept gardens, a number of more modern constructions accommodated the battalion headquarters and two rifle companies and included a mortar-proof dining hall and soldiers' canteen. Outside the stable yard at the back of the house was a granite memorial to men lost by the local Ulster Defence Regiment, who had occupied the base since a local farming family loaned it to the security forces in 1970. Included in the list was Captain Timothy Armstrong, a childhood friend and fellow student at Queen's University, who was shot in the back of the head by cowards as he strolled with his girlfriend one summer's evening in the early 1980s.

We worked in close cooperation with the police. Operations were centrally monitored from our operations centre in Dungannon. From there we would be linked to 3 Brigade in Armagh and to HQ Northern Ireland in Lisburn, near Belfast, by a complex communications set-up. We would dominate our AOR by patrolling either on foot or by helicopter, but we also had a fleet of armoured Land-Rovers. I would regularly attend meetings with the local police in order to coordinate our strategies. I was very clear that the police had primacy, and we were there to support them and provide them with overt protection.

We in 1 R Irish had a particularly difficult line to walk, as we had men from across Ireland, many with close family links in both communities. For instance, there was one man whose uncle had escaped from the high-security Maze Prison in the IRA breakout of 1983 with notorious former IRA man Gerry Kelly, only to be recaptured and extradited back to

Northern Ireland. There were also soldiers with brothers and even fathers who had served life sentences for murder on behalf of the Loyalist side.

When we arrived that summer, the most pressing threat the police had received was from Loyalist paramilitaries, aimed against the Catholic population. Informers within the Loyalist community reported that one of our local Loyalist Volunteer Force (LVF) members was obtaining weapons with a view to carrying out a murder against the Catholic community, any Catholic, in order to foment trouble ahead of the traditional protests at Drumcree[19] in Portadown, due on 5 July. Motivated by a visceral hatred of Catholics, mostly on quasi-religious and racial grounds, the LVF – followers of the now-dead 'King Rat' Billy Wright[20] – were eager to prove they were still in business.

Our duties began in earnest with a series of searches around the home of the suspect. I understand that he was glad of the attention as he was suspected by a rival Loyalist gang, the UVF, of having been behind the murder of one of their leaders. The fact that we, in the security forces, knew he had nothing to do with it made it all seem quite surreal. He was a 'dead man walking' in any case. We just had to make sure he didn't take any innocents along with him. In the countryside of East Tyrone the outlawed UVF were numerically the most dominant Loyalist group, but the LVF made up for their lack of numbers with their sheer aggression.

Our searches were carried out by specially trained teams, with the RSM as the senior search coordinator, while a cordon of troops was set up to protect them and to prevent anyone leaving with contraband. The search teams would break the area into manageable parts and, using dogs and specialist equipment, methodically search each section. Our role was as much to deter and unsettle the terrorists as to actually recover terrorist materiel, and these particular searches drew a blank. But as we waited for the cordon to be taken in, my radio operator noticed that the tax disc on the suspect's car was out of date.

---

[19] The annual Drumcree protest had flared over the insistence of the Portadown Orange Order to march home from their annual church service down the predominantly Catholic Garvaghy Road. This had been a contentious parade for well over 100 years but had recently become a cause célèbre on both sides.

[20] Leader of the Loyalist Volunteer Force, a sickening organisation, known for its murders, Billy Wright's name was much used in 1 R Irish as rhyming slang for a bodily function. INLA man 'Clip' McWilliams shot Wright dead in HMP Maze while Wright was serving a sentence for directing acts of terrorism in 1997.

'Not much to show for our efforts,' the police constable commented as he wrote out a ticket.

'No, but he'll know we're watching him,' I replied.

We carried out a total of four searches within a week, yet all we found were some masks and gloves. We knew, from reliable intelligence, that there were home-made pipe bombs and at least one assault rifle hidden somewhere. Much later it transpired that, as so often, our efforts had paid off in an indirect way. The searches had edged so close to the hides on at least two occasions that the terrorists decided to move the weapons right out of the area.

The Republican camp was far from idle at this time. We learned that there was a big arms shipment coming in – not that they needed it. We already knew that they had surface-to-air weapons in their formidable armoury. During our last tour of duty back in 1998 and just after the Good Friday Peace Agreement had been signed, the local PIRA had tried hard to shoot down a Puma helicopter in Pomeroy, using a Russian SA-7 missile, a crude but effective heat-seeker. Its limitation was that it was powered by a battery pack with a life of only twelve seconds. The firer had to acquire the target through his sights, turn on the battery with a thumb switch and allow the gyro to run up enough for the missile to recognise the target and launch. This took about four seconds. If the target was lost at any stage, then the process would have to start again. After three attempts the firer would have to change battery packs and discard the used one. Proof of this was discovered shortly after we had handed over the area to the Royal Regiment of Wales, when three discarded battery packs were unearthed by cows tramping in a field overlooking the helicopter pad at Pomeroy and reported to the police by a farmer. To us that represented nine attempts to launch at one of our helicopters, frustrated no doubt by the effective flying tactic of the RAF crews who would routinely duck their aircraft behind the cover of trees and hills as they flew.

Late June and early July was the marching season, when the Unionist community celebrated their identity with a series of traditional marches behind bands. Harmless enough on the surface, these marches were an important reaffirmation of that community's identity. Like a Scottish clan's tartan or the carnival in Notting Hill, they were an important expression of culture. But where there were members of the minority Catholic community living on the routes the marches were sometimes seen as provocative and tension could spill over into violence. We knew that we would have to help cope with some of these parades.

Some forty miles from our base, Belfast was the home town of many members of 1 R Irish. If you have never visited the city, think Newcastle full of Glaswegians. The capital of Northern Ireland sits on the Lagan estuary and gets its name from a river, the Farset, long since lost below the streets of the 19th-century industrial city. The Irish name is *Beal Feirste*, or ford on the Farset. The city meets the Belfast Lough at Queen's Island, the man-made site of the now-defunct shipyards, from where the two giant cranes, 'Samson' and 'Goliath', dominate the Belfast skyline. The city then spreads south-west along the Lagan valley, with Cave Hill and the Black Mountain to the north-west and the Holywood and Castlereagh Hills to the south-east. The centre of the town is dominated by the magnificent City Hall, surrounded by the majestic buildings of the boom years when the linen trade, shipbuilding and rope making made it an industrial hub. These then give way to streets of terraced housing that spread out along the city's main routes: the Crumlin Road to the north, the Lisburn and Malone Roads to the affluent southern suburbs, the Falls and Shankill Roads to the west of the city, and the Newtonards Road to east Belfast. Here, passing through the narrow streets of the shipyard workers, you emerge in the leafy suburbs of the well-heeled establishment and reach the Parliament buildings at Stormont on the eastern fringe of the city.

Over the last hundred and fifty years the city has become segregated, with the Catholic minority initially confined to west Belfast, with a small enclave on the edge of otherwise Unionist east Belfast, and another centred around the Ardoyne area. Prejudice and discrimination became institutionalised in the overwhelmingly Protestant-dominated Northern Ireland Parliament after the partition of Ireland in 1922, which left a significant minority of Irish Catholics stranded in a Protestant state. The Catholic minority was effectively sidelined in the prosperity of the late 1950s and early 1960s, until the awakening of radical consciousness across Europe in 1968 manifested itself in Northern Ireland in the form of the Civil Rights movement. The Northern Irish State dealt harshly with the demonstrators, and cynical elements within the establishment played the sectarian card to whip up ancient fears among the Protestant majority, bringing crowds onto the streets to confront the mainly Catholic demonstrators. Civil disorder spread across the province but was at its worst in Belfast and Londonderry. The Catholic minority were besieged in their ghettos. Their only line of protection, the IRA, crumbled, demonstrating it had long since stopped being an urban guerrilla movement and had gone down the path of political ideology. Catholic districts in both cities were burned and there was loss of life on both sides.

Two events followed that were to have long-lasting consequences. The British Army was deployed onto the streets of the province to support the hard-pressed police force, the RUC; and out of the ashes of the defeated IRA rose the Provisional IRA (so called after the Provisional Government declared after the 1916 Easter Rising and in their view still not implemented across all of Ireland), displacing the now-defunct 'Official' IRA to become, arguably, the most sophisticated urban guerrilla movement in the world.

I grew up in the relatively quiet east Belfast but attended school in the centre of the city at the all-boy Royal Belfast Academical Institution, known as RBAI or 'Inst'. My school had been founded in 1810 based on the ideals of the United Irishmen movement. Nonconformist Presbyterian Irishmen had been prominent in the movement towards emancipation for all in Ireland, motivated by the revolutionary ideals of the French Revolution, and they viewed the establishment's anti-Catholic and Nonconformist laws as draconian. The'United Irishmen' had been generally seen as a progressive movement, and one of the champions of that movement, Henry Grattan, had first observed that 'England's difficulty was Ireland's opportunity' and that the American war of patriots and volunteers gave a unique chance to force the pace of political reform. In the decades and century that followed, that unity was shattered and, particularly after the partition of Ireland in 1922, Northern Ireland separated into its politically and religiously aligned groups. Equality and integration coupled with freedom of worship had been their ideals, but by 1970 in Belfast there were very few Catholics studying at Inst.

Travelling to school each day, I saw the huge contrasts between the moderate neighbourliness of the eastern edge of Belfast and the harsh divisions that existed elsewhere. The majority of my friends at Queen's University came from the Nationalist and Republican communities. Comparing their outlook and the militancy of the Loyalist districts just down the road, I despaired of any solution to this seemingly intractable problem. To a great extent it was compounded by the fact that the two opposing factions educated their children separately, while the more moderate, educated middle classes simply opted out of politics, weakening the centre ground and strengthening the extremes. One cynical observer noted that 'the middle classes went to the golf course when the violence broke out in 1969 and haven't come back since.'

Naturally I grew up with some people who later became embroiled in violence, some who went to jail and some who became victims of that violence. When I had casual jobs as a student during the summer holidays I would work alongside men who were deeply involved in the paramilitaries and who could relate first-hand accounts of that violence. Sometimes they were tragic and sometimes they were comical. A character called Tucker related a tale of an attack on a Catholic street in the small Republican enclave of Short Strand in east Belfast. The plan, he was told, was to shoot into the area with a sub-machine gun, but they were concerned about being engaged from a nearby army post on the interface of the two communities. They had read that a wet blanket offered protection against bullets so, armed with their machine gun and carrying a wet blanket, they pulled up at the end of Seaford Street in a black taxi, and while one man stepped out to extend a wet blanket in the direction of the army post, the other fired off a magazine of bullets at the Catholic houses. The amazed soldiers in the nearby post stared in disbelief, then opened fire. The two would-be killers had to abandon their equipment and run for their lives. Not surprisingly, they were arrested soon afterwards, hiding in some bins nearby.

Tucker himself, a Loyalist, spent some months on remand in Belfast's Crumlin Road Prison, for allegedly biting off a policeman's ear, where he was to become very friendly with a Republican remand prisoner called Francis Hughes. Francie Hughes, notorious IRA man, was a legend in his own community and when the police captured him in Maghera, north of Cookstown, after being wounded in a shootout with the SAS, he was hiding in a ditch, his wounds stuffed with twigs to stop the bleeding. Tucker and Hughes shared a cell, where Hughes used his artistic talents to copy photographs of Tucker's relatives in pen and ink, and they were only separated when Hughes was convicted. I often thought that if things had been different, Hughes might have been drawn to the Army, and his undoubted talents would have made him a prime candidate for the SAS. Tucker's unlikely friendship with Hughes did not change either man's outlook, however. Tucker remained a Loyalist on his release and Francie Hughes died on hunger strike in prison on 12 May 1981.

I went to school through the worst of the civil strife – through workers' strikes, power cuts and numerous explosions. In 1972 and 1973 it would go on all night. We were regularly evacuated onto the playing fields because of rioting or bomb scares. I frequently heard shooting and saw some dreadful things. I remember going home at the beginning of the Christmas break in 1973, when I was thirteen years old, and passing the wreckage of a car in which a bomb-disposal officer had been killed the night before. The officer had already defused five bombs that night and was killed as he defused the sixth. The device that caught him was among the most crude, attached to the light in the glove compartment of the car. For an experienced bomb-disposal officer, opening it as he did was a schoolboy error, but a deadly one. He was no doubt exhausted physically and mentally. For his courage he received the George Medal. As I passed the wreckage, I recall being deeply impressed by the man's courage and at the same time frankly wondering why he bothered. Looking at the scene, perched as it was between the Northern Bank on Wellington Street and a bakery, I could see no reason why the bomb had had to be defused. It is probably fair to say that the British Army learned a lesson at about the same time as I did: that people matter, property doesn't. Thereafter the Army was more inclined to have controlled explosions rather than attempt to defuse such bombs. It was also around this time that the first bomb-disposal robots appeared on the streets of Belfast.

The first dead body I saw was when I was nine or ten. My friend Jim and I were playing in the fields near my home one Sunday when we saw a man lying at the side of the field at the bottom of a bank, directly outside the home of the then Lord Chief Justice of Northern Ireland[21]. We thought the man had fallen or was even possibly drunk, until we saw the blood. Without speaking we both ran home to tell our parents. I can't imagine why now, but at the time we each instantly feared that somehow we would be blamed for it.

We went back much later, by which time the police had sealed off the area and removed the body. Brave enough now to lead a small group of children to the scene of crime, Jim and I were rather proud we had helped 'solve a crime' (we had in fact done nothing). Even though I hadn't looked too closely at the body in the first place and nor I suspect had Jim, we embroidered our description for the morbid entertainment of the others, with the particular aim of shocking the girls.

I recall we were all intrigued by the ill-fitting clear plastic gloves the men in civilian clothes wore – presumably detectives. There were no white forensic suits or sanitised areas as nowadays. Then again, I suppose

---

[21] This was in fact Lord John MacDermott, whose brother Robert had been the officer killed in action leading my grandfather' s platoon in the First World War.

the province was just getting used to wholesale murder, having until recently been the place with the lowest civil crime rate in Europe.

It transpired the dead man was 'Witness A'[22] at the trial some years previously for murder of one of the more notorious UVF men of the time, Augustus 'Gusty' Spence. It was their way of saying 'we know who "Witness A" was anyway.' This poor bloke, whoever he was, was just one of the 3,000 people who have died in the last thirty-five years in what the Irish euphemistically call 'The Troubles'[23].

My own parents tried hard to keep us away from the horror that was breaking out all around us. My father, who came from Dublin, had a printer's shop towards the centre of town. I can only imagine the tightrope act he must have had to walk, having customers from both sides of the divide. In any case, in a society where you had to be on one side or the other, many never worked out where his sympathies lay. In fact his sympathy was for all of the victims of violence on whatever side they were. He would become quite sad and reflective if any of us children ever showed any bias. Up until the outbreak of trouble in 1969, my recollection of Northern Ireland is of an extremely peaceful and optimistic place. I was not aware at that time of the discrimination against Catholics. But then again my neighbours, the Boyles, were Catholics and when I played with their grandchildren there was never any mention of religion, and frankly I was completely unaware of any distinction. Of course, in the summers before 1968, when the Orange[24] parades marched through town, we would go and watch, but for my sisters and myself it was just an exciting spectacle. Indeed, I recall going with two of the children from next door and being blissfully unaware of the religious significance of the marches. The Boyles, if they were bothered, certainly never mentioned it. A man at the end of our street was an Orangeman and I can recall, as a small boy, thinking that he looked very grand and important in his sash and bowler hat.

For me at the age of nine, the outbreak of the Troubles and the arrival on our streets of the British Army in large numbers was simply a matter of fascination, and it was curious to look at the soldiers and their equipment and to listen to their unfamiliar English, Scottish and Welsh

---

[22] Oddly the evening news did not give his name even after he had been shot.

[23] In the Republic of Ireland the Second World War was referred to as 'The Emergency'.

[24] On 12 July each year in Northern Ireland and indeed across the world where Ulstermen have migrated, parades are held behind marching bands to celebrate the victory of King William III over the Catholic King James II.

accents. The first black person I ever saw was a British soldier, and I remember staring at the chap, and him smiling back at me in a very friendly way, instantly understanding why I was staring.

We were not a wealthy family and my father had to work hard for everything that we had. My father had lived a fairly bohemian existence before he married at the late age of forty-seven, a couple of decades older than my mother. He had sailed on his own boat, gone shooting with his friends and even dabbled in farming before settling down to work first as a claims inspector with the railways, and later starting his own printer's shop. They went on to have four children, whom he worked hard to put through grammar school and university. He had not attended university himself, although his brothers had, but he believed that education was the way to rise in society. Always smartly dressed, with a magnificent handlebar moustache, he was a man of few words. He smoked a pipe and, even now, the very smell of pipe tobacco can conjure him up for me. Because he had been almost deaf since a bout of scarlet fever when he was seven, he found socialising in larger groups difficult. He couldn't hear what was being said and was frustrated by his dependency on a hearing aid which gave his otherwise soft southern Irish accent a metallic ring to it. He loved the countryside, and he once told me that the one thing he did remember from before his hearing went was the call of the birds, which he knew off by heart. He heard the rest of the world through a device; the birds he heard in his memory. I suppose my decision to join the Army as an officer was much inspired by him. He would have loved to have been in the Army, or indeed any service, and envied his younger brother's success as an officer in the regiment. My uncle, his brother, gave me great encouragement and I grew up fascinated by his tales of the Army and service in Burma with the Chindits, fighting the Japanese. My father was, I know, delighted that I was commissioned after leaving university, and followed my travels with huge interest but passing little comment. Overt displays of pride were my mother's preserve.

My mother came from east Belfast, where her father had owned a grocer's shop. More particularly her mother had run the shop, since my grandfather was constantly unwell after his First World War service. Both my maternal grandparents died before I was born. But from them, through my mother and my maiden aunt who lived with us, I received a sound grounding in the Presbyterian outlook, where discrimination of any kind was frowned upon. My mother encouraged us to work hard and was very ambitious for us.

*

Since the Good Friday Agreement in 1998 between the factions in Northern Ireland and the governments of the UK and the Republic of Ireland, the essential *casus belli* in Northern Ireland has been removed. Power sharing has been enshrined in the agreement and law enforces the equality of both traditions. All sides have signed up to the accord. (In a European context the whole conflict actually looks faintly ridiculous now.) But within Northern Ireland, an almost séance-like atmosphere around the divisions exists, the conviction of many being so strong that it makes it seem very real and even balanced people start to perceive these distinctions. The community divide is especially acute in places like the Ardoyne, a working-class district in the north of the city, where bitter rivalries end in the cemeteries and the flame of hatred burns brightly.

The Provisional IRA in the Ardoyne produced one of the most militant so-called 'battalions', the 3rd Battalion Provisional IRA, as well as some of the better-known personalities in the Republican movement, such as IRA convict Gerry Kelly, the 'Old Bailey bomber' and leader of the Maze Prison breakout, and Martin Meehan, now an elder statesman of Sinn Fein, member of the Local Devolved Assembly, prospective Westminster parliamentary candidate and once, allegedly, a notorious IRA commander. At one point there was an entire regular British Army battalion deployed in the Ardoyne to deal with the threat posed by these men.

It was in Ardoyne that the SAS had last been deployed in Belfast, on 21 June 1978, shooting dead an IRA Active Service Unit comprising three well-known members of the IRA, Dinny Brown, Jackie Mailey and Jim Mulvenna, equipped with explosive devices. (Protestant William Hanna, an innocent passer-by, was also killed.) That evening, as a student and member of the Territorial Army, I was on guard across the city in east Belfast, and I can recall hearing the sustained gunfire of that ambush crackling in the night. There was an outcry after the incident as 171 rounds of ammunition struck the men who died. (One of the IRA men to die that night, Dinny Brown, had previously shown a certain resilience, having been shot thirteen times by the British Army in 1972 and miraculously survived.) In defence of the SAS ambush team who shot these terrorists, they were more used to fighting Communist rebels on the Jebel in Oman's Dhofar region, who had little regard for their lives and would fight to the end, often feigning death to attack anyone who came to their aid. In contrast, terrorists in Northern Ireland want it both ways: they kill without mercy but when they are confronted they want to be shown the mercy they would not dream of showing their own victims.

With the size of the Protestant majority in the north Belfast area having fallen, through demographic changes and flight to the more affluent suburbs, from 20,000 twenty years ago to a figure closer to parity at the time of our tour of duty, the two warring factions faced each other across a series of strategic road junctions. These would come to prominence each summer during the annual marches. Generally, each side kept to its own patch; the fault lines were well marked and respected. There was one tragic exception, however.

The Catholic Holy Cross girls' school was set a couple of hundred metres into the predominantly Protestant end of the Ardoyne Road, a relic of the optimism of the city planners in the early 1960s. It had never been a particular point of concern before, standing as it did beside the state primary school. For years the parents of each tradition had dropped their children off and picked them up with only the most basic pleasantries exchanged. One sultry evening in June 2001 all that was to change.

For some months, the pressure on the Protestant residents had been ramped up by the Provisional IRA. Back in December 2000 a local Protestant taxi driver, Trevor Kell, had been gunned down in cold blood as he waited for a fare, in what was an act of intimidation to effect ethnic cleansing. The IRA denied involvement but the police were able to link the bullet taken out of Mr Kell to a gun used in an IRA shooting in 1997. Loyalists struck back and a Catholic, Gary Moore, was shot dead. Then in June 2001, with tensions running high, there was an angry exchange between Catholic parents bringing their children home from the school and local Protestant residents putting up 'decorations' for the coming marches. Not long afterwards a car raced out of the Catholic end of the road and swept the ladder away from under the man nailing a flag to the top of a lamp-post. A gang leapt out and attacked the fallen man with a screwdriver before running off.

This was the spark that was to lead to the worst upsurge of violence in the area for years. Both sides hurled stones and petrol bombs and the Army was deployed onto the streets in support of the hard-pressed RUC. The Loyalist residents threw up a cordon across their end of the road and vehicles were hijacked and burned. The Republicans responded and the two sides exchanged petrol bombs and blast bombs. By the next day the focus had switched to the children from the Catholic community and their way to school was barred. As both sides stared, eyes brimming with hatred, across the thin line of police and army that stood to separate them, the media gathered and the world wanted to know what was going on. The clash was to drag on over the summer into autumn.

The dispute was compounded by the fact that in the early stages many of the emissaries on each side of the divide were paramilitaries or in close cahoots with them. On one hand there were well-known UVF and UDA men posing as 'concerned residents', while on the other side the 'community activists' were Provisional IRA almost to a man. The scene was hammed up for the world's media by both sides, with well-known terrorists striding up the road among the real parents and insisting they only wanted to take 'their kids' to school. What was lost in the noise was that the real parents couldn't get their children to school without running a gauntlet of abuse, venom and fear that no child should ever be exposed to. By the time local clergymen had emerged as the negotiators to displace the thugs it was too late, although it was the diplomacy of the local parish priest, Father Aidan Troy, in concert with a local Church of Ireland rector, Reverend Stewart Heaney, that was to win through in the long run. A new quarrel had been added to Northern Ireland's already brimming cup of hatred.

1 R Irish was plunged into that bitter scene because we were asked on numerous occasions during our tour of duty to reinforce the 1st Battalion, the Argyle and Sutherland Highlanders, the resident battalion in Belfast, with our operations company, 120-men strong and mounted in heavily armoured Saxon crowd-control vehicles. I would visit them at Girdwood Barracks in north Belfast, where they would wait until they were ordered onto the streets by the police, whereupon they would scramble into their protective gear – cotton long johns, combat dress, body armour, shinpads and arm protectors with a fireproof mask and helmet to top it off – before heading off. The simple strain of dressing like this on a summer's evening should not be underestimated. By the time the men had been relieved of their duties, they would be soaked in sweat and exhausted.

The base itself was a Spartan affair. Over the preceding thirty years the neat camp had hosted countless army units as they passed through on six-month tours of duty. Each had left its mark and the cap badges of regiments, some long since disbanded, with the dates of their tour of duty, adorned the breezeblocks of the curtain walls that protected the Portakabins. These were a precaution against the blast of home-made mortars, which were once a frequent hazard in Northern Ireland. There was an operations room in the base with a sophisticated communications array, a massive illuminated map of the city marked with key points and a bank of televisions carrying pictures from CCTV cameras across the city on one side with another beaming twenty-four-hour news on the other. Often when violence broke out it was amazing to watch the same incident live from two angles, TV news and 'reality CCTV', as the men called it. It was also not infrequent – as I had seen across the world from Zaire to Bosnia – to watch news journalists reporting a scene of unspeakable violence 'live' on the screen and to look at the actual area on CCTV and see deserted streets.

My Irish soldiers would have heavy hearts as they stood uncomfortably between the warring communities, saddened by the state of affairs and disgusted by the hatred spewed forth by both factions. And for some there was the added risk of being recognised, with all the consequences that that could bring. Both Catholic and Protestant soldiers had been murdered while at home on leave. One incident brought this into sharp focus. An edict had been passed down from HQ Northern Ireland that soldiers should not wear their fireproof masks unless actual rioting was under way because it looked too aggressive. A senior officer arrived on the Ardoyne Road, near the disputed Holy Cross school, to visit 1 R Irish and drew my attention to one of my men.

'Look, Tim,' the senior officer said, 'this might not have reached you fellows but I would prefer the men not to wear the masks unless they really have to. It doesn't look at all good on TV and it plays into the hands of those who would do us down.'

'Sir, the message has been transmitted to us loud and clear and we understand the logic. On the other hand, I go out of my way to make sure that everyone in this battalion is treated the same and sometimes that means they have to wear a mask. But we are extra careful to make sure they aren't filmed. Let's speak to that chap and you'll see my point.' I led him down the street. 'Young fellow, would you please explain why you have your mask on for the benefit of this officer.'

'Yes sir, I come fro' doun there.' He indicated the street marked by a giant Irish Republic flag, under which were gathered a number of burly men smoking, laughing and spitting in the manner of hard men the world over.

'Oh,' the officer said. 'Do you suppose any of those men know you?'

'I know them all.' He smiled. 'That's Eddie Copeland, the fat one is Martin Meehan Junior and everyone knows Gerry Kelly, the sneaky-looking one in the glasses. He's the top man in Sinn Fein around here.'

'Mm, I think some of those chaps probably have paramilitary connections,' the officer mused.

The young ranger laughed. 'D'ya think there'll be a fight in the next Jackie Chan movie?'

'Do people round here know you're in the Army?'

'No way! If they did I'd get nutted when I'm home on leave.'

'Nutted?' the officer enquired.

'Y'know, a head job.'

'Oh.' He looked at me. 'Best keep his mask on.'

# —4—

# THE ARDOYNE ROAD

Waiting in the wings for the order to confront a crowd is like being a boxer nervously impatient for his bout or a parachutist sitting on an aircraft. You can only feign interest in the events around you as you focus on your coming role while trying to ignore the inescapable hazards that await you. So it was as the company waited in Girdwood one evening as I went to the operations room to talk with the company commander Sean, my former adjutant, shadowed, as ever, by his CSM, 'Big Eddie', who was now with A Company.

There had been another ugly stand-off between residents. The police had intervened but the already tense situation had been made somewhat worse by the recent death of a Protestant teenager who was run over when a car was driven onto the pavement in nearby 'White City', a Protestant estate adjoining a Republican area. The local Protestants were convinced that this was a murder, while the other side insisted it was a tragic accident. Whatever the truth was, a boy was dead.

The police inspector on duty was pessimistic about us having a peaceful night. 'The Prods are losing on every front and now they've had a kid killed. They're sayin' if it had been a Catholic child, Tony Blair and Bertie Ahern would be calling for a public inquiry. I'd be ready to move pretty fast if I was youse.'

'We're ready to go,' Sean said.

We walked back to the vehicles around which the company were still waiting. Some were chatting and smoking, others were resting, their body armour propped up as a pillow, their faces turned towards the sky, watching the bright vapour trails of the transatlantic airliners in the evening light as they set off for the new world. We sat down on the grass and the conversation inevitably turned to Holy Cross.

The RSM had lived there and he described the tribal warfare that had been a feature of the area for the last thirty-five years. He explained the subtleties of this territorial dispute: the Nationalist Ardoyne is overcrowded but they are prevented from expanding outwards because of the peace wall constructed in the early 1970s to keep the factions apart. The Republicans are attempting to ethnically cleanse a couple of streets across the divide in order to create some Lebensraum by attacking the Protestant residents with whatever they can lay their hands on. The Protestants are moving out from the interface because they've been given such a hard time, but violently challenge any attempt by Catholics to move into the void.

He related the tale of a girl from suburban Holywood, who had returned from a university in England with her English boyfriend, hoping to start a career as a journalist. To their delight they had been offered a flat in one of the Protestant houses near the interface with a rent of only £30 per week. They had quickly learned the reality of the area, however, when they went to visit the flat and had their car bricked as they parked and had to flee for their lives from Republican thugs who opposed any attempt to reoccupy conceded territory.

'You don't have to be on anybody's side to get bricked and shot at up there, as I think we'll find tonight,' he said, shaking his head. 'On the other hand, the Prods are doin' themselves no favours in this protest. They've no political savvy, see.'

My gaze had wandered off to the chimney pots that could be seen beyond the walls of the base and the magnificent chestnut trees swaying in the evening breeze when the company's operations officer ran out with a signal for Sean. He read it as the men watched him expectantly, some already shrugging on their body armour or gathering equipment. He crumpled the message in his paw and stuffed it in his pocket with a shout of 'Mount up. Move in five.'

The armoured convoy rolled out of the camp gates, guarded by a watch tower with a steel-mesh anti-rocket screen and laden with CCTV cameras. The area had once been a smart middle-class suburb of Belfast and had streets of large villas and four-storey townhouses built during the prosperity of the 1900s. The doctors and lawyers and merchants had long since moved away and as the sectarian mix of the area had shifted it had been abandoned to those who had no choice but to live there. By now many of the houses had collapsed or been burned down. A few remained, like ragged teeth in a hag's angry mouth, with wastelands pocked with burned-out cars and debris. Only the odd shred of railing or the magnificent trees lining the broad pavements were left as a clue to the area's former grandeur.

Here a stray dog drinking from a puddle would look up as we trundled slowly past, there some youths would be loitering at a street corner, sullenly ignoring us. We kept the armoured doors open to let in some air in this relatively friendly territory, then our convoy swung right onto the Crumlin Road, now looking like a bombsite with waste ground where the old linen mills had been and the remaining terraced houses adorned with paramilitary murals. A group of nine- or ten-year-old children, still on the streets at nine o'clock, stopped playing on a burned-out car to watch, before beginning to run alongside the slow-moving vehicles, calling, 'Any sweets, mister?'

'Watch out them Taigs[25] don't get ye,' one shouted as he gave up and stopped at the side of the road.

We pulled up at a junction a little short of the Ardoyne Road itself and Sean walked forward to speak to the police inspector standing at the back of the grey armoured police Land-Rover, holding a radio handset to his ear.

The Ardoyne Road is surprisingly narrow for such a well-known landmark. It is set on a slope overlooking the rest of Belfast and one can see the shipyards and the tranquil suburbs of east Belfast across the lough in the distance. At one end is the junction of the Crumlin Road and the Ardoyne Road at a roundabout, with a line of shops and a large pub, the 32 Degrees North[26], facing onto it. These 'Ardoyne shopfronts' are not much to look at, but it is a strategic location that has entered the British military lexicon. Lessons learned here in avoiding terrorist ambushes and rocket-propelled grenade attacks are now practised across the world. The road continues north up past the shops with residential housing on the right – smart new homes built for the larger family in mind – and on the other side the pavement is lined by the railings of a college. Thus far it is Republican territory, as marked by the

---

[25] Pejorative term for Catholics from the Irish translation of the name 'Timothy' (Tadhg) and generally accepted as more offensive than the commonly used term 'Fenians', as 'Nigger' would be to 'Darkie'.

[26] There is a cryptic Republican reference here to the thirty-two counties of Ireland and 'The North', as Republicans call the separate state of Northern Ireland.

slogans on the wall and the green, white and orange paving stones. At the top is Alliance Avenue, a row of post-war terraced houses, once the interface and for a brief time a mixed street, but now predominantly Catholic.

Surly crowds watched from each side of the road. On one side a group of men, some wearing Celtic football shirts over massive beer bellies, stood with their backs to the pub, staring hard at Sean or consulting each other with a guffaw over pints of lager, while putting on exaggerated gum-chewing or spitting displays. On the other side of the road, another mob, some of them in Glasgow Rangers tops, with cropped hair, heavily tattooed arms and knuckle-duster sovereign rings, stared aggressively back across the road.

Sean, still wearing his caubeen with its distinctive green feather, strode forward, his cover man walking a pace behind, glancing left and right ready to meet any threat. Suddenly a shout arose from the Catholic side: 'British bastard, fuck off back to England.' Then as he passed the Protestant gangs, the men growled insults in low voices such as 'Fenian bastard ye, fuck off back to the Free State[27].' A brick smacked the road behind Sean and skidded under the cover man's feet. As he jumped to miss it, the Catholic crowd jeered.

'See, even the fucken Taigs hate ye,' said a man in a T-shirt on the Protestant side, leaning on a telephone junction box, his face reddened by drink. 'Ya wanna get a Scottish regiment or the UDR up here or somethin'; they wuden take that.'

The policemen on duty glanced about nervously as Sean walked past. As Sean consulted with the police inspector up ahead, I dismounted and stood beside the Saxon armoured vehicle. I watched as Sean, having finished his brief, laughed, slapped the police inspector on the back and turned to come back. The platoon commanders and sergeants jumped down from their Land-Rovers and Saxons and gathered around the command vehicle. They walked in a swagger, rolling with the weight of their belt equipment and body armour enhanced with heavy ballistic plates. They had all put on their helmets in anticipation and now it was difficult to recognise individuals. As they waited, they were listening to the earpieces of the radio sets as Control gave an update on the situation. A helicopter hovered overhead, relaying television pictures back to our base.

---

[27] Contemptuous term for the Irish Republic.

Sean began his briefing. 'There's a large crowd of Loyalists gathering at Hesketh Park near the interface and the police want a shield line established. We'll move immediately, I'll lead. OK?'

The commanders nodded and headed back to their vehicles as I jumped into the back of Sean's vehicle with the RSM. As we set off, the high-pitched roar of the armoured vehicles' engines brought a jeer from both sides of the street. We rolled up the Ardoyne Road. Looking out of the hatches, I could see families in the bay-fronted houses to my right watching television as we rumbled slowly past, not even glancing around; they'd seen it all before.

Beyond Alliance Avenue and on up the hill, there are a series of streets of a 1960s build. The houses are pockmarked with bullet strikes, their wire mesh-covered windows smeared with paint bombs. This marks the beginning of 'Glynbryn', Protestant Ardoyne, where the streets and lamp-posts are bedecked with red, white and blue bunting and the flags of the Union, Ulster and a range of obscure paramilitary groups. The streets off to the left on Hesketh Park are of neat 1930s-style suburban semi-detached houses – just what you would find in any city across the UK, except here and there a bunch of flowers or a photograph attached to a lamp-post marks the scene of a murder. As I looked at the smashed homes I was reminded of the bullet-riddled streets of Sarajevo and the smouldering ruins of Brcko in Bosnia, where hostile communities had waged an almost identical hate war.

As we arrived the men spilled out and Sean walked across to speak to another police inspector, standing by his grey armoured car on Alliance Avenue looking up towards the Loyalists. Directed by the sergeant major, and accompanied by jeering and abuse from the Loyalist crowd, two Saxons were brought to face up the Ardoyne Road towards Glynbryn. Men fanned out on either side and in between with six-foot Perspex riot shields, which had a ridge running down each side to allow them to lock onto the shield next to them. This shield line could withstand anything up to high-velocity shots. Once arranged to the satisfaction of the CSM, with the Ardoyne Road now totally blocked and the two sides separated, the men relaxed and stood with one arm supporting the shield and the other hand in a protective glove, holding a hickory-stick baton over their right shoulder. A soldier with a fire extinguisher took his place behind each group of three men. This was the fireman, whose job it was to douse any soldier set on fire by a petrol bomb. We had been told our clothing would offer protection for ten seconds. In practice we knew that was bollocks, which was why the men wore long johns underneath. Beside the fireman was a baton gunner[28]. Baton rounds could only be fired with police permission and this was now rare. Men with rifles moved to vantage points to cover and return fire if the shield wall was shot at.

I had come to watch the company in action, not to take control, so, leaving Sean and the police inspector to do the planning, I strolled with the RSM just beyond the shield wall to speak to some residents who had gathered on the Protestant side. They were agitated but not unfriendly. We chatted about the situation and they explained in vast and sometimes confused detail about the local tensions and violent history since 1969. The rancour of this small group was striking as they recounted events from their perspective with a profound passion, reminding me of similar history lectures I had been given on peace lines in Bosnia and Africa. The residents emphasised the numerous murders that had taken place over the past years, a number within yards of us, and the unrelenting harassment they were suffering. I asked some residents about one of the more recent murders, marked by a bunch of flowers tied to a nearby telegraph pole. They explained how, only a few months previously, a local man had been gunned down as he climbed into his car and how the gunman had walked off laughing as neighbours ran to aid the dying man. (This was the taxi driver we had heard about.)

'Did anyone ever get caught for that?' I asked.

'Are you jokin'? The bastard lives down there!' An angry little man pointed to a group of 'community activists' who stood 100m down the road, clearly directing operations on their side and occasionally speaking into radios while glaring up at us. As he pointed, a stocky man in his thirties with short, gelled hair and a moustache stopped speaking into his radio, looked up and gave a little wave, delight written over his face. The others in his group laughed and slapped his back.

'Is that him?' I asked, studying the laughing man.

'Na, tha's Sean Kelly, the Shankill bomber[29]. Remember him that blew

---

[28] The baton gun fires a non-lethal blunt plastic bung. It is designed to cause a debilitating blunt injury that will allow a rioter to be arrested. The use of these rounds is closely watched by a government adjudicator called the 'Police Ombudsman' and senior police officers are frequently called to account if there is considered to be even the slightest zeal in deploying this crowd-control technique.

[29] 10 October 1993, an IRA bomb killed nine innocent victims including two children. Thomas Begley, the man carrying the bomb, died when it exploded prematurely but Kelly was arrested. He served seven years of a life sentence for nine murders. He was released under licence as part of the terms of the Good Friday Agreement.

up the shops and killed loads of women and children. See, the bastard knows we're talking about him.'

I was intrigued and wanted to know more but my attention was abruptly distracted as four or five low-velocity shots rattled out from the top of the road from the direction of Loyalist houses and struck the window and roof of one of our armoured vehicles, sparks flashing where they hit. I dashed for the cover of the shield line as the residents scattered into their houses.

'Do not return fire unless you can clearly identify a target!' one of the young officers called out as the soldiers and police scanned the gathering gloom with their rifle sights from the cover of the vehicles, their backs to the now-jeering Republican mob.

'Let the fuckers have it!' one man cried. 'Youse'd shoot at us given half a chance.'

'Keep yer cool!' the CSM boomed. 'Have youse changed yer sights for nightsights? If not do so now.'

Behind us some of the 'community activists' marched up Alliance Avenue and began opening the lamp-posts and snipping the wires with pliers, with some kids of ten or twelve following them. As the lights snapped off I turned to the policeman beside me.

'Shall I get some of Sean's lads to stop that?' I asked.

'Na,' the policeman said. 'They're actually doin' us a favour. We're harder to see with 'em off.'

'Fair point,' I said. 'It's a fine line between law and order, and a tactical call.'

'In any case, they'd love us to try it,' the police officer said. 'We'll not rise that easily.'

Not long after the shooting, the crowd on the Loyalist side, which had retreated down side streets at the shots, drifted back to the front of the shield line. A girl of about fifteen, sipping from a bottle of cider, minced over from a group of Protestant youths standing on the corner. She walked up to the CSM.

'Wud youse fellas do us a favour and go and do somethin' about those Fenians?' She indicated the men working at the lamp-posts (which I thought was a bit rich since her side had been shooting at us only five minutes before).

Big Eddie didn't even look down at her as he snarled in his Dublin brogue, 'Sure, we're all Fenians too.'

The girl's face was a picture as she scurried back to her group, pointing at us.

'Taigs!' shouted a plump and much-tattooed youth, flicking a two-fingered salute at us, a baseball cap pulled down low on his head.

'I was at school with that wee fat cunt,' the ranger next to me said. 'I'm gonna knock his bollocks in when I'm next home on leave.'

The men laughed. The situation was quiet but tense. A crowd had gathered where the shots had come from and they were clearly in a mood for a fight. Behind us the Republican bullyboys had closed in too and were leaning on low garden walls about twenty metres behind us. I had no doubt that their gunmen were ready to join the fray when ordered and were probably scanning us with their sights in the now-darkened houses to our rear. Sean sensibly had men covering both directions as the opposing factions watched us intently, swaying from side to side as they tried to see over our shield line to glimpse what the other side were up to.

Now and again a missile would clatter off the Perspex shield wall, or smack off the front of a vehicle, to cheers from one crowd or another. Men with football scarves over their faces would walk down close to the shield line from the Loyalist end, with some of the more courageous, or drunk, banging on the shields with their fists or kicking at them, to the delight of the spectators. When one athletic type began taking running jumps to crash onto the shields with both feet, to great cheers, we briefly considered choreographing a sudden opening of the shields to allow him to sail through into the arms of the RUC.

Soon the crowd settled down and we waited for the next round. Streetlights in the side streets shed some light onto the Ardoyne Road, but it was otherwise in darkness. I was standing to one side of the road chatting to the RUC superintendent in charge of the incident while Sean and A Company got on with covering the road. 'Will we force the way through tomorrow to get the children to school?' I asked.

'The local priest is talking about taking them up the Crumlin and in the back way. I personally would prefer to clear the road. I just don't know yet,' he said, shrugging his shoulders as he took off his cap to wipe the sweat out with a handkerchief.

Just then a Belfast City Transport bus turned the corner above us, some 200m up the road. It was barely visible in the black hole that the switched-off street lights had created against the glare of the city's other ambient light – all framed by the menacing darkness of the Black Mountain in the background. Its lights were out and we could see figures jumping on and off.

'Is dis a normal bus route?' one of the rangers enquired nervously in a Southern Irish accent.

'Depends if ya call hijacked buses normal,' said the man beside him, a local of the area.

'Dat's what I thought – oh, here we go,' the first soldier said, flipping down his riot visor.

As he spoke, a crowd could be seen in the distance, gathering around as if in conference. Then a man ran out, a dull light flickering in his hand, and jumped on board the bus. The flash of a petrol bomb lit the darkness and it burst inside with a *whoomph*. To our mirth, the idiot who had thrown it had got a little too close and could be seen hopping about and beating furiously at the flames on his own clothes.

'Looks like he's got his focken blazer on then,' one of the soldiers quipped.

'Fares please,' another said as the bus began to roll down the hill towards us accompanied by a cheer from the Loyalist crowd.

'The CO will be all right,' a Scouse soldier said. 'He'll have his OAP bus pass.'

'That's the CO standing behind you, you knob,' his platoon sergeant said. We all roared with laughter as he sheepishly glanced behind him.

'Sorry, sir.'

The bus's progress slowed as it mounted the pavement before smashing into a lamp-post, which brought it to a halt about twenty metres from our base line. Orders were shouted and a line of men with shields advanced past the burning vehicle as a soldier stepped on board with a fire extinguisher. Darkness was restored. A hail of stones and bottles clattered off the shield wall as it backed towards our vehicles once again.

This continued until around two in the morning, when the violence petered out. By this time both communities had settled down for the night and the streets were quiet. I turned to the RSM. 'Shall we leave A Company to it then?'

'Aye, sir. Enough excitement for one night,' he said, looking sadly around the once-pleasant streets of his childhood.

Incidents like these were regrettably common during our tour of duty in Northern Ireland and served to underline the need to be scrupulously even-handed in our dealings with the locals. That particular period of violence at the Holy Cross was to drag on into the winter, when local clergy achieved a form of settlement. Between June and October 2001, 262 petrol bombs and seven blast grenades had been thrown, as well as tons of stones, and 113 members of the police and army were injured. Showing amazing restraint, the security forces responded with a total of twenty-nine baton rounds in total over the tense episode. (Had it been left to me and had the technology existed, I would have favoured belt-fed baton guns firing thousands of the things.) The confrontation also served to get the message home to even the youngest ranger that when a mob gathered, common sense went out of the window. Steadiness in the face of such provocation became ingrained in each man after facing crowds hell bent on destruction, with many of them not even knowing why, but simply subscribing to the visceral compulsion of mob violence.

The marching season came to an end and our focus shifted to the growing threat from the Dissident Republicans. One curious episode was when a local Catholic priest stopped at a vehicle checkpoint outside Dungannon and embarked on a long chat with one of our young platoon commanders. His message was that the ceasefire was solid on the Provisional IRA front but that they had no responsibility for the Dissidents. It seemed strange, as if he was an emissary of the paramilitaries, which as an ordained priest he could not possibly be, of course. I had this optimistic viewpoint confirmed one day when I met one of my old adversaries from the Lough Shore PIRA, outside a well-known PIRA haunt. I knew him from my previous tour and regarded him as an authority on the subject. His credentials were impeccable: he had had relatives shot dead by both the SAS and the UVF. He related an incident at a pub in a hamlet where the main man in PIRA had been drinking when Dissidents, he didn't say who, came in. The local boss challenged them over a weapon they had, saying that if the weapon was an IRA one he would have them both shot. They assured him it wasn't an IRA pistol and the boss man accepted this and carried on drinking after he'd let them go. It is one of those rare occasions where an unarmed man can challenge armed men and in doing so make them fear for their lives. It is so 'Northern Ireland' though, and I believe the story was related to me to illustrate that behind the scenes PIRA were still in charge.

In mid-July word came through that the Dissidents were getting ready for a hit. There was activity around their home in Dunnamore to the north of our area. We mounted a large-scale search of farmland near the suspect's family home. One morning at dawn in July 2001, we sealed off the search area, some four square miles.

These searches are meticulously planned. This particular one involved a week of preparation and was aided by numerous specialist agencies and air photographs. Before we went onto the ground the terrain was carefully examined from the air for obvious booby traps and when we deployed we knew we had to be extremely alert to the threat of a concealed explosive device and avoid showing an unguarded flank against which a shooting, mortar or rocket attack could be launched. Unlike searches in Loyalist areas, where the population would be at least benign if not overtly friendly, in hard Republican areas we had to concentrate on the possibility of an attack. We knew that the terrorists who had grown up in the fields in which we now stood could use their local knowledge to mount a deadly assault at a vulnerable flank in a matter of minutes.

The area to be searched was boggy farmland dotted with derelict farm buildings and single-storey cottages, connected by a maze of narrow lanes. Movement across this terrain was slow and the sunken farm tracks and high hedgerows made it difficult to keep an overwatch. As we conducted the search, it became clear that we were getting close to whatever was hidden there, as the main suspect and his brothers, men in their twenties and early thirties, were all out in their fields watching our progress through binoculars. They then started driving in and out of the search area, complaining loudly each time they were stopped and at one stage even appearing in a pony and trap.

What was interesting was that the vast majority of the local community in this overwhelming Republican area turned out to be very understanding and I was even treated to cups of tea at one or two houses. That would just not have happened prior to the signing of the Good Friday Peace Accord.

'Everyone knows they're at it,' one resident said, referring to this Dissident Republican group. 'So what are you going to do about it?'

'What are *you* going to do about it?' I replied. 'We can only beat this together.'

Our information about the suspected hide was sketchy and it was clear that we would have to conduct an almost fingertip search. Day one of the hunt was a frustrating affair and was mainly spent waiting as the specialist agencies checked for the obvious signs of improvised explosive devices. Our chief entertainment was drinking tea with the men who were not on guard. Among them was Ranger Cochrane, the tall lad who had spotted for me on the sniper course in Africa. He was obviously just off duty as the sweat had plastered his dark hair to his forehead where he had been wearing his helmet. As he spotted me he nudged his mates.

'Here, sir, remember in Botswana you said if we went to Belfast you'd eat yer hat. Is that a new one you've on?'

'I meant sent there for the whole tour,' I retorted and immediately regretted rising to the bait, as they fell about laughing.

The second day of the search came and went, with huge effort expended but nothing found. It also pissed down. On the third day, just about teatime, I had a call from the search party deep in the cordoned-off zone. Something suspicious had finally been found. The Ammunition Technical Officer, ATO, went forward to clear the way, checking once more for booby traps. When the all-clear was given, teams dug out a wheelie bin that had been built into a large bank of earth. Inside were 1,000 rounds of 7.62mm Fabrique Nationale Belgian link – ammunition for a light machine gun. The investigation continued.

The evening of the find I was back in Dungannon in my room in Killymeal House when the phone rang at two o'clock in the morning. I expected it to be my ops room but was surprised to hear my sister's voice instead.

'It's Dad,' she said. 'He's not too good. They've taken him to hospital. You'd better come.'

I went to the ops room and got the keys of my car and booked out. When I arrived at the hospital in Belfast my sister and mother were there. My father, who was ninety-one, was asleep but looking frail. I spoke to the doctor. She said he'd had a bad turn but was now stable. I sat with him for a while and then I had to leave and return to the search.

Attention now moved to a farm that was on the very edge of the designated area. I was standing at a gate near one of the cordons when my mobile went. It was my mother.

'Your dad has gone,' she said. 'He didn't wake up.'

'I can't come just now,' I said. 'Will you be OK? We'll need to make arrangements.'

Just then one of the search-team leaders came jogging up. 'We've found a large hide,' he said.

'Well done, I'll be there in a moment,' I replied.

'Is it your father?' asked the RSM, who was standing with me and who sensed something was up.

'Yes, I'm afraid so.'

'I'm sorry for your trouble, sir,' he said, clasping my arm.

'Do you know what he'd want me to do now, RSM?' I asked after a moment.

'Go to your mother?'

'No, the old boy would want me to nail those bastards over there, so let's get to it.'

We headed over to the search area. We had indeed found what could have been a large hide, but it was sadly empty. The bunker was extremely sophisticated. Built a metre below ground, it was about fourteen metres long and one and a half metres wide and had been carefully waterproofed. There were cupboards down each side and carpet on the floor and it even had electric light. Access was through a manhole that from the outside made it look like a drain. Looking back at aerial photographs, it was clear that it had been built in April of that year. We abandoned the search shortly after this, even though we were certain there was a machine gun somewhere to go with the link we had captured. As it happened we were right and two weeks later the Dissidents could be heard test-firing the gun with long bursts in a forest only a mile from the area we had searched. The message was clear: We've still got it!

We buried my father on 19 July from our family church. Without prompting and to my delight, the Pipe Major of the battalion appeared in full regalia and piped the coffin to the hearse. It was the first pipe music I had heard at the church since the Pipe Major's grandfather had piped at my wedding there fifteen years before. A number of the men who were not on duty had also come along, which was a pleasant surprise for me and a show of respect I very much appreciated, as they could not have known my dad.

On Saturdays I would have the company commanders up to Killymeal House for a conference. We would cover personnel, intelligence and operational issues and then I would catch up with details such as reports on compassionate cases and those off sick. It was during one of these conferences that I was briefed that one of my men, Ranger Paul Cochrane, the lad I had met on the sniper course in Africa and had seen only the previous week on the search, was in hospital with an ear infection. I spent the Sunday on patrol with the Home Service company based in neighbouring County Fermanagh. By the Monday evening I was wondering where Cochrane was in hospital when I had a call on my mobile from the commander of B Company, Mike. He sounded shocked. In a solemn voice he reported that Ranger Paul Cochrane had shot himself in the head.

I drove with the RSM to the Craigavon Hospital.

I told the RSM to find out where his mum and dad were (they had been asked to come to the hospital but had not yet been given the heartbreaking news). I then set off to find Ranger Cochrane. I found Mike, who looked grey and sad, and I asked where the boy was. He indicated the emergency room. I asked him to organise a room for me to speak to Ranger Cochrane's parents in private when they arrived. I walked to the emergency room, where a soldier, not one of mine, was peering round the door.

'You – get to your post – you're here to cover us and not to gawp. There is nothing to see.'

He scrambled away. A pretty young girl stepped forward.

'Hi. I'm Jo, the duty doctor. Are you with Paul?' she asked solemnly.

'I'm his boss,' I said.

'He's very bad, I'm afraid he's –'

'I know,' I said. 'Ladies, thank you for your efforts.' I addressed all of the nurses as well as Jo. 'You've done your best for Paul. Can I ask just to have a minute with him, then could you please get him ready for his mum and dad to see him? Whatever you can do.'

They gathered their equipment and I walked over to the lanky lad I had last seen joking with his mates at the search. He was stripped to the waist and had only one boot on as they had tried to get a fluid line into his foot. I could see he had put the gun in his mouth. There was a lot of damage to his cheeks. Thankfully the other wounds were not too bad. I held his hand. It was still warm.

'Paul, what have you done?' I said to the dead boy. 'Why?'

He was only nineteen and looked like a broken child as he lay there. I bowed my head in silent prayer, then after a minute I felt someone close. I looked round to see the nurses and the RSM.

'The parents are here,' he said.

'We'll look after him now,' a nurse said as she passed, pulling the curtains around the bed.

As gently as I could I broke the news that no parent ever wants to hear. Giving them my heartfelt condolences, I left them to their grief and went to see Paul again. The nurses had done a professional job. He was looking much better but nothing could totally disguise the damage of the gunshot. I left it for five minutes then went into a room now filled with sobbing. After a short while I took Paul's parents and brother and sister to see Paul's body.

Outside I met the policeman in charge. 'Will the RUC be handling this?' I asked.

'We already have it. It looks pretty clear what happened, though. I'll be in touch.' He put his cap on and left.

I went to the barracks in Armagh and visited the scene where the police were investigating the death. There was a Royal Military Police

(RMP) warrant officer. He said, 'You may wish to see this. I'll need to keep it as evidence.'

He handed me a blue airmail letter marked 'CO'. Inside was a suicide letter from Ranger Paul Cochrane to me. In it he said, 'You are my hero . . .' but then came a stinging line which read, 'you weren't there when I needed you . . .'

I just wish he'd called me.

I asked the RMP to keep me briefed and returned to Dungannon with a very heavy heart. The men gathered in the cookhouse, our largest venue. They were silent, as word had already spread as to why they were being called together, and the only noise came from the shuffling of feet as more arrived and the whir of the coolers on the drinks machines. I broke the news to them as best I could. The grief was genuine across the whole battalion for this excellent young man, his life cut short, his parents' life in ruins and all of us in this family battalion desolate at the loss. After they had no questions, the men were dismissed and left to low murmurings and the sound of chairs being dragged to one side, each lost in their grief for the lad who had gone.

I went to my office and wrote to Billy and Lynn Cochrane, as a formal expression of condolence to the whole Cochrane family and Lynn's family, the McKees. It was also my personal undertaking to do all that I could for them. I dictated to the Adjutant an instruction for a full and independent Board of Inquiry into the circumstances of the death, before heading off to bed. Sleep did not come easily as I contemplated the lad who had died. I could not even bear to think about what the family were going through. Having lost my father the week before at nearly ninety-two was bad enough, but to lose a child – well, it was unthinkable.

The next day I went to Armagh to visit the company and they were understandably in a state of shock. Suicide is statistically not uncommon among youths, but when it happens in your battalion it is still a numbing blow; and if you knew the lad, then . . . Young men bond closely in the Army and Cochrane was popular across the battalion, with some of his childhood friends even serving alongside him. His CSM was a close neighbour from home. So when something of that nature strikes, it is a bereavement for the whole unit.

But what had caused him to take his own life? We never really found out. There was a great deal of speculation that he was very upset that he could not go home to his parents' house because he was ill with the ear infection. (It seems that one doctor had told him he should go home but that his company commander had delayed this because, as members of the Field Army, my soldiers needed clearance from Headquarters Northern Ireland to go home to Belfast.) But there *had* to be more. I do not know what happened between him leaving the room having chatted with Ranger Tabuya, one of the lads from Fiji, at 1730 hours, overtly quite composed, and the point forty-five minutes later, during his final tearful telephone conversation with his father, when he actually pulled the trigger.

The regimental family immediately rallied around the Cochrane family and sought to give them every possible support. The battalion arranged and paid for the funeral and a church for the service. A venue for a reception was arranged at the British Legion and the battalion provided lunch and drinks. What no one could have foreseen was that in the days after the funeral, the attitude of the family was to change radically. They became estranged from the regiment, the Army and even some of Paul's own comrades. That was sadly at a time when they needed the support of the regiment.

At the graveside it poured with rain as the shots were fired over the coffin. It was a poignant reminder of the extent of the tragedy. Some of Paul Cochrane's childhood friends and schoolmates gave a moving eulogy at the service. Afterwards the men from B Company who had attended en masse were treated to a reception at the Civil Service sports club, a secure location. Paul Cochrane, that lively young man, would be sadly missed.

The company was brought back to barracks and as they were out on an operation the next day they were ordered to bed by 2200 hours. They had been allowed to drink beer at the reception, which was unusual on an operational deployment, but permitted in these circumstances. (Soldiers in the Field Army are only permitted to drink two cans of beer per day when deployed on duty.) The company storeman, Ranger Vance, who had been moved to the stores after he was investigated for a sexual assault on a younger soldier the previous year in Catterick, had different ideas that night. The RMP investigation into the previous year's alleged sexual assault had already taken over a year and in the meantime the most I could legally do was move the alleged offender within the company, in this case out of a rifle platoon and into the stores to work supervised by the Company Quartermaster Sergeant. To do otherwise would have been discriminating against a gay man on unsubstantiated allegations. In any case, on the evening of Paul Cochrane's funeral

Vance identified a young soldier for his attentions and treated him to numerous drinks during the reception. He then, after the company had turned in, got him up again and took him to the bar on camp. There is no restriction on drinking there. We know from the evidence given in court that he plied the younger man with vodka before buying a bottle to take back to the stores where he slept. The young soldier fell asleep. The company was awakened by a commotion and the first witnesses ran into the stores to find Vance raping the now-naked and semiconscious younger soldier.

I can tell you that this was a most unwelcome end to the Cochrane affair. But it did raise a question. He had been alone in the block with the storeman while the rest of the company was deployed on an operational task. I immediately had the RMP investigate the possibility that Cochrane had been interfered with in the last hours of his life. After an investigation and strenuous denials by Vance, amid unwelcome media speculation, the case was dropped. The Board of Inquiry found that there was no more than a circumstantial link between the two events and saw no purpose in pursuing the issue further.

I asked the RUC to keep Vance on remand. We could not have him back. The man who had been raped was from Liverpool, and the other men from there took the assault badly. To add to this, a lot of the Ulstermen were convinced he had interfered with Cochrane and were gunning for him. I explained to my commander that I could not accept responsibility for the life of the man if he was returned to my unit. Fortunately he didn't come back. After conviction in a civil court for rape, Vance served his sentence in Northern Ireland, with another conviction from a Canterbury court for a serious sexual assault to run concurrently. He is still in prison. His victim was emotionally unable to return to duty again and was also discharged at his request.

As the autumn turned to winter and our end-of-tour date loomed, things were increasingly tense in East Tyrone. One wickedly wet evening, towards the end of our time in Ireland, a van carrying offal from a nearby meat-processing factory tried to stop suddenly as it sped along the notorious A4 road that ran past Dungannon. The van slowed but the glutinous offal shifted sideways, tipping the van and smashing it all over the road. The driver was killed instantly. Disastrous as this was – with a wreck and a dead driver – the half a ton of liver, kidneys and hearts all over the road were making slippery conditions even worse and threatening to cause further accidents. The police rushed out from

Dungannon and did what police all over the world do, direct the traffic to safety.

The accident happened near a rural pub and as the drinkers spilled out to have a look, what the vast majority saw was the scene of a tragedy and an unfortunate motorist dead, with a serious risk to other motorists that needed to be cleared. One small group of drinkers saw things differently, however: the East Tyrone Dissident IRA. They saw a lot of policemen with their backs to them and their attention distracted – ideal targets. They immediately mounted an operation and sent for an assault rifle.

When this was detected by RUC Special Branch they contacted us and we threw everything we had out on the road. We had no idea where the shooting was going to be, as the police were deployed widely. We just had to hope to be lucky. That night we had four sixteen-man patrols or 'multiples'[30] on the ground at any one time, all accompanied by policemen. In addition to their basic uniform, ammunition and radios, these patrols carried electromagnetic countermeasures (ECM) equipment to block attacks by remote-controlled bombs, red torches to signal to traffic and 'caltrops', lightweight spikes that could be pulled across the road to destroy the tyres of a fleeing vehicle. One man in four, sometimes one man in two, would have a nightsight.

Across my area of command we went into overdrive. Despite the heavy rain and poor visibility we called in the helicopter based in Armagh to assist us and mustered as many vehicle patrols as we could. We sent the cooks into the watchtowers and woke up sleeping off-duty patrols. We even replaced the infantry on the gate with HQ staff as every last man we could find was dispatched to the area where the crash happened. I called the reserve multiples to stop and search cars on the main routes around Dungannon itself, hoping to intercept the assault rifle as it was moved from its hide. By now over 300 men were silently patrolling through the night, setting up road checkpoints and then collapsing them to cut across fields in the inky blackness and pouring rain. Meanwhile, a helicopter flew overhead, stopping on occasion to search the hedgerows and back roads with a powerful searchlight – 'Nitesun'. On board was another multiple, the so-called 'Eagle Patrol', ready to land and take on any threat.

The tension in the operations room was electric. As the rain beat off the windows, patrols called in to report they were in place and new

---

30 The basic unit was four men – a 'brick'. A 'multiple' was literally a multiple of bricks.

patrols reported themselves ready to deploy. Content that we had the area covered, we were about to heave a sigh of relief when word came from Special Branch that they believed that the terrorists now had their weapon, had found a target and were in the final stages of the attack. What more could we do? We kept up the pressure –and waited for the worst. It looked like our best was not good enough.

By the early hours of the morning the police reported that the accident had been cleared up and the body removed. They were calling their patrols in. We waited until dawn before bringing our soaking wet and exhausted men back in, some of them only having an hour to grab a bite to eat before the next day's scheduled patrols set off again.

I consulted with the police. We must have got something right. No shooting had taken place, though the police were certain that the threat had been very real. Unlike the suicide attackers of Iraq, Dissident Republicans want to survive. They will only attack the unsuspecting and they will abandon a mission if there is the least threat to their skins or liberty. Special Branch later suspected that the attack had been called off when Nitesun illuminated them as they sat in their car or a patrol had passed close by. Convinced they had been rumbled, they fled.

It was one more tragedy averted in an area where they had once been commonplace. This was brought home when I visited the church one evening of a friend who was a local Presbyterian minister. As I looked around the walls of his small rural church I counted twelve plaques to local men murdered while serving in the part-time security forces over recent years. All the plaques told a different, tragic tale. One of the men had been murdered while working in his farmyard one evening in front of his two children. The mother had been at a church meeting in Cookstown and returned to find her children covered in blood, cradling the body of their father, broken open by the gunfire, and steam rising in the cold night from his still warm body. The minister's own cousin had been murdered only yards away at the front of the police station. His crime? He was a reserve police officer. Numerous local Nationalists had fallen victim to the random Loyalist paramilitary killings too. They had no memorial, except grieving families and shattered lives. The suffering was not all one-sided, though. The Republicans and Loyalist paramilitaries had not escaped unscathed. The SAS had taken a significant toll of the terrorists in East Tyrone. It would be fair to say honours were about even across the region.

The lesson we had learned above all was that operations such as the one we had just conducted in East Tyrone could not hope to be successful if you did not seek to harness the good will of the local population. That was where we expended ninety per cent of our efforts. Some were on your side from the off and they were a great help, providing an outer layer of defence as they watched out for the signs of potential attacks. Some were indifferent. They just accepted you were there and lived with it. Others were hostile, whatever happened. You could do little to sway them.

In my view, the key to success was to establish your humanity and then take every opportunity to reinforce that. That meant not being too uniform. We wanted the public to recognise individuals. Where possible the men wore caubeens rather than helmets to make them recognisable. I constantly encouraged them to engage the public in conversation during their duties and to get to know the locals. 'If you stop a car, get your head right in the window and talk to everyone onboard. Chat about the weather; tell them where you are from. Connect with them.' The simple fact is that it is easier to kill a uniform than to kill a person.

We reaped the fruits of our labours in East Tyrone. If you set high standards and kept to them, even the hard core sometimes came down on your side. It might have been the excesses of their own side or weariness of violence. It might have been that they recognised you as a human, like their brother, son or father. But when they did take your side, even fleetingly, what they could tell you and warn you about was the most precious information, and the most likely to save lives. Lives were undoubtedly saved by such information during our tour of duty in East Tyrone. It was clear that winning the hearts and minds of the local communities, and thereby isolating those who chose the path of violence, was more valuable than ammunition. It was a lesson that we would take with us and apply elsewhere.

# —5—

# OPERATION FRESCO

We returned from the Northern Ireland tour of duty in mid-December 2001 to a welcome Christmas leave and then began re-forming the battalion into its air assault role. This meant a series of heavy-weapons cadres, an NCO cadre and a period of intensive training for the battalion headquarters staff. The culmination of all this would be a trip to Canada for a live firing exercise. One piece of good news was that our recruiting efforts had begun to pay off and it was clear that, having taken over the battalion at 250 under strength, we had now reduced that by half and, with the Gurkha company now returned from the Falklands as reinforcements, we were even slightly above established strength of 690. My aim was to deliver the battalion at the end of my tour fully manned.

The period leading up to deploying to Canada proved to be a testing one for me as a commander. There were around 100 men in the battalion from second-generation Irish families in London, Manchester, Birmingham and in particular Liverpool – the 'Scousers'. Often excellent soldiers, the shame was that a small minority of the Scousers behaved as anything other than the hard-working men we got from the land of their forefathers in the Republic of Ireland. It could all have been dealt with, except they brought into our ranks a previously unheard of problem – drugs.

Compulsory drugs testing, or CDT, is a necessary and effective way of ensuring that the Army remains a drug-free environment. We had four CDTs during my time in command, two at my own request. Generally, I took as fair a line as I could. Class-A drugs brought an automatic discharge from the Army unless a special appeal was lodged. I lodged a number of these – but only for men under nineteen years who had tested positive for a small amount of ecstasy. I believed that at that age they deserved a second chance if the forensic tests bore out their full and contrite confession. However, the rate of reoffending of these 'second chancers' was disappointingly high. With cannabis I took a less harsh line. For a man who was prepared to confess all and who was not a regular user I would launch an appeal. The fact of life was that the stuff was freely available in many of the pubs and clubs of Canterbury, a university city.

I would have no truck with the drug suppliers, however, especially of ecstasy. It became clear that we had some men who acted as middlemen for more sinister types back home in Liverpool. I am in no doubt, nor are the Kent Police, that there was an attempt to corner the drugs trade in the area by these men. I had a blitz on this trade and ended up having to dismiss about forty-seven soldiers. The strange thing was that though they were ruthless in pursuit of their hobby they were affable people to speak to and often very good at their jobs. I was not without compassion but I had to be careful of becoming too sympathetic towards them. One particular lad, aged seventeen and a half, was a constant absentee and was suspected of drug dealing. He was not a particularly good soldier, but he was young and vulnerable. We had been in the process of discharging him during one of his long absences when I had a tearful phone call from his mother begging for him to have a second chance. I relented and he was returned to the battalion on the Wednesday fresh from Liverpool to start anew. Sadly, he was to let down both his mum and me. He was arrested on the Friday night by Kent CID for openly dealing drugs in a local nightspot. I was always very conscious of the duty of care I had to all of my soldiers and the responsibility I had to the parents of the younger men to provide a drugs-free and bullying-free working environment.

Canada is an excellent training ground for the British Army. We were destined for Wainwright in Alberta, right in the middle of that massive country and two hours' drive from the nearest airfield at Edmonton. Camp Wainwright had been a Canadian POW camp in the Second World War and there was one of the old guard towers still standing. At one point it had also been a reserve for buffalo, but now only about six of the animals were kept in a field next to the front gate.

The exercise began with a rotation where the companies would do their live firing and then go on adventure training, followed by a week off in Edmonton. They would then return as the battalion came together for a march-and-shoot competition followed by a battle group field exercise. The adventure training was at a location called Trail's End, just outside Calgary. The activities on offer included white-water rafting, rock climbing, snow and ice climbing, mountaineering and canoeing. The men of course loved it, even though some had a close encounter with a bear, which are pretty common in the beautiful Canadian wilderness.

It was an optimistic time for me too with the news that I had been selected for promotion to colonel. While this was welcome news, it would also mean I would be moving on early from command. In addition, the Northern Ireland operational honours and awards list had just been issued and I had been awarded a Queen's Commendation for leading the battalion during the last tour of duty.

The field firing had been going well. One company was under-achieving, however, and they would clearly need some extra tuition. I was aware that the Brigade Commander would be visiting soon and the rotation of companies meant that this would be the company he would see in the field. I wanted the company to be seen in a good light. I visited them on a night-firing range and to say it was perfunctory was an understatement. They were simply turning live rounds into empty cases and the men looked bored. When I asked them what they were supposed to be doing no one knew. I was sorely tempted to make one of the eager young captains up to local major to inject some order and to give leadership to this otherwise enthusiastic company, but I was keenly aware that this would spell the end of this particular company commander's career and I wanted to give him every chance to snap out of his daze and achieve something. I allowed him the benefit of the doubt as he was a recent graduate from the Joint Services Staff College and perhaps he had dwelt too heavily on theory and lacked experience.

Live firing at night at company level in the British Army is an exhilarating affair but if everyone is not a hundred per cent switched on and doing exactly as they should, it can be extremely dangerous too. The targets are set out like a real enemy, in prepared positions that can be spread out over a square kilometre, but arranged to ensure that when engaged by friendly forces the shots are directed in a safe direction. The exercising troops are briefed on the safety rules, then they go into operational-rehearsal mode. They will not have seen the position and are expected to navigate silently to the target area from around five to ten kilometres away. At the end of their march they meet safety staff whose task it is to orientate them to the range and to issue 'Cylumes' – coloured lights which they wear at the back of their helmets, blue for exercising troops, orange for safety staff. The rest is free play.

The targets are a mixture of electronic targets, three-dimensional fibre-glass figures which pop up on the press of a button from the safety staff and which can also have sound effects of firing, and figures of running men pasted onto target boards. These are usually set out on the depth targets – the target areas farthest away from the start. In our exercises the supporting guns, 105mm howitzers, would blast the depth targets for twenty minutes with high explosive. The mortar platoon would join in with 81mm high explosive and switch fast between targets to practise cutting off any hope of escape or reinforcement on a real mission. In Canada we had the fire adjusted by the battery to within 250m of the troops under the watchful eye of safety staff from the Royal School of Artillery. The troops could feel the pressure waves strike their faces as the rounds detonated and smell the sticky residue of the ink-black blasts of the high-explosive shells illuminating the target with deep red flashes as they struck with a deafening crack (for those who dared to look up).

Rounds completed, the troops would rise and swiftly sweep in at a jog-run into the midst of the objective through lanes cleared by the engineers, either by hand or in this instance by the blast of a 'Bangalore Torpedo' (an explosive hosepipe passed silently under the enemy's barbed wire) – known to the boys as a 'bangs galore'. As they moved into the enemy position, closely followed by safety staff commentating quietly to each other on a separate safety radio net, the targets would be activated and would snap up with a burst of simulated machine-gun fire from gas bottles in the mechanism. Invariably these would just as swiftly disappear in a hail of well-aimed shots fired through precisely zeroed nightsights, with those with optics only firing towards the tracers marking the target. The British Army is still woefully under-equipped with night-vision devices and we managed only one between four on operations, a much worse ratio than comparable armies.

It was around this time that we had another brush with fate. One of the Fijian lads, Ranger Bulimaibu, known to us as Bo, had a freak accident while mountain biking. He was about to cross a stream when his wheel hit a rock, throwing him forward. He struck a large boulder with his nose and was stunned. A Canadian helicopter medivacked him to Edmonton, where I went to see him in the neurology ward. It didn't look good. There was a danger of the bleeding pressing on the part of his brain that controlled his breathing. We immediately called his family in Fiji. The crisis lasted for five tense days, until he seemed to recover and was moved to a general ward.

I returned to Wainwright to start planning the field training exercise (FTX). I was in my room when the phone rang. It was a very solemn-sounding operations officer.

'Sir, I have some very bad news for you.' I immediately assumed Bo had relapsed, but he went on: 'Ranger McMaster has had a parachuting accident. I'm afraid he is dead.'

I could hardly believe it. I had spent a week worrying about one lad and seen him recover only to have another snatched away without a chance.

'I'm coming over,' I said, then called my driver. 'There's been a disaster. Wee McMaster's bought it parachuting down in Byker. Are you up for another drive?'

There was silence. It dawned on me then that he was a good friend of Stuart McMaster; they had been in the pipe band together. 'I'll bring the wagon round,' he said quietly.

When I came out, the RSM, Doug Beattie,[31] was in the staff car, a massive Chevrolet Suburban.

'Has the Adjutant informed the next of kin?' I asked.

'Aye. You know it's Jimmy McMaster's lad?'

I hadn't met Jimmy McMaster before but he was known to me through his work for charities at our regimental depot in Ballymena. A deeply religious and gentle soul, he had served in the Army with the Royal Irish Rangers. We drove the three hours in silence, lost in our own thoughts. I cherished every one of my men, they were all my children and they looked to me as their chief. Now here we were, having survived one of the most dangerous Northern Ireland tours of recent times relatively unscathed, with another teenager dead – and to a sporting accident, not even a shot fired.

The inquiry into Stuart's death began immediately. It transpired that he had been a star on his sports parachuting course. He had completed his training jumps and had taken up the option of buying more jumps. During this particular descent he had left the aircraft brimming with confidence. However, just as he deployed his main canopy, the risers, or

---

[31] The previous RSM, Jim Pritchard, had been granted a commission and Warrant Officer Dougie Beattie took over on St Patrick's Day 2002.

cords that hold the parachutist to the 'chute, got caught on his automatic opening device, which opens your parachute if you fail to operate by a certain height. The effect was that he had an uneven canopy and was doing loops and losing height more quickly than is desirable. He manfully fought to correct this but wasn't able to. He eventually cut the tangled 'chute away and tried to deploy his reserve, but alas too late. He hit the ground before it was fully deployed and died instantly. I am in no doubt he was so busy dealing with his main 'chute problem that he was dead before he realised the danger. He was to the last a very determined and courageous soldier and would have been a star. His love of life was second to none and a more polite and talented young man you could not have met.

I travelled back to Northern Ireland for Stuart's funeral. It was in many ways a strangely uplifting affair. Stuart's mum and dad and brother and sister were buoyed by their strong religious faith. If anything they were a tower of strength to us all. The arrangements for the funeral were taken care of by the commanding officer of our depot, who laid on a superb farewell for Stuart. The turnout for the funeral was large and as the cortège passed through the market town of Ballymena, we halted outside Stuart's house before heading off to the cemetery. I returned to Canada with a very heavy heart.

It was, it must be said, an eventful training trip of over seven weeks. We achieved a very high degree of readiness, learned much and burned down most of the training area at some point. We also had a couple of other close misses. A young officer was struck by a ricochet when a round struck some metal out on the training area. Luckily it hit his nightsight and was deflected away from his head. One of my corporals also had a stern lesson from one of the new and very potent grenades. He threw it but then failed to get into proper cover. The grenade followed its instructions and went off in all directions, hitting everything it could see, including the corporal's arse. Both lived, but we all learned a great deal from the exercise. Teamwork had improved, commanders at all levels had a better grasp of what was required and we had recognised and addressed some of the problem areas. We were without a doubt ready for operations.

On return from Canada the Board of Inquiry into Paul Cochrane's death a year before was finally held. The evidence was confused by some serious allegations from our battalion padre, Reverend NAP Evans, which were subsequently proved to be unfounded. By the time it was completed, the Board of Inquiry could find no conclusive reason for him to take his own life. In the section entitled 'Findings of the Inquiry' it stated:

> Inevitably, the single question that remains unanswered is why a young man, arguably with a promising career ahead of him, supported by his family and under no apparent pressure, other than a curable physical compliant, should take recourse to what the autopsy describes as self-harm.

In the summary it says:

> As indicated, it has not been difficult to reach considered opinion on any of the issues the Board has been asked to review, recognising that there will, in perpetuity, be a question mark over the state of mind of Ranger Cochrane at the moment he appears to have inflicted injury upon himself.

The final section that records the 'Opinions of the Inquiry' states:

> ... that there was no indication that Rgr Cochrane presented a suicide risk. The Board considers the coy chain of command, from Team leader through Pl Comd and CSM to OC to have been exemplary in its involvement in Rgr Cochrane's situation. Even Rgr Tabuya, the last person to see Rgr Cochrane alive, saw at the time no signs of the sort of distress which might indicate what would happen. Short of placing Rgr Cochrane under some form of escort, it is considered that there is nothing the coy could have reasonably done at the time to anticipate or prevent the incident.

We remain none the wiser to this day. A full copy of the Board of Inquiry was passed to the family.

In the late summer of 2002, after a month's leave, C Company, now under Colin Marks[32], returned to North America to exercise with the 101st Airborne at Fort Campbell, Kentucky, while the 101st's D Company, or 'Delta Dogs', were sent over to us in exchange.

---

[32] C Company was commanded by Major Colin Marks. He was a bright young graduate of the Joint Services Staff College, and an officer of wide operational experience.

I went across to the USA to visit C Company on exercise in Fort Campbell. The training went at a fast pace and C Company was expected to fit in with everything. I was able to observe the superb deployment of the US Airborne brigades with three helicopter battalions in support. It was an awesome spectacle. The terrain in the Kentucky/Tennessee border is a lot like England, green and verdant, but much hotter. The wide open spaces of the training area was in places quite beautiful.

But visiting Tennessee had a deeper resonance for many of the Ulstermen serving in 1 R Irish. Everywhere we looked – in the names across the front of a shop or the deep religious conviction of the Southern Baptists – we were reminded that this state, like many in the region, was founded by Ulstermen who had emigrated to escape religious persecution in the 18th century. By 1770 there were some 200,000 Ulster settlers in the Appalachian valleys. Many of the men had been unaware of this connection before the visit and this discovery added to the depth of the understanding and friendships that were developed during the exchanges.

The commander of the battalion, Lieutenant Colonel Steve Bruch, set a fast pace in his battalion in every way. I went to watch one of their training exercises. The US approach is very different from the approach of the British and Canadians. Firstly they are superbly equipped. Each man not only has a night-vision device but many have laser pointers and laser aiming devices on their rifles. They are equipped with the M4 rifle, a compact upgrade of the M16 Armalite, regarded by the troops as the Cadillac of rifles, unlike our SA 80, which is more of a Morris Marina. They have the light Minimi section weapon known as the 'Squad Automatic Weapon' (SAW) and a modern version of our GPMGs, which they call the M64B. The close-support weapons, especially the 60mm mortars, are impressive too.

I was intrigued, however, by the way they conduct live firing training. It was performed in almost 'exam' conditions, reflecting the cut-throat competition for promotion and advancement in the US Army. Their exercises were watched over at the next level of command throughout. This meant Steve Bruch would supervise his company commanders, while the brigade commander would supervise his efforts. Though the actual training was conducted at a much slower and deliberate rate than ours, the peer pressure was immense and added a tension all of its own.

Overall we gained quite an insight into each other's way of doing business. It was clear that the US Army was run on very authoritarian lines and engendered a culture of military elitism with a bloodcurdling undercurrent of ferocity to any and all enemies. I admired much about its professionalism but I was concerned about the rigidity of its command ethos and what I perceived as a significant absence of individual initiative. The Americans in contrast found our groupings of Irish, Gurkhas and so on quaint and exotic. They sympathised with our plight over equipment and probably regretted the lack of missionary zeal in our global outlook and our live-and-let-live attitude. Steve later visited us in Canterbury and went to the north of England to the Kielder Forest to watch his boys in action against the Gurkhas. I was personally satisfied that we had made the most of this exchange and we finished with a much clearer understanding of each other's working practices and strengths, as well as making some lasting friends.

While C Company was in the USA, my A Company had gone to Gibraltar to exercise with the Royal Gibraltar Regiment. The Royal Irish Regiment and the Gibraltar Regiment have much in common and their CO, Francis Brancato, had served as a company commander with the Royal Irish Regiment. A Company had a splendid welcome waiting for them in Gibraltar and enjoyed an exciting time, during which part of the company went to Morocco to train in the desert with the Moroccan Army. I visited and spent some time with the men, enjoying the hospitality of the Rock and taking the opportunity to sail over to North Africa with some of the boys. The variety that this training offered once again added to the cumulative experience of the battalion. The opportunity for all the young soldiers to live and work in unfamiliar environments undoubtedly strengthened the foundations of our expeditionary army.

Back in the UK we were told to prepare ourselves for what was to be our one and only operation of 2002. The firemen were set to strike for higher wages – up to £30,000 per year from the £21,000 a year they received for their four-day week. As usual the Government relied on the Army to cover the eventuality of a strike. Soldiers, with a ranger earning £12,000 a year and a corporal £15,000, were able to take this job on after three days' training. This was to be Operation Fresco: the 2002 fireman's strike. (Had it not come along 1 R Irish would have been without an operation for the first time in eight years – 1995 Fermanagh, 1996, 1997 and 1998 East Tyrone, 1999 the invasion of Kosovo, 2000 Sierra Leone, 2001 East Tyrone – and now Bedford and Nottingham!)

The task was very straightforward. We were equipped with the venerable 'Green Goddess' Bedford fire tenders dating from the early

1950s. (I observed that the number plates on the ones we were issued were probably worth more than the actual vehicles.) The men were issued specialised personal equipment – gardening gloves and donkey jackets and industrial wellington boots. I visited the training.

'How difficult is this?' I asked one of the fire officers.

'What your boys lack in technical skill, they more than make up for in enthusiasm,' one senior fire officer told me.

We were to be under the command of 49 Brigade and the Brigade Commander, Donald Wilson, could scarcely disguise his delight at having an operation on his hands. A series of high-level meetings were held and study days were encouraged. During one of the conferences a debate began between the CO of a Royal Artillery regiment and the Commander about the finer details of training the operations room staff (this unit had not been on operations recently and were beside themselves with excitement). The CO of this regiment was describing the complexities of the command post exercise that he had run over the weekend. We had run one too. It hadn't taken us a weekend, though. One wag described it like this: 'OK, lads, look in. You're sitting watching the telly and the phone rings. You say: "Hello, 1 R Irish Fire and Rescue Service. A fire? Where? We'll be right over!" Then you tell the peeler sitting drinking tea where the fire is and you crash the lads out in the Goddesses. You set off for the fire at speeds of up to thirty-five mph [top whack for the Goddesses] with the bell going for all it's worth. When you get there, attach the hoses to the fire hydrant and point the hoses at the fire. Then it's water on, fire out, water off, roll up yer hoses and home for tea and medals. Questions?'

I did get the battalion together for a pep talk, as I do before all operations. My main point was that we were not strike-breakers. We were there to assist the civil authorities and we were not in confrontation with anyone in this strike or on anybody's side. I reminded the men that their oath of allegiance was to the Queen and not to any government. We were there to protect lives. This was the next point. We were not to take risks for property. We were being deployed with fifty-year-old vehicles and dressed like McAlpine's Fusiliers with a minimum training, and we could, with our ingenuity, courage and resolve, provide a safety net to the taxpayer until the Government and trade unions had finished squabbling. Finally, I reminded the battalion that during the last firemen's strike in 1977 we had lost a man in an accident in Manchester – I wanted no repetition.

The country was on a knife edge. We deployed to Nottingham and

Recce platoon
1 Royal Irish training
the new Sierra
Leonean Army on old
British self-loading
rifles outside Freetown

Senior officers from one of
Africa's leading insurgent
groups, the West Side Boys,
assemble for an evening at
the officers' mess

One of the West Side Boys'
weapons instructors discovers he
has no working parts in his rifle.
Even the bandage around his
magazine will not help that

A Republican youth greets 1 R Irish in the traditional manner…

(PETER MORRISON/AP)

… and not to be outdone, a warm welcome to 1 R Irish from a Loyalist mob on the Ardoyne Road

(PAUL McERLANE/REUTERS)

As the violence subsides, a ranger reflects on the scene

(PA/EMPICS)

£30,000 for a four-day week – equivalent to £50,000 for a soldier's week – yes, please!

A venerable Green Goddess. Number plate spotters will be able to date this one to the early 1950s. This is one of the hi-tech varieties with air horns on top instead of a bell

(PETER BYRNE/MERCURY PRESS AGENCY)

St Patrick's Day, Kuwait – the traditional parade. This one got out of hand and ended up marching to Al Amarah

WO2 GILES PENFOUND © CROWN COPYRIGHT/MOD

The Drum Head Service on St Patrick's Day. The Drums were actually on loan from the Black Watch – ours were in a lost container

(SARAH OLIVER/MAIL ON SUNDAY)

C Company during the chariot race

Bedfordshire. The strikes were to be staged so that the firefighters would lose the minimum amount of pay. It was an interesting time but not exactly what we had joined for.

I was based at a hotel in Nottingham. There was to be a mammoth logistics effort to keep the strike covered. The first strike was set for a Wednesday evening at 1800 hours. With no hope of a compromise, the strike began on time. Our first fire started thirty minutes later. A hedge beside a fire station was set on fire and our Green Goddesses deployed, only to be met by a large group of firefighters with banners who jeered and stuck their yellow stickers on the vehicles. I had frankly expected better of them. I was delighted with the restraint that the soldiers showed as they ignored the protest and quickly put the fire out. The next fire was equally malicious. A pub went ablaze at around seven o'clock. It was in a tough part of Nottingham and this particular pub had closed on the Monday evening. It caught fire to order and our fire crews raced to the scene. Luckily the police escort with us explained the situation and warned the men not to take any risks. I went to the scene and watched as the lads played their hoses on the now fiercely burning pub.

'That's a first-class effort,' one of the senior fire officers said as we watched. 'Our regular crews could do no better.'

Every now and again there would be an explosion inside the pub as a beer barrel or gas cylinder went up. I noticed the crowd that had gathered was a pretty tough-looking lot and the local police were having some difficulty controlling them.

'This reminds me of the Holy Cross dispute,' I said to one of the policemen. 'I would be deploying a shield line if this was Belfast.'

'Well,' the police inspector said, 'I don't want to take anything away from Belfast, but they're pretty tough here. Over there,' he indicated some houses across the nearby playing fields, 'there was an execution on Saturday night. A girl was made to kneel and shot through the top of the head. The guy we suspected of doing it was stabbed to death last night at his house not far from here. It was all drugs related.'

'We recovered a sub-machine gun from his coal bunker,' added a constable standing nearby.

'A sub-machine gun?' I said in disbelief.

The policeman laughed. 'Oh that's par for the course.'

I looked at the crowd circling the fire. Tough men with T-shirts and tattoos with lots of gold jewellery despite it being a cold winter's night. They stood, arms folded, legs apart, talking out of the sides of their mouths – not unlike the 'community activists' in the Ardoyne, in fact.

There were groups of young girls, most with pushchairs with slumbering babies. They were dressed in the regulation leggings and bomber jacket with their hair pulled tightly up into ponytails with coloured 'scrunchies' holding it in place in the coiffure known as a 'Croydon facelift'. They spawned a joke poster that appeared on notice boards soon afterwards in a take-off of the old Fairy Liquid advertisement. There was a mother washing the dishes and a little girl watching her, saying, 'Mummy, why are your hands so soft?' To which the mother was saying, 'Because I'm only twelve.'

A group of youths in baggy jeans, their arses showing and wearing hooded jackets with only the peak of a baseball cap and a cigarette showing, capered around on tiny bicycles doing stunts and stopping to draw on their smokes, pass some comment and then set off with another stunt. Small children, even though it was 2200 hours now, played around the feet of the teen mums and laughed, cried and fought, while a small group of wine victims and druggies huddled together, passing a can of Special Brew while smoking and spitting mournfully as they watched the pub burn.

Another Green Goddess from B Company arrived and the men leapt out to join the effort as the fire was huge by now and we were simply preventing nearby buildings catching. The lads threw the side lockers of the Goddess open and grabbed tools and equipment. One of the NCOs, a burly Dubliner, struggled to open the fire hydrant with the hydrant tool. He suddenly threw it down with one of the most unusual but in its own way eloquent, descriptive and accurate sentences I've heard in the English language: 'Ah, fuck, de fucken fucker's fucken fucked!'

After the first forty-eight-hour strike it was hoped that a second strike would be averted by last-minute talks. I listened to their progress as I drove up to Nottingham from Bedford in my staff car with Corporal McAleer, my driver. 'Looks like we'll be headin' home, Mackers,' I predicted. Then, to my amazement, the Deputy Prime Minister, John Prescott, failed to show for the talks. He claimed he had nothing to say. Suddenly we became the fire and rescue service for two counties once again.

On the Saturday morning the local MP visited us in our Nottingham base – none other than Geoff Hoon, Secretary of State for Defence. There was much media excitement. Geoff Hoon was a little cagey as he first arrived – no doubt wondering what reception he would receive. He needn't have worried. Many of the men were aware that he had given the order for the rescue in Sierra Leone and held him in some regard. He soon settled in and was drinking tea and chatting with the soldiers. I was praying that they wouldn't rib him too savagely about John Prescott ('Thunderbird 2' as he had become known) and his antics on TV. The men opened up and chatted about their experiences during the strike. There had been surprisingly few fires but some other serious incidents. One group described how they had been called to save a workman who had fallen down a hole and had then been disembowelled by a mechanical digger. They explained that they had kept the injured man calm and rescued him to the surface, giving him life-saving first aid before the paramedics arrived.

Geoff Hoon then repaired to a small Portakabin to conduct a telephone interview for a Sunday paper. The issue of the hour was whether any more modern 'red' fire engines (recently discarded by the firefighters) would be sent across to the Army in place of the ancient Green Goddesses. He was in expansive mood and was clearly – and rightly – proud of the MOD's performance during the strike. 19,000 service personnel were providing excellent cover, much to the annoyance of the firefighters sitting around their braziers. With prompts from myself and the RSM he explained that the existing equipment was working well and newer equipment would require more training. (The fact was that despite the slow speed of the fifty-year-old Goddesses the pumps worked as well as the pumps on modern fire appliances and as well as the pumps on the red fire engines being discussed, which had just been retired after fifteen to twenty years' service.)

Perhaps the most remarkable part of this whole operation was a rescue that the men were called on to perform some thirty minutes after the strike had ended. As they were bussed back to Canterbury a car passed their coach at a terrific speed, only to swerve and then somersault into the air. They stopped and piled off the bus, to find a woman in the car, her leg caught by the door and practically severed. She was conscious but clearly going into shock and losing a great deal of blood. The driver had been ejected by the force of the turn and had shot off into the air to land on his head. As the men tended him they could see that his brains were exposed. He was still alive but only just. Sergeant Breckell, the senior man on the scene, took charge. He correctly and coolly realised that while the man was clearly in a very bad way, the girl was dying. He ordered the medics to treat her first. Corporal Campbell applied a tourniquet to the leg and covered it from view. Once the girl was stabilised they turned their attentions to the boyfriend. 'All I could do was keep the wound moist and put a shell dressing on top with a neat bow under the chin to stop anything popping out,' Sergeant Breckell later explained. Because of the upset caused by the changeover of services, it took thirty minutes for the police and paramedics to arrive. During this time the men directed traffic and kept the two casualties warm and stable. Both lived. She lost her leg below the knee but was otherwise fine and he miraculously made a good recovery. They later married.

Once again this experience, frustrating as it was at the time, provided an excellent grounding in the process of working with civil authorities and attending to the vital needs of the community. As 2002 faded, the men of 1 R Irish had gained experience of operations and hard live training that covered the whole spectrum from war fighting to aid to the civil power. What they were soon to find out was that in modern wars moving quickly from one to another, with no time for extensive briefing or specialist help, would prove vital.

In the meantime, 1 R Irish returned to Canterbury to await the next call. My period in charge was coming to an end and I was looking at the rather bleak prospect of leaving the battalion within a month. My successor was preparing to arrive and arrangements were made for my farewell. I would not be the only one leaving 1 R Irish, however. Time was up for the Gurkhas too. 1 R Irish was now almost at full strength and so there was no longer any need for a reinforcement company. I would miss my battalion; and the superb Gurkhas, who had become an integral part of the battalion, would be missed by all.

# —6—

# PREPARING FOR WAR

**C**hristmas is a time for unwinding in Army battalions that are not on operations. It was often a time for farewells too. I was heading off to be Chief of Deep Operations in Kosovo and would officially leave the battalion on 6 January 2003. Before that, though, I was due to be 'pulled out' of camp. It is the tradition in a British Army battalion that the CO is pulled out of camp in some vehicle or other, with the men lining the route to cheer and say farewell.

'We could pull you out in a Green Goddess,' the RSM quipped.

'Not in the least bit funny,' I replied.

As I packed up my office in preparation, however, I received a call summoning me to a meeting at Brigade HQ in Colchester.

'I'm glad I'm missing this pulling-out thing,' I told the RSM.

'Och, we had the Goddess beautifully polished too,' he added.

With the storm clouds gathering over Iraq, the meeting would turn out to be one of many held over the Christmas holidays. I was only glad to be doing something that might get the battalion on some real operations. While I had no desire to start a war, if there was going to be one, I wanted 1 R Irish to be there. It was what I had trained the whole unit for over the last three years.

An Air Corps helicopter took me from the sports pitches in Howe Barracks off to Colchester. On arrival at the conference I greeted the other commanding officers, all of us animated by the prospect of action. There was a great deal of debate as to the chances of 16 Air Assault being used. I was of course in no doubt that we *should* have a role. Whether we *would* was a different matter. The problem was that the brigade had been getting a lot of action lately and there were Army politics and jealousies to contend with. The key staff of the brigade gathered around the table and began to discuss the potential for operations. The CO of 1 Para, Tom Beckett, sat nearest the Brigade Commander. Tom was a courteous Dubliner who had transferred from the Queen's Royal Irish Hussars to lead 1 Para. John Lorimer, who led 3 Para, was extremely bright and by far the youngest CO of us all. He was an Arabist and from an old Army background. Our commander was Jacko Page. I knew him of old and we got on well, although he found me rather eccentric. Young and with an impressive pedigree, he would morph from no-nonsense Para to gracious social host to intense Oxford don almost before your eyes.

The planning for the UK participation in operations in Iraq was a follow-on from contingency planning that had been going on in the USA for some while. The UK did have a presence in the area for Operation Southern Watch[33] but now a more substantial contribution was needed. The options immediately available were Special Forces only and/or the use of in-place forces (air and maritime, plus bases in Cyprus and Diego Garcia[34]). These could be increased by the addition of one or more aircraft carriers, a land contingent, ranging from a UK brigade embedded in the US forces through to a division comprising three brigades or more. It was clear that the US commander in the region, Tommy Franks, favoured a light option, that is to say light, helicopter-borne air assault troops, as US thinking by that stage had moved beyond just Baghdad to concern the southern oilfields. They would have to be secured quickly if the world's largest reserve of oil was to be protected. Our own Chief of Joint Operations favoured sending two light brigades – 16 Air Assault Brigade and 3 Commando Brigade – or just one of these as a token gesture. It was clear to everyone in the room that if only one was to go, 3 Commando Brigade had the best chance of going, as 16 Brigade had been picked for the last series of operations and there was tri-service pressure to spread the experience. HQ Land at this time preferred an armoured option. This was not surprising as it was always a struggle, during the treasury rounds, to justify the rather expensive armoured forces that the UK maintained. At that time, we had an

---

[33] The coalition operation to protect the Marsh Arabs of southern Iraq against Saddam's military. It prevented the overflight of the southern marshes.
[34] The US airbase on the tiny but strategically important UK island in the middle of the Indian Ocean.

armoured division in 1 (UK) Armoured Division of three brigades equipped with Challenger 2 tanks and Warrior armoured fighting vehicles (AFVs), with a substantially armoured division in 3 (UK) Division, which had 1, 12 and 19 Mechanised Brigades with a mix of AFVs and Saxon armoured personnel carriers (APCs). In reality these were armoured taxis, most useful in defence. I didn't rate them. When I commanded a company of these white elephants, I personally favoured driving them to the enemy's most likely axis of advance and letting the tyres down then filling them with concrete for use as roadblocks.

It was thought that the politicians would favour 16 Brigade, however, as it was agile and cheap to move. One distinct possibility for a short-notice move was to place 16 Brigade under the US 82nd Airborne Division. There was also an active lobby in the MOD that would have preferred the UK forces to act as follow-on forces for the stabilisation and reconstruction phase, avoiding actual operations. With hindsight I realise that this was the first manifestation of the anti-war lobby within Government.

It was also clear at this time that strategic planning had built a 'Northern Option' involving Turkey into the equation and this needed to be ruled either in or out. This would see a coalition force based on the 4th US Division striking from Turkey to catch the Iraqi military in a pincer. Our Permanent Joint HQ hoped for a decision from the Turks by 15 January. So, no doubt did the US, otherwise the 4th Division, afloat in the Mediterranean, would have to sail south through the Suez Canal to Kuwait, two weeks away.

If 16 Air Assault Brigade did go, we could be configured in three ways. We could go as a 'light' brigade, with just an aviation regiment and some infantry plus guns and logistics. We could go with the brigade as it stood, with three battle groups of infantry guns and engineers plus reconnaissance troops. Or we could go with the brigade 'enhanced', with added units including a multiple launch rocket system (MLRS) regiment and perhaps even armour. Our direction from the Brigade Commander was to wait and watch, saying very little, but to think about training for the worst-case scenario – war fighting.

I was convinced that 16 Brigade was the best option for a number of reasons. We could move quickly and exploit an early fracture in the enemy's resolve. Additionally, if the Northern Option were not forthcoming then there would need to be a rapid readjustment of forces, which we were best suited to deal with. On the downside there were the severe conditions in Kuwait, the only available basing option in the region. This small nation was already full of troops and any newcomers would have to live in the desert. And there would be issues arising from integration with the US. Our radios were from the Stone Age for a start. The US Marines alone had more planes than the UK and if we could not talk to these aircraft to direct them towards the enemy and away from us, experience in the First Gulf War and Kosovo showed that any future conflict would be a very dangerous place to be, with a serious risk of what the media euphemistically call 'friendly fire' incidents and what we in the military call 'Blue-on-Blue' incidents.

The Commander laid out his concerns for our troops in order of priority. Top of the list were Weapons of Mass Destruction (WMD). We were pretty certain that Saddam had these and, if threatened, would use them. (He had form on this.) The intelligence passed onto us with regard to these weapons seemed fairly conclusive. Then came mines and booby traps, and the risk of Blue-on-Blue incidents. The traditional threats to armies in the field could not be ignored, of course, such as disease and disability resulting from harsh environments and living conditions, as well as the more modern threat of road-traffic and air accidents, which are almost inevitable when modern military forces are concentrated together.

Stern warnings were issued about our dealings with the press. It was a sensitive time and the last thing we wanted was an unguarded thought or action being communicated to the media and throwing the whole plan into jeopardy. With all the concerns about sites of special scientific interest and the need to exploit intelligence gained in a timely manner it was clear that this was going to be a very modern war. Commanders would need to brief their men carefully, as it was the most likely scenario that Iraq, once liberated, would become a gigantic scene of crime that would need to be examined if the regime of Saddam Hussein and his henchmen were ever to be brought to book.

I returned to the battalion and immediately called in the main staff. I warned them that operations were now a real possibility and that as I was changing over shortly, they would need to be in a position to brief the new CO when he arrived. Meetings continued into the Christmas period and beyond. Finally I received a call on 28 December. It was Jacko Page. He explained that the Commander in Chief HQ Land Command, General Mike Jackson, had decided that the commanders who were due to change over would stay in place, which meant that both I and John Lorimer – who had also been promoted and was due to leave his unit on posting to a new job – would be staying.

'Does this mean we're on the order of battle?' I enquired.

'One thing at a time,' Jacko replied.

Within days we were given a mission. The brigade was to 'Mount and deploy as a brigade, working under 1 (UK) Division as coordinating HQ as an integrated part of the US 1 Marine Expeditionary Force [1 MEF] and dependent on it for J2 [intelligence], deep and close fires [artillery], some lift [helicopter support] and key CSS[35] natures [logistic supplies].' We were to be prepared to act – 'on orders to hold the Rumaylah oilfields, secure Basra Airport, conduct rear area security and to protect the key logistics route [Route Tampa].' This was in order to 'allow 1 MEF to exploit rapid fracture and maintain momentum'. The operation was to be Operation Telic[36].

I returned elated to the battalion. There was an obvious buzz of excitement as I briefed the key commanders on the mission and tasks. That was it: 1 R Irish were going to war. But there was so much to do. In just a single month – less now – I would need to train the men to the peak of performance, the Quartermaster would have to load the equipment and issue the men their desert kit and we would need to get to know every detail of the enemy and his ways. Major McClean, Jackie, who had replaced Paddy as QM when he went off on posting, didn't flinch as I detailed the necessary tasks. He was extremely professional and had seen deployments many times before. I looked around my team. They were solid and dependable. The difference was that this was to be a real war, not some intervention or peacekeeping mission. I knew that some would shine out as stars on the operation, most would be as good as one expected from professional soldiers, and inevitably some would fail. My job was to watch for the failures before they happened and act for the common good.

On 6 January, 1 R Irish returned from leave. The whole battalion was ordered to the QM's hangars, a large indoor venue. As they gathered men could be heard asking, 'What are the Gurkhas still doing here?' The RSM called the battalion to attention. There was an audible gasp from some quarters as I walked in.

'You'll notice that I am not the new CO,' I began, having taken my place at the head of the men. 'You can guess that something important is

---

[35] Combat Service Support.

[36] The UK uses computer-generated code names that have no significance to the operations and mean nothing. The US military opt for more bloodcurdling names to act as statements of intent like 'Desert Storm', 'Desert Fox' or for this war 'Iraqi Freedom'.

95

going to happen.' I carefully explained the circumstances we in the UK had found ourselves in with the other members of the alliance. 'This means that it is now very likely that the UK will contribute ground troops to any future operation and 1 R Irish will be part of that contribution.'

There was a hush, then excited chatter. The RSM told the men to pipe down. As he did so there was a cheer from the Gurkhas as my words were interpreted by the better English speakers. They all understood, of course, but were checking with each other, as they could not believe their ears.

'We must be equal to the task,' I went on. 'That means a great deal of hard work and what may seem impossible deadlines to meet. Meet them, surpass them, excel. We will be deploying overseas within a month. Be ready.'

I could feel there was a real sense of purpose and commitment across the ranks and as I walked among the men to return to my office, I could see them watching me. I was as conscious as they were that I was about to lead them on a momentous enterprise and that the reputation of the Army and the regiment – and the lives of every one of them – depended on how well we performed.

Training began almost immediately. In the cold January weather we marched the 26km from our base in Canterbury to the ranges in Hythe to test-fire our rifles and machine guns. We needed to get hardened again; two weeks of easy living and Christmas turkey had to give way to preparation for war. There was much to do on all fronts. In the first weeks I held regular study days in the hangars where I sought to pass on my experience to the officers and senior NCOs. I watched to see who was absorbing the information and who it was passing by. Documentation went on late into the night as passports were checked, wills written and identity discs issued.

Everyone needed to ensure that their inoculations were up to date and the medical sergeant became a feared figure as he and his team sought out those who needed boosters. Nobody was safe from their enthusiasm. One or two men even got a knock on their doors at home late at night, to open it to shadowy figures who would greet them with 'Roll up yer sleeve'. I was sitting in my office when these hoods turned up with a computer printout. I set down my phone as they closed the door. 'Roll up yer sleeve, sir.' They left me feeling like a second-hand dartboard, though I did manage to win one concession – I was CO after all – persuading them to put the last couple into my other arm and one in my arse.

'Ye'll enjoy this fucker,' the medical corporal said, jetting a squirt of gamma globulin from a gigantic needle as I posed, trousers at half-mast. I could hear the Adjutant snigger in his office next door when I groaned as the needle was rammed home. 'Pleasure doing business,' the medic said as he packed his kit to leave.

The first batch of desert clothing arrived and was broken out. What a load of crap it was too. The clothing and hats were so small I remarked to the QM I could wear two – one on each horn. Jackie, the elder statesman in the battalion, was stoic about the plight.

'Sir, you get on with sharpening this battalion, not that it needs much; I'll speak to the other quartermasters in the Paras and we'll figure something out.'

Their kit was no better. We were to find that a constant shortage of gear would follow us into theatre and almost across the border into Iraq. We had body armour but no covers to wear them with. There were sleeping bag liners, presumably for some sleeping bags we never saw, and the odd camouflage net. The clothing was also very old and of mixed batches and colours and mostly in tiny sizes. My concern was to get a battalion into theatre, dressed in a semblance of military clothing and with the vehicles painted. There can be no doubting the psychological importance of dressing soldiers properly so that they feel equipped for whatever awaits them. Frankly I would have preferred to lead the men into Iraq in our European dress rather than looking like some ragged third-world army.

The training focus switched to Sennybridge. This was a harsh, boggy training area in southern Wales, now in the grip of winter. I was clear that some form of testing external backdrop to the preoperational training was needed in order to encourage the troops to look beyond the ambient weather and focus on the task in hand. While I expected the backdrop of the actual war to be the exact opposite, it is crucial for troops to focus on their personal administration and this takes time and discipline, whether you are struggling with the environment to try to stay warm and dry, or hydrated and cool.

The companies were to be deployed in long-abandoned hill farms now converted for use as troop shelters, with each setting up operations rooms and antennas as well as makeshift cookhouses and ammunition stores. But first there was the approach march. I had planned that the men should be awakened to the realities of war with a bit of exercise, so the farms had to be reached after a 20km insertion march across the Black Mountains.

It was a crisp afternoon as we prepared to set off from the car park of the small camp in Sennybridge village, where first line scales[37] of ammunition, 200 rounds of 5.56mm ball per man, link for the machine guns, mortar rounds and pyrotechnics, were issued. With food and warm clothing, most men had 100lb of kit on their backs. The men in the heavy weapons platoons (mortars, anti-tank and heavy machine guns) would carry up to 150lb. As with all the commanders, my own 'bergen', or rucksack, was tipping the scales closer to the 150lb mark, thanks to the extra batteries I carried for my two signallers, each of them similarly burdened by the weight of either an HF or VHF radio and supplies. My senior signaller, 'Reggie', a full corporal, would walk close behind me with a spare handset ready to pass to me if a call came on the net. A quiet County Donegal man with a cheerful personality, he was always calm and steady, a trait which had stood him in good stead during his time in captivity in Sierra Leone. Corporal Magowan, or 'Magoo', carrying the HF radio, would walk close by him.

The RSM set off at a steady pace, his distinctively camouflaged helmet buckled under his chin. In 1 R Irish the RSM was king of the field as well as the number one soldier. He took this role seriously and set a high standard in field discipline and tactics. Snow had fallen the previous night and, when the sunlight faded, the scene was soon lit by bright starlight as we moved through the tree line to the bare mountains above us. The hills were at their most dangerous, however, with a hard frost turning the snow to sheet ice underfoot. There was much mumbled cursing as men slipped on the ice as they climbed, balancing their heavy loads. Every fifteen minutes or so we would stop and 'vent', opening our clothing to allow clouds of steam to billow out as heat generated by the exertion was released. One dare not keep this in, as it would quickly turn to sweat and soak one's clothes, only to freeze once you had stopped. At these halts I would consult with the RSM to check our navigation and search the hillside through the nightsight on my rifle, to see against the snow the black specks of the men in the rifle companies plodding across the wastelands.

As the night went on increasing reports were coming in of injuries caused by men falling on the ice or twisting ankles in the tufts of grass concealed by the blanket of snow. By the time we in the battalion HQ party had come down off the mountain and reached the road the news

---

[37] That which the soldier carries into battle in his pouches. The second line would be in trucks just behind and the rest would follow with the logistic tail of vehicles.

was that five men, including three section commanders – crucial to my chain of command – were down. Two had broken legs. With 8km to go to our farm, I sat down beside the RSM.

'Can we keep this going?'

'We can,' he replied, 'but we can't afford to. We need good section commanders. But there's been no slacking here. I reckon honour is done. I'd bus them in on lorries from here, sir. We can't afford any more injuries.' He was, as always, right.

'Reggie, close the battle group in on us and call forward the transport. We're going to truck them in from here. Can you get an up-to-date casualty count too, please. Some tea, I think, Magoo,' I said as I fished my flask out of my bergen.

I dropped my gear and now, with just my operations waistcoat holding my personal-role radio, ammo and water and carrying my rifle, I set off with the RSM to meet the men as they arrived off the mountain. The inside of my helmet was soaked with sweat, which was dribbling onto my chin and freezing fast on the stubble.

As the long lines of soldiers trudged in from the darkness I was relieved to find morale was still buoyant. 'If Saddam goes and hides up a fucken mountain at the fucken North Pole, we're the boys to get him, sir,' a ranger said as he stomped past, bent under his burden.

'It's dat cold, ya could hang a focken wet duffel coat off moi nipple,' said another as he stamped his feet, standing beside his bergen propped up at the side of the road.

We stood and waited for thirty minutes, watching the hillside through nightsights. The men who had arrived began to brew up tea on their hexamine solid fuel burners and chat in low tones, which grew almost festive as word spread that they were to be driven the rest of the way. As I walked among the waiting soldiers, they laughed and joked, ribbing each other about the march. When new troops arrived I could see them drop down backwards to the hedgerows as they sat back to release the straps on their loads and then, like old men, stretch to their feet, the steam rising as they opened their clothing to vent, while the men who had been there some time were wrapping themselves against the chill again.

'Minus 6,' I said to the RSM as I looked at the temperature on my Suunto watch.

'Fucken Baltic,' a soldier nearby commented.

Limping with stiffness in the freezing cold, the men made their way over to the four-tonne lorries as they arrived and loaded their kit. Soon a shuttle was clearing the 690 men of 1 R Irish off to their various farms, where bivouacs were erected, sleeping bags laid out and all, apart from the unlucky sentries, fell into a deep sleep.

The next day I went around the company locations. As usual there was a buzz of activity and enthusiasm as the platoon commanders trained their men. Then I busied myself in our own farm, going over company manning strengths. The battalion was close to being fully manned but we would need to call back some men who were on loan to training establishments to complete our numbers. We had as a reserve our Territorial Army (TA) regiments, the Royal Irish Rangers and the London Irish Rifles company of the London Regiment. I had been a Territorial Army soldier when I was at school and university and I knew that the TA, like Paddies, fight best when under their own officers and serving together. I decided to spread the men of my slightly under-strength machine gun platoon out across the battalion to back-fill gaps caused by injury and ask the Royal Irish Rangers for a fully formed machine gun platoon. I knew that would mean the platoon from Enniskillen in County Fermanagh. A request was sent and for the twenty-five places we had available seventy-four men volunteered.

The real business was training, however. I knew that if we were to avoid casualties in combat I had to ensure where possible that each man regarded his weapon system as an extension of his body and could react at an instant when a threat arose. This involved not only training the men to shoot straight but to do so at night, under pressure and when exhausted and even frightened. After Canada we were still in pretty good shape, but the ranges we constructed in Sennybridge would challenge the men to the limit. They would culminate in a daytime live-firing exercise that would be supported by the 105mm guns, 81mm mortars and Milan wire-guided missiles. As the men advanced they would do so under covering fire from the medium machine guns and the heavy .5 inch guns mounted on the stripped-down Land-Rovers. The training attacks would be conducted at company level and there were targets for the whole range of weapon systems, including the hand-held antitank rockets, the 94mm light anti-armour weapon (LAW), and the 51mm hand-held mortars.

As the training gathered pace in the freezing conditions we had another setback. It was Wednesday 15 January. On one of the ranges it was possible to approach the target along a river. Some enterprising sections even crawled through a tunnel built for the river under a road in order to complete the attack. It was during one of these attacks that a section from A Company, led by Corporal Parkin, leapt into the freezing water, which came up to their waists. As he led the way though the tunnel the man behind lost his footing and fell. He gripped his rifle as he plunged into the icy water, striking it against the side of the tunnel. One of the shortcomings of the SA 80 he carried was that the safety catch protruded from the side and was not a 'thumb switch', as on most other weapons. The safety was knocked off and the trigger operated, firing eight rounds of 5.56mm ammunition into the tunnel. Corporal Parkin dropped, hit several times. Medics were on the scene instantly and a dripping wet Corporal Parkin was recovered from the stream and placed on a stretcher. After initial first aid to wounds in his arm and legs he was evacuated to a civilian hospital in Abergavenny.

The ranges were closed immediately and an investigation began. It was later to conclude that it was a rare training accident, tragic but ultimately no one's fault. As soon as I heard of the accident I went to the hospital to find young Parkin. When I arrived he had already been operated on and was awake. It was a serious set of injuries, but to my delight and utter amazement, Corporal Parkin, a tough Manchester man, was cheerful and alert.

'You're in a bit of a two and eight[38],' I said. 'How does it all feel?'

'Like I've been jumped on. I've got me morphine for the pain but I want to stay clear-headed to see the wife.'

'Is she on her way, RSM?' I asked.

'Aye sir, should be here soon.'

'Will she be OK with you in this state – you know, the shock of it all?'

'Oh, we've been together since we were young. She just wants to see me and me her. When I was pulled out of that river I thought I was a goner.'

'You're lucky . . . we're all lucky. Get some rest now.'

I spoke to the surgeon as the RSM chatted with Corporal Parkin.

'We had a lucky break there with him getting medical help so soon,' I said.

The surgeon, a cheerful Welshman, took off his glasses and placed an X-ray on a light board. 'We're not out of the woods yet. The energy transfer from the bullet has shattered his leg, as you can see. Here and here,' he indicated black, ragged shapes, 'are fragments of the bullet and this, in his abdomen, is the warhead. It's done a great deal of damage.'

'Sadly, doctor, that's exactly what they are supposed to do.'

---

[38] Rhyming slang = state.

He bit the end of his glasses. 'You know, the wounds from these 5.56mm bullets are the worst I've seen, and I've seen a few.'

'Its because they shatter,' I explained. 'The energy exchange is right inside. It rarely passes straight through.'

'Yes, it causes us significant problems and generates a lot of dead tissue,' he mused.

'So what do you reckon then? Pins and reconstruction?'

'No. Gracious no. I think it may well have to come off.'

'Off? Does he know yet?'

'I thought we should leave him till we know for certain.'

'Good God. Amputation. Is everything else OK?'

'Well, as OK as you can be after receiving multiple gunshot wounds. We've had a couple of your lads in this week. Pressing it a bit?'

'We're getting ready for war, doctor,' I replied.

'God help you,' he said. 'You'll be seeing a lot more of this, I expect.'

'If we train hard and I get it right on the ground we'll keep this to a minimum – on both sides.'

'I wish you luck, my friend,' he said, patting my arm gently. 'I think all commanders and generals should come to these places to see what their wars cause.'

'We don't start them, doctor. That's a politician's job. We finish them.'

'There's a fact, boyo.' He smiled.

Corporal Parkin was soon joined by his wife. His mum and dad wanted him close so we had him transferred to a hospital in Manchester. The weather closed in so the flight we had planned was cancelled and he had to drive. A couple of days later I got an update from the doctor. 'He's lost the leg, I'm afraid.'

The accident with Corporal Parkin and the injuries to the other men was something that I could ill afford. Replacements would have to be found. I was very clear, however, that we needed to continue this level of training if we were to avoid potentially disastrous casualties when we faced the enemy. I could see that the effect of the injuries on the rest of the battalion – once the initial shock had worn off – was to galvanise the more experienced soldiers and to leave the newer lads in no doubt: this was for real.

As the build-up continued, for me the days became an exhausting round of training and conferences. I would finish observing a night-training manoeuvre, only to set off for a conference in Colchester, some 200 miles away, before returning to join another training exercise. I spent much of my time with the commanders on the ground, teaching and sometimes addressing whole companies. I needed them to have the basic building blocks – advance to contact with the enemy, the set-piece night attack and meeting the engagement – all perfectly understood and practised, as I knew that there would be no time to think when it was for real. In modern war battles are won by tempo and shock action. Troops must all know the actions in any given situation and be able to carry them out with the minimum of instructions. The slow learners who need constant detailed orders and time to think are the weak, slow beasts at the back of the herd who will fall prey to the faster, more agile beasts who rule the battlefield.

By mid-January the plan was taking shape and it was clear that 16 Brigade would go to theatre with three battalions and an aviation regiment, plus artillery, engineers and reconnaissance troops, from the Household Cavalry, or Combat Support (CS) in Army parlance with logistical supplies, or combat service support (CSS), provided by my Quartermaster or the Royal Logistics Corps. We would be under command of 1 (UK) Armoured Division and under the US Marines' 1 Marine Expeditionary Force (1 MEF) led by Lieutenant General Conway. The UK team was to be led by Air Marshal Brian Burridge. 1 (UK) Armoured Division would retain its commander (who like myself had been due to change over), Major General Robin Brims. The division would include 3 Commando Brigade and the 7th Armoured Brigade, the Desert Rats, led by Brigadier Graham Binns.

The plan was to compress the Iraqi regime with Special Forces, who would act to restrict movement of the enemy forces and direct air power at opportunity targets. Air power would produce 'shock and awe', with the land component standing by to exploit the fractures and effects. The US air power was truly impressive. It could mount twenty-four-hour-a-day air cover and could surge to provide a 'taxi rank' of aircraft ready to attack for shorter periods. We realised that in such an environment combat identification would be vital[39].

As we broke up from a meeting in late January we knew that the signal to move would come soon. We had to attend to pressing though mundane issues such as spraying the vehicles and finding enough equipment to look like an army beside the superbly equipped Americans. We had to get our vehicles ready for sea movement, which meant removing anything that could be stolen while on board – something our

---

[39] An electronic or physical means of identifying friend or foe.

experience of the First Gulf War had shown to be a certainty. They would need to go to Marchwood, the UK military's maritime point of exit near Southampton, and to be moved in the face of potential protests by the growing and increasingly vocal anti-war lobby.

We were warned that the media would be the third force in the conflict, in the light of the increasing disquiet across the world at the prospect of the impending action. This was something that I must admit did not impact too much on the men and myself at the time. But we were aware that CENTCOM[40] were expecting 18,000 members of the media in theatre, of whom only 6,000 would be registered. It was announced that the media were to have unrestricted access, right down to battle group level. This came as something of a surprise to me. I was not personally well versed in dealing with the media. I recognised, however, that media operations were not simply public relations stunts, they were information operations and if handled badly there could be some serious downsides to such exposure, and that speculation and misunderstanding were as much a threat to the mission as anything. The Brigade Commander urged us to present the media profile of a confident brigade but to remain understated, portraying ourselves as 'quiet professionals'.

One of the big issues that remained was the question of Turkey. Time was running out for a decision on the Northern Option. By now we at 16 Brigade were concentrating more on Iraq itself, the topography, climate and people. I was surprised to hear that Basra, the largest city in the area we were going to, had a population considerably larger than Northern Ireland. General Brims was concerned about being drawn into fighting situations in the cities in what he described as 'urban suck'. We all recognised that we had neither the time nor resources to become involved in a prolonged urban war. With this in mind, on return to the battalion I ensured that we practised, albeit in a modest way, on the village specially built in Sennybridge training area for these operations.

The call to deploy came at the end of January and I took my essential staff, the company commanders, Intelligence Officer and Operations Officer, off to the Air Mounting Centre at South Cerney in Wiltshire. The QM and his staff remained with the second in command, my executive officer, to deliver the men into theatre when the time came. We travelled to South Cerney for an early flight, arriving the night before for the Movement Control Centre, where logistics officers would pretend that they were airline staff but take a lot longer to do much less.

---

[40] US Central Command, responsible for the Middle East and under whom we would serve.

We were not to be disappointed. I arrived at the massive hangar at around 2300 hours to join the 300 or so others who would be flying out to Kuwait. Entering into the spirit of the game, the movement clerk greeted me with a cheery 'Good evening, sir, and where are we off to?'

'Majorca,' I replied.

'Oh, sir's having a laugh.'

'If you know where I'm going just give me my boarding pass.'

I sat down with the other COs, who had already been through the process.

'I don't know what the rush is,' Tom Beckett from 1 Para said. 'We'll be here for days.'

He was right. We walked outside to take some air. There was snow on the ground and the sky was clear and sharp as we recognised the stars of the Great Bear and Cassiopeia. I took a long look at the Wiltshire countryside bathed in moonlight and wondered if I would see the UK again. I was certain that for some this would be their last experience of their home.

The first news of delays was coming in. The routes that had been reserved for flying to Kuwait were becoming difficult as the countries that would have to be overflown withdrew their permission. These ominous announcements spoke clearly of a deeply divided international community. It struck me as so very different from the unity of resolve that had characterised the First Gulf War twelve years previously. There is going to be a reckoning, I thought. Even as the international community lined up behind the pro- and anti-war lobbies, I resolved in my own mind that we were on the right side.

Three days and two visits to the departure airfield at RAF Brize Norton later, we finally boarded an RAF Tristar aircraft and took off for Kuwait and whatever lay ahead.

# —7—

# FÜHRER RALLY

Our flight finally touched down in the dark at Kuwait International Airport late on Wednesday 5 February 2003 and immediately I could see that there was little normal about the place. There were numerous aircraft manoeuvring across the pan and lining up to be unloaded. Our aircraft taxied for what seemed to be an eternity before coming to rest in the midst of what looked like a Hollywood film set. The scene was illuminated by arc lights and armed men mingled with contractors in hard hats driving forklift trucks with the nonchalance of London cabbies. As our RAF Tristar came to a halt the passengers stood up and began stretching and gathering their belongings, ready to disembark – until it became clear that we were going nowhere fast. Individuals started to sit down again as the stewards and stewardesses moved among us explaining that the ground crew were looking for some steps.

After what seemed like three hours, some steps were found and we emerged into the light chill of a desert evening. The first thing you notice is the smell, a dusty, almost spicy fragrance carried on the wind that smells exotic and beckons one to the desert. Some of those who had been there for a while were dressed against the evening but for us new arrivals from the UK's winter the temperature was very pleasant. We were loaded onto buses and driven through the organised chaos of the airfield to the reception area. This consisted of long rows of large marquee tents, white on the outside but lined with a decorative yellow material inside. The tents were bare inside except for some urns of hot water set on trestle tables from which the new arrivals could get a hot drink by adding tea or coffee from a box of sachets. Most people sat on their day sacks – our 'hand luggage' in RAF parlance – and chatted over the hum of generators, while the nicotine slaves stood outside enjoying their first smoke for many hours. Outside there were rows of Portaloos, chemical toilets, and there was an understandable demand for them after the long journey. I was intrigued to see US military police checking the booths after each occupant had left.

'Is this some form of turd survey? Is there an extra charge for excess weight or length,' I wondered out loud.

'Naa,' said an obese contractor in US army fatigues and trainers, sporting a baseball cap on his shoulder-length hair, 'they're checking for smoking and graffiti.'

'I suppose they're bound to smoke a little in the evening chill – body heat and all that – but I really can't image how you would set about writing on them,' I observed.

'Not the crap, the walls of the john,' the contractor explained helpfully.

This was not my first experience of the rigid discipline that pervades the US military.

A pasty-faced British logistics officer stepped into the tent and tapped his clipboard. 'Could I have everyone's attention!' he said in a rather camp voice reminiscent of Sergeant Wilson in TV's *Dad's Army*. He explained that we would be called forward for processing into theatre.

Dutifully we lined up to show our passports and ID cards and argue with the medic about how many anthrax injections we had enjoyed, some rolling up sleeves to display their scars as proof. After a brief on driving safety we were sent to board more buses. These were elderly but heavily furnished with lavish curtains that had also seen better days. It was dark but through the cracked windows I could see more passengers arriving and boarding buses, set in lines with baggage trucks in front and behind. We were then invited to get off the buses again to go and identify our bags before reboarding. This happened a couple of times – part of the all-too-familiar military routine of 'on the bus, off the bus'. By now it was two o'clock in the morning and we were all becoming fairly tired. To help us relax, the Arab drivers helpfully switched on the radio to blast Arabic music into our exhausted ears. It made little difference, as most people were asleep before very long.

There had been a number of attacks on the US forces in Kuwait and so each bus convoy had an escort of US Humvees[41], manned by

---

[41] High mobility vehicles. A sort of squat jeep.

Marines in our case. At one point a Marine sergeant hopped onto our bus.

'Camp Eagle?' he wondered. There was silence.

'I think we're for Camp Commando,' said one of the logistics officers.

A lucky escape, as it turned out. At this point in history Camp Eagle, the intended coalition military city, was a barren sea of sand. Before long we set off towards Camp Commando, a Kuwaiti military facility, our first stop and our entry point for the war. As we left the airport we passed Kuwaiti army patrols sitting on top of their Humvees, chatting and smoking, determined to sit this coming war out.

Camp Commando was approached down a bumpy track that ended at a massive concrete and barbed wire barrier, manned by about thirty US Marines. They waved us on and we drove through a busy camp with tents, vehicles and people crammed into every available space and a great deal of activity, even at this late hour. Much of the camp was illuminated by bright arc lights, something we would become accustomed to over the next two months. When we finally stopped, Brigade staff who had flown out some weeks earlier came to greet us. I cannot begin to describe how good it was to see a friendly face after the uncertainty of the previous few days. We collected our baggage and settled into our new accommodation, tents with bunk beds. We dragged out our sleeping bags and fell into a deep sleep.

Morning brought the opportunity to examine our new surroundings. Camp Commando was about 15km from Kuwait City. The tents in the British compound were set out in lines behind some disused Kuwaiti Army barracks. In the places where there was tarmac the rosettes left by the impact of shell splashes could be seen. One resident who had already spent three weeks there explained that Camp Commando had got its name from the fact that it had been a Kuwaiti Army Commando barracks before the First Gulf War. It was one of the few places to offer organised resistance to the Iraqi invasion. When the Iraqis had finally captured the camp, the majority of the Kuwaiti defenders had been dragged to the assault course, a massive structure that stood over the camp like a tower block, and hanged.

The British camp was set around two large tents where the food was served. At first there was an officers and other ranks distinction, but when the Paras and Royal Irish advance parties arrived that went out of the window. The food was provided by a contractor of Pakistani origin, and the food had a bizarre US/Middle Eastern theme. Breakfast would be scrambled eggs and well-fried bacon, or flatbread, chapattis and honey. It was curious that the British servicemen overwhelmingly favoured the Middle Eastern alternatives and at supper you had to be early to ensure some rice and chicken curry or you would be left with ribs and salad with a dizzyingly wide assortment of dressings.

As more people arrived the lunch queues got longer and became a social event in their own right. Deals were struck, information exchanged and missing relatives were traced as we waited to shuffle out of the blazing sun and into the tent. Eventually we would reach the hotplate with a prison-style serving tray to be greeted with a scene that was like a mix of Dante's inferno, the stock market and Gordon Ramsay's kitchen on a busy day. The food was fine, however, and was a miracle of organisation in many respects, given the numbers to be fed. The only crisis was the tea problem. You could have all the colas or fizzy orange drinks you wanted but tea was in short supply. Those who had conceived the menus and catering had simply had no idea of the British Army's tea habit.

The ablutions were long, mobile wash houses fed by great white water tanks, which would be filled each day. There were more long queues and only those prepared to rise an hour before reveille could be assured of a swift wash. I once tried waiting until the afternoon to enjoy a hot shower, but as I stepped out of the cubicle and bent to dry myself, paying little attention to the other occupants, I glanced up, only to realise that the afternoons were reserved for the few female signallers, who whooped with mirth as I scurried off clutching my belongings. I was content to queue in the cool morning air after that.

We were allocated planning tents near our accommodation and soon these were filled with chairs and makeshift planning tables, with maps stretched on large boards set against the wall. The Brigade HQ was in one of the large tents, with a reception desk and a sentry guarding its entrance. The various cells, operations, logistics and movements were laid out along the walls and at the end was a quiet area for the Chief of Staff and the Commander, which is where we would have our evening briefs.

There was a constant threat of terrorism and alerts were frequent. A number of bunkers had been constructed for the troops to shelter in if an attack occurred. This was no over-precaution. There was at least one mortar attack on Camp Commando and a shooting at the gate by terrorists while we were there. The biggest risk was from Scud missiles, as we were well within range of Iraq[42].

---

[42] On the first day of the war proper Camp Commando received a hit from a Scud.

The camp was set below the famous Mutla Ridge, the escarpment that separated the shores of the bay of Kuwait City from the beginning of the desert, and the main Basra highway intersected it beside our camp. This had been the 'Highway of Death' at the end of the First Gulf War and had been the scene of carnage as the fleeing Iraqi forces were cut to pieces by allied aircraft and long-range artillery. Those who had been there at the time described how the wreckage and dead were spread either side of the road for hundreds of yards. Tom Beckett, who had served with the Royal Irish Hussars at the time, recalled how he had seen an Iraqi tank almost untouched by the carnage but on closer inspection realised that the neat hole in the turret had been punched by one of the depleted uranium rounds in use at the time and decided it was not a good place to be. Another veteran of this first war against Saddam remembered coming across some dead bodies at the side of the road, where they had lain for a couple of days. As he looked he realised to his horror that one of the corpses was following him with its eyes. He summoned help, but the woman died shortly before it arrived. There was no trace of this devastation now and a Kuwaiti police post stood at the centre of where the destruction had been, checking documents as people travelled into the desert.

The day after we arrived the Command teams from 1 R Irish, 1 and 3 Para and 3 Regiment Army Air Corps were briefed that we would be flown over the area and on towards the border. We assembled at the helicopter landing site (HLS) and before long a US Army Blackhawk flew into view. As it landed we were called forward and we walked bent over to take our places and buckle in, fitting earphones as we settled down. The aircraft took off in a cloud of dust and climbed high over the desert. Kuwait suddenly seemed rather small as I looked out towards the city and the port beyond and then north, the highway and some power lines streaking away into the desert towards Iraq. Below, the detritus of the annual holidays was visible – many city families from Kuwait had headed off to camp in the desert and now large piles of rubbish and makeshift goalposts marked where they'd been. As we went further north we could see some real Bedouin settlements with their low tents and small corrals where goats and sheep were herded. Sometimes we would fly over a shepherd, who would invariably wave, shielding his eyes from the strong desert sun.

As we headed north we flew over some large plantations and date groves gave way to irrigated fields, contrasting sharply with the surrounding desert. After some minutes, the pilot informed us over the intercom that we were restricted on how close we could go to the border by international treaty. We swung left and as we did so I got my first glimpse of Iraq. The most immediately striking feature was Safwan Hill, the large mound that rose out of the desert and which was shared by Iraqi signallers and intelligence staff and observation posts from the UN monitoring force. The hill was a couple of hundred metres high and would become crucial in the plans for invasion. To the north of Safwan, we could see the smoke from the southern oilfields. We could also see the border stretching out across our front. A kilometre wide, it consisted of a berm[43] around five metres high and beyond that a tank ditch some two metres deep and four metres wide, then a stretch of bare desert and an electric fence. Past this was a further ditch and finally the Iraqis' berm. Observation posts were dotted along both frontiers and UN monitoring HQs could be seen in the area between the boundaries. By international agreement there was a five-kilometre demilitarised zone on either side of the border.

As the helicopter swung south again we could see tank scrapes from the previous war. These were ditches excavated out of the desert that allowed a tank to drive in with only its turret showing above ground. Most faced south or west and had been dug by the Iraqi invaders. Further south, as we approached the Ali Al Salem airbase, we flew over the most remarkable junkyard in the world. The wreckage of thousands of Iraqi vehicles from the last war was spread over an area of ten square kilometres. Row upon row of tanks, artillery vehicles and armoured personnel carriers were gently rusting into the desert. Ali Al Salem itself was, in contrast, a scene of order, with scores of aircraft – transport planes, fighters, helicopters – lined up in every conceivable part of the airfield. Taken with the thousands of aircraft in other bases in neighbouring countries or afloat on the US or UK aircraft carriers, this brought home to me the sheer size of the coalition air force.

We circled over Kuwait City, the hotel-lined seafront corniche giving way to palm tree-lined residential neighbourhoods, which in turn gave way to the high-rise estates of the guest workers. We could see Kuwait International Airport and its approaches once more crammed with transport planes and helicopters, another indication of the massive force that was gathering in this small country.

*

---

[43] Hindi word much used in the British Army to describe a linear bank or low earthen rampart.

The next day we concentrated on the Iraqi Army. It was clear that the allies had a pretty good handle on the troops facing us. Across the border was the Iraqi 3rd Corps. This comprised the 51st Division, centred in Az Zubayr, with the 6th and 11th Divisions, and 10th Division in support, centred on Al Amarah. The 6th Division, which was thought to be in the area to the north and west of Basra, was said to be seventy-five per cent Sunni Muslim and therefore likely to fight more determinedly than the 51st, which was overwhelmingly Shia. The 6th Division was reported to be equipped with GHN-45s, long-range artillery capable of firing chemical and biological munitions, with a range of 35km. There were reports that the 25th Brigade based in Al Qurnah was strongly dug in. There was a possibility that they might be moved west to centre on the town of Al Medina. The 25th Brigade was reported to have Soviet-era D30 122mm field guns with a range of 29km. Their preparedness was in sharp contrast to the reported state of the 11th Iraqi Division in An Nasiriyah, which was apparently not in such good shape and in a ragged line which in the military we call linear defence.

During this time men from the ANGLICOs[44], US Marine reservists and mainly originating from Camp Pendleton, California, joined us, including Major Stan Coeur, a Cobra pilot who had retired from the military to attend the JFK School at Harvard; Brian Borlet, his US Navy colleague; and the redoubtable Sid Heal. Even at fifty-three, Sid was one of the most physically impressive men in the battle group. Sid had first seen active service aged nineteen in Vietnam and now was bringing that military experience and knowledge to 1 R Irish. Sid was also a captain in the Los Angeles Sheriff Department, the equivalent of an army general, and he carried an unspoken authority, judgement and wisdom that would be invaluable in the weeks to come.

Gradually the men filtered into theatre. Arriving in batches of fifty to a hundred, they would be bussed off to transit camps before being claimed and brought to our expanding base. Our concerns now turned to accommodation for us all. An area in the desert had been set aside for 16 Air Assault Brigade and its constituent units, all part of the massive Camp Eagle, the coalition camp. There would be four 16 Air Assault camps and ours would house 1 R Irish and the 7th Royal Electrical & Mechanical Engineers (REME) Battalion. Jackie, my QM, would preside over the turning of our patch of desert into home.

---

[44] Air Naval Gunfire Liaison Coordinators.

In the meantime, we moved into a camp that had been constructed for the use of the brigade, including the headquarters staff, now numbering some 180 souls, reconnaissance unit and signals unit, and would, on the arrival of the men of the brigade's defence platoon, drawn from the Royal Irish Rangers (Territorial Army), become Camp Killaloo. We shared it with the other brigade units and set up a temporary operations room in the main tent. At night we slept on the floor along the sides of the tent. We would be woken early by the sounds of the men of the Household Cavalry Regiment (HCR) exercising in the square behind us. We got to know many of these men as we queued for our meals and they were a well-disciplined and handy-looking bunch of guys. Their vehicles had not yet arrived and they busied themselves around the camp with lectures and physical training.

At night we really felt the cold and would wrap up in all the warm clothing we had. For some that was not much. I had been in the desert many times before and had fought in the First Gulf War and knew what to expect. Temperatures can drop to two degrees or even freezing at night. Where we were it was the wind at night and the damp mist at daybreak that made it really cold. Others had been minimalist in their packing and grew to understand the old British Army adage 'Travel light, freeze at night'.

We had a series of visits from our senior commanders. I recall the first time I met Air Marshal Burridge, who was to be our overall commander. It was Tuesday 11 February 2003. Before the meeting there was growing frustration among the commanders at the idea that the UK seemed to be opting for the supporting tasks; those of us from regiments with a long fighting tradition did not want to play second fiddle to anyone. When we quizzed him about the UK's role, his message was that the UK had no particular strategic objective beyond attempting to foster some unity within the UN at that point. Geoff Hoon, the Secretary of State for Defence, was in the States and it was hoped that some direction for the UK military would be forthcoming as a result of that visit.

He emphasised that the final statement from Hans Blix, which was due on 14 February, was critical. It was hoped that this statement would bolster the evidence for the presence of weapons of mass destruction. That would make the case for war, and therefore our presence, much stronger and help justify the preparations we were making at a rapid pace. We were pessimistic, however, as it was clear that the inspection regime would be useless without intelligence-led targeting of the inspections and there was concern that this was not happening.

We were also told that there was to be a UK-led second resolution, but that it was unlikely to enjoy unanimous support and might take two to three weeks to get through. This resolution was critical to the position of Tony Blair, the Prime Minister. The question remained, however, as to how long the US President was prepared to wait for these UK efforts to bear fruit. The international order seemed to be splitting into two camps, war and anti-war. The war party was led by the US, but the UK was working hard to build some consensus for that policy. It appeared that the US had already made up its mind to strike but they were prepared to allow the British, their closest ally, a little time to strengthen that position before they went ahead. The UK's traditional European allies, including Denmark, Spain, Italy and Holland, supported the US coalition, along with a number of the new members of the European Union from the old Soviet satellite nations, most notably Poland. The anti-war camp, led by France, Germany and Belgium, had also lined up Russian support, the so-called 'Axis of Weasel'. There was a very real prospect that this war would result in a fracture of the alliance that had seen Europe emerge from the Second World War and provided the framework for the existing international order. Not surprisingly, the Middle East was unified in opposition to military action, no doubt with regimes in Syria, Libya and Iran asking themselves 'If Saddam goes – who's next[45]?'

As I sat in the desert after this meeting, watching the sun go down over another day of 'sitzkrieg', I reflected that it was looking increasingly likely that the war would go ahead. It would, it was now clear, be fought on four fronts. The Iraqi front we would win, I was in no doubt. The military capability of the Iraqis was overmatched significantly, though I certainly had a very healthy respect for them. The Iraqi soldier is a force to be reckoned with if well motivated. Some of the fiercest troops my regiment had faced in Gallipoli during the First World War were Mesopotamians (now Iraqis). They had also fought well in the Iran–Iraq War and, after my experiences in the First Gulf War, I knew that their capabilities, even under pressure, were not to be taken lightly. However, I just did not believe that they would fight for Saddam.

A second, international, front had evolved, which resulted in our being at diplomatic odds with some of our closest allies. A war for the hearts and minds of the old established world order was being fought out in the UN. For the UK, it was a watershed. Our old allies within the

---

[45] What we did not know was that even as this was happening Libya was working behind the scenes with the UK to rejoin the international order.

Commonwealth were split, something that was almost unknown hitherto. Australia was with us and was led implacably by John Howard. But Canada was firmly against military action, as was South Africa and New Zealand. India and Pakistan were ambivalent.

There would also be a third, regional, front to the coming conflict. The nations that surrounded Iraq had lived in the shadow of its dictator for the last twenty-five years. Most had been touched by his activities. Iran had endured a life-or-death struggle with the Iraqis. The Turks had conducted a war against the Kurds based in Iraq, yet had provided the base for the allied intervention on behalf of the Kurds at the end of the First Gulf War. At stake for the Turks was US friendship and UK support for their bid to join the European Union in the face of opposition from some, including Greece. But they also had their Islamic population's anti-war stance to consider. Syria had long been in dispute with Iraq, because of both the rivalry between the two dictators of those countries and Syria's sympathies towards Iran in the Iran–Iraq War. Hafiz Assad, dictator of Syria, had been replaced on his death in 2000 by his son, Bashar, who was actively attempting to gain international understanding of his position as he tried to maintain the difficult balance of being a Ba'athist leader of Syria and a power broker in that crucible of conflict, the Israeli-Palestinian dispute. The Syrians were no innocent bystanders in the cauldron of Middle Eastern politics, though. While having 14,000 increasingly unwelcome troops deployed in Lebanon, Damascus was also the base for a number of the most virulent anti-Israeli and US organisations, including the Iranian-backed Hamas and Islamic Jihad. The Hashemite Kingdom of Jordan, led by the statesmanlike King Abdullah, had sprung from the same seed as Iraq after the rule of the Ottomans. A moderate and progressive nation with a moderate tradition, it had a difficult balance to strike between neighbourly relations with Iraq and a close alliances with the West, most notably the UK. Saudi Arabia was a potential cauldron of turmoil in itself, as the march of democracy and the spread of Islamic fundamentalism combined to threaten the rule of the House of Saud. Finally Kuwait, wealthy and opulent, lived every day with the threat of its northern neighbour and their claim on their territory, surviving by the aid and succour of the West. More widely the Gulf states and Egypt, allies of the West, watched in uncertainty as the case for war against Iraq was made, uneasy that the real destabilising issue, the Israeli question, was effectively sidelined. What, they might have wondered, was this really all about? The question that the UK and US administrations should have been asking was, At the end of this war, would our traditional allies in the region survive and what steps were being taken to ensure that they did? In short, was it all worth it?

Then there was the fourth front, the home front. The impending war was, to say the least, controversial at home in the UK. It appeared to me that Tony Blair had bet the house on the war issue and was now using every available ounce of energy to make the case both to the country and to his own party, and even to the cabinet. War was not supported in Ireland, North or South. A close ally of the US, the Republic of Ireland was against war but it was later reported that George Bush had given the Irish Prime Minister short shift when he had raised the issue of the refuelling of US military aircraft en route to the region during a visit to Washington.

As the plan matured, it became increasingly clear that the four major units that comprised 16 Air Assault Brigade – 1 and 3 Para, 3 Army Air Corps and 1 R Irish – would, as expected, be sent to secure the southern oilfields in Iraq. Our task would be to ensure that the oil reserves, which represented one of the largest oil deposits in the world and which would be crucial to securing the future of a new Iraq, were taken intact as far as possible and that they were guarded against any eventualities until they could be brought back to full production. We were left in no doubt that our task was of strategic importance. For this reason we had to learn a great deal about the oil infrastructure and quickly.

It had been estimated that there would need to be 2.3 million barrels of oil a day flowing from the oilfields after the conflict to feed the new Iraq. The oil came out of the ground at a pressure of 10,000 pounds per square inch, a mix of natural gas, oil and water, and flowed into wellheads known as 'Christmas trees'. From these it went to the gas-oil separation plants (GOSPs), where it was separated into its three constituent parts and piped off to collection tanks or, in the case of the water, discarded. In our area there were six main GOSPs and a number of minor ones. The main pumping station was at Az Zubayr, where the oil and gas went into storage tanks. From there the oil would go to the distribution centres at Al Faw and Umm Qasr, on the coast, where it could be loaded onto ships for export. The GOSPs were potential bombs. If they were neglected or attacked they could explode. They were designed to turn themselves off if in danger but we were warned that after twelve years of sanctions their failsafe devices might be inoperative. Then there was the likelihood that the Iraqi State Security Organisation

(SSO) would try to destroy the GOSPs to deny the allies this strategic resource. (Some would argue then and now that the whole war was about oil.) It was noted in our briefings that an exploding GOSP would go off with a flare that would reach 300–600°C, with a lethal area of some 2,000m. Because of the danger of accidental explosions we would be not able to use radios within the GOSP compounds and we would need to be alive to the threat from noxious gases. We were assured, however, that we would have expert help on hand to assist and that there would be professional oil well specialists, or 'wildcatters', who would follow up and deal with any fires.

The build-up continued and men and kit continued to dribble into theatre. The main problem seemed to be that because the decision to mount the operation was taken at such a late hour in the UK the response from industry and the shipping organisations was behind our hopes and expectations. By now we at least had a set of desert combat clothing each, and Jackie had managed to get our vehicles painted at a Kuwaiti barracks.

By 21 February we had moved into our own camp, christened Camp Blair Mayne by the men after a Second World War SAS hero from our regiment. Blair Mayne had been pivotal in the SAS's war in the western deserts of Libya and had won four Distinguished Service Crosses, the Croix de Guerre and Legion d'Honneur in a brilliant career. It was considered fitting that the camp should bear the name of this desert warrior.

Within sight of the Iraqi border, the perimeter of the camp had been formed by the bulldozing of a protective berm around three metres high and a kilometre square, which would take the edge off the desert winds and act as a barrier against opportunist attack. Within this, there was a central cookhouse and two dining hall tents, then rows of Bedouin-style tents running away at right angles, each forming a street, which the boys soon marked out with familiar street names: 'Shankill Road', 'Newtonards Road', 'O'Connell Street'. The troops lived in large tents with up to forty men in each and the senior officers shared six-man tents. I was fortunate to get one of the smaller tents to myself. The alignment of the tents would have done justice to one of Scipio's legions, and but for the vehicles drawn up at the front of camp – mainly four-tonne lorries and stripped-down Wolf-series Land-Rovers laden with machine guns and rocket launchers – it was not hard to imagine Arab horsemen racing through it, or Hannibal's elephants appearing over the horizon.

The desert at this time was still in the flush of spring. Rains had brought patches of green where grass had sprung from the parched landscape and evening walks could be a wonder. The colour of the desert changed every day as the temperature climbed. Here and there, visible only close up, were beautiful desert orchids, purple and delicate against the harsh sandy background. I picked one each for Caroline and my mother and pressed them in letters home.

In mid-February, a number of Iridium satellite telephones were issued, along with a twenty-minute phonecard per week to each man. Being able to call home proved a considerable boost to morale. Surface mail was all very well, but it was terribly slow, something the forces postal system didn't do much to help. On one occasion I was sitting outside my tent when a clerk presented me with three airmail letters. 'Looks like they're from your wife,' he announced.

Curious, I took the letters and checked the address boxes for the sender and addressee. 'No, you clod,' I said, 'these are *to* my wife. I put them in the post yesterday.' He took them back and scurried away.

As the camp filled with men we continued our preparations for war. Many of the platoons opted to do their physical training in the cool of the dawn, and I usually joined one of them or set off with the RSM for a run. After a wash (the showers, at least initially, being solar-powered) we had breakfast. I personally opted for some real coffee that had been sent out in a parcel and some of the Arabic flatbreads with dates or honey, which could be bought at a roadside shop in the middle of the desert called the Mutla Stores. As I ate, I would listen to the BBC World Service on my shortwave radio.

While troops headed off to the ranges to fire their weapons, trying to acclimatize themselves to the increasingly hot conditions, I would have a morning briefing session at 0900 hours, when we would look ahead at the day and discuss the latest intelligence. During the day I would normally visit training and then spend some time conducting planning sessions with the commanders or discussing logistics matters with Jackie and his team. After an evening brief I'd travel to Brigade HQ for a conference chaired by the Brigadier. This meeting was to update us on recent developments and to provide an opportunity to compare notes with the other commanders. We would also be given the latest passwords, which to my delight no one could remember, such as 'Challenge: Hipbone. Reply: Pin. Running password: Talon.' One of my clearest instructions to my men was to stay well away from US installations at night. Several incidents where vehicles had driven close to US installations in the dark and had been fired on had made it clear that the American sentries were very jumpy, and if in any doubt they would shoot, password or not.

Much of one's time was spent keeping the place clean, as the desert winds carried a fine sand into the tent that shrouded everything in its icing sugar-like covering. Books were important and I found reading a welcome distraction from the routine. The food was basic, though there was now a plentiful supply of tea. Lunch would be a bottle of water and a US MRE (Meal Ready to Eat), and we'd have a form of stew most evenings, with a Gurkha curry on a Wednesday night. In my tent I kept a small petrol stove to brew tea and coffee and a supply of cigars, which I would puff as I thought or wrote reports.

We also invested a great deal of time in talking about the Iraqis and their background. Unusually for a commanding officer, I took the lead on this training. I wanted very much to impart to my men my sense of comradeship with the Iraqis and engender an understanding of all the peoples of this region. Iraq had been a British creation at the end of the First World War. It took in the unlikely bedfellows of the Ottoman provinces, or 'vilayets', of Mosul, predominantly Kurds and Turkmen, Baghdad, predominantly Sunni Muslim Arabs, and Basra, dominated by the majority Shia Muslim sect. It had been part of the southern Ottoman Empire and was known as Mesopotamia. It was based on the ancient civilisations of Assyria and Babylon, the ruins of which are not far from Baghdad, and boasts a rich cultural and archaeological background. Abraham was born near the ancient city of Ur, close to modern An Nasiriyah, and the site of the Garden of Eden is supposed to have been close to the modern city of Al Qurnah. It is said that the legend of the Great Flood is also based in Iraq.

The state of Iraq, galvanised by the turbulent nature of its birth, spawned a series of nationalist movements, including, in 1949, the Ba'ath party, a movement based on the ideals of a Syrian Christian advocating Arab unity and a form of socialism. Discontent boiled over in 1958 with a secret organisation of 'Free Officers' staging a coup which culminated with the King being murdered, torn apart after being tied between two of his favourite cars, which were then driven off in different directions. After a period under a nationalist government and a short taste of power for the Ba'athists in 1963, the Arab disaster in the Six-Day War of 1967 set the conditions for a return of the Ba'athists and by 1968 they were in power once again. The history of this time is unsettled and bloody, with atrocities against the Kurds and the Shia majority, culminating in the seizing of power in July 1979 by Saddam

Hussein and the execution of 500 leading Ba'athists, as well as the leader of the Shia, Ayatollah Mohammed Baqir al-Sadr, and his sister Bint al-Huda.

In September 1980, sensing the weakness of Iran after the overthrow of the Shah and his replacement by Ayatollah Khomeini, who had purged the once-formidable Iranian Army, Saddam attacked Iran. He was emboldened in his decision by support from the monarchist Arab states and from the West, most notably the US, who were angered by the recent US hostage crisis in Iran and the humiliating failure of a rescue mission. (Notable visitors to Saddam at the time included a rising US political star, Donald Rumsfeld.)

Saddam's early gains were quickly reversed and the conflict descended into a long, vicious war, involving the use of weapons of mass destruction, all at a cost of over a million lives. In the face of the deadlock, the Arab nations that had once so encouraged Iraq drew back. The war ended in stalemate in 1988. Furious at the lack of support and unwillingness of most of the Arab states to write off his war debts, Saddam invaded Kuwait on 2 August 1990, ostensibly to recover Iraq's 'nineteenth state'.

The international community rallied round and the First Gulf War of 1990/91 saw the routing of the Iraqi Army and modest incursions into Iraqi territory before the forces were pulled back on orders from the US President, George Bush Senior. I served in that war with the 22nd Special Air Service Regiment. It was after this that a UN inspections team was sent to Iraq for the first time with the aim of examining the country's capacity to produce weapons of mass destruction. This continued until their withdrawal in 1999, still uncertain whether Saddam's capacity to produce such weapons had been removed.

The Iraqis themselves are a generous and welcoming people. They are of a settled nature, unlike the nomadic Bedouin of the Gulf States, although there is a large Bedouin population in the south and west of Iraq. Iraq also has a unique ancient people in the form of the Marsh Arabs. With a civilisation dating back 6,000 years, the Marsh Arabs were one of a notable group, along with the Kurds and the residents of Fallujah, who were a constant thorn in the side of the Tikriti clan-dominated government. The regime resorted to any means available to suppress them, including an infamous gas attack against the Kurds, which left 5,000 dead, many of them women and children. Attacks on the Marsh Arabs after the failed Shia uprising of 1991 led to the establishment by western powers of an exclusion zone over the area.

The religious make-up of the country is complex and indeterminate. The best estimate of the total numbers of Iraqis is drawn from the population declared by Saddam's regime in their returns to the UN in the 'Oil for Food' project. It may be wildly out; no one really knows how many Iraqis there are. This survey showed that the population was approximately 53.5% Shia Muslim, 42.3% Sunni Muslim and 3.5% Christian. The ethnic make-up is supposedly 77% Arab, 19% Kurdish, 1.8% Turkmen, 0.8% Persian and 0.8% Assyrian. Again this is a 'bestimate'. Of the 1.5 million Shia Kurds, the 'Faili Kurds' who lived in the central region, for instance, many are in exile in Iran and elsewhere. They are not counted as Kurds but as simply Shia or Iraqis of Iranian origin. This boosts the 'Arab' numbers. The fact is that they are Kurds, belonging to one of the oldest civilisations in the world. But since Saddam decided they don't exist – they don't.

As planning became more focused we visited our opposite numbers in the US Marines. 1 R Irish was due to cross behind 1st Battalion of the 5th Marine Regimental Combat Team (RCT) – a brigade-sized formation. The 1st of the 5th (or 1/5), as they were known, were led by Lieutenant Colonel Fred Padilla. Softly spoken and thoughtful, with a 'jarhead' US Marines haircut, he was widely respected. His team were as eager as our boys to get on with the job. US Marines – indeed US soldiers in general – always wore neat, high-quality uniforms and their identical haircuts and strict uniform guidelines made them look businesslike, in contrast to our hand-me-down desert combat clothing and longer hair.

We had a 'study' day where we walked through our respective parts in the plan on a large diagram the Marines had made in the sand. These were known as 'rock drills'. We would stand at the edge of this large grid covering several square metres, with features such as rivers and roads depicted by ribbons and towns by cardboard markers and symbols showing allied units and enemy units. Soldiers with coloured bibs would slide our symbols around the model as we described our actions at each phase. This process provided a detailed insight into each other's plans and allowed questions about pace, coordination and so on to be resolved and recorded. Essentially the plan was to advance to report lines or features on the ground, which were given code names, such as 'phase line Tampa' or 'phase line Georgia', that would have no meaning for the enemy but allowed us to accurately track our own troops and our allies.

After we had finished on the model we would take some refreshment in the Marines' dining hall, where discussion would continue. I exchanged background information on my troops with Fred and he pointed out his commanders and their young officers. This was vital. In the mist and dark of battle we would be meeting with men we had broken bread with and would recognise. Any adjustments to the plan had this mutual basis to work from. I felt we had begun to get to know our opposite numbers and found the optimism for the success of the mission and for the future of Iraq heartening. I was both proud and glad to be working with the US Marines, an organisation much more like the British Army than the US Army. Watching the steely determination of these high-grade warriors, I was also relieved to be on their side.

My headquarters was expanded with the arrival of a rear link detachment from the Royal Signals, in the form of Corporal Stevenson and Signalman Cascarino. 'Stevo' and 'Cas', as the boys called them, fitted in perfectly and turned out to be witty and able men and also very effective signallers. My first real introduction to Stevo and Cas was an almost fatal encounter. We were on a night exercise and had been sent on a long drive through the desert to various rendezvous points. At one of these someone had made mistake and set out a traffic lane that involved crossing a two-metre-high berm. As my 'Comms Camel' – my command vehicle, a Land-Rover bristling with antennas – went over it had to put on full revs to scream up the bank before almost taking off to land with a crash on the far side. I told Herby, my operation warrant officer, who would often drive the Comms Camel, to stop, then I climbed out with the intention of telling the next vehicle to wait until I could find another way round. But too late. I suddenly saw the looming shape of Stevo and Cas's Land-Rover sailing through the air. I dived out of the way and felt the two-ton vehicle whoosh past as it blasted into the back of the Comms Camel. The Camel came off with a bent bumper while the Land-Rover was destroyed. Luckily Stevo and Cas walked away from the wreckage.

Life continued with more anthrax jabs and an increase in activity as training reached its crescendo. We managed to hold our Barossa[46] dinner night, to which all of the Royal Irish who were in theatre were invited, in a tent decorated as if it was an officers' mess, with the Battalion Colours proudly displayed. A splendid meal cooked by our own chefs was served,

---

[46] This dinner, held on 5 March each year, commemorates the seizure of the first French Imperial Eagle, touched by the hand of Napoleon, by my regiment at the Battle of Barossa, in Southern Spain, in 1811.

along with alcohol-free beer, before we turned out once more into the darkness of a desert night to return to our tents.

The following day we had a visit from the Chief of the General Staff (CGS), General Mike Jackson. His aim was to see the preparations for himself and he was to have a press call while visiting 1 R Irish. He had the Director of Corporate Communications (Army), or DCCA, Brigadier Matthew Sykes, in tow. We took tea in the mess tent until it was time to go out to see the troops in the presence of the media. The General was clearly not enamoured with the journalists. He finished his tea and, placing his beret on this head, said, 'Time, I think, gentlemen, to deal with the reptiles.'

He spoke to the boys and then made a statement to the press, echoing what we had heard from our own commander, General Brims. The big issue that the media had seized on was a shortage of toilet paper, which some Royal Marines had written to their local MPs to complain about. As the CGS fended off loo paper questions with a booming 'Let's not get bogged down with this detail,' I allowed my gaze to stray north towards Iraq. The RSM saw and leaned forward to whisper, 'Don't worry, they'll have loads of bog roll up there – we just have to go and get it.'

Near our camp we found a lot of evidence of the last war. On one occasion I was driving through the desert when I spotted a massive lizard that must have been a metre long. I stopped the vehicle and followed it to get a good look and over a sand dune I saw a large fenced area with a berm covered with barbed wire. Oddly there were a few desert dogs sitting inside the area in the shade of a dune and the odd rag or discarded boot lying around. As I walked back I found a 7.62mm cartridge case with Arabic markings showing it was made in Iraq in 1991. A relic from the last war, I thought. The following day at Brigade I indicated the area on the map where I had seen the fenced area and said to the training officer, 'Could we use that for training? We could practise blowing wire and berm-crossing techniques.'

He smiled. 'No, too realistic. There's an Iraqi battalion dug in there.'

'Dug in? Iraqis?' I said. 'I didn't see a soul.'

'You wouldn't. It's a mass grave from the last time.'

The next day I was standing outside my tent when the final members of our battle group arrived, the journalists, sent by the Army to follow our every move. From Sky News there was Greg Milam, a big, dark-haired chap with a friendly face, and Ronnie Dewhurst, a Geordie with an impish expression. Then from the *Mail on Sunday* there was Sarah

Oliver, slight of build with flame red hair. I had not dealt with the media before to any great extent, but I was increasingly a believer that, in addition to their overt role of informing the public, they could play a key part in Information Operations in the modern military landscape. With the advances in modern communications they could be used as a vehicle for reassuring allies, as well as putting the fear of God into your enemies. I resolved to give them full access. My only caveat was that future operations and planning were off limit, as were the ANGLICOs – unless they invited them to talk. The rest was free play. I was also conscious that the media were mostly very bright people and realised that the individuals they would send to a war would be of their finest. From an early stage I was convinced of the good will towards us that existed within the UK's media, almost without exception, reflecting perhaps the store of good will that the UK public has for the armed forces.

Training had reached its peak now and with night firing complete we knew we were ready. Planning was an almost twenty-four-hour-a-day business as we fine-tuned our preparations. The expectation was that we would be crossing the border in ten days' time. On 16 March we went to the ranges to conduct daytime live firing, supported by our mortars and artillery. It was essentially a fire control exercise but it would practise the coordination of our fire support, including the heavy machine guns and Milan wire-guided anti-tank missiles. We arrived in good time and the first few companies went through at a cracking pace. However, I was still concerned about the number of stoppages we were getting with our weapons and the only solution seemed to be lots more oil on the working parts, which is exactly the opposite of what you would expect in sandy conditions. Suddenly a call came to cease fire. All activity was to be suspended.

I called brigade to find out what the problem was. There was a simple explanation. A troop of Challenger 2 tanks from the Scots Dragoons had had a little problem with their map reading and had crossed into the demilitarised zone, and now the commander in Kuwait had ordered all training to halt. I went to the back of my vehicle and lit a cigar. It looked like an enforced tea break. As I smoked I opened my body armour to let out some heat. I leaned back on the vehicle, waiting for the problem to sort itself out so I could get on with the training. But live firing was not reinstated and we returned to camp in the gathering darkness via the Mutla Stores, where I bought a large thermos flask so that the crew of the Camel would always have tea.

The next day we were awakened by the pipe band reminding us that while we might be in Kuwait it was still St Patrick's Day. As tradition had it, we took tea around to the men. The best kept secret – up to now – was that it was well laced with whiskey, which came as quite a surprise to the boys. Contrary to the stereotype of Paddies, a lot of the young men did not drink – at eighteen and nineteen they preferred coke and sweets to whiskey – so for those who liked the stuff there was plenty to go round.

As he took his tea one ranger lifted the flap of his tent and looked out into the desert sunshine. 'There'll be a parade in my town at home,' he declared. 'They've got lovely weather for it.'

'Don't be so daft,' his mate said. 'They're three hours behind. It could be raining by then.'

St Patrick's Day was a day off of sorts and for the men of the Royal Irish battle group this meant sports and a chariot race, where 'chariots' made of junk that was found around the camp were raced around the fort, with a lot of flour and eggs thrown and water slopped over rival chariots. The afternoon saw a parade and a sunset service outside the camp. In keeping with Irish tradition, Major General Brims came to inspect the parade. It was an opportunity to allow the men to see their chieftain. After the battalion marched off, we had a ceilidh, where the turns by the companies included a number of short plays, mostly taking the mickey out of me and the HQ staff, and the usual round of Irish songs.

Dawn on 19 March 2003 was much like any other day. It was the third day of a desert storm; sand as fine as talc coated everything and filled ears, noses and equipment. New kit was gradually finding its way into theatre, but there was never enough to go round. What we did not know was that in Washington, nine time zones away, an opportunity had been seen that would change our world for ever. Unknown to the waiting world, the Information Operations campaign had been targeting the Iraqi regime as well as the Iraqi Army. Part of this had been a lure to get the regime to confirm the physical location of its key players. A number of ruses were used but it was an almost schoolboy prank that was to prove most effective. Having circulated a story over the previous days that Tariq Aziz, deputy Prime Minister and Saddam's right-hand man, had defected or had been arrested for leading a palace coup, Tariq amazed western intelligence by calling a press conference at which he would appear personally. It was really too good to miss. Cruise missiles erupted from beneath the waves of the Arabian Gulf and off towards

Baghdad and the podium where Tariq stood. Somehow he survived. Staggering from the wreckage, he was a wiser man. The assault on Saddam's regime had begun.

As the sirens wailed over Baghdad once again, more missiles followed, streaking away from US surface vessels and B-52s from Diego Garcia, or erupting from the UK's Trafalgar-class submarine fleet. The onset of actual hostilities brought a buzz of excitement to the camp. I became aware of the outbreak of war when some of the men saw it on television, sheltering from the winds and sand in the dining tent. I immediately asked Sergeant Major 'Herby' Herbert to get my close staff ready for a move.

I was having a brew and completing some reports in my tent when my field telephone buzzed. A signaller with a broad Belfast accent introduced the Brigadier's Chief of Staff.

'Are you up for a chat with the Brigadier?' a familiar voice asked.

We both laughed.

'Any particular time?'

'No rush. Just as soon as you can get here will do.'

'I'm on my way.'

I picked up my pistol belt, from which hung my Gurkha kukri and a small, battered pouch containing my folding knife and teaspoon, and buckled it over my desert combats. Then I shrugged on my fishing vest, which held my map, satellite-navigation devices, prismatic compass, cigars and lighter. Finally, I grabbed my helmet, chemical warfare kit and respirator as the RSM threw back the tent flap.

'It looks like we've gone off a little ahead of schedule,' I said. 'Can you make sure everyone is cutting about, please? I have a feeling time will be short when I get back.'

He laughed. 'Sir, they don't need telling.' He tilted his head towards the queue forming outside the Quartermaster's tent. 'They've been watching the telly.'

'See you later,' I said, making my way to the Comms Camel. 'I'll need to speak to the head shed[47].'

'I'll get the Adjutant onto that right away, sir.' He glanced at the Arabic kettle boiling its brass head off on my petrol stove and added drily, 'Do ye want me to turn off that brew before ye burn the camp down?'

'It's all yours,' I said with a grin.

*

---

[47] The commanders of the various components of the 1,225-strong Royal Irish Battle Group.

'Youse lot again . . .' The sentry at the HQ of 16 Air Assault Brigade was wearing a shemagh and sand goggles, but his broad Enniskillen accent was unmistakable. 'I thought youse were warned off from here!'

These were the Air Assault Brigade's defence platoon from the Royal Irish Rangers, the Territorial Army reserve of the Royal Irish Regiment. This particular lot were from Tyrone and Fermanagh, like my machine gun platoon.

'We just can't keep away,' I said.

'And you TA lads are just as scruffy as ever,' the Sergeant Major added from behind the wheel.

The sentry pushed his helmet back and leaned into the Land-Rover. 'Is this it, sir? Has it really started?'

'Ask me on the way out,' I said.

He smiled and stepped back as we drove in.

Forts Killaloo (16 Air Assault Brigade HQ), Pegasus (1 Para) and Longdon (3 Para) had been constructed alongside Blair Mayne in a diamond formation, a kilometre apart. They reminded me of battle cruisers in squadron formation.

Staff officers and signallers milled around inside the Killaloo complex, looking important, answering telephones and marking maps. One rather earnest individual was busy pacing from one desk to the next, waving a piece of paper, then racing back to his own desk to scribble another note before beginning the process all over again. I pictured the headline: FIRST CASUALTY! OUR BRAVE LADS WATCH IN HORROR AS BRITISH STAFF OFFICER DISAPPEARS UP OWN ARSE!

We were in a tent the size of a small aircraft hangar, whose sides were billowing in the desert wind like the lungs of a warhorse. It was divided into functional cells (intelligence, logistics, air and so on), with a large table in the centre, the 'Bird Table', upon which lay a plastic-coated map marked with troop dispositions. Brigadier Jacko Page sat, phone glued to his ear, at an identically marked but smaller planning table in one corner, his Chief of Staff alongside him.

'You're all saved,' I boomed as I entered. 'The Paddies are here, and this time we're on your side!'

'*Shhh* . . .' the staff officers chorused.

I gripped my notebook like a clutch bag to my chest and, miming affront, walked over to the planning table. As the other COs arrived or sat studying their maps, I whispered to Simon, 'Who's on the phone?'

'The General,' he whispered back.

'Relax, boys, the Paras are here . . .'

I looked up to see the COs of 1 and 3 Para making their entrance. This time I led the '*Shhh* . . .' chorus.

The Brigadier rolled his eyes at the tomfoolery, but none of us could ignore the gravity of the moment. There were some genuinely worried faces around the room – the virgins who had never tasted conflict before. I was mildly concerned that the plan would change again and that the Royal Irish, currently in pole position, might get dropped into reserve or given a less aggressive task.

The call completed, the briefing began. 'This is it,' the Brigadier said, polishing his glasses and checking them against the light. 'From what I could gather from the GOC[48] – once Collins here quietened down – we are to move to dispersal areas straight away. Everything will go ahead according to plan, but to a new timescale. We can expect an immediate response from the Iraqis in the form of Scuds, so be on your guard and respond to the alarms immediately. Questions?'

Of course there were.

When we gathered up our notes and maps and made our way to the exits, I stopped for a moment beside the Brigadier, an old friend since our days in the boxing club at Sandhurst.

'So here we go again,' I said.

'Once again, Tim,' he replied, reaching for his tea. Then he looked at me over his glasses. 'And don't cock it up, there's a good chap.' As I left, he nodded at my fishing vest. 'I'll see if the DCOS[49] can get you some proper kit, shall I?'

I tilted my caubeen at a jaunty angle and responded appropriately in my best stage Irish.

The boys had the Comms Camel drawn up outside. I waved to Tom Beckett, commander of 1 Para.

'Good luck,' he shouted.

'See you over there,' I replied.

For the trip back to Fort Blair Mayne, Corporal Magowan was in the driving seat. 'Where's the Sergeant Major, Magoo?'

'Gone back to sort out kit, sir.' He paused, looking straight ahead. 'So,' he said eventually, 'we're off to Iraq?'

I nodded.

---

[48] General Officer Commanding.

[49] Deputy Chief of Staff – the HQ staff officer in charge of discipline and supplies.

'I don't want to seem funny here, sir,' he said awkwardly, 'but the blokes don't really know why this is happening. That's to say, we know Saddam is the devil incarnate and all that – but why now?'

Magoo was a bright young man, with more operational experience than most. He'd seen active service in Kosovo and Sierra Leone, as well as East Tyrone. I thought for a moment. 'Do you think I should get them together?'

'Aye, sir.' He smiled. 'I'd say it's time for one of your Führer Rallies.'

Back at camp there had been a transformation. Most of the busy little town had been packed away into vehicles. A menacing line of Wolf-series Land-Rovers stood poised for action outside the fort.

I briefed the command group on the latest developments at Brigade, just as I had been briefed, then asked them to gather the boys together for a central briefing.

'On the square in ten minutes,' the RSM boomed. 'Scale X.' A Scale X parade meant everyone apart from sentries.

As the RSM and I walked to my tent, the wind whipped around us. Soldiers doubled back and forth, loaded with ammunition, water and rations. Once inside, I sat on my American camp bed and he pulled up one of the chairs.

'What shall I say?'

He looked me straight in the eye. 'I think you know, sir. We've talked about this moment for a long time now; you'll not be stuck for words. Just give the boys what you have just told the command group, plus a couple of jokes to keep them alert.'

Alone again, I glanced around the tent. It was a rather smart affair, about six metres by four, and about two and a half tall, with strip lighting and power points. I looked at the board on which I'd pinned a large-scale map of Kuwait and Iraq. Scenes like this would be playing out on both sides of the border. I thought of the Iraqis I knew. Good men, good friends. Then I thought of my own boys. I couldn't have been prouder to be leading Ireland's oldest surviving regiment into battle, but I knew I could be leaving some of them in shallow graves in the desert, if not getting dug in myself.

I said a short prayer then looked up as the tent flap was hauled back.

'We're ready, sir,' the Adjutant said.

I stepped outside. The wind had dropped as suddenly as it had risen, leaving an uneasy calm and an ominous light. It had whipped sand high into the atmosphere, blanking out the sun. The temperature had dropped too; it was now around thirty degrees.

I could see nothing much beyond the walls of Fort Blair Mayne, except the massive oil fires that already raged deep within Iraq, but I knew that hundreds of thousands of British, American, Australian and Polish soldiers, tanks and trucks were taking up their positions somewhere near the specks of bright orange light that danced on the horizon, beneath the ink-black clouds of smoke that hung like a pall in the northern sky.

The men were gathered on the square. I stood facing west. I could see the officers on one side, and A, B, C, L and Headquarters Companies Royal Irish and D (Gurkha) Company forming a hollow square, with the Gunners, Engineers, Intelligence and Military Police mixed in. The US Marine Corps ANGLICOs were with their respective companies, yet easily recognisable by their camouflage suits. Seeing them so fully integrated reminded me sharply that I had some twenty nationalities in my battle group. While the vast majority were Paddies from the north and south of Ireland or second-generation Micks from England, there were also Canadians, Australians, Nepalese, South Africans, Zimbabweans and Fijians. Among the US Marines – all reservists – there were even a handful of Mexicans.

The Battalion 2IC, Andrew Cullen, called the parade to attention. I had known him for fifteen years, and at six foot four and seventeen stone, he was my executive officer. He spun around and reported that the 1st Battalion the Royal Irish Regiment was assembled and awaiting my instructions. I asked him to stand them at ease.

As I took my place I noticed our embedded media gathered to my left: Greg and Ronnie from Sky News, and Sarah Oliver from the *Mail on Sunday*, dwarfed by the hulking camouflaged men around her. A photographer from the Army's Directorate of Corporate Communications hovered at the back.

This was what Magoo had called a Führer Rally. My bit came partly from the head, partly from the heart and mostly from the shoulder. I noticed Sarah Oliver taking out her notepad.

I knew that by the end of the brief the men had to look on their task as the rescue of the Iraqis from tyranny, rather than the vanquishing of an enemy. I invited them to close in.

'We are going to Iraq to liberate and not to conquer,' I began. 'We will not fly our flags in their country. We are entering Iraq to free a people – and the only flag that will be flown in that ancient land will be their own. Show respect for them.

'The enemy knows this moment is coming too. Some have resolved to fight and others wish to survive. Be sure to distinguish between them. There are some who are alive at this moment, who will not be alive shortly. Those who do not wish to go on that journey, we will not send; as for the others, I expect you to rock their world. Wipe them out if that is what they choose. But if you are ferocious in battle, remember to be magnanimous in victory.

'Iraq is steeped in history; it is the site of the Garden of Eden, of the Great Flood and the birthplace of Abraham. Tread lightly there.

'In the near future you will see things that no man could pay to see, and you will have to go a long way to meet a more decent, generous and upright people than the Iraqis. You will be embarrassed by the hospitality they will offer you, even though they have nothing. Don't treat them as refugees in their own country. Their children will be poor. In years to come they will know that the light of liberation in their lives was brought by you.

'If there are casualties of war, then remember that when they got up this morning and got dressed they did not plan to die this day. Allow them dignity in death. Bury them with due reverence and properly mark their graves.

'It remains my foremost intention to bring every single one of you out alive. But there may be those among us who will not see the end of this campaign. We will put them in their sleeping bags and send them back. There will be no time for sorrow.

'The enemy should be in no doubt that we are his Nemesis and we are bringing about his rightful destruction. There are many regional commanders who have stains on their souls and they are stoking the fires of hell for Saddam. He and his forces will be destroyed for what they have done to their people. As they die, they will know that it is their deeds that have brought them to this place. Show them no pity. It is a big step to take another human life. It is not to be done lightly. I know of men who have taken life needlessly in other conflicts. I can assure you that they live with the mark of Cain upon them.

'If someone surrenders to you, remember that they have that right in international law, and ensure that one day they go home to their family. The ones who wish to fight . . . well, we aim to please. Remember, however, that if you harm your regiment or its history by over-enthusiasm in killing, or cowardice, know that it is your family who will suffer. You will be shunned unless your conduct is of the highest order, for your deeds will follow you down through history. We will bring shame on neither our uniforms nor our nation.

'As for chemical and biological weapons, I believe the threat is very real. We know that the order to use these weapons has been delegated down to regional commanders. That means he has already taken the decision to use them. Therefore it is not a question of if, it is a question of when they attempt this. If we survive the first strike, we will survive the attack.

'As for ourselves, let's bring everyone home safely and leave Iraq a better place for us having been there. Our business now is north. Good luck.'

Activity continued that night with ammunition being broken out and the final bits of equipment being issued. Even at this late hour kit was still arriving. The night was not without incident. As the men of C Company HQ staff packed their kit, the clerk from the Adjutant General's Corps walked in with a loaded rifle, pointed it at each man as they sat packing and pretended to shoot them. Not surprisingly he was jumped on and quickly overpowered. He was judged to be unbalanced and arrangements were made to take him to a field hospital for psychiatric care. I was informed and he was on his way to the field hospital in chains within half an hour. I spoke to him before he left.

'I expect you thought this was a good way to get out of this war. Well, it worked. One word of caution. Had you done it in front of me I would have killed you on the spot. Be in no doubt of that. Sheer luck has kept you alive.'

I had heard of such incidents before. Men, their minds unbalanced, have run amok before combat and often killed their own. It was yet another of the things that commanders had to watch for. A tragic instance was to follow a few days later in Camp Commando. A Muslim US soldier, a sergeant from the unit we had exercised with the previous summer, 101st Airborne, cut out the generator near his lines to plunge the camp into darkness before tossing a grenade into tents full of sleeping men and shooting into the darkened interiors. A young captain, Christopher Seifert, was killed and fifteen others were wounded, some seriously, before the man was overpowered.

Within an hour of the arrest of our clerk the doctor was shuffling around outside my tent. She had another conscientious objector on her hands. I went to see the man. Sadly he was from the Royal Irish. He was in his mid-twenties and I had known him for a long time.

'I'm scared, sir,' he told me. 'I don't want to go.'

I knew he had a brother in the battalion so I asked to see him before sending the man away. After a few minutes, as I sat writing in my tent, a voice announced that the brother was there. I lifted the tent flap to see a corporal waiting for me. He had clearly been packing kit, as he was stripped to the waist, and as I emerged he was looking straight at me, his eyes burning, staring intently and his face taut and angry.

'I've decided nothing yet,' I said immediately, sensing what he was thinking. 'That is why I've asked to speak to you. What shall we do?'

We both turned and, heads bowed, walked in silence into the desert until we were out of earshot. Finally he turned to me.

'Sir,' he began, 'my family has been in this regiment for generations. If my brother is allowed to run, then we are shamed. The whole family.'

'What do you want to do then?' I asked.

'What I want is to strap the fucker to the front of the leading Land-Rover as a mine detector, but what I'll settle for is for you to leave him to me. I'll take him over and then we can send him home if he wants once he has crossed. But he's gotta cross – you know why. He did this in Kosovo too, you know,' he added.

'I know,' I said, 'but in Kosovo he finally went of his own free will. You realise I can't tolerate this – it sets a bad example and upsets the other men. But I understand it's family business for you. As I trust you, you can deal with it now, but this is the last time, OK?'

'OK.' He paused and then said, 'And thanks. Permission to carry on?'

'Carry on,' I said. He turned to go. 'I'd do the very same if I was in your shoes,' I added as he walked off to find his brother. He glanced round and nodded. As I watched him leave I could see him ever so slightly shaking his head. Family is strong in our regiment and is a support and an inspiration – but it can be a burden too.

We waited in Fort Blair Mayne until morning. By 0600 I got the message to move out to dispersal locations and dig in. The Scuds were flying. Within an hour we were gathering around our vehicles. There were high spirits that belied the seriousness of the moment as we loaded the last gear. We were brimming with equipment as the Operations Officer, Graham Shannon, passed around some Tayto crisps, a brand from Northern Ireland. It was truly odd to see a wrapper that was so familiar in the leaded skies of Ireland here in the bright desert light and on the eve of war.

Once packed, we drove outside the berm and the vehicles were lined up. Now joined by our attached elements, the Royal Irish battle group stretched for more than a mile. The mortar platoon 2IC, Sergeant Major 'Aunty' Billy McKenna, passed some Havana cigars around and we had a final smoke before we set off. And not a moment too soon. Several tremendous explosions announced that the Scuds and Al Samoud missiles were responding in kind to the cruise-missile attacks. It had all gone noisy.

We drove off into the desert. Our dispersal areas were patches of desert where no troops had been and which could not have been pretargeted by enemy missiles. There had always been the fear that the enemy had spies in Kuwait who were taking the coordinates of camps so that Scuds could be targeted. There had been a number of attacks on coalition forces by terrorists since the build-up had begun. At our dispersal area, shell scrapes were dug and I listened to the radio as reports flowed in. I regret to say that a certain jumpiness from a nearby battle group who donned their anti-gas respirators at the least alarm – a Kuwaiti police car driving past, someone dropping a shovel – was beginning to affect my men, who would respond to the neighbouring unit's alarms, donning gas masks and setting off their own alarms. I soon tired of this and called in the company commanders.

'You are to tell your men to stop acting like women. If they want to join the [battle group who will remain nameless] then fucking go. If you want to stay with the Irish then dig a trench and stay in it until I tell you to move. OK?' They set off and soon the flapping next door became a source of amusement to us.

We moved on to our final dispersal area near the international border and settled down for the night. On my Blue Force Tracker, a satellite-controlled device that allowed me to see all friendly forces, I could see that there was a huge build-up on the border and there we were, part of it. I attended a conference with the Brigade Commander and we discussed the situation. Finally he said the words we wanted to hear: '1 R Irish will cross the border at 0600 hours. The US Marines will have crossed before and there will be a breach in the border, cleared of mines and obstacles. You should be ready to move from 0300 hours. Good luck.'

I decided that the only thing to do was to brew some tea and have a cigar. As I sat smoking contemplatively, the kettle gently wafting steam from the spout, my petrol stove began to make an odd spluttering noise. I peered at it and then looked closer. I reached forward and adjusted the valve. A sudden flash caused me to reel back. Fucking idiot, I thought to myself. CO 1 R Irish would be meeting the Iraqi Army with no eyebrows and a very short fringe of hair.

# —8—

# INTO IRAQ

As we sat waiting I knew that ahead of me the US 3rd Infantry Division had pressed up the main highway and was well on its way towards the crossings on the River Euphrates, having burst through the international border at 0430 hours. The UK 3rd Commando Brigade had carried out an attack on the oil terminals on the Al Faw peninsula to our east and to the south of Basra. From here had come the sad news that a US CH-46 Sea Knight helicopter had crashed in the Kuwaiti desert and that eight Royal Marines had been killed. The US Marine Expeditionary Force had crossed to our west that morning at around 0500, and soon the US 1/5 Marines, with Colonel Fred Padilla's 63-ton Abrams tanks and amphibious Amtrack personnel carriers leading the way, would press forward to take the southern oilfields. The 1 R Irish battle group would follow in our Land-Rovers, four-tonners and Humvees.

Military victory was assured, I was certain, as I watched the columns of armour stretching as far as the eye could see, queuing to cross the border. Fighter jets screamed low overhead. There was no sign of the Iraqi Army ahead of us, just columns of black smoke on the horizon. But it would not be for the military victory that this war would be remembered, it would be for the quality of the peace that followed. I wondered how the 1.2 million inhabitants of Basra were feeling as they watched this drama unfold around them.

As darkness began to fall on 21 March I had to concentrate to believe that there was a war on. Skylarks sang as they darted over the shell scrape trenches where we waited. Then, in a heartbeat, night had fallen and numerous fires burning with a bright orange glow lit the horizon. Were the oil facilities we had come to rescue for the good of Iraq already in ruins? We would know at dawn.

As ordered, 1 R Irish crossed the Iraqi border at 0600 hours on 22 March. The first vehicle bumped onto Iraqi soil as the second hand swept over the numeral 12. My vehicle led the Headquarters packet through the gap in the border that had been created by the Royal Engineers. It was a gloomy morning, not unusual for the time of year, but the murkiness was significantly increased by the pall of smoke from numerous fires burning all around us. As we drove along the road into the no man's land between Kuwait and Iraq, I was reminded of the internal Cypriot border I had once patrolled, a despised empty space where men literally feared to tread.

As we drove deeper into Iraq we paused near one of the gas fires raging in the morning air, a searing 600°C ball of flame, bursting from the fractured pipe with a roar and a pulse that made the very air quiver. Around us lay the detritus of an earlier war, shattered T-72 tanks and smashed self-propelled howitzers, destroyed by coalition air power as Saddam's forces fled the 'Mother of All Battles' in 1991 and which no one here had ever seen the point of recovering. In Kuwait, a mile away, the tanks had been carefully gathered and placed in a secure area to rust and radiate away from humanity. I was surprised that they hadn't even been harvested for scrap value. Then I remembered that in a land where everything is managed by the party and without free enterprise, scrap has no value. In any case, after twelve years of sanctions, the very oil infrastructure that generated the country's wealth was virtually scrap itself.

As we headed for our rendezvous we passed considerable amounts of fresh battle debris and weapons scattered around, and among those who lay where they had fallen were two corpses sprawled on the road beside electric-blue Jawa motorcycles. When we linked up with Fred Padilla at the most southerly oil facility, he looked tired and drawn. Coffee in hand, he described the battle of the preceding hours to me during our handover of command. Fred described how the Iraqis, taken by surprise initially, had fought then fled, but die-hard elements sniping at the Marines had claimed the life of one of his young lieutenants.

'I heard he was wounded,' Fred said, 'and we had a priority "dust-off"[50] inbound. Then I heard it had been downgraded to "routine".

---

[50] Helicopter casualty evacuation.

I knew the worst. He was a good kid.'

He shook his head and glanced at the ground. His master sergeant, squatting beside him with an unlit cigar clenched in his teeth and a mug of black coffee in his hand, looked towards the desert, then spat some tobacco juice aggressively. Fred's men had surprised an Iraqi brigade three times their number and overcame all before them.

This scene was played out within yards of the body of a young Iraqi conscript of about eighteen years old, killed in the fighting. Some Marines stopped to look at the dead boy. He had a peaceful look on his face as if sleeping, but the ragged holes in his chest swarming with flies that crawled into his mouth and nostrils told a different story. I asked my RSM to have the boy buried. This particular lad's war was over, and we sought to identify him so that his mum and dad could know he had died heroically defending his country. The reality of war is much less glorious and very grubby.

Fred wanted to wait until all my units had completed their handover before the formal change of command and so in the meantime I set off to drive the length of my area of responsibility. The numbers of Iraqis around the oilfields astounded me. We had been told to expect a battalion across the whole area. It was clear from what Fred had said and what I could see that at least a brigade had been dug in here. The evidence was also clear that they had not wanted to fight. The barrels of the 122mm D-30 field guns were pointing north and the shells neatly stacked away from the guns. These were now being looted by the Bedouin and as I walked over to shoo them off and inspect the guns I looked around to see Stan Coeur and Sergeant Aryolla from the ANGLICOs following me closely.

'You don't know what to expect,' Stan explained, 'and we're not goin' to lose our boss on day one.'

All around the area civilians were looting weapons from the piles of abandoned equipment and dead bodies scattered on the battlefield. At the Gurkha company location there was a group of 150 prisoners in a pitiful state. As we discussed their plight, a bus drove towards us with Iraqi Army markings but driven by a Bedouin. It was stopped and commandeered in order to take the prisoners to the central POW cage that had been created back at the oil-processing plant where we'd rendezvoused with Fred, which had now been given the name 'Oxford'. I gave the driver $10 for his trouble and made an enthusiastic Iraqi major the 'bus monitor'. As the bus drove off, a lieutenant from a signals detachment that had also stopped asked, 'Won't they just escape?'

'I told them that there was food and clean water there and that they would get a blanket each – they'll go all right,' I replied as I watched the dust trail head off towards Oxford.

There was in fact a shortage of food and water in the early stages because supplies had not crossed the border and were behind the fighting echelon, and therefore many hours – or even days – behind. The RSM was looking after the prisoners and was arranging supplies where he could get them. We still had a war to fight and I had given strict instructions that they were not to be issued my soldiers' rations. The men guarding the POWs had discovered a store of dates and, with some clean water they had boiled up, brought these to the prisoners, who told us they had not eaten for days. I arrived back at Oxford just as the feeding process was beginning, with some men covering the prisoners as three men tried to give each prisoner a cup of water and a handful of dates under the watchful eye of the RSM. As they started to distribute the food, what had begun as a ragged queue degenerated into an outbreak of frenzied and vicious fighting as the Iraqi POWs fought to grab a handful of food or scoop a cupful of water from the water container, which was duly spilled in the struggle. As the clean water soaked into the dust, the struggling men pushed and fought to scoop a little off the ground and retreat to a corner to eat or drink their prize. In the end shots had to be fired in the air to restore some semblance of order and stop the fighting. The prisoners drew back into the shed we had put them in like sullen beasts to hunker down in the corner, some licking their wounds and some rocking to and fro, watching the guards with the intensity of hungry animals. The dust settled over the scene, littered with a ragged combat shirt, ripped off someone's back, an abandoned shoe and the spilled water butt.

As the men of the 1st of the 5th US Marines RCT prepared to move off to concentrate on their next attack, Fred and I posed for the embedded journalists with a handshake to signify the handover. Then he climbed into the massive Amtrack, the automatic door closing like a spaceship before it rumbled off into the desert.

I set off to speak to the most senior Iraqi officers I could find. The officers had been separated from the men and were held in the chemistry laboratory within the oil-processing plant. I went across to it with a translator, Phil Ballard, a captain in the REME who was half Egyptian. He was without doubt the best interpreter in the brigade. An engineering graduate, Phil was in his late twenties, with the unmistakable olive complexion and dark brown eyes of an Arab. He spoke Arabic with his mother's Egyptian accent and could read it at a glance. He was also a tough and pragmatic officer with a great deal of personal courage, but to me perhaps his most valuable asset was that he could think like an Arab. It was through Phil that I was to understand the Iraqis, their likes and dislikes, hopes and fears.

Inside the laboratory the layout and smells were instantly recognisable from school days. The room was filled with the acidic smell of the chemicals packed neatly into glass-fronted cupboards around the walls and there were solid benches in rows, with here and there Bunsen burners and test tubes. A large periodic table with a chart showing chemical formulae for oil products covered one wall. The big difference was the figures huddled on the floor in cheap blankets, their down-at-heel shoes set neatly beside them. One man stood and stared out of the window. I walked in past the sentry and announced, through Phil, that I wanted to speak to the most senior officers. The sleeping men stirred and sat up, glancing at each other and then me. Without speaking two men got up and pulled on their shoes.

The first, in the uniform of a lieutenant colonel, walked towards me, blanket under his arm. I said that he would not need it and then told him to leave it with the guard. Phil asked his name. I was introduced to Lieutenant Colonel Kasim. He was unshaven and smelled of sweat and sleep. A second man shuffled over, his hands buried deep in the pockets of a parka jacket and the hood up over his bowed head like a surly youth on a housing estate. I was surprised to learn that this was Lieutenant Colonel Rait, who had commanded a battalion. Kasim was the deputy commander of the 148th Brigade. They had been captured in the early stages of the fighting and were brought to us by men of my A Company, who had rooted them out of a bunker. Kasim was in his late thirties and was a stocky man with a black moustache and wavy hair that was long on top. He wore the red strip on his badges of rank that indicated that he was a graduate of their staff college and so would be well briefed on the plan. Rait was less impressive, but I decided to bring him along too for a chat. Older, with a paunch and thinning grey hair, he did not look like the picture of a Ba'athist loyalist.

We walked out of the lab and then off across the courtyard towards my makeshift HQ, which was in reality a cluster of vehicles. As we passed the grave of the youth, Kasim glanced down. I paused and raised both hands as if in Arabic prayer and Kasim nodded to indicate he understood it was a grave. We went to my table set up at the back of the Comms

Camel and sat down. I invited Phil Ballard to sit on my right. Tea was brought and we gave them some MREs. I opened Colonel Rait's and showed him how the self-heating cooker worked. He watched, licking his lips as the packet bubbled and fizzed, warming the food in the foil container. I could see that there would be no business done until he had eaten. Colonel Kasim was much more measured, sitting back and waiting patiently, then casually enquiring if I was going to eat before launching himself at his rations.

Over their meal they described their experiences over the last twenty-four hours. Little by little they relaxed and before long they were smiling and chatting freely. It seems that they had received the Information Operations campaign literature that had been sent over in leaflet raids and broadcast on radio, and understood the messages, but were uncertain how to act on them. The Iraqi Special Security Organisation (SSO) had been around so they had all been wary but the SSO had cleared off shortly before the invasion. Once the attack started they said most troops in their brigade just took cover and waited to be captured. I enquired as to where the brigade commander was. Kasim said nothing but scowled and waved his hand as if to say 'off' in a dismissive manner. I then steered the conversation around to my main areas of interest. Were there any booby traps in the area?

Were there any wounded still lying out in the open?

Were there any groups still at large who might offer resistance?

Where were the minefields?

What was the plan for the GOSPs?

Who had started the fires on the oilfields and were there any SSO still around?

Kasim could not have been more helpful. Rait was of little help, as he was genuinely not in the picture, but he watched us intently, his eyes swivelling from face to face as he gobbled his rations, the packet held close to his mouth. Once I had established the answers to most questions, I asked if they would take me on a tour of the area. The one way I could be certain there was no danger of booby traps was to go and see – but with these two as mine detectors. They readily agreed.

As we walked around I noted the layout of the brigade position and the camouflage techniques they had used. The positions were carefully sited and concealed and we would not have found some of them unless they had opened fire. Most had chosen not to. Here and there was evidence of fighting, a blasted trench, an abandoned vehicle riddled with gunshots or a pile of bloodied bandages, but these were exceptions. I was surprised by the quantity of the ammunition that had been abandoned. There can be no doubt that had these men chosen to fight it could have been quite a job to shift them. Once or twice we happened on 14.5mm anti-aircraft guns with belts of ammunition loaded ready to fire. I made a mental note to have these destroyed, as the last thing I wanted was for them to be used against us.

The main command bunker was quite large, ten metres square and about two metres deep, with a cooking area at one end. They had clearly been there for a while. Reed mats covered the floor and in one place they had created two or three small rooms with iron bedsteads and small bedside lockers. On the walls were calendars and tattered orders in neat handwritten Arabic. Filthy cooking pots and spoiling food suggested that when the final attack had come they were cooking some of their meagre rations. Above all, the thing that struck me about these positions was the smell. There is a particular smell in Iraq and it was very pronounced around the prisoners and their trenches. It is a mixture of sweat and diesel with an intangible spicy ingredient. It was so distinctive that on two occasions, when it was suspected someone was hiding in a building, I was able to walk in and sniff and be in no doubt they were there by the smell alone. But that was at the start. By the time I left Iraq I fancy that I smelled that way too.

As they led me on a tour of the area in order to satisfy my curiosity about their set-up, I noted that they both picked up items that would be useful in captivity, such as another blanket, a pot or some abandoned cigarettes. They clearly expected to be prisoners for some time. I asked them about all the money that was lying around and they explained that they had been paid just before the attack. Fearing that it was useless, they had thrown it away in their desire to be taken as a 'clean prisoner' with no incriminating evidence on them. 'Why would money be considered incriminating?' I asked. They looked at each other. Neither spoke.

Content that I had extracted as much as I could from these two, I led them back to the lab. As we returned, our escorts carried some Iraqi flags that we had picked up. It was a strange sight as this rather odd colour party made its way past the POW cage. The prisoners stared in silence, now totally confused. When I bade them farewell back in the laboratory, another officer, a captain, came over and introduced himself. He had been trained, he explained, at the Royal Military Academy, Sandhurst, and was well versed in British ways. He explained that his platoon commander had been James Cameron of the Princess of Wales' Regiment – who I actually knew well – and he enquired after a couple of his old mates from the platoon in Alamein Company. 'They're probably in the invasion force,' I pointed out. He smiled. We chatted for a while and as we parted he said he was really glad to be out of the war and in British hands.

As I left there were more questions than answers in my head. I resolved that what I needed was an adviser, someone who could interpret what I was seeing and hearing. He was not far away, as it turned out. On my way to Brigade HQ, I saw Sergeant Major Murphy with a large crowd of prisoners. They were in a sorry state, squatting on the ground and looking dejected. Two white doves were fluttering nearby and the prisoners were trying to tempt them over with bits of grass and twigs. I realised they wanted to eat them.

'Best get these boyos back to the cage,' I said to Murphy. 'The QM is trying to get some food through for them.'

Just then I spotted one old boy with the rank slides of a lieutenant colonel. I asked Sergeant Major Murphy about him. He explained that he spoke English and had been most helpful during the day. It turned out that this was Colonel Atiff, who had been put in charge of the Iraqis' oil-protection group. Atiff looked around fifty, careworn and stooped. He later explained that he had received a back wound in the First Gulf War while serving in the Navy but had been recalled for service recently. Although he looked grey and unassuming, I thought he would be able to answer a number of questions for me. But I was late for Brigade and set off with Colonel Atiff in the back of the Comms Camel.

At Brigade HQ I briefed the Brigade Commander and handed him one of the Iraqi flags we had found as a souvenir. I was able to report that we had met very little resistance but that I was concerned about all the ammunition that was lying around on the battlefield. The Marines had reported being shot at and the last thing I wanted was to take a casualty when it could be avoided. The official line, he explained, was that where possible ammunition and weapons would be held back for the new Iraqi Army.

We returned to my makeshift camp and I treated Colonel Atiff to an MRE. As we ate he was not very forthcoming about his specific roles. Fair enough. He was most illuminating on some other issues, however. In particular, he told me that if I wanted to understand the things I saw, I should try to think like a Ba'athist. The starting point, he explained, was that the system in Iraq had ultimately been about a single man, a psychotic sociopath, Saddam Hussein. Everyone was a threat to him, so he had to be a bigger threat to everyone else in order to survive. It was that simple. The trick was to make everyone think that the whole system was watching them and the best way to avoid suspicion was to report – enthusiastically – on whatever you saw. In doing so, everyone was in fact watching everyone else. He was the common denominator and the only certainty. Those who were laggard about submitting reports might be invited along to the Ba'athist HQ to explain themselves. He painted a picture of a country run by a system that was completely auditable, top to bottom, at a moment's notice. By running groups against each other there would be resentment and the only source of continuity or focus of loyalty could be the leader, Saddam. Zeal in filing reports was encouraged so that top officials acting on Saddam's behalf could show mercy or act harshly. Where a wrong was done, they could point the blame at the originator of the report and not the leader himself. After all, the leader was all merciful.

'So where does this information go?' I asked.

'To the local Ba'ath party HQs, of course. Get them intact,' he stressed, 'as it is all in there. Nothing did happen, can happen or will happen unless it is recorded there.'

'Where,' I enquired, 'is the nearest of these Aladdin's caves?'

He indicated Az Zubayr and Al Rumaylah on the map I had placed beside my vehicle. 'Here, Tim,' he said. 'Get these and you will know all.'

I walked over to the officers' prison with Colonel Atiff. As we left he thanked me. 'It's only normal courtesy,' I explained.

'No, you, the allies, the Americans, the British, thank you for coming here. I hope the nightmare is now over. I am tired. We need peace. Too much fighting. Now you bring us peace,' he said before walking into the laboratory, the guard stepping to one side as he passed.

I slept under the stars that night. The morning brought a scene from a science fiction movie. There were oil-well fires burning all around. The RSM had organised a party to go and bury the numerous dead that littered the area. I was concerned about disease and, having lived in Sarajevo during the siege there in late 1994, I recalled the well-fed dogs that stalked the streets and I had no intention of allowing them to get fat on the corpses of men who had only been defending their country.

At one location, where the Iraqis had opened up on the US Marines lieutenant whose death Colonel Fred had described, the men responsible still lay where the lieutenant's comrades had cornered them as they tried to escape. The Iraqis had been in an open-backed Russian-made Gaz jeep, mounting a 12.7mm heavy machine gun and had foolishly tried to shoot it out. They now lay literally shot to pieces and scattered across the ground. Sergeant Major Millar from C Company had buried the men with the assistance of some of his lads – placing a fair share of arms and legs into each grave. I arrived just as they finished.

'You've missed the fingers,' I said, pointing to some severed human fingers in the back of the truck. 'This bloke needs a manicure,' I noted, picking one up.

'Share 'em out among the graves, sir,' he replied.

This may seem ghoulish, but it is just how we dealt with the horror. Take it too seriously – or yourself for that matter – and you're on the slippery slope to depression. Two of our men, burying an Iraqi, generated one such moment. He had been searched after he had been shot and his belongings were scattered around him. One of my men stood guard with his rifle as the other stuffed the belongings into the dead man's pockets, finally putting a packet of cigarettes into his top pocket and patting them down in preparation to put the body in the grave.

'What's ya doin' that for?' the gruff Belfast cover man said.

'Ah well,' the cheery little ranger replied, 'he might want a smoke in the hereafter. He's had a bit of a day after all.'

'Don't be so fucken daft,' the Belfast man said. 'Sure, everybody knows that it's all non-smokin' up there now.'

The dead boy from the day before had made an attempt at resurrection, and was found half out of his grave. The Iraqi prisoners we had set to burying him, no doubt debilitated by low morale and exhaustion, had done a poor job, digging a grave less than a foot deep. The dogs had dug him up and begun to eat him. Rigor mortis had caused him to bend into a sitting position. A party of Paddies made him a proper grave and he was laid to rest once more.

By daybreak on 23 March, 3rd US Division was deep inside Iraq and now only 150 miles from Baghdad after one of the fastest advances in history. The oil terminals at Umm Qasr and Al Faw were secure and we had control of the southern oilfields. The US Marines closed in on the town of An Nasiriyah. As they approached the town they were met by the first well-organised resistance from the Fedayeen[51], who halted the US advance and began what was to become one of the sharpest actions of the war. To the south the UK 7th Brigade poised outside the towns of Az Zubayr.

Prisoners were to be brought in from 3 Para, who held the area to our north, so as to consolidate the captured enemy for transfer to a centralised prisoner cage. 1 R Irish had around 1,200 POWs by this time. Jackie had worked another miracle and food finally arrived for the POWs. The atmosphere was now a lot lighter, with the prisoners contentedly eating special rations that they would instantly recognise as both wholesome and halal[52]. From the road I watched them being issued their rations and water and then walked back to my HQ. It was a bright warm day and the wind was slight, allowing the billowing smoke from the oil-well fires to rise into the sky.

I was outside the buildings, alone, speaking to Brigade HQ on my secure radio in my vehicle about ammunition, when I noticed a large group of up to 100 men coming towards me in an excited state. Some had ration boxes, the same ones Jackie had recently delivered for the Iraqi prisoners. I immediately assumed they had looted these from the stocks at the roadside. Telling the watchkeeper at Brigade I would call back, I walked into the road and waved at them to stop. The men pressed around me and I told them in pidgin Arabic that the *acle* and *moy*[53] was for the POWs – '*Jash Iraqis*', not civilians – '*Lah Bedouin*'. They protested that they were not POWs. I agreed, but told them to clear off.

---

[51] Iraq had been beset in the early 1980s with an upsurge of abandoned children whose parents had perished in the Iran war. In a stroke of genius, Saddam had them all gathered in special schools and brought up as his own. The numbers were swollen by the fruit of the systematic rape of female prisoners. Many of them believed they actually were his children. In a manner of speaking they were. It was an idea copied from the Ottomans. They ate and drank Saddamism, and at twelve became trained killers – Saddam Martyrs or 'Fedayeen' – swearing on their lives to defend him. In actual fact they had no conscious loyalty to anything other than him in their lives. In the prelude to this new war he sought both to expand his pool of fanatical killers and preserve the Fedayeen. He cleared out the jails on the understanding that the released prisoners 'owed him one'. The deal was, one hit against the allies and your debt was paid (fail to act and the real Fedayeen would not rest until they had got you for welshing on the deal). The nastiest of the ex-prisoners were easy to spot: they wore blue tattoos, mainly on their hands and neck. The hand-reared Fedayeen would be the nucleus of any resistance to any invasion of Iraq. Knowing no other way, they would fight to the death by any means they could.

[52] The prisoners would have eaten anything, but the rations they had been given conformed to strict Muslim dietary rules.

[53] Food and water.

(I decided to let them have the food as they were probably pretty hungry too.) They thanked me and as one of them did so, he raised his hand. I could see a POW number on his palm. I then realised that they all had numbers on their clothes too and that I was surrounded by more than a hundred escaped POWs.

Struggling out of the group, I dashed over to my vehicle to get a gun. All my gear and weapons were inside the building and the only thing in the vehicle was an AK-47[54] that I had picked up off the road earlier and tossed into the footwell of my vehicle. The men realised I was planning to recapture them and started to run off. I fired a shot in the air and they stopped. I called for help and then motioned for them to lie down. Most complied, but some hesitated, obviously contemplating an escape into the desert. I motioned again with my captured rifle. As they lay down it occurred to me that the rifle might have very few bullets in it. It had certainly had one. I would have to bluff it out. As Corporal Stevo Stevenson arrived, stripped to the waist and also without a rifle, I ordered him to get help. As more of my men arrived, I sent a runner to find out how the prisoners had escaped and began making arrangements for them to be gathered in and searched. I was now standing in the middle of the prostrate men. I could literally smell fear from them as they lay all around me, glancing up and pleading in Arabic.

As my signallers and teams from the US Marines rushed to my aid, one man kept grabbing at my leg and babbling in Arabic. I told him to keep his head down. Pushing his head with my hand, I turned around to see a convoy of vehicles approaching. I waved at them to stop. As I did so the man on the ground grabbed the barrel of my AK-47 and my leg – but in a plaintiff manner. I shook him free and pushed his head down once more. I glanced up to see that the convoy approaching consisted of passenger coaches escorted by Land-Rovers. It was clearly a POW sweep-up. Indicating to Sergeant Aryolla and his men to cover the prisoners, I ran over and, standing in the centre of the road, flagged down the convoy. At the front a warrant officer from the Duke of Wellington's Regiment slid open the window of his Land-Rover.

'I've got about a hundred prisoners here who have tried to make a break for it,' I told him. 'Where do you want them?'

He looked at the prostrate men. 'Are they processed?' he asked.

'Some. Most have numbers, but I'm not sure if they have –'

---

[54] An assault rifle of Russian origin. This one had a folding stock and a fifty-round magazine.

'I assume you are an officer, sir,' the warrant officer said. 'I'll be honest, I don't want 'em and I've nowhere to put 'em. Why don't you just fuck 'em off into the desert.' He then added, 'I'm not being funny here, but that's our brief. Any loose hands, let 'em go.'

I shrugged my shoulders. 'OK.' I turned to the signallers and US Marines and shouted, 'Turn 'em loose.'

'Roger that,' Sergeant Aryolla said, shrugging his burly shoulders. Then he turned to the men and shouted, 'You heard the Colonel, send 'em on their way.'

'Oh,' I called after them, 'and let them keep the rations.'

The men started to get nervously to their feet as the convoy of buses set off once more in a cloud of dust. Slinging my AK, I dusted my hands together in theatrical style towards the prisoners, now free men, then shouted, *'Khalas! Yalluh!'*[55] and started waving my arms towards the desert. Grabbing their boxes, some bowing towards me, the men ran off towards some buildings in the distance. I could see that a lot of them were tall and muscular. These men were not Bedouin. I guessed they were conscripts and if our brief on the 51st Division was correct they came from central Iraq. They had quite a walk to get home – most would circle round and head for Az Zubayr, about two hours' walk to the east – but they were at least free and the walk home was their problem.

A call from Brigade earlier that morning had warned that there was to be a journalists' visit. At around 1000 hours, I was squatting in an Iraqi mortar pit behind my HQ at Oxford, answering a call of nature, when the helicopter flew directly overhead. Enjoy the view, I thought to myself.

I had returned to my temporary HQ and was making tea when I saw a bearded figure walking off towards the POW cage at 'Oxford', having separated himself from the main group of journalists who were shambling up the road. I was concerned about journalists photographing the POWs, which according to the Geneva Convention demeans them and is forbidden. This chap certainly had a camera, but he was actually chatting to the prisoners and for the first time I could see them smiling and laughing. As I walked towards him I could see from the way his shemagh was wound around his head that he had been in the Oman and, putting this together with his familiarity with the Arabs, I guessed he was ex-SAS. I was right. I saw to my delight that it was none other than my old squadron commander from B Squadron 22 SAS, fellow Ulsterman

---

[55] Finished. Get going.

and good friend Alex Gardiner. We enquired after each other and it transpired that he now worked for Abu Dhabi TV.

Alex had been talking to the prisoners in Arabic and had established that many of them were actually Bedouin and farmers. I asked Alex to translate for me and he was able to ascertain that the men had got caught up as the British forces advanced. Through Alex, they appealed for me to show them some sheikhly lenience. I lectured the men about the dangers of the battlefield and especially picking up weapons, which I knew the farmers would heed and the Bedouin would ignore (they define themselves as armed men), pointing to the grave of the Iraqi conscript but telling them it was a Bedouin boy who had made the mistake of having been seen with a gun. They gasped and began to chatter. I then told them to go in peace. Alex translated and instant jubilation broke out, with handshaking and gratitude, before they set off north, following the trail of the group I had released earlier.

We walked down towards the prisoner compound at the main installation at Oxford and went inside. There were long lines of prisoners queuing to get their food boxes, small cardboard cartons with script in English and Arabic. These new arrivals were in coarse, threadbare uniforms and many had bare feet. Hardly the proud Babylonian Army that Saddam had boasted of. It was bizarre but cheering to see the disbelief on the traumatised Iraqis as each shambled forward to receive his food package to the accompaniment of Irish banter, which they could not understand, but which by the smiles and kind gestures of the soldiers they knew to be friendly.

I asked Alex to help with some more translation and we walked among the Iraqi prisoners, chatting and assuring them they would soon be fed and given water. The men touched their chests in thanks. I walked behind him and the men glanced furtively at me, being careful not to catch my eye. Some recognised my badges of rank and drew themselves stiffly to attention as I passed – the Iraqi Army was founded by the British and their rank system and badges of rank are the same. Alex explained I was the British commander and that they were in safe hands. The men listened and glanced at me nervously as they did so.

'They don't look too happy, do they?' I said to Alex.

'In their army when a colonel stops to talk to you it's usually big trouble,' he explained.

Alex then asked if any of the men were wounded and immediately a man was brought forward, supported by two comrades. He was grey with shock and pain and one of his mates pointed to blood seeping from the man's ripped combat trousers. I called for the medical officer, who came across with one of her medics. I took the man's shoulders as we lowered him onto a stretcher and asked Alex to assure the man he would receive good treatment. The other prisoners now crowded round, helping the man and grinning in thanks to me, their dusty faces and stained teeth breaking into smiles for the first time. I could see that this most natural of responses had touched off a sense of relief among the captured men and they knew it was going to be OK.

'What chance is there of joining you as an embedded journalist?' Alex asked as we walked off towards the other journalists, who were preparing to leave.

'Every chance. You know where to find us,' I said as his rather stressed-looking visit coordinator waved him back to the group waiting to head off to Kuwait.

My biggest concern at this stage was the quantity of weapons and ammunition lying on the battlefield. With large groups of displaced men wandering around it could have posed a real threat, but there was so much else to do and by now all of my forces were deployed. I had a mind to destroy it, but Brigade was clear that it should be kept for the new Iraqi Army. We struck a bargain. The stuff we could recover and secure we would keep, which was very little indeed. The rest would be destroyed.

I returned to the POW compound to find the RSM, who revealed some confusion over the prisoners. He said that he had released the men I had encountered earlier as there was doubt that they were soldiers at all. Once they were disarmed, they had sat patiently waiting to be processed all night. He had decided that they posed no threat and as there was nowhere to put them he had let them go. He then pointed out that a large number of those in the actual cage, taking up space and rations, were probably farmers. I related the tale of the group I had met outside the gate with Alex.

'Aye sir.' He nodded. 'And there's plenty more too.' He pointed to some old men squatting nearby with an odd-looking youth sitting with them. 'We've got half a care home here and a backward sixteen-year-old who the doctor has segregated as a minor too.' He shook his head. I felt my hackles rise at the thought that some units to the north (not in 1 R Irish) were arresting everyone in sight, regardless of age or appearance.

I had all the old and young and the obvious farmers gathered together. I included anyone with an oil company uniform on too. I told them to raise their hands and then separated out the very young (sixteen and under) and old (over fifty). Then I separated out all those with oil company ID cards, and all the farmers by judging their hands. There were about twenty prisoners set for release when a burly man – marked 'Number 19' – stood up and asked to approach me. Off to one side and speaking through an interpreter, he explained in hushed tones that two of the men who claimed to be oil workers were in fact soldiers. 'Look in the wallets,' he said. We pulled the men out and sure enough in their wallets were military ID tags. They went straight back into the POW cage. The rest were placed on a bus for release with more handshaking and thanks.

I walked back to my temporary HQ for a conference with my key planners and the Royal Engineers. As I walked up the dusty road, buses with prisoners passed, while released farmers and marauding Bedouin filed up and down the road. It was a scene that was to become the norm. Heavily outnumbered by the population, we just had to exist among them. With my rifle companies deployed forward, we had no choice. Modern wars are not what you see in the cinemas. With rapid advances and blurred front lines, it is often hard to tell who is friend and who is potential enemy. The one sure way I discovered was to look them in the eye. Most looked away and rushed off. Some stood and with a guilty gesture would raise their hands to show they were unarmed. I would motion them to go and they would take off out of sight.

I arrived at my HQ in the single-storey oil workers' office and our meeting began immediately. I had given the engineers the task of destroying the weapons and ammunition that was lying about. The quantity was immense and ranged from loose ammunition to wire-guided missiles, some with Milan mark III firing posts, more modern than our own mark IIs and clearly recently imported from France, where they are made. They explained that it was a mammoth task and they could not hope to achieve it in under a week. My engineer squadron commander then pointed out that there were massive pits that the Iraqis had dug then filled with crude oil. They had set fire to these to try to blind allied aircraft and armour as it attacked. Why not throw the weapons into the pits? The heat and the sludge would render them unusable. It was an excellent idea and before long thousands of weapons were being decommissioned in this way.

I drove up to the north of our area and along the way passed a number of vehicles that had been abandoned by the US forces on their advance, including an M1 Abrams tank. As we drove along the Bedouin circled the vehicles like vultures. One massive fuel tanker had obviously had a gearbox problem and could not be moved, but I did find a Humvee that had had its tyre damaged by a mine. We drove this back to our base and our ANGLICOs were able to report it up their chain for repair. It had the markings of Fred Padilla's 1/5. I said to Stan that if we got it repaired he could have it for his fleet.

The Bedouin were snaffling up anything left unattended. At one point I washed the thick arctic socks I had been wearing since we left Fort Blair Mayne. I hung them on the fence of the oil office compound to dry, only to discover an hour later that they had been stolen. Somewhere a Bedouin is sporting a pair of well-used socks more suitable for wear in boots in the cold northern climes. Good luck to him, because they really stank.

# —9—

# AL RUMAYLAH

On Monday 24 March, 1 R Irish were warned to be prepared to move to take over the area as far as the Hammar Bridge. This was across the 'Loyalty to the Leader Canal' (constructed as part of the project to drain the southern marshes) and the boundary between allied territory and territory controlled by the Iraqi Army, in this case the 6th Division. This tactical area of responsibility now stretched from the Kuwait border to the canal in the north, 90km in total, and comprised a corridor 20km across, embracing all the oil installations, including the village of Al Rumaylah. I now had to consider my options for the series of new tasks with which I was presented.

I visited 3 Para, who were in the area just south of the Hammar Bridge and some 20km north of Oxford at the time and who had my C Company under command. That battalion was being put into reserve for other tasks. 3 Para HQ was settled in a hide just outside the oil pumping town of Al Rumaylah, with C Company 1 R Irish in control of the actual town. I sought out the CO of 3 Para, John Lorimer, and we had a swift conference and studied the map of the area. He took off his glasses to get a better look. We agreed that there was a lot to be done and time was short. It was a huge task. This was now nothing less than a race against time to secure the wealth that would create a future Iraq before they could be attacked by insurgents. I returned to Oxford to give orders that evening.

The following day I boarded a Gazelle to fly north to Al Rumaylah for a ground brief from the commander of my C Company in the town. The POW cage was just beside the helicopter pad and as we strapped ourselves in I could see more prisoners arriving, an army of tired and hungry men, devoid of any military bearing and as compliant as sheep taken to market. Tattered remnants of military uniform hung off most of them, except those who had tried to slip through allied lines disguised as Bedouin. They sat, cowed, waiting for who knew what. Some looked up as we took off, but most just stared ahead, barely bothering to shield their faces from the dust whipped up by the rotor blades.

We flew for about fifteen minutes across the abandoned battlefield. The lads I had seen at the broken-down American battle tank had also cleared off, leaving it stranded like a beached whale. I could see Bedouin still looting anything they could find, mostly wood and scrap metal but sometimes live shells, around the gun battery we had chased them from on the first day. Its barrels were still pointing north, in compliance with allied instructions for surrender.

This stretch of desert was as flat as a billiard table, with six or eight installations rearing out of the sand at about one-kilometre intervals, linked by a pattern of pipes and access roads, shrouded by the acrid smoke of the still-burning oil fires. In the midst of it all, an Iraqi battalion had dug in before fleeing the allied advance, leaving a trail of discarded blankets, ammunition boxes, mortars and assorted weapons.

I told the pilots to circle when we reached the outskirts of what looked like a small town. A series of refineries and a storage facility radiated out from a two-kilometre-square grid of streets lined with trees and the latest and shiniest Land Cruisers, and a rather less prosperous village with a sprinkling of matchstick men, children and dogs.

The oil compound was a massive affair that housed the vehicles, offices, workshops, replacement pipes, drill bits and all the other paraphernalia of the oil business. While the town itself seemed virtually deserted, you couldn't move here for looters. They ebbed and flowed like the tide in the grey light that followed the storm, carrying off whatever they could: tools, barrels and even sinks from the toilets. The place looked as though it was being stripped by locusts[56].

---

[56] I remember being confronted by a similar vision of hell when I served in Africa. There, the walls and floors alone remained of the looted buildings. Furniture, wall coverings, door frames and even light sockets had been ripped out, often only to be discarded a few feet away. One group of scavengers had formed a human chain to pull a still live generator out of the ground. They sat where they had died, in a bizarre, fly-covered tableau, each man still clasping the one in front, a dazed expression on their fast bloating faces. In a room nearby lay another sixteen who had attempted to prise a high-pressure pipe carrying toxic gas off the wall with an axe. Others still lay against a wall, crushed by the frenzied greed of those behind them.

I spoke into my mike over the noise of the aircraft. 'This –' I motioned to George, my AGC[57] Detachment Commander, with my finger – 'is what we have got to stop. I need you to persuade them it's better to work than loot.'

George nodded. 'Understood, boss.'

I was met by Nada, a civil liaison officer from Brigade, who emerged from the mêlée as we landed. C Company was barely holding the ring of yelling Arabs, some fighting to hang on to their loot and others looking on in dismay. Nada led me to the imposing entrance of the Southern Oil Company facility and introduced me to a group of oil workers.

Through Nada, the locals explained that they and their families had been drawn from across Iraq, not only because of their skills but because the old regime liked to divide and rule. They explained that they were now virtually under siege by rail workers (who had been brought to the village some years before and then abandoned as sanctions bit more deeply and the regime could no longer afford – or rather be bothered – to pay them), as well as groups of marauding Bedouin and gangs of prisoners released from the civil jails by Saddam the previous November. These people had armed themselves from the battlefield and were intent on attacking them.

'Why should they do this?' I asked.

The self-appointed leader of this small group, a man in his fifties with a dirty blue dishdash and rotten teeth, spoke up in broken English. '*Sidi*,' he said, 'it is because they want what we have, though that is very little.' He turned and translated this for the benefit of his companions, who eagerly agreed, pressing around me, shouting complaints in Arabic and gesticulating towards the rail workers' dwellings in the scruffy village I had seen from the air.

'Whoa,' I said. 'One at a time.'

'They sense you are in charge, and can't wait to debrief you!' Nada smiled, waving his right hand, fingers pursed, at the group in the Arab gesture for patience.

I extracted myself and smiled at the exasperated George. As I did so I saw the commander of C Company approach, wearing his habitual grin. 'How's it going, Colin?' I shouted over the din.

'Powerful,' he said. 'Sure, it's been like this all night. We had to shoot the tyres out of that forklift when they tried to ram the gate.'

---

[57] Adjutant General's Corps.

'How's it going, lads?' I asked the men standing beside the abandoned vehicle.

'Serious, so it is,' said one lanky youngster in a Belfast accent. 'They're focken mental here, no mistake.'

'Aye,' a tough-looking little Scouser added. 'It's like the 'Pool on speed.'

'Can't we turn that thing off?' The forklift's engine was still running, and making quite a racket.

'We've tried,' Colin said, 'but they've hot-wired it. We were just going to let it run out of gas.'

'What about this lot?' I indicated the group of Arabs behind me. 'Nada, ask them if there's anyone who could turn this thing off.'

A large man began to jostle his way through from the back of the group. 'This chap is the transport coordinator, apparently,' Nada said. 'He got lifted by the first unit through and he's saying something about you being his mate.'

I pushed forward to get a closer look at this long-lost friend of mine and sure enough there was Number 19, one of the men I had released from the POW cage near Oxford and who had warned me about the soldiers who had been hiding among them. He still had his prisoner number on his dishdash. He beamed at me and held up his callused paw with the figure 19 marked on it and wobbled his head like a snake charmer.

After an exchange of salaams I pointed at the truck. 'Nada,' I said, 'ask yer man here if he can stop that racket.'

Number 19 nodded enthusiastically and puffed out his chest then, accompanied by a small group of admirers, walked over to the forklift with Colin and clambered on. I followed with a couple of the rangers and our own retinue of small children and onlookers. As Number 19 got to work on the wiring, I realised how new the vehicle was. He pulled and twisted, and I chatted to the lads. Beyond them, I could see a couple of characters watching us from the far end of the compound. I climbed onto the forklift as its engine sputtered and died.

Number 19 looked up and smiled. '*Khalas*[58],' he said, spreading his hands and then wiping them on a rag.

'*Mumtaz*[59],' I replied.

At that instant two shots flew past my head with the vicious crack of high-velocity rounds. I ducked and slid off the side of the forklift.

---

[58] Finished!
[59] Wonderful!

Number 19 was well ahead of me and, as if by magic, my retinue had melted away. There was another series of shots, both single and automatic fire, some chopping past us, others kicking up spouts of dust on the road and whining into the air. The people up at the gate dived for cover.

'Well, you couldn't fault their reaction to enemy fire, and dat's a fact,' said a Southern Irish Ranger beside me.

'Dey don't seem too keen on ye messin' wid der truck,' said another.

From behind the forklift I could see the gunmen standing in the open about 200m away and firing AK-47s from the shoulder.

'This, lads, is what we're paid for,' I said to the rangers nearby, with the full weight of a lifetime's experience. Colin called for back-up and issued a string of orders to the men around him. 'Now in situations like this,' I continued, 'you have two options.' The rangers were scanning the enemy with their sights but glanced nervously at me as I spoke. 'You can either do nothing, or you can take the problem head on.' There was another burst of gunfire. 'Now,' I said, 'if we do nothing, someone will be killed. It might be a villager, or it may be a looter. It could even be one of us. But if we go in hard and do what they least expect, then we stand a very good chance of disarming those bastards and doing some good.' I paused. 'What do you think?'

There was a moment's silence.

'Yer focken mad, sir,' the ranger nearest me said.

'Do you want us to go for it, boss?' Colin asked.

'It's the only way. Trust me.'

Colin rolled half over, raised his hand and shouted, 'ATMP!'[60]

An ATMP roared towards us and tipped forward as the driver stood on the brakes. In his helmet and goggles, rifle slung across his chest, he exuded determination. A number of the rangers leapt aboard, followed by Colin and me. He looked at me as if to say, Where do you think you're going?, then thought better of it and nodded to the driver.

We sped off down the main drag, racing through the gears. I took out my Browning and cocked it, my leg braced against the rollbar. One of the rangers fired a single shot. 'Aimed shots! Aimed shots!' Colin yelled.

The gunmen stared at us in amazement then turned and tore at each other in their haste to push back through the hole in the fence through which they had entered the compound. As the ATMP sped

---

[60] All terrain mobility platform – a six wheel, flat-bed buggy about 2.5m long with six bulging tyres.

towards the firing point, Colin called teams[61] into depth, left and right, on the radio.

Jumping off the ATMP and running towards the firing point, I stopped by the spent cases while Colin continued to direct proceedings. There was shouting as more of C Company arrived. I rounded the corner to find a bunch of looters trying to steal two Toyota Land Cruisers parked outside a small single-storey office building, so new their specification dockets were still stuck to the windows. As the thieves struggled to start the 4x4s, they were grabbed by the rangers and pushed to the ground. One plucky lad was still trying to hot-wire the lead vehicle when a burly corporal pulled him from the driver's seat. Those who had turned tail as we appeared were now hovering by a hole in the wall they had crashed through with a stolen JCB.

'They're wonderin' if we're gonna give up and let them have the loot,' one of the sergeants said.

Colin turned to me. 'What should we do?'

'Move 'em on – with gusto,' I replied.

As the men of C Company did just that, we checked the area. It had clearly been the vehicle compound – empty now except for the two Land Cruisers. As the men took up cover positions I walked over to the broken wall, just in time to see our friends with the AK-47s running up a railway embankment and jumping into a white Toyota pick-up with a horse motif in the rear window. One of my men adopted the kneeling firing position as the vehicle took off at high speed. 'D'ye want me to give 'em a couple?'

'Na,' I replied, 'I've no doubt we'll see them again. But you could put a couple over that lot there.' I indicated the crowd escaping in the direction of the Pikey[62] village – as we came to call the rail workers' shantytown – barrows laden with office desks and jumbles of cables and pipes.

He loosed off a couple of shots into the air, and most of the crowd dropped everything and ran. But some of their more determined companions carried right on. One punter had managed to manhandle a vast industrial air conditioner onto a cart.

'Wud ye look at de focken size of the fan on that thing!' said the corporal nearest me. 'If he gets that fitted to his wee shack and turns it on, he'll loop the focken loop.'

---

[61] Half sections (four men).
[62] Slang for Gypsy.

The crowd had swooped off to the right like a flock of birds, so we ran across to see what had attracted their attention. There was another large hole where a bus had been driven through a wall into the oil company storage yard and loaded with tools, desks, chairs and more air-conditioning units. It had burst a tyre in its attempt to make its way back over the rubble and some men were trying to replace it with a spare.

I had the rangers empty the bus of looters and disperse them across the waste ground. One turned to strike out at a soldier, only to receive a stiff boot in the arse for his trouble. As another of our boys reflected later, 'Caught him a cracker – he'll be farting outta his shoulder blades after that.'

The men working at the tyre carried on as if nothing was amiss. As I stood watching them they explained their problem by dusting their hands and pointing at the flat. I explained mine by indicating the Oil Company motif on the side of the bus and shaking my finger.

'Nam, Nam[63],' they chorused, impervious to the thrust of my argument. They had clearly decided that possession was nine tenths of the law.

I had my men try and push them away, but it was past 1700 hours and I could see the fatigue and strain on their faces as they jostled with the thieves. Suddenly I felt thirsty and desperately tired. I decided it was time for more drastic action. 'I've had enough,' I said. 'Keep them back. I'm going to fix their tyre for them.' Then I shouted, 'Stand clear!' and shot the spare tyre where it lay on the ground. I circled the bus and shot the other three good tyres and the punctured one again for luck.

One of the soldiers cleared his nose with his Paddy's hankie[64]. 'That one's goin' nowhere!' he said with some satisfaction as the crowd dispersed. The bus was now an immovable block in the wall.

Back at my HQ in Oxford, I estimated that we probably had until the next day to restore order or fail in our mission to protect what little oil-production infrastructure was left. We had struck so swiftly that the planned sabotage by Saddam's SSO had been botched; they had only managed to start some fires. However, things were falling apart before our very eyes, mainly because of the looting and associated damage; no one could have foreseen the level of wanton destruction and theft that threatened to achieve what the Ba'athists had failed to.

---

[63] Yes, yes!
[64] Hand.

I held a meeting of the company commanders, Operations Officer Graham Shannon (known as 'Shaggy'), Richard Woolwark, the Battery Commander (BC), and just about everyone else I could think of, including the young doctor. This was more of a brainstorm than a planning group and certainly not an orders session. As we talked I was constantly interrupted by calls from 16 Brigade, and I would have to walk out to the Comms Camel parked outside, where my secure radio was, to get details of the situation as it was developing elsewhere. Outside, I could see tracer in the sky towards Basra and hear the deep tones of artillery rumbling in the distance to the north. The air was filled with fine, cloying spray from a fractured oil pipe, probably caused by a stray round, leaving the constant smell and taste of crude in our clothes, food and tea.

I listened on the secure radio as the Brigade Commander outlined to the commanding officers on our conference call that the main preoccupations at Brigade that night were the attacks against coalition forces by Ba'athist loyalists and the recent capture of two British servicemen who'd got lost near the town of Az Zubayr. He warned us that we faced the threat of asymmetric warfare[65] and that there was real concern that the Republican Guard was weaving itself into the civilian infrastructure to avoid being targeted. We were further warned to maintain an aggressive posture.

He explained that 7 Brigade, to our eastern flank, had requested that a divisional rear security area be created so that they could build up forces for the push through Az Zubayr and on to Basra. This meant that the troops originally earmarked to take over our POWs were going elsewhere. I mused that this left 1 R Irish with around 1,500 hungry and thirsty prisoners, the southern oilfields to protect and a right ruckus in Al Rumaylah.

As the conference call ended and we signed off, I walked to the back of the Comms Camel where I met the RSM waiting to update me on the situation at the POW cage. As we spoke we stood outside the makeshift HQ building by the light of a fierce gas fire that burned some 200m away to our side. 'What's the form on the prisoners?' I asked.

'Not brilliant, to be honest,' he said. 'They're in a shit state and a lot of them are wounded. The doctor's team is doin' a great job but they're not happy.'

---

[65] Where a small, often covert force of terrorists takes on a conventional army – hampered by its size, conventions and public scrutiny.

'What sort of wounds?'

'Gunshot wounds mostly. One poor bloke had had his face shot out and was just sitting patiently, covered in flies, till we noticed him. Then we had one who'd been shot in the chest. He got spotted because he wasn't eating his grub and when we got him out he threw up over the doctor. Oh, and a lot of superficial wounds too.'

'What about food and water?'

'We're not bad now,' the RSM said, 'but it's like the zoo at feeding time.'

'Are you saying we've a security problem?' I asked.

'To be honest, these people are broken; we're the only people they trust. They'd kill each other over a fag. And that happened, you know,' he added. 'Aye, we tried to give 'em some smokes and it ended with us having to rip them apart. Never again . . .'

In the darkness outside my HQ I reflected on the information that had come down from Brigade. By the fourth day of the campaign, the US forces had isolated the town of An Nasiriyah, but a convoy of logistics vehicles from the 507th Maintenance Company had got lost and was ambushed in a hail of AK and rocket fire.

The commander of 1 Marine Expeditionary Force (1 MEF), Lieutenant General Conway, was ordered to seize the bridges over the Euphrates. There was heavy fighting in An Nasiriyah to our north-west. 3 Para were defending in the north, reinforced by L Company[66] of the R Irish and in contact with the enemy, with two companies cut to act as the divisional reserve. The main body of 1 (UK) Division put a block in south of Basra to our east. Two servicemen from 33 Engineer Regiment (EOD)[67] – Sapper Luke Allsop, from North London, and Staff Sergeant Simon Cullingworth, from Essex, were reported missing that evening after their convoy was attacked. Staff Sergeant Steven Roberts, from Bradford, a Challenger 2 crew member from the 2nd Royal Tank Regiment, died when he left his tank to reason with a mob blocking the advance of his troop in Az Zubayr. He could have crushed them, but believed it was his responsibility to save life, not take it.

As refugees fled from Basra and Az Zubayr, the heroes of the Fedayeen

---

[66] I had brigaded my heavy machine gun and Milan anti-tank weapon vehicles together with my snipers and recce to form a mobile company called L Company after the officer commanding them, Sean Lundy.

[67] Explosive Ordnance Disposal.

mortared and machine-gunned them. The UK's 3 Commando Brigade had finally defeated resistance in the port of Umm Qasr[68]. 7 Brigade was poised outside Basra and the Black Watch was getting ready to take on the fierce resistance in Az Zubayr.

There was still resistance in the town of Safwan on the Kuwaiti border to our rear. 16 Air Assault Brigade had 1 R Irish on the oilfields and 3 AAC covering the western desert. 1 Para were standing by for a possible airborne assault on Qalat Sikar airfield, ninety miles to the north behind enemy lines.

At this stage the main objective of the coalition was to protect the oil production infrastructure.

I returned to the conference, my eyes hurting as I walked into the light of the room lit by storm lamps. 'Well, where did we get to?' I asked.

The company commanders glanced at each other, then Marcus, the OC of the Gurkhas, spoke up. 'Basically, we need to isolate the Pikey village then do a house-to-house search for weapons and stolen goods.'

'Or give them the opportunity of an amnesty,' Andrew Cullen, the 2IC, added.

'Or both,' I said. 'Shaggy, what can we afford to take up there?'

'Depends on the situation elsewhere. We can't afford to leave the oil complexes unguarded . . .' The Operations Officer looked thoughtful. 'But we could release elements of D and some of B – at risk. A Company is off with the Air Corps battle group on the flank and I gather Sean Lundy is having a bit of a to-do up on the Hammar Bridge with L company and 3 Para versus the 6th Iraqi Division.'

'OK, we'll take up to two companies to the town, with a view to seizing control of the rail workers' village and conducting a search for arms. Kick-off tomorrow morning.' I outlined my plan, reassured that men as clever as these had reached the same conclusion. Frankly, things had happened so quickly, this was the best we could do. I recalled the Chindits' motto: 'The boldest measures are the safest.' In my book, that meant go at the problem and say sorry later. 'We need to get a recce in tonight. It will include the company commanders and the BC. Shaggy, you'd better come too. That leaves you, Andrew, in charge.'

I turned to Mike Murdock, OC B Company. 'Mike, can you bring

---

[68] The UK Secretary of State for Defence was to arrive shortly after this for a 'morale boosting' visit. At a press conference he announced, 'Umm Qasr is just like Southampton!' A Royal Marine disagreed. 'There's no prostitutes, no beer and they're shooting at us. It's more like Portsmouth!'

Sergeant Wilson from the ANGLICOs? Stan and Brian have a previous engagement with some gentlemen up on the Hammar – I think they've got a little something for them[69]. Once the recce is done we can have a brew then a *schnell* planning session, back-brief, then orders for the job. Time is short, so let's get cracking. Questions?'

They scribbled down the briefing and shook their heads.

'BC, time check, please.' I turned to Richard.

'It will be 2145 in two minutes,' he said, looking at his watch.

'We'll do a bit of map appreciation for our wee walk now,' I said to Shaggy.

'Roger,' he replied.

I looked for Magoo. 'Any tea, Magoo?'

He was squatting against the wall, cleaning his rifle. 'Coming up!' he said, leaping to his feet.

'Ten seconds,' the BC said.

'D'ya want something to eat, sir?' Sergeant Major Herbert asked.

'Please.'

'5, 4, 3, 2 . . . 2145 hours.' Richard stared at his watch, holding up his arm to catch the light from a Tilly lamp.

My plan was to rendezvous with two of my rifle companies, each some 120 strong, 60km up the road at Al Rumaylah, seal the town that night and conduct a recce with the company commanders and a cover party from what we were led to believe was the comparative safety of the oil workers' village. Armed with whatever we found, we would then perfect our plan and issue detailed orders.

We left Oxford at around 2200 hours, a convoy of blacked-out vehicles moving slowly up the narrow road that had been given the code name 'Route Dallas'. Visibility was not too bad, despite the distortion of the glare from the oil fires. As we drove I could follow the battle across the whole of southern Iraq on my Blue Force Tracker, seeing the friendly forces as icons on a map. I could also see the US forces pressing towards Baghdad. Every now and again an American unit would hammer past from the opposite direction, driving with night-vision equipment, so I turned down the backlight on my BFT display.

After about an hour we spotted a swinging red light at a road junction, which marked our rendezvous with C Company. A ranger walked

---

[69] In fact, the ANGLICOs directed a Cobra attack helicopter strike across the river that night in support of L Company 1 R Irish, destroying two enemy T55 tanks and some artillery.

forward and I leaned out of the window. He returned to his vehicle without speaking and we set off, following the glow of the vehicle's convoy light. After driving for about a kilometre, we parked up. As I stepped from the Land-Rover and allowed my eyes to adjust, I recognised men from C Company. Some were in their sleeping bags, resting, some made brews and smoked, an occasional stifled laugh breaking the silence, while others just stared at the 'Hexi TV[70]'.

A dull light led me to the C Company planning cell, where I met the other company commanders and those who would make up our patrol, including arguably our most valuable asset, Phil Ballard. I briefed them on what was to happen and the CSM organised us into four-men bricks.

I waved each vehicle in the convoy past before jumping into my Land-Rover. Herby set off, lights out, for the junction of the road into the oil workers' part of the village in Al Rumaylah, where we had a quick comms check and sorted ourselves into patrol order. As we headed for the centre of the town I ordered a multiple[71] to move to the streets either side of me. I aimed to travel the length of the oil workers' village and then swing right towards the Pikey village from the cover of the railway.

It was a beautiful starlit night with a full moon, so we took particular care to stay in the shadows. Much to my surprise, I was hardly into the oil workers' village when I spotted an armed man through my nightsight. He was dressed in paramilitary gear – a combat jacket and shemagh, with a chest rig containing magazines for the AK-47 with folding stock that he cradled in his arms – and he was not alone.

A cigarette glowed bright and then spun to the ground as I called for them to put down their weapons. The patrol fanned out to cover me. As we surrounded them, they dropped their weapons and competed with each other to see who could raise his arms highest above his head. One of the men started babbling what I recognised as the Arabic Lord's Prayer. With the help of Phil we gathered in the rest and realised we had captured around forty men.

I was immediately struck by the quantity and quality of their weapons. 'Where did you get these guns?' I asked the nearest prisoner, a man in his late forties, with a couple of days' stubble and a grey moustache. 'That Romanian AK[72] – that's not standard . . .'

---

[70] We cooked on hexamine solid fuel blocks and the men – if the situation permitted – would sometimes light one and just stare silently at the flame, no doubt thinking of home.

[71] Group of 16 men in patrol formation.

[72] The Romanian version of the AK is a better-tooled version and has a pistol grip on the front stock as well as the one with the trigger.

'I found it on the battlefield, *Aqeed*.' He drew nonchalantly on his cigarette, but I knew he was studying my face closely and watching my every move.

'You cleaned it up well,' I said, examining it more closely. I turned to the first man I had challenged. 'What's the form then; why are you out here?'

Phil translated.

'*Sidi*,' he began, 'the "Ali Babas" have warned us they will attack tonight. They have told us we will die this night. We must protect our families!'

'The British Army is in control here now. Nobody will be attacking anybody. I'll deal with the Ali Babas tomorrow. In the meantime you need to understand that I require you to cooperate with me. That means tomorrow I want you to come to the gates of the oil company at 0900 hours, so that my men can register the guns. I will agree a limited number of issues, after which anyone in possession of a weapon without a licence will be arrested – or shot.'

The men listened intently as Phil translated, with the exception of Mr Romanian AK. He lit himself another cigarette and examined me with quiet disdain. His expression reminded me of the sceptical observer at a kitchen gadget stand, watching the demonstrator and ignoring the demonstration. He was starting to irritate me, but instead of asking what his fucking problem was, I managed to continue my speech. 'Night is no cover,' I said, 'for you, or for them . . .' I motioned towards the Pikey village. I took the magazine off my SA 80 and cleared it, then handed it to the nearest of them. 'I can see you as if it is bright sunlight.' I pointed at the sight. 'All my men have these.'

They passed the rifle around, each taking it with exaggerated respect and squinting through the rubber eyepiece, letting out the occasional gasp or '*Wallah*[73],' then passing it on to the next man as if it were crystal.

Not taking his eyes off me for a second, Mr Romanian AK waved it away, indicating he wasn't interested or he'd seen it all before. I found myself avoiding his gaze, suddenly unsure about how best to respond. As the CO of a British battle group, my options were limited. The method recommended in training was to ignore him. My instinct was to stand on his fucking head. I went with the training.

The rifle was handed back. I reloaded and made it ready. 'So, tomorrow at the gates of the oil complex,' I said. 'And if there is shooting

---

[73] Oh God.

tonight, get into your houses, because my soldiers will kill anyone seen with a weapon.'

'OK, OK!' said one man ahead of the translation, indicating that at least someone understood English.

As I turned, the first man I had stopped placed his hand lightly on my sleeve and smiled gently. 'See you, *Sidi*,' he said.

Mr Romanian AK continued to watch me impassively as we moved off, his gun hanging at his side, smoke leaking out of his nostrils.

It was a quiet night, as it turned out. The rest of the troops had arrived, but on return from the recce patrol I decided to stand down the plan and briefed Brigade that things were not entirely as they seemed.

I awoke the next day at about 0700 hours to find a brew of hot chocolate and a ration pack of corned beef hash beside my makeshift body-armour pillow. I ate my breakfast, taking in my new surroundings. Things always look so different in daylight. In the corner of my gatehouse were the watchman's neatly stored possessions. I imagined he'd long since gone into hiding. If only he knew, I thought, just how much I'd like him and his mates to get back to work. That was the goal I had set myself.

I flicked through a pile of Arabic newspapers, whose pictures and cartoons formed an eloquent commentary on life leading up to the war from an Iraqi perspective. I put on my gun belt, picked up my rifle and headed off to chat to the men, steal some of their tea and get a look at the place. It was a beautiful day. Birds sang from the gum trees and a stray puppy circled me, hoping for food. As I stretched in the cool morning air I saw the face of Saddam leering at me from a massive mural outside the gates. A fairly new minibus, its wheels shot out, stood in the middle of the road, and the doors of the fire station hung open, with not a tender in sight. Those won't be hard to spot, I thought, as I made my way to the Comms Camel.

# —10—

# BA'ATHIST CHALLENGES

The weather played its hand on 25 March in central Iraq. With a sandstorm obscuring the battlefield, a thick blanket of sand driven along at 80kph brought confusion and disorientation. A British tank from the Royal Tank Regiment mistook another Challenger 2 for an Iraqi tank and engaged it with one of its 120mm armour-piercing fin-stabilised, discarding sabot rounds. Striking the tank with the force of an InterCity 125 train, the powerful ammunition tore the turret off the massive tank and killed two of the crew instantly, seriously injuring the other two. Meanwhile, the fighting in An Nasiriyah was intense. The 1st Marines had taken Qalat Sikar, 1 Para's planned target, which placed them back in reserve. To our south in Safwan, an attempt to distribute rations by doling them off the back of trucks had turned into a riot. It was a mistake I had no intention of making. On my front line on the Hammar Bridge there was an uneasy peace and in the town of Al Rumaylah the looting seemed to have abated as the locals waited to see what we would do.

I arrived in good time for the meeting with my retinue of advisers, including Phil and Nada as interpreters. Satisfied that C Company had secured the area, I was now keen to re-establish the utilities and get the place back to work. Some of the oil workers reappeared for the meeting at 0900 hours sharp, but I noted that the vigilantes did not show up. I waited for a short while then I accepted that they had either decided not to bother or had been warned off coming. Both were equally unacceptable to me as an excuse but I set that particular problem aside to be addressed later. My highest priority was to start taking a grip on the town or risk losing the initiative to the unfolding mayhem. The absence of the vigilantes was a significant spur to my efforts.

I asked the group of men to tell me their most pressing need. '*Mai*[74]!' they replied. I dispatched one of my young officers with two men who claimed to be water engineers to see if they could get the water running. Noting there was barely any electric power in the village, the next thing was to establish where the power source was. They explained that the village depended on the oil depot, and all the generators had been turned off. I was hoping they had not been looted as Nada sent some locals off to commandeer any generators they could find to supply power to the two villages. We would address the power needs of the depot itself later.

As this meeting ended, a frenzy of looting broke out across the town once more. Looters were streaming into the town in lorries, shouting loudly and cheering, clearly having spontaneously decided that we were not willing or able to stop them. It was every man for himself. I had a call from C Company telling me that there was a load of abandoned weapons at the local army barracks and they were wondering what to do. We had climbed into the Comms Camel, Shaggy reporting to Brigade on the radio net, and set off to join C Company when a convoy of looters passed us heading into town. We turned round and stopped them. I stepped out of the Camel and walked to the front of the vehicles, where an angry crowd was forming. Phil, who had followed in another vehicle, joined me. They told me, through Phil, that they demanded their share of the loot. I had him explain that it was not a case of 'shares' and that what they perceived as Saddam's property was in fact the property of the free people of Iraq. 'Fine,' they replied, 'then we are the Iraqi people. Give us our share.'

At this the mobs on board the lorries surged off in their vehicles, shouting and gesticulating as they did so. Soldiers ran to and fro, trying to contain this degenerating mêlée. The MO was called to a car further down the convoy containing an elderly Bedouin and his sons. The old boy didn't look too chipper.

'He has a heart condition,' she explained. 'I simply don't have the drugs to treat him!' She looked tired and careworn as she searched my face for a solution.

---

[74] Water.

'Couldn't we just give him some M&Ms?' I asked. 'At least he'll enjoy them! That's what I prescribe,' I added. 'Two M&Ms four times a day taken with hot sweet tea. Here,' I said, handing her a bag. 'Seriously.'

She had a minor sense of humour failure. On reflection, it was wrong to interfere in her territory and I sensed how upset she was that she simply didn't have the drugs to help everyone. I resolved to go and apologise later. The dear old Bedouin just watched this little vignette impassively, gasping for air and panting. This was my selfish little distraction in this sea of chaos. I was beginning to get rather fed up with the mayhem.

Things at the trucks were turning nasty. I realised that I needed to regain control at the point when my interpreter couldn't be heard above the noise. I took out my pistol and brandished it. This had no effect, so I cocked it. This was also lost in the scramble. I then aimed at the ground for maximum safety and fired one shot. There was silence.

'Right,' I said to the Bedouin nearest to me. He looked like Brutus, Popeye's chief rival. He was a stocky man in a dark blue dishdash and a dirty white shemagh. He was clearly the man in charge. 'Leave town now or I will have you arrested and sent to a prison!' This was translated.

He began to argue even more forcefully, with others joining in, waving his fist in my face until one of my senior NCOs, sensing that I was annoyed with him, grabbed him by the scruff of the neck and pushed him towards his lorry. After a last hard shove Brutus headed off to his cab, his hands raised in obsequious 'yeah, yeah, I'm going' fashion. Muttering like a London cabbie, he started the engine before reversing and heading off into the desert, angrily crashing through his gears.

As they left, my attention was drawn to a riot at the end of the road. We jumped into our vehicles and sped down towards the gates of the oil compound. At the centre of the angry crowd, I could see the Toyota pick-up from the previous day with the horse motif on the back window. 'Tell OC C over the net to secure the weapons at the barracks,' I shouted to the signallers in the rear of my wagon. 'Tell them it's all kicked off down here and I'm going to see if we can calm this down!'

As we drove through the crowd, they parted and gestured towards the men in the white pick-up, some drawing their fingers across their throats and pointing at the men. I wasn't sure what they meant, but it didn't look good. We stopped and soldiers hopped out of the vehicles and began to push the crowd back. I walked around to join Phil at the back of the pick-up. I ordered it to be searched. Though it was loaded with loot, no weapons were found. We had the men lined up and interrogated them through my interpreter.

The leader was a menacing-looking blighter, tall for an Arab and very wiry. He was dressed in a dirty white dishdash and had a red shemagh wound around his head. He had a passing resemblance to long-remembered pictures of Jesse James staring out of wild west Wanted posters. He said in a mock plaintiff voice that they were just locals getting their share. The rest of the crowd shouted them down and said that they were from an out-of-town criminal gang. Some of the residents began jostling me and pressing forward. Phil did his best to appeal for calm, sensing that I was losing patience with my audience.

I could see that the driver and two of his companions were covered in prison tattoos. I asked the tall thug about these. He just shrugged. I told them that I knew that they were the gang who had shot at us the day before, which they denied – of course. Even though this exchange had to be shouted over the din, in Arabic translation, half of the oil workers joined in. I would estimate that the crowd consisted of up to 200 Arabs and about twenty-five soldiers. As tempers became heated and the crowd pressed in, the thieves pointed out that we couldn't possibly recognise their vehicle, as there was mud on the number plates. When this was translated, the 'home team' of villagers went ballistic. I did my best to find out what had been said, with three or four locals shouting their version in Arabic at me and Jesse James shouting back and pointing at the number plate. Phil was trying to translate a little of each for my benefit. At this point it was hard to make myself heard and one man had taken to pulling me from behind to get my attention.

As this was happening Jesse James and his friends had begun to scuffle with the oil workers. Once more I brandished my pistol. This got their attention. I told them to get out of town and never return again, on pain of losing their vehicle. As this was translated they stood, mouths hanging limply open. They didn't like it at all. When Phil finished they became really angry again, shouting at me and gesturing at the oil workers. The crowd sensed the tension and became more animated and involved. What concerned me was the return of stolen property and identifying the vehicle because of the mud on the number plates. These guys had tried to kill me the previous day. At this point I could see that the whole thing was about to break down so I decided to fire a shot once again. I sought to reinforce my point while firing in a safe direction. I fired once into the number plate and under the vehicle. There was a crack from my

Browning Hi-Power and a cloud of dust. Immediately everyone went silent. Jesse James stared in disbelief. I explained that if this vehicle was ever seen again – unmistakable now because of the horse motif and hole in the rear plate – it would be confiscated and the occupants arrested. It seemed to have the desired effect.

They then changed tactics and pleaded poverty. I noticed that Jesse James had no shoes on. I'm certain that he had had a pair of flip-flops to begin with but these had somehow been lost in the scuffles. As a sweetener I let them all have one pair of stolen boots each and a single water tank. I then told them to leave. I made it clear that this was an order. The men clambered into the front of the white pick-up and started the motor. After a brief exchange with the oil workers out of the driver's window, they sped off at high speed, with the jeering of the locals to help them on their way. As they did so a little fat man in a nylon shirt with brown trousers and mules pushed forward to speak to me in rather formally accented English.

'*Sidi*, this is bad! These Ali Babas are not Bedouin. He has lost face. You must be careful! *Sidi*, when you see him next you must arrest him or he will bring you trouble – they have guns – yes, rifles!'

As usual Phil turned and translated this for the crowd, who yelled their approval in the form of a cacophony of comments, pleas and statements. The man who had been pulling at me from behind was there again, jerking my gun belt and reaching to turn my face to look at him with a callused hand.

I told the little fat man not to worry, that it would be the last we would see of Jesse James one way or another[75]. I then turned to the little 'Klingon' behind me. Phil asked him what he wanted.

'He says he has lost his daughter and needs help to find her.'

'What? Where was she lost?' I asked. 'When?'

The man stood impassively now, cupping his hands in a pleading fashion and with a genuine look of despair on his face. He was a little chap, dressed in a dirty and tattered dishdash with a grey shemagh wrapped tightly around his head. He was darker than most and had an exceedingly pockmarked face.

In a voice that was breaking with emotion he described to Phil what happened and then watched, his face a mask of pain, despair and pleading, as Phil turned to me.

---

[75] As it turned out, some days later the vehicle was stopped and confiscated as an oil company vehicle that had been looted. I believe up to four occupants were arrested and sent to the POW cage.

'He says that yesterday or the day before . . .' Phil turned to speak to the man. 'On Friday?' The man confirmed. He turned back to me. 'On Friday when the US troops came through, his daughter got burned. He took her to the US troops and they took her to a vehicle – I think he means ambulance.' He consulted the little man again and turned once more to me. 'He says that they kept him away but he watched from the road, then a helicopter came and they put her in the helicopter and flew off. Then they packed up and went. He just wants her back.'

I agreed to come to his house later. As this was translated, he began kissing my hands and feet and had to be pulled away by my men. I walked to my Land-Rover. I could feel the little man's eyes following me and as we drove off I glanced up to see him watching me earnestly from the side of the road, a pained smile on his face and an expression that was a cross between despair and hope.

After driving down through the oil workers' village and over the rail tracks we drew up in the centre of the rail workers' hamlet, much scruffier and more run down. We dismounted and my escorts took up cover positions. To my left was an abandoned caravan site, which had originally been used by some Russian workers who had helped build the oil installation. The village elders came out to meet me and a crowd pressed around. They shook hands very formally and, sensing the moment, I took off my gun belt and helmet and handed them to Herby, who put them in the Camel. The elders led the way to a dwelling. We went inside and the crowd raced around to look in through windows as we sat down on the carpet. Tea was served and a small child circled. The room was quite large but sparsely furnished. The walls were unpainted plaster and a motionless fan hung from the ceiling. There were some plastic flowers and on the walls some pictures of children and a large black and white picture of a youthful Saddam. Phil sat to my right and two of my signallers stood near the door. We introduced ourselves and I began by explaining that we had come to liberate Iraq and that I was disappointed to see the people destroying their own country. The chief spokesman responded by explaining that it was in fact the oil workers from the other village who had been doing all the damage and that they also despaired at the waste. It was just like the Ardoyne Road in Belfast, I thought. It's always the other side's fault.

I launched into my speech about looting being theft and that it was against the Muslim and Christian faiths. I explained that what had been state property was now the property of the Iraqi people and that it must be respected. I then turned to the question of weapons. We made it clear that we would have no choice but to shoot anyone who was armed and we thought posed a threat. Obviously the elders denied they had any weapons.

I then asked them for their thoughts and concerns. They explained that clean water was the top priority but that they were worried about thieves from the outlying area coming into town to steal. They wanted to discuss detailed deployments around the town to protect them. I waved this idea away and explained that the company commanders would liaise but that they would ultimately decide where there would be checkpoints. I stood up to leave and glanced at the picture of Saddam. The house owner looked at it and then took it off the wall and threw it outside. There was a pause and then the crowd started jumping on it and stamping on it with cries of 'Saddam Khallas!'

We returned from the rail workers' village and went to visit the small hospital in the main town. One of the major complaints of the elders that I had just left was that this hospital had been reserved for the oil workers alone and that they wanted access. I wanted to speak to the doctors to explain this.

The hospital was on the edge of the oil workers' town and on the main road that ran towards the rail workers' village. It was a single-storey building of fairly modern construction with a well-maintained garden shaded by trees. Inside there was an entrance hall with a dispensary and a treatment room, with a number of consulting offices along a corridor. The place was not obviously looted, but on closer inspection I could see that all the medical stores and office equipment were missing. I asked about this and the staff looked at each other. Then a medical assistant shrugged his shoulders and said it had all been taken. I told the hospital staff that I would post guards there to prevent any more looting and went on an inspection.

As I was walking around with Phil I stepped into an office and as I did so the medical assistant closed the door behind us. I could see he had something pressing to say and he spoke in a low voice to Phil, glancing at me and looking nervously at the closed door.

'He says that the Ba'athists are planning to counterattack tonight,' Phil translated. 'He says that you disturbed their meeting the night before but that they had issued weapons for the assault as a result.'

The man watched my face as Phil spoke. Suddenly it was all clear. The men we had met on the reconnaissance patrol were not village guards but a cover force for the Ba'athist meeting. I asked where the weapons were. Phil listened and then explained that as far as the man knew, most had been issued but that the grenades and some ammunition were still at the Ba'ath party headquarters.

'Where is this headquarters?' I asked. 'Will he take us there?'

Phil translated but the man shook his head. 'He's too frightened. He will draw us a diagram but asks that we do not involve him.'

I left Phil with the medic and went out to the Comms Camel to call for back-up. I did a hasty asssessment of our available forces with Shaggy then called D Company on the radio. Phil arrived with the medical assistant's diagram and we plotted it on the map. The supposed Ba'ath party HQ was actually pretty close, less than 200m away, in the centre of the town and beside the school that we could see from the road. I briefed D Company that they were to surround the area. I then gave quick orders to the men gathered at the hospital and, as unobtrusively as possible, set off on foot with a small cover group to meet D Company at the alleged HQ.

There were very few people around in the village at the time, wary no doubt of the new liberators and watching nervously to see how the Ba'athists who had ruled the country with a rod of iron for living memory would react. I must admit to a certain satisfaction and anticipation as we walked through the mist that had descended. If what Colonel Atiff had told me back in the camp was right, the HQ could be an Aladdin's cave of information.

We got there to find that the birds had flown minutes ahead of us, but we did get the whole HQ intact. It included tons of food, an armoury holding some old rifles and hundreds of grenades and rounds of ammo – and thousands of documents. As Phil leafed through them he looked up and smiled. 'It's all here: names, serial numbers – the lot!'

We sent most of the documents to Divisonal Intelligence, but first I had Phil glean a list of local activists from them. This was not hard as the records were very comprehensive, including addresses and weapon serial numbers. One particular treasure was a detailed diagram of the village with houses individually marked with coloured symbols and in the corner a key with details such as 'Al Quds[76]' or 'Fedayeen'.

As my troops consolidated in the village, setting up road blocks and orientating themselves with foot patrols, I walked around the Ba'ath party HQ with Phil. Greg and Ronnie from Sky News turned up and I allowed them to film as we explored the building. I cut down a large portrait of Saddam with my kukri. I walked into the largest office, where

---

[76] Reserve Army.

there was a desk with a white telephone on it and a conference table and chairs. I noticed a board on the wall and asked Phil what it was. I could see names and dates written on it. He explained that this was a record of the heads of the local party over the years, in the same way a golf club might record past captains. We called this the 'Leader Board' and it would come in handy as I sought to understand the local Ba'athist structures.

'So who's in charge now?' I asked.

Rising to the challenge, Phil noted the name, leafed through a large book and announced his address. 'Shall we have someone pop round?' he asked.

'Rude not to,' I said. 'His village and all that. Perhaps he'd like to join me for tea?'

Phil walked out, a posse of cover men gathering behind him. I settled down and took off my equipment while Magoo and Reggie set up our communications and some Gurkhas got the tea on. Around half an hour later, a head appeared around the corner.

'Visitor for you,' Phil said with a grin.

'Is it him?' I asked.

Without replying he turned and spoke in Arabic and a man walked into the room and stood in front of the desk. He was in his late forties and balding with a pullover and suit trousers on. 'Have a seat,' I said and Phil translated. I studied his face. I knew that he was suffering the humiliation of sitting in his own office with me sitting in his chair at his desk. He sat terrified in a chair facing me as I savoured the moment.

The Ba'athist leader looked like a harmless chap and shrugged his shoulders when quizzed. I wanted to know about life under the Ba'athists and actually felt well disposed towards him. At first he denied being a Ba'athist. I then asked Phil to read out what was written on the Leader Board behind my head.

'Took command 12 December 2001,' Phil read out to us.

'Oh, that. Well, of course, since you put it like that . . .' he began.

I held up my hand to stop him. 'Just explain how it all works,' I said, leaning over the desk and stabbing my finger into the table. 'Who do we need to talk to?'

He was very guarded but once tea was served he put his cards on the table. 'Look,' he said. 'I cannot help you at all. It would be death for me. There will be a lot of people who will talk. I want to go to your jail. I want you to get me out of here.'

I tried to establish a rapport but I could see that he was a worried man. I realised that I would be getting very little out of him. 'OK, Phil. Send him off,' I finally said as I rose and left the office, the man watching me as I went.

I wondered why he was so cagey. Later, after he had been sent off, I was rooting through a drawer in his desk, drinking his tea and eating his biscuits, when I was stunned to see a pistol, some knuckle-dusters and a set of handcuffs. I fished them out and without saying anything held up the handcuffs to show Herby, who was setting up a camp bed in the office. He looked up, paused and then began working at his bed again. 'Those will come in handy for the wife,' he noted.

That night the heavens opened and the roads were flooded. Soaked to the skin, the rest of the battle group made its way into the village as my Tactical HQ set up in the former Ba'ath party HQ. The message I wanted to send was clear. Rumaylah was under new management. I was the new boss. I accompanied Phil to the now-deserted home of the head of the party and we looked around. In the kitchen Phil showed me some documents: a weapons certificate and a Ba'ath party member's card. As I stood looking around I noted how they had lived. The house was a bungalow with a large living room and kitchen and three bedrooms. It was in a row of around ten identical houses, surrounded by a shoulder-high wall and with a small but well-maintained garden shaded by trees. I did note that as well as pictures of Imam Ali there were also Christian pictures. This was clearly a mixed marriage, but I had no idea if he or his wife were the Christian. It did not actually matter, of course. He was head of the Ba'ath party and had an office full of guns and a set of knuckle-dusters in his drawer – that was what mattered.

The next morning, 25 March, the downpour had cleared the fug of the preceding days and it was bright and sunny. I went for a walk around the village with Phil as my men, guided by the diagram we had captured, went on a door-to-door round-up of Fedayeen. (Not surprisingly they had all gone.) I stopped to chat with some youths and we discussed their delight in liberation. I then asked whom I might talk to in order to get a feel for local affairs. They chatted among themselves and then one lad said in good English, 'We will take you to the house of Abu Rifat. We respect him and he is not party.'

We walked for a short distance through the town until the youth pointed out the right house and left. I knocked. It was a terraced house with a small yard, smaller than the house of the head of the party, and when the door opened a young man looked out.

'We have come to see Abu Rifat,' Phil said.

The man asked us to wait and then came back and beckoned us in. Women were scurrying out and in the centre of a neat room stood a stocky man with a moustache and stubble on his chin. He was wearing a cardigan and an open-necked shirt and had a white Arabic skullcap on his head. He had kind eyes, yet he looked worried.

'I am Abu Rifat and these are my sons. Whatever business you have with me, leave them out of it.'

This was translated and I laughed. 'You misunderstand. I am the British leader here and the people of the town have told me that you are a man of honour and respect. I have come to introduce myself and ask for your help.'

He smiled and then waved his hand. 'Sit,' he said in English. 'Welcome, leader of the British. My home is your home.'

We sat and tea was brought. Over the next hour I learned a great deal about the village and what had gone on, then I asked him to accompany me as I continued my walk around the village. I wanted to be seen in public with this respected man and as we walked we talked to locals and I felt that the mood across the village turned from one of great anxiety to one of relief as they watched us chatting like friends. I sensed Abu Rifat relax. Before we parted I asked for help in recovering the weapons that I knew to be in the town. He said he would try.

We had already captured fourteen weapons at our vehicle checkpoints, but by the early evening Abu Rifat sent a runner to say he had gathered a further twenty-three weapons and we should come and pick them up. Meanwhile, my main HQ moved into the abandoned school.

The following day, 26 March, a UK Civil Military Cooperation (CIMIC) team arrived and set up. Made up of reservists, they were a mix of serving policemen and social workers. They were detailed to take on the responsibilities such as deliveries of fresh water by tanker. They had brought supplies of bottled water and POW rations, which were, however, totally inadequate. In their innocence they had wanted to distribute these from the backs of lorries. I forbade them to do this, as that was what had started the fighting in Safwan. I had a long-standing policy of not permitting soldiers to throw sweets at children, as it seemed to me to be demeaning to a population that we meant to liberate, and would cause resentment, which could lead to violence. It was also grossly arrogant and ill-disciplined and was bound to attract large groups of children and young adults, providing perfect cover for close-quarter attacks. (This was once common in Northern Ireland.)

The journalists with the battle group were able to visit widely around the area and had more material than they could use. Alex had joined us by now, arriving in a rather smart Chevrolet Suburban, and in the evening we were able to snatch moments to catch up on events in our lives since we last served together some ten years before. The Sky team, Alex and Sarah lived in the school with my Main HQ, while I lived in the Ba'ath party HQ.

The relationship with Abu Rifat continued to flourish. As he came to visit he began to bring others. Among these was Mawood Jaber, a bespectacled medical student in his twenties, and sometimes a timid young oil engineer called Ahmed. Ahmed was a small man with a pockmarked face and a serious expression. He rarely came out of his mother's house but he was sensible with something to say and I liked to see him at these advisory meetings.

One afternoon I got him along to the office with Abu Rifat and Mawood Jaber to discuss one of our greatest blights – the oil-well fires. Around us there were fifteen or so, started by the fleeing Ba'athists. An oil-well fire is an awesome sight. Oil burns a deep orange and spouts flame about thirty feet into the air. Gas manages twice this, and the heat is so intense that it would be impossible to go within seventy-five metres of it without suffering severe burns. Its roar can be heard more than a kilometre away. The specialist wildcatters from the US and Kuwait were due to arrive to put out the fires, and I was eager to be able to furnish them with some locals who could help. I asked my new advisers over tea if they knew any way to put them out. Their response taught me an interesting and critical lesson about this sadly abused and deformed society. Of course they could put the fires out – easily! I wasn't certain what I was hearing. They could put out the fires? How? Abu Rifat explained that the Ba'athist SSO had come to them to arrange the attacks on the oil wells and pumping stations as they fled. They, the locals, had shown them where to place the explosive so as to render the plants useless. In fact, unknown to the SSO, they had made them place the charges in areas where they could easily repair the damage.

'So,' I enquired, 'we could put these fires out?'

'Of course,' Abu Rifat said. 'We just turn off the supply of oil to the fires and they go out. Simple.' I wondered why they hadn't done so.

'Well,' they replied, clearly confused, 'no one has told us to – or even asked if we could!'

'So,' I said, 'if someone asked you to put out the fires, you would?'

'Yes, of course,' they replied.

'Then I'm asking you to,' I said.

The last fire was put out that same evening. We discussed their needs in exchange for this help. What they still needed was clean water, they told me. They had lots of water but they needed clean drinking water. When I offered to share out the stores the Ba'athists had been hoarding they said they had an abundance of dried goods but some fresh food would be nice. Meanwhile the farmers outside the town had a lot of fresh food but it was spoiling because there was no market. We needed to sort this out. As we strolled outside the building after the meeting I asked Abu Rifat about the whole nonsense of the oil-well fires.

'You must understand,' he explained, 'in our society having a good idea can get you killed. In Iraq you do not have ideas. You do as you are told. It is how it is.'

'It is how it was,' I corrected.

'No, Aqeed, with respect, it is how it is. We do as you say. It is too dangerous to have ideas even now.'

I was a little confused. 'But Ba'athism is finished,' I continued.

'We only do as you say,' he insisted; 'there are things you do not understand.'

'Fine,' I said, 'then I need you to help me understand what needs to be done.'

'Is that not why we are talking now?' he asked.

'It is,' I agreed.

My main focus was replacing the Ba'athist menace with visible signs of normality. Andrew became the main coordinator of the village activities and divided his time between the oil workers' village and the Pikey village. The people from the latter were a more basic if trusting and pitiful lot. He formed the Village Action Decision Group and Executive or 'VADGE'. How we tittered when this term became currency and was mentioned by Geoff Hoon in the Commons during one of his reports on the War. Little by little there were tangible signs of progress. On my first visit to the hospital it had been clear that it had been looted. There was nothing left of the stock of medicine that had clearly been there recently, judging from the dust marks on the shelves (the dust is not a sign of mismanagement but a fact of life here). This was looting with a difference, however. Once we had regular foot and vehicle patrols through the town, within a day or so all the stores were quietly returned from the hiding places where the staff had taken them for safety and the clinic was reopened. The hospital was not the only facility that was protected in this manner and I took the voluntary self-help as a vote of confidence by the locals in my troops.

One day during one of my walkabouts, I asked Abu Rifat where the mosque was. He looked at me in amazement. 'Mosque? Would you not object to a mosque?' he asked.

I was confused until he explained that the Ba'athists hated mosques. He told me they had closed down the mosque years before. I asked if there was an imam. Of course there was. That Friday they had the first call to prayer for fifteen years. We borrowed the public address system from Brigade and loaned it to the imam. It all went swimmingly and was recorded by Sky News and Abu Dhabi TV as well as the *Mail on Sunday*. When I asked if they would like to borrow the PA system again for evening prayers the imam said, 'It's OK – we have our own! We just wanted to use yours for the first one in case it was a trick to capture our system!' Tortured and abused for so long, the people of Iraq were deeply suspicious and loath to trust. Careful understanding would be needed if the coalition forces were to win their confidence.

I discovered that there was a barber's shop. A haircut was 200ID – about 5p. I marched down one day and had 5p worth. The barbers were a gregarious pair who were delighted to see me. They were burly men in their thirties, with the standard moustache and a couple of day's growth of beard. The chap who cut my hair wore a loose-fitting polo shirt with a blue pattern and baggy pants. On his feet were what became known as Iraqi desert boots – flip-flops. The barber's shop was a single room with a few chairs for customers along the wall. There were mirrors in front of each chair (not barber's chairs) and the usual array of creams, potions and brushes set in front of each workplace. Trumper's of Mayfair it was not. The walls were decorated with Islamic charts and plastic flowers, and startled-looking infants looked out from framed pictures set before each barber's chair.

They gave good value and my hair didn't grow back to a respectable length for months. Still, I enjoyed the conversation and learned more about the town, the people and the various wars – the Iran–Iraq War, the First Gulf War, the Shia rebellion and the second war – from them than I had from any other source. There was something different about them and I wondered how they'd ended up scraping a living as barbers. They

The battle group close in with the RSM to my rear and the embedded media to my left

Immediately to the left of me in this picture is Chris McDonald who was to lose his life in post-war Iraq

POWs arrive at Oxford

Pikey Reynolds brews up on a hexamine stove

A ranger on foot patrol through Rumaylah with a GPMG

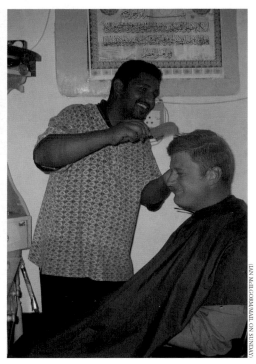

Some of the rifles and rocket launchers Abu Nawfel had 'forgotten about'

Greg Milan from Sky News regrets a visit to the barber in Al Rumaylah

The children

Ali translates as I count my blessings on my Arabic beads

I consult my map in a WMIK before we set off to cross the Euphrates

Two of our Australians hitch a ride home on an Al-Samoud missile

revealed that they were former Marsh Arabs, the Madan. They were part of an ancient people who had dwelt in the marshes since prehistoric times – well back to the Flood, according to them.

'So,' I asked, 'where are these marshes?'

'Gone!' they said. Saddam had had the marshes drained some years back. The civilisation no longer existed.

This struck me like a brick to the temple. Why had we not been told? What the fuck was the use of Operation Southern Watch – twelve years of flying over the place – if the people it was supposed to protect had ceased to exist and we hadn't noticed – or cared? Indeed, why did we have the operation at all? Were the Marsh Arabs and their ancient culture and environment just a convenient *casus belli* for other, more sinister purposes? I was angry and cynical as I left and deeply sorry for the noble, unbreakable people who had turned to (bad) hair-cutting to survive. We had failed them.

# —11—

# NIGHT PATROL

The previous day had seen the British engaged in their heaviest fighting of the war, with the Royal Scots Dragoon Guards facing a concerted attempt to break out of Basra. Fourteen T55s were destroyed while allied air power pounded a second column, accounting for nineteen enemy tanks. It was the end of the first week of the war.

During the morning of 27 March, I conducted a walkabout to allow aid workers in DFID[77] to assess the town. I was in the hospital when I saw that the medical assistant who had helped us in the past appeared unusually nervous and furtive. I sent for Phil Ballard.

We took him off to a side room and, as the DFID team chatted outside, we stood in front of a large medicine cabinet and acted as if we were talking about the medicines. He revealed that he had been told that he was going to be shot that evening, along with Abu Rifat, our cooperative town elder, and the young medical student, Mawood Jaber, who had reopened the clinic. We asked why they had not just run away. 'It would go hard on our families,' he replied[78].

---

[77] Department for International Development.

[78] The tactic used by paramilitaries in Ireland, but it's even more sinister here; the victim feels there really is nowhere to turn. Once, an Air Force general suspected of plotting against Saddam was called to the Intelligence HQ in Baghdad, where he was forced to watch men gang-rape his nine-year-old daughter. She was then thrown to dogs trained to eat human flesh and torn apart before his eyes.

'OK,' I said, 'you tell us who these heroes are and we'll sort them out.'

Initially hesitating, he gave us detailed descriptions of the people involved, their weapons – which we were able to cross-reference with documents seized in the Ba'athist HQ – and the addresses of the three known by him to be involved. I knew from my experience of paramilitaries in Ireland that providing this sort of detail did not come easily to a victim and the man showed great courage in confronting these people – even though he knew he would be killed whether he did or did not help us. This is a reflection of the power of the bully. Once more, as in Ireland it was not at all unusual for the victim to know the identity of their would-be killers – in fact, it is part of the terror process. Then he helped Phil prepare another diagram showing the location of the houses of those he knew of. Finally we told him to go home for the rest of the day and not to answer the door to anyone except the British. As he left, he warned us that the idea was that once he and the others were dealt with, there was going to be a move to rally the Ba'athists in the town and take us by surprise. They had as many as 150 armed men, but he explained they were reluctant to act unless victory was certain. They believed that if the informers could be dealt with, it would encourage the populace to rise up, if only to protect themselves.

There had been other such attacks in areas which the British forces thought had been liberated. It is hard to say if these were coordinated. In one, a thirteen-year-old girl had been found guilty of the crime of waving to British troops as they drove through Safwan. The Ba'athists led her to the lamp-post where she had stood to wave and, as an example to others, hanged her from it. Other parents had also had their children killed in front of them that day in Safwan, for refusing to fight against the allied forces. I was in no doubt the Ba'athists meant business. But so did I.

The Brigadier, Jacko Page, visited early in the afternoon. 'How are things here?' he asked, settling into a chair in my office in the Ba'ath party HQ with a cup of tea.

'Fine,' I replied. 'Except we have the threat of a major hit on us tonight.' I described the intelligence from the medical assistant.

'So what do you plan to do?' he asked.

'We need to try to get a cross reference on this. We have lots of names and details but no faces to put to them.'

'Well, I have nothing to offer you in the way of additional assets. What you can't afford to do is to lose this situation. And,' he added, 'remember what has been threatened may never happen! It may all be in the mind of the frightened medical assistant. But you should be aware that this village has become a focus and so have you. The progress here in Rumaylah seems to be outpacing progress everywhere else. You are likely to have a problem when all the "do-gooders" want to come here and get a slice of the action, and you will also have to keep out the refugees who want what they think you have in here. An influx of refugees will lead to more resentment than anything else. In short, Tim, you're going to have to be very careful how you handle this one or you'll lose control. Just wait till DFID turn up. They'll want to take charge and get credit for all this!'

'They've been already!' I laughed. 'This morning!'

I invited him to come and see our main HQ in the school. As we walked outside, we were met by the sight of a convoy of US Humvees manned by heavily armed soldiers. Those in the lead vehicle were scanning the area with a rack-mounted Mk 19 automatic grenade launcher. Others crouched or stood as if about to conduct a house assault. I could see at a glance that these guys weren't regulars. Overweight and all shapes and sizes, they were strictly Dad's Army.

Suddenly I was alerted to activity on the market square, as mothers swept up their children and rushed indoors and groups of young men started to gather. Land Cruisers sped through the back streets as even more youths emerged from houses. I had grown up in Belfast during the worst of the troubles. Sensing the approach of a riot was second nature to me. This was Belfast's Ardoyne Road all over again and a sixth sense told me we were a heartbeat away from violence.

Some of the US soldiers were shouting and lining up the children from the Pikey village outside the school. The children had come across to the oil village, tagging along behind a delegation of thugs – headed by none other than my old friend Brutus the looter – who had had their stolen cars confiscated and were planning to persuade us to give them back. Translating for Brutus was a mischievous-looking beggar with a large 'soup-strainer' moustache and a filthy dishdash. I had met him before and the prison tattoos on his hands and neck suggested he had an unsavoury past. He spoke English in a slow, condescending and exaggerated manner.

It seemed that the US patrol had taken it upon themselves to become involved, brushing aside all the work of previous days, to negotiate with this delegation while throwing sweets and candy bars at the children. It was instantly clear that the oil workers had taken deep exception to all of this. I turned and motioned to them with my hands that I would deal with the situation, then walked towards the man who seemed to be in charge, saying, 'Excuse me, could you stop that,' louder and louder until I was shouting above the din.

The man was chatting to Brutus and his translator and just held up a hand, without looking round, as if to dismiss me as I walked towards him. He was a US Army major, a fat little man with a helmet and body armour and a pistol belt around his substantial waist. He looked me up and down and said, 'What exactly is your major issue, mister?'

'This area is my responsibility,' I said as evenly as I could, 'and I want you to stop that right now. This is a disgrace.'

He shrugged his shoulders. 'I'm just doin' my job,' he said, then, putting his face close to mine, sneered, 'so why don't you go do yours?'

He turned and nodded to his companions, as American footballers do when they've just scored. Brutus and his mate shuffled away, clear that they weren't getting their cars.

I was furious. 'I am CO 1 R Irish, this is my area and stopping this sort of behaviour is precisely my job! And,' I added, 'the man watching this pantomime over my shoulder is Brigadier Page, Commander 16 Brigade.'

He glanced back at me. 'So?'

'I think that you and I need a chat in private. Please go to my office; I will be along shortly.'

As I walked off he stood in a lazy pose, following me with his eyes and ostentatiously chewing his gum or tobacco. I went to the HQ in the school and showed the Brigadier around. After the Brigadier had returned to his vehicle, I emerged from the school alone, only to see the handouts by the US soldiers still going on. Rather than go to my office, the US major had totally ignored me.

'Stop that right now!' I said to the soldiers. Then I turned to the little fat officer and said, 'You – follow me!'

I walked to my office and the major strutted along behind me. I was by now incandescent with rage. Things did not improve after we reached my office. Initially I tried to be firm with this insolent man, then I changed tack and attempted to reason with him. I took him across to the armoury to show him the weapons we had captured so far and explained that these – I knew – were the tip of the iceberg. Things went from bad to worse.

'So you're tryin' to impress me with some old weapons, huh?' he sneered.

It was clear that he would not accept that I had any authority at all.

Finally, when I had had quite enough of him, I turned to leave but told him to wait exactly where he was until my return.

'Are you arresting me?' he enquired as I walked off.

I halted and paused then said, 'Yes, if you like, you're under arrest.' (Of course we both knew that I had no power to arrest a US officer, but if that's the way he wanted to see it . . .) On my way out I saw Herby and said to him, 'That man is to stay there and he is not to leave.'

Herby later told me that after I had gone, one of the American's men ducked into the hall and shouted, 'Everything OK, Major?'

'I'm under arrest!' he replied, then added, 'If I'm not outta here in two minutes you know what to do!'

'Hooa! We'll not leave without you, sir!' squeaked some little action man in a high-pitched voice.

Herby was leaning against the door drinking tea at the time. He decided to take an interest.

'If you come near here in the next hour I'll stick that rifle up your arse – understand?' The rescue party scuttled off, leaving the major standing in the corridor with Herby watching him as a cat watches a mouse.

After a brief consultation with Brigadier Jacko Page at the back of the Brigadier's vehicle (he had been speaking to our Divisional HQ to see if they could not get the American civil affairs team withdrawn before they did some real damage), I went back to the office, picking up the US Army major's second in command on the way. He was an elderly captain and was clearly most embarrassed and concerned with the way things had gone. As he walked into my office, past the now red-faced major in the corridor, he removed his helmet.

'May I sit, sir?' he asked.

'Please do,' I said, indicating a chair. I asked his name and he introduced himself as Captain Stoll. 'We've a bit of a problem here,' I said.

He raised his hand. 'Sir, I cannot apologise enough for the major's behaviour. There's been a serious misunderstanding here. Things have got badly out of hand. Now, I'm certain the major meant no harm. I don't think he knew who you were.' He explained that they were reservists and that the major, who was called Re Biastre, only wanted to get his photograph taken talking to an Arab so he could show the folks back home.

'Back home?' I said, exasperated. 'Has he any idea what is going on round here?' Captain Stoll just looked at me. His lips pressed together. 'Get that utter buffoon in here,' I ordered him.

I called the now visibly shaken US major into my office and was about to tell him to leave town when, to my utter astonishment, he began shaking and then sobbing. I could see the name 'Biastre' on his helmet.

'Sir,' he sobbed, 'I have the greatest respect for you and the Royal Irish – the Irish above all – you see, I'm a New York cop and –'

'I'll stop you right there. Enough! Just get out!'

As he left he said, 'I swear I'll never be back, sir.'

'Good!' I said as I walked past him and out of the building.

As Biastre and his sorry band limped out of town, tails firmly between their legs, things began to hot up for real. D Company was Division reserve. Fighting outside Basra meant that it was needed and was to leave ASAP. A short time later I had a call to say that we were to be prepared to deal with an attack on the Hammar Bridge. I managed to claw back a platoon of Gurkhas for this by negotiating on the radio with Brigade HQ as the Gurkhas, at this point in time still in the village, mounted their vehicles. As the remaining Gurkhas drove out of town, I drove with my Tactical HQ vehicles, the Comms Camel and one other up to the bridge. Sean Lundy was there to meet me.

'We've been getting some from their GHN 45s[79]; they're good for range but they haven't got our line yet.'

Richard, the BC, nodded. 'When they do get the range, it's going to get exciting here. They are large-calibre guns.'

'One of the battery commanders from another battle group came up when we were getting shelled last night,' Sean said with a laugh. 'He suggested we move. "Do you realise who we work for?" I asked. I told him we'd rather be shelled than piss off TC.'

I inspected the preparations around the bridge and spoke to Brigade again on the secure radio. The orders had changed and there was to be a fighting patrol that evening by 3 Para across the bridge. If there were enemy artillery observers out there across the river that would settle them. I set off back to Al Rumaylah in my little convoy of Land-Rovers.

With the information on the planned murders, I called an impromptu orders session. I knew that with the pace of operations we had very few uncommitted forces. Brigade likewise had nothing to offer in support. We were on our own. It was a tense night and there was fighting outside Basra. Our surveillance radar had picked up movement on our eastern

---

[79] 152mm long-range artillery, with a range of 30–35km.

flank – possibly enemy tanks – but I had all my forces committed: A Company to 3 Army Air Corps Regiment in the west; B Company on the GOSPs and covering the Kuwaiti border; C Company in positions around the town, covering outwards and very thinly spread; D Company with 7 Brigade as Divisional reserve; and L Company on Hammar Bridge covering 3 Para and in contact with the enemy.

Before I left the UK I'd fished out my copy of Niccolo Machiavelli's *The Prince*. More than four centuries after it was written, this slim treatise on the use and abuse of power remains vital reading at times like this. It was written by a man who wished to gain favour with the notorious Medici family on their return to power in 1519 Florence. Niccolo Machiavelli, educated in the ways of the Republic and heavily influenced by the writings of Aristotle, recognised that to survive in a harsh world man must adopt some lateral thought. He wrote a text based on his life's experience as an aide memoire to the Medicis. I had spent many hours digesting it over endless black coffee and cigars. I thought now of the lesson contained in Chapter 17: 'Of Cruelty and Clemency and Whether it is Better to be Loved or Feared'. This had particular pertinence for me as I considered the problems besetting my command that night. Machiavelli said that, on balance, it is safer to be feared than loved. The prince who seeks to be loved will be despised, as popularity is an elusive goal and a fickle mistress. No one can give everyone everything they want and envy and jealousy soon corrupt the underlying attempt to gain favour. Conspiracies flourish and the prince becomes a victim of his own vanity. I made a mental note to lend my dog-eared copy to Tony Blair on return. If the prince is firm, however, things will turn out differently. Firmness is understood and, in a war-torn country, reassuring. As Aristotle said, men do not fear justice, but they hate the lack of it. Provided the prince does not give them a reason for hatred, then they will learn respect. Order and justice are the real goals, and to achieve them the Prince must above all be fair. And a wise prince must rely on what is in his power and not on what is in the power of others.

I had been in situations like this before. Bullyboys were the same the world over, from Ulster to Bosnia, from Colombia to Iraq. If you stood up to them, they would crumple. Where, I wondered, was the weakness of this lot? As I drew on my cigar I began to chortle to myself. They were amateurs. They had crumpled the first time I'd met them. As it turned out, we now knew the armed men we had encountered that first night were not anti-robber vigilantes but the local Ba'athists plus a few conscripts who had been protecting a meeting when we stumbled across them. Their complete panic at the very sight of my men gave me the measure of them.

I had been naive too. I'd wanted to believe that we would be greeted as liberators, with crowds throwing garlands. I wanted to think well of the Iraqis. But now I had to face the fact that the evil bastards I had described during my Führer Rally at Fort Blair Mayne were much closer than I'd thought. I was going to need to be a little more cautious in my dealings with the locals. I recalled Machiavelli's thoughts on the matter. After rebel territories are reconquered, they are not so easily lost again, he wrote. The reinstated ruler will not hesitate to enforce his position by severely punishing offenders, unmasking suspects and reinforcing himself in weak places.

I was haunted by my naivety. I'd been wandering around Al Rumaylah unarmed and seeking to empathise with the locals. Most of them were decent people, of course, but I had failed to look beyond this. I hadn't fully appreciated that there were still those among them who wanted only to regain power and were prepared to kill us, and anyone who cooperated with us, in the process.

There had been a Shia rebellion in the south after the last Gulf War. I knew little about it, except that it had failed. I did know that after the 1991 war the allies had advanced as far north as Al Rumaylah. President George Bush Senior decided at that point that Saddam should be allowed to stay in power, so the troops withdrew to Kuwait. In the south, however, a disillusioned Shia officer returning to Basra was arrested by the military police on suspicion of desertion. He fought back and others joined in. Before long, the Shia south was in open rebellion. Jails were thrown open and prisoners were released from underground caverns; some had been there so long they loudly denounced the regime *before* Saddam's.

Sadly, the rebellion lacked focus and leadership. Saddam, initially shocked and then relieved that neither the West nor the Iranians leapt to the aid of the Shia, dispatched Ali Hasan al-Majid al-Tikriti, aka Chemical Ali (he already had form for gassing Iranians in the Iran War and the murder of between 250 and 400 Kurds in Balisa on 16 April 1987), to quell the rebellion. This he did with his customary gusto and brutality. It was clear that the Ba'athists hadn't kept control for thirty-five years by accident. It was – I believed – safe to assume that they would have made sure that a repeat performance was unlikely. That meant that there would be some mechanism to divide and conquer; most likely a tangled web of informers, backed by a pretty robust threat of force. I realised in the darkness of that night that I, like the coalition, needed to radically readjust my approach.

I didn't know it on that first afternoon, but the jokers who had nearly blown my head off at the factory gates were released prisoners put up to it by the Ba'ath party. Thanks to Abu Rifat and the others, I now more clearly understood the relationship between the released prisoners and the Ba'athist Fedayeen.

Machiavelli believed that there are two methods of fighting, by law and by force. The first is employed by men, the second by beasts, but man, he went on to say, must at times emulate the beast. The lion cannot protect himself from the trap and the fox cannot protect himself from the wolf. One must therefore be a fox to see the traps and a lion to frighten the wolves. There were quite a few wolves in our town – about 150 of them, apparently – and I had little idea who they where. I had lists of names, but no way of putting faces to them. Then I recalled the Irish proverb *Ni gnach cosaint ar dith tiarna*: 'The fight is rarely continued when the chief has fallen.' If I could take out their chief in one go, without making myself too vulnerable, then we would succeed.

My principal advantage was that the Ba'athists didn't know I was on to them; they didn't know I had the three addresses that the medical assistant had given Phil plus a detailed diagram of where their houses were in the village. I needed to act decisively; I needed to send a clear message to these guys, up close and in person. Once more *The Prince* reminded me that men must either be caressed or annihilated. They can avenge themselves for small injuries, but cannot do so for great ones; whatever I did to the Ba'athists that night had to put an end to the matter. Annihilation was not an option, so I had to find a way of subverting them instead. I'd take a leaf out of the Romans' book. In every newly captured province, the Romans empowered men who, moved by their new status and fear and envy of their former masters, would draw attention to any threat of rebellion to protect their own security. A possible solution was beginning to take shape in my mind.

It was a velvet dark night. My tactical group was now living in the former Ba'ath party HQ, but the Main HQ, with signallers, intelligence staff and the planning and operations cells, was controlled by my second in command from the school at Rumaylah. I walked across. The planning room was a sparsely furnished history classroom, with slogans like *Nam! Nam! Nam! Saddam* daubed across the wall and illuminated by tactical lighting kits and Tilly lamps which shone brightly on the map but threw gloomy shadows above chest height. Radios babbled, phones rang and runners came and went in the background.

The main players were waiting for me at our planning table, faces set. It was around 2000 hours. The war wasn't going exactly to plan, not just in Rumaylah, but across Iraq.

'Well,' I began, 'what do we think?'

'If what the informers are saying is true, we're badly outnumbered,' said a strained voice from the gloom. 'We're down to the Battalion HQ and the CIMIC – forty men, all up. By all accounts they've 150 plus.'

'Yeah, but they're not Paddies, so we've still got them outnumbered by about two to one,' I said rather irritably. I placed my hands on the table and looked at the map. 'Has anyone got any ideas as to how to deal with these particular nutcases, or shall we just panic?'

Jim, my former RSM and now a captain[80], leaned forward into the light. 'It's just like home. These people need to be gripped, or they'll run amok.'

'What would the boys in Belfast do, Jim?'

'They'd find a Granada full of volunteers rolling up to their focken door!'

'I agree,' Phil said. 'I am half Arab, as some of you know. They will not respect any display of weakness – in fact they'll exploit it. Sir,' he added, 'at the risk of sounding melodramatic, what you decide this evening will set the course in this whole region for the rest of this campaign, in the eyes of the local population. I have spoken to them. They are frightened. They are looking to you. If you fail them, you will never regain their trust.'

I began to think out loud. 'We need to rediscover our centre of gravity. The security of the oilfields – which the Commander told me only today the Prime Minister and President are watching with interest – depends not merely on their physical security, but on the security of the people. It's a microcosm of the current situation in the country as a whole. Firstly there are the oil workers, then their families, then the US and international oil workers and the civilian support staff and contractors. If *any* of these people are harmed, no amount of tanks, aircraft or Northern Ireland-style security forces and bases with watchtowers will convince the people vital to our mission that it is safe to work in the oilfields. No workers means no oil. No oil means no money. No money means no new

---

[80] Commissioned from the ranks, Jim had been brought up in one of the most violent areas of Belfast in the most turbulent years of the Troubles. I valued his judgement on such matters!

Iraq and that means we've wasted our time and effort; Corporal Parkin lost his leg training in Wales for nothing, and those Iraqi lads that we buried down on the border died for nothing.

'As I see it, we have four options: do nothing; call in the C Company cordon and raid the suspect houses, sealing off the inner village, in the hope that the suspect radar contacts prowling around outside town – whoever and whatever they are – don't come our way; wait and risk an attack from the Ba'athists, then get the RMP to flop around the place like a lot of would-be Inspector Morses; or we could pay a friendly visit to the suspects but make it clear that we will not be taking no for an answer on certain subjects.'

I turned to the Adjutant. 'Rules of engagement, David. What's the form?'

'Well,' he began, 'as named members of the Ba'ath party, any of these wankers with weapons are classed as combatants. We are authorised to use force against this sort of lowlife, provided that it is proportional, directed towards the threat and fulfils a military necessity.'

'Thanks, that's clear enough.' I looked around the table. 'Do we have a consensus?'

'Stick it to the bastards – that's what I say!' said Scotty, a tall, blond, Aussie captain, from the side of his mouth. But after another five minutes of heated conversation, it was clear to me that there was no real agreement. I could see that some senior people were really frightened by the whole situation, and there was a strong 'do nothing' lobby, but I knew 'do nothing' was not an option. I didn't have the time or specialist manpower to cordon and search, so that was out. I did have high-grade intelligence though, and decided that if I opted for a 'friendly visit – with a difference', we might get away with it.

'Do you know, fellas,' I said, 'I was just telling a couple of the C Company lads the other day that sometimes, when faced with a problem, the best course of action is to take it head on. You might fail, but you might so surprise the opposition with your boldness that he crumples. The trick, as I say, is to surprise him, not to bloody astonish him!'

A ripple of laughter ran round the room. There was now a hive of activity at the Bird Table, but the group of men in desert fatigues at the planning table – an identical table to the other, with the same map, but with future intentions marked as opposed to reported fact, as with the current operations of the Bird Table – remained deep in thought.

'So do we send the boys round, or what?' I asked, more than a little rhetorically. There was silence. 'That'll be a "Yes, sir" then.' I pushed myself back from the table and clapped my hands in satisfaction.

Usually when I went to visit Iraqis in their houses, I'd go unarmed and with just an interpreter, with the sacred tenets of Arab hospitality as my guardian. On this occasion, I opted for full body armour, complete with helmet and head torch, service pistol and spare magazine. I was greeted by the Adjutant, RSM and BC in the darkness of the hallway of the school. It was almost 2100 hours.

'What's this?' I said, looking at the most highly paid cover patrol in history.

'Well, it's us or the mortar platoon – in which case *we* would be doing sangar[81] duty,' Andrew Cullen said from behind me.

I spun round to see his massive frame in the gloom. *'Et tu, Brute?'*

I began the final brief in suitably sombre tone. 'We are gathered here this evening to pay a wee visit on some sinners who have lost their way and reckon that they're going to bump off all of our touts. We will advise them against this course of action and take the weapons they have at home into safekeeping. Depending on how cooperative our new friends are, we will decide if they go to the nick or not – but I'd prefer to encourage them to work for us, all things being equal.

'Phil, have you got the list of names, addresses and weapon numbers?'

'It's here.' He held up his red notebook.

'Could you talk us through the town plan and layout of the suspect addresses?'

He nodded, and unfolded the Fedayeen diagram of the town which we had found on the first day and which was now our tour guide for the town. It was annotated in Arabic script with the locations of all their operators, collaborators and Al Quds members. 'Can I have some light here?' he asked. The diagram was instantly caught in the crossbeams of a dozen torches and headlights. He briefed the group on the intelligence in some detail. 'So we have three main suspects,' he concluded. 'Jari, Deputy Head of Security to Tariq, who I gather is no longer in town. Jamil, his driver and sidekick and the man that Abu Rifat thinks is to be the shooter. And the school headmaster, Ayoub Younis Nasser, or "Abu Nawfel[82]", who seems to be the key man here. We must be careful,

---

[81] A sandbagged sentry position.

[82] Meaning literally 'Father of Nawfel' a familiar term used throughout the Arab world for men with sons.

though. These people have been brutalised for more than thirty-five years. They'll tell you what they think you want to hear, and some are not above dropping a neighbour in it for a laugh.' Phil pointed to the three houses with his pencil. 'OK,' he said, 'any questions?'

No one spoke.

I stepped to the front of the group. 'Right, boys! This could work out to be a real coup for us, or a disaster. The birds may have flown or they may fight. Bearing in mind what they have planned for this evening, I suggest we stay on our guard. In an earlier life I recall the case of one punter – a particularly nasty piece of work – being lifted in Bosnia for war crimes. He was minding his own business one day, fishing by the river with his lunch hanging from a tree to keep it cool, but armed – as usual – when he saw the boys coming to arrest him. Now, he was the sort of chap who delighted in torturing people in ways I won't describe, and assumed he was going to be on the receiving end of what he'd normally dish out on a surprise visit. So he tried to shoot it out.'

'What happened?' someone asked.

'Tragically, he shuffled off this mortal coil, with a little help from a hail of lead,' I replied. 'But only after wounding one of ours, of course.'

We loaded our weapons and made ready, and after a brief check set off.

There are patrols every night in places like this – but very rarely led by the CO, with the 2IC and Adjutant in tow – and the fact that I had allowed 1 R Irish to become so thinly spread worried me. But needs must when the devil drives, and I knew I had to bear the brunt of the risk.

The sixteen-strong multiple consisted of four 'bricks'. We were connected by Personal Role Radios (PRRs), which had a range – depending on conditions – of a couple of hundred metres, so we could spread out, each brick covering two or three blocks. Each man wore body armour with ceramic plates that would withstand a high-velocity round, a helmet, radio and belt kit with water rations and white phosphorus and high explosive fragmentation grenades.

Each brick was commanded by a team leader, usually a corporal but in this case the 2IC, RSM, Adjutant and BC. With nightsights fitted to our rifles, we had a distinct advantage over the opposition, who had a handful of first-generation nightsights at best. We moved silently along the streets of baked clay, still tacky from the previous evening's rainstorm, whispering into the mikes of our PRRs. It gets warm in body armour, even at night, so as one man grabbed a gulp of water, his buddy would scan the area for trouble with his nightsight as the team of four divided into two twos.

The town was quiet. People were staying off the street, even though we had lifted the curfew. As we made our way across some waste ground towards the better houses, we stopped every now and again to scan the area. We paused at the medical centre and consulted the diagram. By now we were in a maze of streets which, while they may have been familiar in daylight, remained a blur in the darkness.

Phil kept his voice low. 'I think this is it!' The house was a flat-roofed, seventies-style estate agent's nightmare with peeling wooden fascia and crumbling paintwork.

'OK, let's go,' I whispered.

We knocked. The door opened a fraction and a man peeked through the crack. When he saw me he drew it wide.

'*Salaam Aleikum,*' I greeted him, suddenly feeling self-conscious about speaking out loud.

'*Aleikum Salaam,*' he replied.

I recognised him as one of the men I had disarmed the previous night. '*Kaif Halak*[83]?' I enquired.

'*Bikhair alhamdulillah*[84].' He smiled, bidding us enter.

'Great,' I whispered to Phil. 'The first house we call at, and it's the wrong frigging one!'

We moved through the spacious hallway, past the kitchen, which was lit by a low-power bulb hanging limp and naked from the ceiling, and turned right into the living room. It was large and sparsely furnished, with a rug on the floor on which perched some of the vigilantes, who I now knew to have been protecting the Ba'athists, drinking tea. They shuffled apart and invited Phil and me to join their circle.

I slipped off my helmet and opened my body armour. Tea appeared.

'We're out on a bit of a prowl and heard you were having a bash!' I explained through Phil. They looked at one another, amazed.

'So, how does freedom feel?' I asked, settling down on one arm.

'We were just talking about it,' one of the men said. 'You've been here before, did you know that? Not you personally, but the allies.'

'When was that?' I asked.

'At the end of the last war the Americans came,' they explained. 'They camped outside town and they gave us food and gas for our cookers. They gave the children sweets. Then one morning they were gone!'

'Gone!' echoed one of his companions, dusting his hands.

---

[83] How are you?
[84] Fine, by the grace of God.

'What happened then?' I asked.

They all lowered their eyes. No one spoke. I realized I had struck a nerve.

'I mean, wasn't there a Shia rebellion here?'

'Not here,' one of the men said. 'This is mixed. I am a Christian.' He nodded at the householder. 'He is Shia.' Then he indicated the two men sitting across from me. 'And they are Sunni.'

'I am Sunni too,' Phil said.

'Egyptian!' they chorused.

This was so Irish, I thought to myself. Everyone has to establish what tribe they belong to before conversation flows (mainly to avoid a faux pas). The Gurkhas do it too. 'So, what did happen?'

'General Ali Hasan al-Majid al-Tikriti came with his men,' said one, looking fixedly at the carpet.

'Chemical Ali[85],' another said. 'It was very bad.'

'Things happened,' the first said. 'Bad things.'

The group fell silent.

'Like people disappearing at night – that sort of thing?' I prompted.

'No,' one of the Sunni said, shaking his head at my naivety. 'Not disappear, not at night.' His eyes suddenly filled with passion. 'In public – in daylight – and we all had to watch.'

'What did they do?' I winced; it was as bare a question as the one I had been asked about the Bosnian War Criminal. I changed the subject. 'Will it get hot?' That wasn't much better.

'Yes, *Aqeed*,' the Christian said. 'Very hot.'

'Much must be fixed,' the house owner said very seriously. 'Or it will be very hot in many ways.'

We finished our tea.

'We're going to pop in to see Jari,' I said. 'I think he lives nearby . . .'

'Back, back,' they all said in English, indicating the house behind this one.

'He's promised me a cup of tea.'

'Jari?' the Christian said. 'You know Jari?' He seemed surprised.

'Well, no . . .' I gave them my most menacing look, 'but I soon will.'

'God go with you!' he said, looking at me earnestly.

I put on my helmet at the door.

'*Sidi*,' the house owner said, gripping my hand. 'Look after yourself.'

---

[85] Which was what we also called him in the West.

'I will look after everyone,' I said expansively.

'No,' he said. 'Look after *yourself*.'

After more *masalaams* and much additional handshaking, we went in search of Jari and his wife Sabbah. We knew from documents in the HQ that she was employed at the school as a teacher. It was an ordinary enough house. The sentries and close cover group took up position. I stood to the left of the door and Phil to the right, both in cover. I remembered a policeman in Belfast who went to serve a summons on a terrorist who saw the outline of a peaked cap through the door and cut him in half with his AK-47.

Phil knocked and a voice asked who was there.

'*Jaish Britani*[86],' he said. '*Wen* Jari[87]?'

The door opened and a man peeked out. He was in his late forties and clean-shaven but with the standard-issue Ba'athist moustache. His expression changed from sheepish to shocked.

'Jari!' I boomed at him. 'You are Jari, of course?'

'Yes, yes,' he replied.

'We've a bit of a misunderstanding and thought you could help us,' I said. 'Can we come in?'

'Yes, come, come . . .' He opened the door wide and waved us in.

'We have a report that you're to be involved in a shooting tonight, and we need to sort this out.' Though he clearly understood English, I didn't want any misunderstandings. I asked Phil to translate.

'Not me!' he said. 'No, not me.'

'Can we have the pistol number?'

Phil glanced at his red book. 'A6032C.' He then established Jari's and his wife's credentials from the Ba'athist record.

At that moment our host looked like a man who had just met the devil. 'Sabbah!' he called.

A very large woman in a black burka and headscarf emerged from the sitting room and moved so smoothly towards us I wondered for a moment if she were on wheels. She remained expressionless. They whispered urgently to each other in Arabic and then Jari spoke to Phil.

'He says that the pistol is actually Sabbah's,' Phil said.

'What the fuck does a schoolma'am need a pistol for?' I asked. 'They're not even armed in Middlesbrough.'

---

[86] 'British Army.'
[87] 'Where's Jari?'

Phil shrugged his shoulders. 'Well, that's what he says.'

The layout of the house was identical to the one we'd just been in, but much more homely and brightly lit. They showed us into the sitting room, which boasted a three-piece suite, a coffee table, a dining table and chairs. There was also a well-stocked bookcase and a TV in the corner, in front of which sat three bare-headed young women. 'Daughters, daughters,' Jari said with a wave of his hand.

We sat down at the dining table and Sabbah left the room with one of the girls. We made small talk until they reappeared, the daughter with tea and Sabbah with a bag she handed to Phil, who passed it to me.

I opened it to find a brand new Browning Hi-Power and about fifty rounds of Belgian 'Fabrique Nationale' 9mm ammo. It was loaded, so I took out the magazine and set it on the table. I cocked it and made sure it was clear before letting off the action towards the ground with a loud click and handing it back to Phil. 'This thing is spankers,' I said. 'I'd say it's worth maybe £500 in the UK. What do these characters get paid?'

Phil asked Jari, who consulted Sabbah, then turned back to me and said, 'They say about 40,000ID a month.'

'That's about £27,' I said. 'So I'm holding a year's wages.'

'Probably more,' Phil said.

To my amazement, Sabbah placed a piece of paper with some Arabic script in front of me and took out a pen.

'She wants you to sign for it!' Phil laughed.

'Certainly.' I wrote 'Gerry Adams' with a flourish and handed the receipt back to her.

Pleased, she folded it and placed it in an ornate box on the sideboard. As we took our tea, we watched some Iraqi TV and saw 1 (UK) Division in Kuwait. I made a mental note to ask intelligence how they did that, when we had been assured that the TV relays had been bombed and the TV stations destroyed. 'Good, good – British!' Jari said. 'Very strong,' he added, crossing his fists.

'Oh yes,' I agreed.

I glanced at Sabbah, who seemed to be upbraiding him, and raised an eyebrow in Phil's direction.

'He's fucked when we leave,' Phil said, 'and not in a nice sense!'

I nodded. 'I'd say Johnny Vegas there is gonna knock the bejasus out of him when we leave, for being such a creep!'

Phil choked on his tea.

We got up to leave and as we put on our kit, I turned to Jari and waved my finger at him. 'You'd be a very silly little Ba'athist to come to my notice again, understand?'

'Yes! Er, no!' He shook his head vigorously, in a pretty passable impression of Muttley the cartoon dog.

'Who else is involved?' I asked.

He glanced across to make sure Sabbah was out of earshot. 'Ayoub Younis Nasser. Schoolteacher,' he hissed, his mouth inches from my ear. 'Dangerous!' His breath hit me like a garlic-flavoured hurley[88] bat.

The door was closed behind us with due deference.

Andrew met us in the street. 'How did you get on?'

'Piece of cake,' I said. 'He's shitting himself. We'll have no trouble from him, and he's given us Abu Nawfel.'

'*Confirmed* Abu Nawfel,' Phil said. 'They think you can read their minds.'

'Let's keep 'em guessing.' I laughed.

'What do you make of them?' Andrew asked.

'Tosser. Big fish in a small pond.'

'Not sure about her, though,' Phil said.

'Not sure? We were lucky not to get pulled up for dirty boots on her carpet. She's definitely in charge!'

I noticed some men standing nearby in a small group and we went over to talk to them.

'*Masa'alkhair*[89].'

They greeted us, but were nervous and not very forthcoming. We chatted through Phil as the patrol moved to cover us.

'Let's go,' I said, and turned to bid the men goodnight. They smiled and raised their hands in farewell, then looked around in surprise as a dozen soldiers emerged from the shadows and moved silently past them.

The next house was owned by a man we had down as Jamil, the driver. I wasn't certain of his status, but he was strongly tipped as the shooter. We took up our positions around the gate.

'It's locked,' Andrew said.

A dog began to bark.

'Shout and see if we can get them out.'

Phil called from the gate. At first there was no reply, then some youths looked out.

---

[88] Irish hockey stick.
[89] Good evening.

'Where's Jamil?' Phil asked in Arabic. The youths replied in a state of high excitement. 'They said that Jamil has gone to Basra.'

'Well, that is a pity. Tell them to open the gate.'

A woman inside began to cry and then Jamil appeared, large as life. He was a small, skinny man in a dirty white pullover, stained grey slacks and flip-flops. He was sporting a few days' growth and had a sparse, or what the men would call a 'five-a-side', moustache rather than the bushy 'Saddam specials[90]' sported by most of his fellow countrymen.

'*Ureed ma'lumat an al musaddas*[91],' I said to him, grabbing and snapping the flimsy lock on his gate with a flick of my wrist.

'*Ma fi musaddas*[92] . . .' he pleaded, backing off.

Once inside the house he had a hurried conversation with Phil. After a minute Phil turned and said, 'He wants to come clean. He has a pistol, but he swears he was not involved in a plot to murder.'

'We know he has a pistol. So it's a no-brainer to cough for that.' I turned aggressively to Jamil. 'OK, where's the gun?'

Jamil turned to the youths and told them to take Phil to the cache. With Jamil and his wife, a tiny woman in a pale blue kaftan, in front of me, I moved into the not very tidy lounge. A ranger stepped in to cover me and bar the door. A cockroach scuttled past. Mrs Jamil started to cry again.

'We could be mistaken here, but your name has been given to us as being involved in Ba'athist terrorism,' I said to Jamil in my pidgin Arabic. He perched on the edge of a sofa, chain-smoking, beside his wife.

'No, no . . .' He spoke quickly, shaking his head and touching his chest as she rocked back and forth, sobbing.

My cover man leaned over to me and whispered, 'I've never seen a more guilty bastard in my life, sir. Look at him! He's shaking like a shitting dog!'

'Do you know what Jamil means in Arabic?' I said.

Jamil looked up at the mention of his name.

'Go on, sir, amaze me!' my cover man said.

'Happy.' I beamed.

'What's the Arabic for "shitting myself"?' the ranger asked.

Jamil's wife began wailing again, and he stared in open-mouthed horror, imagining perhaps that we were discussing some horrible end for

---

[90] It seems to be an odd coincidence that most despots have facial hair.
[91] I want to know about the pistol.
[92] There is no pistol.

him. In desperation, he told me they had relatives in America and sent his wife off to get a letter with a US address. She returned clutching an airmail envelope with a Chicago postmark. I glanced at it with a blank expression and handed it back, explaining that if he did not cooperate, this would be of no help to him at all. He started to catch my drift and left the room, beckoning to Phil to follow him.

After a while, Phil reappeared with some AK-47 magazines and a Tokarev 7.69mm pistol. 'Result,' Phil said as he cleared the gun.

'You've been a very naughty boy!' I said to Jamil in my best Dinsdale Piranha voice.

He didn't look at all happy again. He obviously wasn't a Monty Python fan. I gave him a pep talk, through Phil, laced with as much menace as I could muster. He turned and nodded eagerly to me as he listened to the translation.

We left with the thanks of Jamil and his wife ringing in our ears. I turned to Phil. 'Not a bad night's work, so far. I'm ready for some tea.'

'Let's see if the schoolmaster has any,' he said, consulting his notebook.

'The bloke Jari dropped in it?'

'The very same.'

It was late – after 2300 hours – but we needed to finish this. The house was no more than 100m from the base. We fell out about half of the patrol and set off to the house. With a little difficulty we found the place, and the lead man tried the gate. It was locked, so I had a man climb in and knock on the door. After a short wait, two men emerged. Ayoub Younis Nasser (Abu Nawfel) was in his nightshirt and looked to be in his fifties. He was about 5' 10" and pretty well built. His son was a strapping lad in his early twenties. We talked in the porch light for about ten minutes and I became convinced that we had the wrong man.

'There's no way yer man here is the kingpin,' I said to Phil, Andrew and Richard.

Phil took out his book. 'I took this down from the HQ Leader Board. Abu Nawfel gets a mention as a minor official and here, below, is what the informer said.' He traced the script and read, '"Ayoub Younis Nasser – schoolmaster". And this says, "head of the youth wing – deputy head of internal security".'

'Or, as they say in the IRA, "the nutting squad".' I looked at Ayoub Younis Nasser again, and couldn't help remembering a well-known paramilitary I had encountered in Northern Ireland. He's a local councillor now, and a prospective parliamentary candidate. But back in the seventies the old hood wasn't (allegedly – he was never convicted) above removing the toes of his victims with bolt-cutters, and ironing their shirts while they were still wearing them. I thought of the DIY torture kit I'd seen in the party leader's office at Ba'ath party HQ.

I turned to the patrol. 'You and you, cover me,' I said, pointing to the men closest. 'Phil, we're going to take this blighter inside. Whatever I yell at him, yell the translation too. We'll try the angry bit.'

'Well, you're fucking good at that!' Andrew said, moving out into the street to cover us.

I drew my pistol and began shouting immediately. 'Why are you lying? I know you have guns. Give me the guns or I'll have your house ripped apart . . .' That sort of thing.

The blood drained from Abu Nawfel's face. His son began to protest loudly and made to come between us.

'Back off, sonny!' I yelled at him, my nose virtually touching his. He bounced back in shock. Lights were appearing in windows all around us. I grabbed Abu Nawfel by the front of his nightshirt and ran him backwards into the house. There were two figures just inside the door; as we plunged into the darkness of the hallway he rocked back and landed with a thump at their feet, legs flailing. I hauled him up and he began shouting 'Get the guns' in Arabic.

Phil said, 'I think he's remembered who he is. He's telling his son to get the weapons.'

'Yeah, got that,' I said.

Phil went through the kitchen door with the son. I pushed Abu Nawfel after them and he fell over again. There was a light in the kitchen and I could see that we were both covered in blood, but I had no idea where from. Some women appeared from a side room and pushed their way through and when they saw Abu Nawfel they began to scream. Abu Nawfel put his hand to his head and looked at it, seeing the blood for the first time. He began to scream too.

'Shut up,' I shouted. *'Khalas.'* The blood alarmed me as well, and I could hear shouts from outside, over the screaming. I told one of my men to shut the door and get the women into the bedroom. Abu Nawfel was crawling about screaming and I was yelling at him to sit down. I then told him to shut up again and cocked my pistol. He covered his face and the screams grew louder. I looked around and saw a soft surface under the sink. I aimed my pistol, eased the safety off and fired once. Then there was silence.

I dragged Abu Nawfel to his feet and pushed him outside.

The cover team looked thunderstruck. Andrew asked what was happening.

'Don't ask,' I said. 'It's all gone pear-shaped.'

'We thought you'd topped him!' Andrew said. Then, looking at the schoolmaster's bloodied face, added, 'You haven't, have you?'

'Of course not. He just tripped over in the hall.'

With me trying to get him to kneel, holding him by the scruff of the neck, and him spinning around, I tried to trip him with my foot until he was put – pretty firmly – into the approved kneeling position[93] and glanced nervously at me as I went inside again.

Phil shouted from the garden, 'I think we have a result – is everything OK?'

'He's still alive, if that's what you mean.'

Ranger Malcolmson emerged from the bedroom. 'You'd better come and take a look at this,' he said. He held up a plastic shopping bag.

'What's in it?' I asked.

'Hundreds of thousands of Iraqi dinar,' young Malcolmson said. 'I think they must have won the lottery.'

'Take it outside,' I told him. I didn't bother to look in the bag.

Outside, Abu Nawfel caught sight of the bag and toppled over. I hooked him up with my hand. 'Why couldn't you just cooperate?' I shouted.

Andrew pointed behind me. 'Sir – look . . .' I turned to see young Magoo carrying a large white sack. I took it from him and emptied it out in front of a now weeping Abu Nawfel. Two rifles and a selection of bayonets clattered to the ground.

'So, if you're just the schoolmaster, what the fuck are these?' I asked. Phil appeared at my shoulder and translated.

Magoo ejected a cartridge from one of the rifles – a Soviet SKS 7.62mm with a folding bayonet. 'They're made ready, boss.'

The prisoner squirmed away, sobbing, '*Sorry, sorry.*'

'You will be.' I pulled him to his feet. 'Lift the son as well.'

We set out in procession for the Ba'ath party HQ, curtains twitching as we went. I sent a runner ahead to get a medic.

I could hear Abu Nawfel crying '*Lah, lah*[94],' as he was led towards the office. I can just imagine what he was thinking. I didn't have much

---

[93] Hands on head where we can see them, kneeling with one foot over the other so he needs assistance to get up and can't leap to his feet and run off.

[94] No, no.

trouble guessing what he and his playmates got up to in there; you only had to catch a glimpse of the hooks in the ceiling or the knuckle-dusters and handcuffs I had found in the head of the local Ba'athists' desk.

I left this little procession and turned towards the school. Inside I called the Commander on the secure radio.

'Things aren't looking brilliant out there,' he said. 'It appears the two British servicemen who were captured the other night have been murdered. The Americans are getting it pretty bad around An Nasiriyah and Basra is a cauldron.'

'I heard about the thirteen-year-old girl in Safwan.'

'Yeah, I heard about that too.' He paused. 'So, do you think you've got this sewn up?'

'They're disrupted, but only time will tell if we can get them to cooperate,' I said.

'Be careful with the old boy. I don't want him dying on us.'

'Nor do I,' I said. 'He's with the medics now.'

I went over to the Ba'ath party HQ and had Abu Nawfel brought to a bare civil affairs interview room, with a desk and three chairs, and the 'Leader Board' propped against the wall.

Abu Nawfel was freshly washed and sipping from a bottle of water. I showed him his name on the board. 'Do you think we are stupid?'

He wobbled his head obsequiously, but with a great deal more composure than he'd managed at the house.

'You realise that none of this would have happened if you'd just cooperated like everyone else?'

He touched his head. 'With this, I can be very cooperative,' he said. 'The blood – the shot – I can now go to my people and say "cooperate or we are all done for". You see, before you acted as if you deserved respect. Here in Iraq respect has to be earned. I was injured resisting. I now have respect. Now *you have respect*. We can work together now!'

I shook my head in amazement as this was translated. Could this be the same man who was wailing just an hour ago? Well, it seemed Abu Nawfel and I were big mates now.

Finally the medic arrived. I told him to start straight away. He showed me the cut; it was small but there was a great deal of blood. I asked the medic about this and he said the scalp was very 'vascular' and this was usual. I asked if he needed stitches and he said he could do two but because it was a blunt injury it was arrow-shaped, so he recommended three. I left the medic stitching Abu Nawfel and went back to the Main HQ at the school to read the reports from my deployed companies.

As well as intermittent firefights with enemy patrols, L Company had been getting artillery fire from across the Hammar Bridge on the 'Loyalty to the Leader' Canal and there had been a sharp firefight between the Gurkhas and a large group of Iraqi Army across the canal. No one had been hit and no hits were claimed. In the distance I could hear the rumble of heavy artillery.

'That's some poor bastard off to the moon fer their holidays, so it is!' mused Brian, one of the officers commissioned from the ranks and that evening's watchkeeper, in his broad Ballymoney accent. He didn't look up but continued to fill in the logbook that would record the history of that night by the light of a lantern and the glow of the lights on the radio sets. It awakened me to the reality that we all lived with. While Brian's two brothers had long since left the battalion I knew he had friends and relatives from his native County Antrim fighting. I knew that his thoughts were out there in the darkness of the battlefield, praying that they would all see the dawn.

He suddenly looked up, smiling eyebrows raised, his face gaunt in the mean light of the ops room. 'Cuppa tea, sir?' Then before I could answer he said over his shoulder, 'Youngster, get the CO and mesel' a cuppa tea there.' As he continued writing, I sat in silence while the radio hummed and the distant rumble continued to our north. Soon, a signaller brought some tea, scalding hot and welcome against the evening chill.

I had just settled down to drink my brew when a message reached me that Abu Nawfel was being very helpful indeed. He wanted to cut a deal: if we released him to his family he would get all the weapons in the village handed in and he would produce a list of all the Al Quds members and Fedayeen. I sent a message back saying that we would release his son and then if *he* got the weapons Abu Nawfel could go the next day. The runner returned with a note to say that Abu Nawfel had made it clear that his son had no authority to collect any weapons and that he alone in the village possessed the authority to gather in *any* equipment. 'What the hell!' I thought. I agreed to his release.

The Adjutant came to tell me that the money found in Abu Nawfel's bedroom came to 375,000ID (£200). The average wage was £3 per week so this was big bucks in Iraqi terms. Abu Nawfel at first said that it was his life savings. He then changed the story to claim it was for school salaries. I noted that 375,000ID split three ways is 125,000ID – the going rate for a hit in Iraq at the time. We had been reliably informed that the hit squad was to have been three strong. I do not know to this day if the three we visited were to have pulled the trigger – but I suspect not. They were the paramilitary commanders and the shooters would probably have been others detailed by them. But with these three under arrest or suffering from explosive diarrhoea, there would be no shootings – not that night anyway.

I went across to the old Ba'athist HQ to go to bed. As I undressed I said to Phil Ballard, 'Tomorrow we need to make some sense of all of this. I want some answers off these people. Either they're with us or against us. Start with that toerag Jari. Make it clear that if I don't feel a whole lot better about this by tomorrow evening I'm sending him to jail!'

As I climbed into my sleeping bag I glanced at my watch, 0215 hours. I fell into an exhausted sleep.

Abu Nawfel was as good as his word. He turned up the next day full of smiles with a list of serial numbers and Fedayeen members. 'How many weapons does he think he can get?' I asked.

Phil looked at his list. 'About 150.'

My jaw dropped. 'Well, that's what I was expecting,' I lied. That evening our haul of arms passed the 130 mark, including brand-new weapons and rocket-propelled grenades manufactured in Russia – not the crap that littered the battlefield. I spoke to Abu Nawfel outside the Ba'ath party HQ as we packed to leave to our new HQ just outside town and thanked him.

'Now, you will get the school open for me by Monday morning, OK? We will leave here, but we will not be far away.' As this was translated he was all smiles and nodding – until the 'leave here' bit. He reacted with horror and began babbling to Phil. 'What's he saying?' I asked.

'He wants to know who will protect him now. He says he is in great danger and you must stay to keep him safe.'

'Tell him I will always be there, even if he can't see me[95], and sweeten it with the fact that I've told the CIMIC to use the money from the hit for the school.' I then asked him to paint out all the slogans at the school. He readily agreed but then said he was unable to paint over the ones on the outside of the school. I wondered why, but as it was getting on – after 1800 hours – I said I had to go.

I hopped into the Comms Camel and set off, with a rather worried-looking Abu Nawfel staring after us and waving limply. He was a sight.

---

[95] This was a tactic that I was to employ successfully in Rumaylah and Al Amarah. Not only did they fear I was around every corner, they also thought I knew everything – and I wanted to keep it that way.

Here was a man whose house I had raided the night before waving at me with tears in his eyes as I drove away the very next day. He also struck quite a dash now in his western-style suit and a bandage that covered the whole of his head like a rather camp turban.

# —1 2—

# TARGET FOR MURDER

The Battalion HQ moved out of the village to a large chemical-processing plant just outside the town of Al Rumaylah and occupied the offices of the oil company, from where we had launched the night patrol on the first night. It was a series of low sand-coloured buildings in reasonable condition. It could only have been ten or fifteen years old. It covered an area of around 500m square and was surrounded by a sturdy fence. The RSM set up in the fire station. He established a POW holding cage behind this and this is where any Ba'athists arrested would be brought, searched and documented before being collected by staff from the Divisional cage. This facility was operated by the defence platoon, supervised by members of the Military Provost staff from Colchester – effectively the Army's prison service. It was a fenced area about 10m by 10m. It had a roof, and therefore some shelter, but it was illuminated at night and the guards could see the prisoners at all times.

The site itself was a tangle of pipes and storage tanks dominated by a fifty-metre-high structure, which had a series of gantries and a ladder up the side. The gantries were large enough for a few men, and our Para gunners struck on the brilliant idea of setting up an observation post on the top gantry. It turned out to be quite a vantage point, and we were able to use radar and high-power viewing devices to look, unseen, right into the village and keep a watch twenty-four hours a day.

My room was an old office with plastic sheeting for a window. It had a couple of chairs and a large table. A swivel chair had miraculously survived the looting and was wheeled into my office by one of my signals corporals, Stevo, who was delighted with his find. I spent many long hours in this during the campaign, chairing planning sessions or visits. My camp bed, a box of small luxuries such as real coffee and some maps on the wall completed the room. The only picture was a list of ten top tips from Saddam Hussein, but written in ornate script like a passage from the Qur'an. Such arrogance!

The operations complex was set up in the plant control room. This was like the control room of a power station, complete with *Starship Enterprise*-style desks and chairs facing a now-defunct control panel with a massive diagram of the plant marked out in coloured lights. We overlaid these with maps of the region, signallers rigged antennas and before long we had a first-class set-up established, which was coordinated by Andrew. At night we would hold 'prayers', as we called our evening debrief. This would begin with the intelligence staff and be followed by the operations staff with an update of the battle. The QM would give points on logistics and I would hold forth on something or other. We would then have a look forward to the next activities and have a time check from the gunners. On some occasions we would allow the media to be present if something of interest had happened. They couldn't be briefed in advance about any planned operations, for their security as well as the nation's. We were also joined by a field Human Intelligence section, who set up in an old chemistry laboratory. We left them to their own devices and I have no idea what went on in there. What I can say is that no one got hurt and they came up with some timely and extremely accurate information – some of which saved lives.

Proper washing facilities were scarce but we were fortunate to have a number of fire hydrants. One was used for washing clothes and one – with particularly high pressure – acted as a shower. We were not bashful and we would strip off and stand in front of the water as it blasted us clean. In the heat of the day it was extremely refreshing. There were other showers that we constructed for the more modest but they weren't half as good.

Commerce was difficult for the locals. They were paid in Iraqi dinar and most had a considerable supply of these. The problem was that there were no markets to spend them in and in some circles of the coalition forces there was a determination to stamp this currency out. It had Saddam's face on it after all. When I asked what would replace it the answer came back – 'Why, dollars, of course.' The problem was that the daily wage, which everyone was happy with, was 1800ID. That was the equivalent of 69 US cents. Anyone got change of a dollar? There was a delicate relationship in this area between supply of labour, receipt of remuneration and market prices. This balance had survived the Iran–Iraq War and the First Gulf War. My vote was to shut up and listen to the locals. What did they want – what did they need? But we were drowned out by shouts from the rear echelon: use US dollars – triple the wages! I knew this well-meaning ignorance was laying the foundations for trouble in the future. I regarded it as my job to insulate these people from the friction for as long as possible.

We were eventually able to get a float in Iraqi dinar issued by the Division and it was my aim to get commerce going again as soon as possible. Although we had captured millions of dinar on the battlefield, they had been sent to Division to be incinerated. The blood money for the hit was an exception. We said nothing about it to Division. It was put towards re-opening the school, which had been closed by the Ba'athists two weeks before the war for use as an ammo compound. I was certain that the people I cared for in Al Rumaylah needed a school more than anything else. It was worth the risk to defy the bureaucrats and get the children back learning and off the streets.

I realised that most Iraqis had a bundle of dinar and an AK-47 under their beds. I was also well aware that rifles played an important part in their culture and knew that it would be naive in the extreme to expect them simply to hand them over when ordered. On the other hand we could show them a different way, by giving them an outlet for the dinar and building a sense of security and partnership that would render the rifles redundant. To this end I coopted some of the locals to join me in a 'think tank', where we discussed what had happened and our hopes for the future.

I also continued my policy of walkabouts in the villages. What often struck me during these visits were the children. Often when we appeared they would dash indoors and then emerge dressed in western clothing, as if to be associated with us. It was sweet to see. Little girls in Sunday dresses, boys in T-shirts and jeans. One little chap of about eight would always hold my hand. He was missing his front teeth and wore a T shirt with the motif 'Pretty girl' and some coloured ladybirds on it and sky-blue tracksuit bottoms. A little innocent who would no doubt have died with embarrassment had he known what the shirt said. Long after we left, a collection was organised in Canterbury among the Royal Irish families for these people. I hoped that my soldiers absorbed and understood why we had to refrain from constantly giving out treats and they seemed to be compliant, or so I thought – but the amount of discarded British Army chocolate wrappers and boiled sweet papers told a different story. Irish soldiers are sentimental beasts at heart. So long as it was done with due respect and discreetly, I would turn a blind eye.

I recall chatting to one father as he was presenting his sons. I placed my hand on the head of his eldest (who was wearing a set of oversized and obviously looted oil company overalls and boots) and said, 'I have one about this age – eleven or so?'

'No,' he said, 'sixteen!' I looked in horror.

'It's the malnutrition,' whispered the doctor who was with me.

It was hard to come face to face with the result of sanctions, but we also had some happy moments. A man, clearly beside himself with worry, once approached me with a blood test result written in English. It meant little to me as I read it. He was holding the hand of the most beautiful little girl of about five years old. He indicated her and pointed to the note. I beckoned him to follow me and I sought out the MO. She read the note, turned it over, studied it and shrugged her shoulders.

'What?' I asked.

'Normal,' she said. 'That's what it says – it's fine!'

For a moment I was choked as I tried to explain in my poor Arabic that everything was all right. But he just stared at me, half in study of my face and half in dread. I had to take him to find an interpreter. Suddenly his face erupted in glee and he hugged me close then lifted the girl for me to hold. What I learned from this was that the Iraqi medical services were in fact as good as you would find anywhere and the drugs they prescribed were the same ones as my doctor would have prescribed in the NHS.

I visited the home of the man who had been pulling at my clothing the first day in Al Rumaylah, wanting to find his daughter. He described how she had been tending the fire to boil some water for drinking when her dishdash had caught fire. It had spread to her hair and she'd been badly burned. This happened the morning of the assault on the town and so he took her to some US forces nearby. The last he had seen was her being flown away in a helicopter with a drip in her arm. He gave us some photographs and her ID card. I promised to find her. This became a cause célèbre as the order went out: 'Find her!' The difficulty was that there were quite a few injured children in the system and she had gone onto the helicopter with no ID. She couldn't speak English and with her accent it might be hard for a non-Iraqi to get her name accurately. In any case, there was a good chance that a little girl as ill as that would be sent to the big medical ship sitting in the Arabian Gulf or even to the States.

We had seen the result of the fighting on the children. I'm sure that there were some injured by allied action but I didn't see any. 1 Para did come across a little brother and sister who had been in bed at home when the cowardly Ba'athists fled Ad Dayr. As they left, they shot up their own town, having a crack at their rival Shia neighbours. One of these heroes fired an RPG which passed through the bed the children were sleeping in, cutting off their feet.

I saw the father of the burned girl on many occasions and he often came to see me with little gifts and to hold my hand between his and thank me as I explained the latest twists and turns of the search.

The briefing I received at Brigade on the night of 30 March 2003 was heavy with pessimism about the potential for insurgency in Iraq and the activities of the Fedayeen. We were told of several incidents where Fedayeen had displayed white flags and then attacked those who came forward to take the surrender. In one incident near An Nasiriyah nine Marines had died in one of these ambushes. We were also warned of cheese wire being strung across road to decapitate drivers of armoured vehicles. There was, we were constantly warned, no front and no back to this war. Vehicles were to travel in a minimum convoy of two vehicles, each with a minimum of two crew. Prisoners were to be approached with caution and we were urged to take the utmost care in planning travel and providing route protection. While we had dealt with our threatened insurrection in Al Rumaylah it was feared there was much more planned and we had to brace ourselves for attacks. The final message was that the conflict was now event-driven and not time-driven. We should, the Brigade Commander warned us, prepare for the long haul mentally and physically.

It was clear that with our move against Abu Nawfel and his followers we had struck a major blow against organised resistance. But were they finished? It was hard to tell and for evidence we had to depend on the locals. Proof of sinister elements was not long in coming. One local who I did not know at all, but who was a true friend, was a person or persons known as 'Kingfisher'. Kingfisher would contact us by passing notes to the regular patrols we sent through the town. His information was passed in a manner that spoke volumes for the oppression of the preceding years: tiny notes screwed into tight tubes, meant to look like the innocent gift of a cigarette, with details written in fine, closely packed Arabic script.

On the Saturday Kingfisher warned us that I had become the main target of the resistance and said that an individual called Tariq was behind these moves and was bringing pressure on a number of people to get close to me and set me up. Tariq was one of the names we had come across at the Ba'ath party HQ, and the note explained that he had now returned from Basra, where he had fled initially with some other Ba'athists. One of these was named as Abu Bashir. I called the company commanders together and briefed them. I wanted Tariq and Abu Bashir arrested as soon as possible. It was a race against time. If their influence was re-established then we could potentially face an insurgency which would cost many lives and which we might not win.

Patrols went into the town but there was no sign of this Tariq and the men reported that the locals looked genuinely frightened when they mentioned his name. However, Abu Bashir was tracked down and arrested. I had him brought to my office to take tea with him. Abu Bashir was a tall man in his fifties, with a high forehead and a thick mop of white hair. His bushy white moustache was combed upwards, giving him the look of an Edwardian colonel. He spoke good English and would talk in the animated way of a storyteller when in his stride, gesturing with his hands and fingers. He explained that he had family in Basra and that he had many pressures on him. He explained that he was a 'Saddam' poster artist and a civil and gas engineer.

By the end of the interview, I liked the man but didn't believe a word he said. He was very convincing, I must admit, but somehow too good to be true and too sharp and streetwise to be a simple poster artist. In any case I had him released. All I asked was that he went to Basra and told his bosses that I would like to meet. He smiled at this and explained that he thought that my wish would be granted very soon as his bosses were actively after me. As it turned out, when released he did not return to Basra, opting instead to remain at my side as an adviser. In a short time he was to become a close friend. I later reflected that of the many people and politicians I had met over many years across the world, Abu Bashir stood out. He was a shrewd politician for sure, yet, unlike many politicians, I later discovered that he never once, despite my initial misgivings, told me a lie. He avoided questions all the time, and constantly changed the subject, but he never lied. One often hears it said of people that they are honourable and trustworthy, but I can point to Abu Bashir and say that he was a true man of his word.

Abu Bashir eventually went home to Basra for a few days once things had settled down to see his family and life continued in the village, yet there was still a menacing atmosphere. The school was due to open on the Monday morning and I drove into town on the Saturday to see how things were progressing. There was an air of excitement and the whole community was joining in to get the place ready. There was a great sorting of books and equipment and the inside was being painted and the Saddam slogans had all gone – but from the inside only which was strange.

I returned to the GOSP and received a call from OC A Company. 'We've had another contact from Kingfisher,' he explained. 'We need Phil down here to read the note.'

Phil left immediately. The note, I was later briefed, contained a tip-off that Tariq was definitely in the town and that there was something planned for that night. It claimed that Jamil had been involved in targeting our patrols as they moved through the town and it explained that he had built up a careful record of our movements. He had noted in particular that the entry point to Al Rumaylah was particularly vulnerable. I had ordered a checkpoint to be constructed there, both to control access and to slow down vehicles entering the village, because I feared that a child would be knocked down as a result of all the speeding that went on. It also happened to be right outside Jamil's house.

A Company went onto a higher state of alert but overtly nothing changed. We didn't want to startle the locals or warn Tariq that we were planning an arrest. Then, as light fell, A Company mounted a snatch operation. Moving directly to the addresses we had been given by Kingfisher, troops sealed off the area and arrest teams went into the houses. A total of five suspects were arrested, including Jamil again. They recovered 3,375,000ID and two assault rifles from his house. When questioned, Jamil explained that it was his savings – and he swore he knew nothing about the guns. A receipt was written for the money and when Jamil's wife was handed the receipt she insisted there was 4,000,000ID. The money was counted for a second time. Still finding 3,375,000ID, the sergeant in charge grabbed Jamil by the scruff to march him out, with Jamil's wife still complaining loudly about the missing money.

Turning to Phil, the sergeant said, 'There's definitely 3,375,000. Ask her if there's a bookies in town – I suspect this little bollocks could tell her where the rest went.'

A Tokarev and a pistol were captured in one house, and it was reported that there was another pistol in Tariq's house. Tariq himself had disappeared again, unfortunately, but when challenged by a squad from A Company, Tariq's wife had pushed her hand into a large bowl of flour and drawn out the pistol.

The first I knew of all this was when the vehicle convoy arrived at our POW cage and I saw prisoners being unloaded. I asked if I was right in thinking that Jamil had been arrested again. The RSM confirmed this but told me that we had failed to get Tariq. I ordered Jamil to be taken for immediate interrogation by the Field Human Intelligence team. The RSM explained that he would go just as soon as he had been cleaned up. (Jamil had literally crapped himself when he was arrested.) The RSM wondered out loud what had possessed Jamil to become involved once again.

'Jamil is what the Superintendent in Dungannon, Davy Pickering, would call a cushion. He bears the imprint of the last person to sit on him,' I concluded.

I went back to my makeshift office. That was not good, I thought. I contemplated what the Commander had said about there being no front or back to this war. It was clear that in the areas where the Iraqi Army had surrendered people like Tariq *were* the war. We needed to get him or this town would soon become pretty dangerous. We did manage to get some photographs from his house. One was a snap of him as a younger man for a Ba'athist publication. Others were him with his family and one showed him in uniform in a large trench with three or four other men. The Iran–Iraq War, I guessed. I studied his face. He looked strangely familiar.

By 2300 hours I was sitting in my room writing a letter home when Phil appeared.

'We've had another note from Kingfisher. He says Tariq is still at home.'

'Bollocks, I knew we should have turned the place over,' I said, looking up. 'Get him, wreck the place if you have to, *but get that bastard.*'

Within the hour the convoy was back and I looked out to see a figure being led into the fire station blindfolded. A runner arrived to inform me that we had him. I put on my jacket and walked across to the fire station. As I took my seat the RSM warned me that Tariq was a cool bastard and had already apparently regained his composure. Tariq was brought in and his blindfold was removed. He was a well-built man with little spare on him. He was in his late forties and had a greying moustache. Standing in front of me he looked relaxed, although his eyes were still getting used to the light of the room, lit by lanterns. I still couldn't place him.

'Are you Tariq the murderer?' I asked.

He shrugged his shoulders. He was to do this several times during the interview and I realised his English was good as he didn't wait for Phil to translate. I quizzed him about the proposed hit that had been reported. He claimed to know nothing.

'Why have we had such a hard time tracking you down?' I asked.

He listened carefully as this was translated and then replied with a shrug. I suddenly realised that he was using a well-known anti-interrogation trick. Take your time, however you can, to answer questions, so that you'll have a chance to think about your answer. (The famous British traitor Kim Philby affected a stutter during his interrogation by MI5 for this very purpose.) He was taking full advantage of the translation in order to get time to think. When he could get away with a gesture he would do so. Then he suddenly volunteered in Arabic, 'But we've met before.'

'Where?' I asked.

'The first night you came to town. In the town square. You were showing off your nightsight.'

It struck me like a flash of light. He was the man with the Romanian AK. Yes, he was that cocky bastard, all right. The talk continued for a while. I could see that he was too skilled to reveal anything to me and I had no interest in building a rapport with this creature. I explained to him that he was off to jail now. They would find out what he knew there.

'But I'm an innocent man,' he claimed in Arabic, addressing Phil.

'Look at me,' I shouted and he turned, almost casually. Once again I told him solemnly that he would go to jail and that when the Iraqi people were ready we would give him to them. 'You can lie to me all you want, Tariq,' I explained through Phil, 'but they saw you doing your crimes.' His face fell. 'They will decide your fate. I expect they'll hang you for what you've done.'

For the first time he looked worried. He was immediately blindfolded and frogmarched off to the cage. As the door closed behind him there was a silence in the room. I looked up at the RSM and Adjutant. I was very glad that we'd got that man out of circulation. He was trouble. It dawned on me that there must be many like Tariq throughout Iraq.

They clearly had a sophisticated plan and were prepared to wait to attack the invaders once we were well spread throughout the country. Could we ever find them all, I wondered. How could we know who they were? It was clear that we could do neither without the help of the Iraqi people. I realised that all the success I had enjoyed in the area so far – opening the school, putting out the fires, arresting the suspects and so on – had been done with the compliance if not direct support of the Iraqi people. We had done little on our own, in fact. More than ever, it was clear to me that the way forward was in partnership with the people of Iraq.

The next day, Sunday, the vicar held communion and I silently gave thanks for the delivery of Tariq into my hands. I sauntered around to the cage to see him but he had already been moved on to the Divisional POW cage as a high-value prisoner. The day brought further challenges. Two busloads of refugees heading into the town were stopped. All claimed to have relatives in Al Rumaylah. I knew that to allow them to stay would have brought them into competition with the locals for resources and that it would have become a point of friction. I had them sent away. We had enough to deal with. Like any war zone the issue of displaced persons was to become increasingly significant.

On Monday morning, I went down to the school and to my amazement there was new paint on the walls, obliterating the Saddam slogans. Men and youths were still painting as I walked in, an obsequious Abu Nawfel bowing and scraping before me and proudly showing off their work. It was now apparent that the spectre of Tariq had been behind the reluctance to cooperate. With him gone, it was as if clouds had parted to let sunlight through.

Several teachers stood in front of blackboards, writing in chalk and questioning eager children, with a forest of small arms shooting up in response to questions. As I passed they would glance out and continue with a barely concealed smile of pride as they once more brought learning to the future generations. In their enthusiasm I could see the ray of hope that would build the new Iraq.

I wandered into the marketplace, which was now busy once again. As I stood there, pleased with the progress, Abu Bashir appeared and asked permission to carry out a survey of the storage facilities to check gas pressure.

'Please,' I said, 'don't ask in future, just go.'

'I always prefer to ask,' he said with a smile as he set off. The incident reminded me we still had a long way to go and a lot to learn about Iraq. But the people had been so badly abused they would need careful handling if their self-confidence was to be restored.

# —13—

# OPERATION FURY

Tuesday 1 April 2003 brought heavy clashes up beyond the Hammar Bridge, and tragedy. One of our Scimitar reconnaissance vehicles manned by men of the Household Cavalry Regiment overturned and an officer, Alex Tweedie, was seriously injured. He later died. This came as a shock. It was the second disaster to hit the HCR in a matter of days.

On 28 March, the night after the incident in the town and Biastre's dismissal, the Household Cavalry Regiment had been caught in a Blue-on-Blue incident, when one of their Scimitar reconnaissance vehicles – small, tracked armoured cars – had been attacked by a US aircraft as it probed the area forward of the Hammar Bridge. It was during this engagement that a young eighteen-year-old, Trooper Chris Finney from the HCR, was to win a George Cross, the highest decoration available for gallantry not in contact with the enemy that Britain has to confer. I had only seen Finney when we shared a camp in Kuwait prior to the construction of Fort Blair Mayne. The HCR were to lose two NCOs, Lance Corporal of Horse Matty Hull and Lance Corporal Karl Shearer, in this incident. His citation for the George Cross reads in full:

On 28 March 2003, D Squadron Household Cavalry Regiment were probing forward along the Shatt al Arab waterway, north of Basra, some thirty kilometres ahead of the main force of 16 Air Assault Brigade. In exposed desert, their mission was to find and interdict the numerically vastly superior, and better equipped, Iraqi 6th Armoured Division.

Trooper Finney, a young armoured vehicle driver with less than a year's service, was driving the leading Scimitar vehicle of his troop, which had been at the forefront of action against enemy armour for several hours. In the early afternoon, the two leading vehicles paused beside a levee to allow the troop leader to assess fully the situation in front. Without warning, they were engaged by a pair of Coalition Forces ground attack aircraft. Both vehicles were hit and caught fire, and ammunition began exploding inside the turrets. Trooper Finney managed to get out of his driving position and was on the way towards cover when he noticed that his vehicle's gunner was trapped in the turret. He then climbed onto the fiercely burning vehicle, at the same time placing himself at risk from enemy fire, as well as fire from the aircraft should they return. Despite the smoke and flames and exploding ammunition, he managed to haul out the injured gunner, get him off the vehicle, and move him to a safer position not far away, where he bandaged his wounds.

The troop officer, in the other Scimitar, had been wounded and there were no senior ranks to take control. Despite his relative inexperience, the shock of the attack and the all-too-obvious risk to himself, Trooper Finney recognised the need to inform his headquarters of the situation. He therefore broke cover, returned to his vehicle which was still burning, and calmly and concisely sent a lucid situation report by radio. He then returned to the injured gunner and began helping him towards a Spartan vehicle of the Royal Engineers which had moved forward to assist.

At this point, Trooper Finney noticed that both the aircraft were lining up for a second attack. Notwithstanding the impending danger, he continued to help his injured comrade towards the safety of the Spartan vehicle. Both aircraft fired their cannon and Trooper Finney was wounded in the buttocks and legs, and the gunner in the head. Despite his wounds, Trooper Finney succeeded in getting the gunner to the waiting Spartan. Then, seeing that the driver of the second Scimitar was still in the burning vehicle, Trooper Finney determined to rescue him as well. Despite his wounds and the continuing danger from exploding ammunition, he valiantly attempted to climb up onto the vehicle, but was beaten back by the combination of heat, smoke and exploding ammunition. He collapsed exhausted a short distance from the vehicle, and was recovered by the crew of the Royal Engineers' Spartan.

During these attacks and their horrifying aftermath, Trooper

Finney displayed clear-headed courage and devotion to his comrades which was out of all proportion to his age and experience. Acting with complete disregard for his own safety even when wounded, his bravery was of the highest order throughout.

On Wednesday 2 April, we were visited by Major General Robin Brims, the General Officer Commanding 1 (UK) Armoured Division. It was the first we had seen of him since St Patrick's Day and he was in high spirits. I brought him up to speed on our progress and gave him a blow-by-blow account of the arrests of Abu Nawfel and Tariq. I then briefed him on our positions in the north facing the Iraqis. Afterwards we drove together into town and visited the Ba'ath HQ, where I had the CIMIC teams give him an update. We talked for a while of the town and Iraq in general. I explained to him how we had developed a good rapport with the townsfolk but expressed my concern at the long road ahead. I illustrated this with a book from the school. It was an English language reader and what was fascinating was that after the usual stuff on British life – cinema tickets, sport and trains and so on – each section ended with an Iraqi or Arabic historical story – 'Saladin', 'The Tale of the Iraqi Army', 'Tales of the Palestinian Uprising' or 'The Story of Nebuchadnezzar II' – that concluded with a comparison to Saddam Hussein.

'I think we have a mountain to climb,' I explained. 'For many, Saddam is the embodiment of their history, culture and here,' I said, indicating the book, 'language. If we cannot break, I mean lead them away from, the mindset carefully put in place over the last twenty-five years, we will fail to win the peace.'

'What do you need from me?' he asked.

I explained about the market – deserted when we arrived and now bustling – and the money. 'But the most important thing is that the eighteen-year-olds must sit the baccalaureate exams this summer. If we fail in this there'll be a generation cast adrift, and who can answer for their actions? We've seen it in Ireland. The youngsters are better off in school than on the streets.'

He left with a copy of the book. He was as good as his word and the process of sorting out the exams for the summer was set in motion.

I wasn't to know it but my time in Rumaylah was running out. As I arrived at Brigade HQ for a briefing the following day, the Brigade Commander spotted me and took me to one side. He told me that orders had come down for a strike against the Iraqi 6th Division and that

1 R Irish with 1 Para were in the frame. We chatted for a while then headed into the briefing room.

The Brigade Chief of Staff explained the current position to the commanders of the battle groups as we sat aound a large map. It was the task of the commander of 1 (UK) Division to get ready to deal with any attempt by the enemy to withdraw in good order from the city. His deployment was as follows: 7 Brigade was poised south-west of Basra and 3 Commando Brigade had fought its way to the outskirts of the town from the south-east, capturing some senior Iraqi officers. 16 Air Assault Brigade were now poised to cut off Basra from north-west and the rest of Iraq. 3 Para had crossed the Hammar Bridge, guns blazing, in a night-time raid some days earlier and the Iraqis had fallen back towards the towns that lined the Shatt al Arab and the north–south highway. The road to the north of Basra towards Baghdad was dominated by the town of Ad Dayr and even further north the crossings of the Euphrates and the only intact bridges towards Baghdad were commanded by the town of Al Qurnah. It looked from satellite photography as if the main position of the 6th Division was south of the river guarding this crossing. 1 Para was to strike east and destroy the enemy in Ad Dayr to set the conditions for an attack by the 1 R Irish battle group into the middle of the 6th Division. It is not as crazy as it sounds. The 6th Division had already received a pounding from the coalition air forces and was being fixed by the recce screen of 16 Air Assault Brigade. We would move to split the enemy and exploit as far as we could to shatter any resistance.

I studied the maps and air photographs in the makeshift intelligence cell at Brigade HQ, and took some material away to brief my own team. It was in some respects a relief to be getting ready to fight an enemy you could see, even if it was the remains of a division. In any case it was an Irish battle group and 1 Para up against an Iraqi division – two British battalions versus potentially nine Iraqi battalions, so they were well outnumbered, by my reckoning – and we had surprise on our side.

I ordered the companies to begin to train at an abandoned Iraqi Army barracks outside the town. We planned to perfect our house-to-house fighting there and to test our weapon systems against the buildings, which were typical of the region. We found that the 5.56mm rounds had little effect, nor did the Iraqi 7.62mm (short), fired from their AK-47s. However, the 7.62mm from our GPMGs ate their way straight through the buildings, and the .5 inch heavy machine guns punched fist-sized holes through the walls. A burst of five to seven rounds could blast a hole big enough for a man to climb through. Our anti-tank weapons were of less effect than we expected, roasting the interior of the rooms but leaving only a small hole. We elected to keep these for use against any armour. The star of the show, however, was the new grenade, which had only been on issue since the previous summer[96]. It absolutely trashed the inside of any room it was put into. I directed the men to use them where possible with white phosphorus, as the noxious smoke and heat had the effect of drawing out any enemy from cover, while the fragmentation grenade would shred them. We also constructed wall charges, which would be placed against a house to blast a hole, allowing the troops to then fight through into the building. I attended as much of this training as I could to ensure it was being conducted both safely and also up to the limit. I fully expected to be engaged in close fighting soon and the men had to react automatically to any situation they found themselves in.

On return to my own HQ I had a planning session with the Battery Commander, Engineer Squadron Commander, Operations Officer and Adjutant. The RSM popped in to listen. The trick I needed to achieve was to make 1 R Irish as combat-effective as possible, with as many shooters as feasible, yet still maintaining an effective logistics tail. A rough idea of what was needed was hammered out and we looked at our resources. Because of our recent success in recruiting, 1 R Irish had been able to field four rifle companies, including the Gurkhas in D Company, as well as a mobile manoeuvre company, L Company, based on the machine gun and mobile antitank platoons, who were all Land-Rover mounted. The addition of recce cars from the HCR released my recce platoon to L Company. This gave us a mobile and pretty potent strike force of twenty-eight WMIKs, mounting a variety of .5 heavy machine guns, Milan and Gimpys. At the suggestion of the Engineer OC, I added some engineers to my defence platoon (these would normally guard the HQ) and extra watchkeepers and the like to form a third platoon, to give us yet another company known as M Company or the 'Militia'. They would be led by the Adjutant, David Middleton. This gave us a fifth rifle company – with L Company, a total of six manoeuvre groups – but only for a limited time. The men who made up M Company had day jobs. The recce troop from the HCR, which would come with their squadron HQ, led by Richard Taylor, a tall, languid cavalry officer who went under the sobriquet of 'Lettuce' (but would go on to win the Distinguished Service Order, one of the UK's highest decorations for gallantry and leadership for his actions; he has since become known as 'Rocket' – a crisper

---

[96] Like the one that had injured one of our men in Canada.

227

lettuce), gave us some armour and more thermal sights. With a troop of Engineer recce and the guns the battle group would be 1,225 strong.

The enemy were strung out over a front of around 2km with the Euphrates and the Tigris to their north and another river, the Shatt al Arab, to their backs. The area between the enemy and us was drained marsh given over to agriculture and intersected by wide ditches topped by narrow tracks. Movement on these was very exposed. I knew their tanks could not manoeuvre except on very predictable lines. But if they could not manoeuvre, nor could our WMIKs. The enemy's only escape would be south towards the waiting Paras or north across the Euphrates. As the Paras were to attack first I expected a rush of escaping enemy to push north up towards the river.

Initially my plan was to present the enemy with so many problems that command and control would break down and they would halt and surrender in the confusion rather than try to fight. I would have preferred them to surrender. It seemed to me that if we could get an Iraqi Divisional HQ and its commander intact we could cut a deal and encourage a wholesale surrender of all Iraqi forces. Many lives would be saved. If it became clear that the enemy had chosen to fight, then I would not risk my men in a confrontation straight away. I would invite the ANGLICOs to strike at the enemy, with the Cobra Venom gunships and A10 Thunderbolt aircraft strafing the road north to south. If they still held out then I would finally launch a ground attack. My plan for the ground manoeuvre would be to smash two rifle companies (M and A Companies) into the western flank of whatever was left of the retreat, mainly as a distraction while force-marching two rifle companies around to the northern flank between the river and the enemy as cut-offs. I would hold L Company and the Gurkhas back and throw them in as my reserve, reinforcing success where I found it. I would strike at opportunity targets with my artillery, mortars and air.

The final version of what was to be Operation Fury was drawn out on the wall of the fire station, where the planning team sat and considered it in silence, some drinking tea, others smoking, each mentally searching the plan for flaws and testing it with 'what ifs'.

Once again I wondered about the possibilities of employing large intact Iraqi formations and the demoralising effect it might have on any Ba'athist resistance. If the coalition assaulted Baghdad with volunteer Iraqi troops, we could win a substantial Information Operations victory. It would be like Paris in 1944, where the British, Canadians and Americans had done the vast majority of fighting up to Paris, but the

Free French Army led the liberation of the capital in order to energise the vanquished French people into rising up against the Nazis and Vichy French traitors. We could do exactly the same and foment a revolt against Saddam. Naturally, as in 1944, the coalition forces would be on hand to do any real fighting. I believed that would be enough to win the war quickly and set the conditions for a lasting peace.

At midday on Saturday 5 April I held an orders group at our HQ. That night we drove north to the Hammar Bridge and across it to visit 1 Para, who were now dug in some 5km north, 3 Para having secured the crossing of the canal some days before. They were to attack the next day, 6 April. It was inky black as we traced our way to 1 Para's HQ, where inside a blacked-out building they had maps laid out and radio nets humming as the plan of attack was finalised. 1 Para would go forward using a relatively wide west-to-east road as an axis towards the town of Ad Dayr (known to our boys as 'Mad Dog' after the Loyalist paramilitary Johnny 'Mad Dog' Adair). The Paras would advance on Mad Dog behind an artillery barrage and destroy any resistance in close, dealing with tanks using their hand-held weapons or Milan. Air cover would ensure the enemy wasn't reinforced.

Tom Beckett was there as we arrived, ready to lead his Paras into battle, face blackened, rifle hanging from its sling at his side. They were itching to go, having spent a lot of time in reserve; they clearly relished the prospect of action. We had a cup of tea together and a laugh. A typical Irish toff, he was in expansive mood and was more like a man off to a day at the races than someone about to go into battle. As I looked around at the many familiar faces of my friends in 1 Para, I could see Tom's calculated cool was reassuring and motivating his whole battalion.

Poring over a map with Tom, I made sure I understood his plan so that we could be certain to avoid Blue-on-Blues, then we left them to their final preparations. We set off for our base in darkness, the convoy blacked out and with only the flashes of explosions on the distant horizon to remind us we were at war.

A recce was carried out on Sunday 6 April. 1 Para's attack had been successful and they had rolled forward, meeting little resistance and accounting for a couple of T55 main battle tanks as they went. The enemy, very sensibly in my view, ran. Shortly after 0400 hours, even as the Para attack was under way, I led a small convoy of Land-Rovers and Humvees north to a spot 45km north-west of Basra and 15km north of Ad Dayr, where we met a patrol from the Brigade Pathfinder platoon.

These were special recce troops and the forward edge of the coalition forces at the time. We made our way to their positions by traversing raised roads constructed through the partially drained marshes and passing the place where the HCR armoured car had overturned the previous week, killing Alex Tweedie. We stopped most of the vehicles there and I crossed onto Sean Lundy's WMIK, leaving Herby to set up a radio mast to get comms to base and Brigade. Andrew Cullen took charge of this drop-off point for the majority of our vehicles, such a tactical car park being known as a 'Zulu Muster' in military parlance. We followed the Pathfinders who had met us in some WMIKs to the last safe area out of sight of the enemy, where their vehicle halted and we too dismounted.

It was getting light. We made our way towards the front, crawling or walking in a stoop to avoid being seen by the enemy. We were separated from the main enemy position by a lattice of drained fields and irrigation ditches. Skylarks swooped and sang overhead and insects hummed in the thick grass growing on the edge of the ditches. We had no real idea where the enemy's forward positions were but we knew they could be only yards away.

By now the sun was up and the temperature was in the high 30s. After a walk of around 2km I met up with one of the Pathfinders. He had been living within sight of the enemy for the last two weeks and the strain showed. His kit was filthy with dust and it was ingrained into his face. His bearing and equipment were both fresh and well maintained, however, a well-oiled SA 80 clutched in his grimy paw and grenades, fragmentation and white phosphorus, hanging ready from his webbing equipment.

'Follow me, boss,' he hissed after we had been introduced in whispers and we crawled forward towards the Iraqi lines. We stopped at a low embankment. We both took off our helmets to reduce our profiles and to get a better view before gently raising our heads over the parapet to look east towards the Shatt al Arab river and into the enemy's lines. The scene that met my eyes was a flat landscape with bumps and ditches, which I knew were more irrigation ditches running off to the river. I could see the line of the river marked by date palms in the distance. I knew that there was a lot in front of us that was out of sight, or as we say in the Army, in 'dead ground'.

The Pathfinder sergeant orientated me with a precise brief given in a whisper: 'Look east and to your front. The tall water tower is on the main Ad Dayr to Al Qurnah road and is 1.2km distant. That will be known as

"Water Tower" and is the centre of arc as well as the centre of their position. Look right. The tall mast is beside the point where a bridge crosses the canal and is your right-hand boundary. This will be known as "Mast". Look left. The tangled ruin of a large mast and some buildings is a destroyed radio station and is the left of arc and your left-hand boundary. It will be known as "Ruin". Look at five o'clock of Water Tower. Can you see the Mickey Mouse ears there, there and there?' he whispered, pointing out domed shapes 500m away with black half circles standing out above them like mouse ears. 'Those are the T55s we know about and the ears are the open hatches. You might even see the crew now and again as they move about. There's plenty more out there but you can't see them. As you can see, they're "hull down[97]". You can't make out the gun because it's pointing straight at us. Look to eight o'clock and the bushes that run for around 200m towards Mast. That is the area where their self-propelled artillery appears at last light to shell us. We believe they have a hide to the east of the main road. Enemy infantry are believed to have a series of positions to the front, which they occupy at last light and leave before first light to return to shelters between us and the road. Questions?'

'Yes,' I said, looking through my binoculars. 'Who are those people?' I indicated a small group of women in black burkas digging 125m to my front.

'Those are the farmwomen. They come out each day to work on the fields. The person she is talking to, and we cannot see, is the enemy. They leave a few behind during the day.'

She stood resting on her rake and chatted towards the ground, glancing up now and again and pointing towards us with a flick of her chin as she spoke.

'Fack, they're close,' I whispered, gripping my rifle and easing off the safety. 'Do they know you're here?'

'Oh yes, they most certainly fucking do,' the sergeant confirmed. 'We can hear them at night.'

I looked at the area where the road should be with my binos. There was a lot of road movement. 'Is this usual, I wonder? It looks like the West Link[98],' I whispered to Sean, who was right beside me.

'I've not seen that sort of activity before,' the Pathfinder sergeant said.

---

[97] The hull is concealed below ground in a excavated 'tank scrape' or large hole where only the turret shows.
[98] Belfast's main commuter route.

We crawled back. I thanked the Pathfinders and we walked to our vehicles, parked well to the rear. I jumped onto Sean's WMIK and we set off back to our main body, who were waiting where we left them. There was a lot to do but I was content that my basic plan for Operation Fury was sound. As we approached the Zulu Muster through the fine silt sand clouds I could see Andrew's massive bulk standing ahead of the vehicles, clearly waiting for me.

'Looks like trouble,' I shouted to Sean over the engine noise. I jumped down from the vehicle and landed at his feet. 'Well?' I said as I caught my balance.

'Fury is off and we are to return to base immediately. It looks like Basra has fallen.'

'That explains the Wacky Races on the roads. Looks like we've missed the boat. Right,' I shouted to the recce group. 'We're going back to base.'

# —14—

# AL MEDINA

That morning the staff at UK's 1st Armoured Division, who had been keeping up pressure on Basra for days now, had detected movement that indicated a collapse of resistance from within the town. Special Forces and their contacts in the city reported that the Ba'athist leadership had flown and that only the desperate Fedayeen remained to fight a forlorn rearguard action. General Brims, loath to fight a house-to-house battle against well-prepared troops, now saw his opportunity and had no hesitation in striking for the centre of town. The GOC, General Robin Brimms, ordered 7th Armoured Brigade, led by Brigadier Graham Binns, forward in a three-pronged assault. H-Hour was 0530. The Iraqi defenders could feel the earth vibrate under their feet as the Royal Tank Regiment and the Warrior armoured fighting vehicles of the Black Watch struck forward, the high-pitched roar of the twelve-cylinder 1,200bhp Perkins engines driving the massive 52-ton hulls of the Challenger 2 main battle tanks, turrets swinging left and right seeking targets while the tracks smeared makeshift sandbag bunkers and their occupants across the tarmac of the roads into Basra. On their flank the Royal Scots Dragoon Guards thrust into the city, crushing the hopeless bravery of the foreign fighters from Egypt, Lebanon and Yemen who threw themselves at the tanks. The CO of the Royal Scots Dragoons later reported that his men had had to fire on each other's tanks to sweep these would-be martyrs off the turrets as they desperately clawed at the hatches. One tank had to use its windscreen wipers to see out of the blood-covered sight blocks, and effect sharp moves left and right to throw the dead

Fedayeen off the turret. With fanatical bravado, the enemy still came, firing rocket-propelled grenades, which bounced off the armour of the Challengers. We had been making our way forward to the Pathfinders as this assault went in far to our south, but it was now clear that the vehicles on the road had been the fleeing Iraqi Army.

I drove directly to Brigade HQ from the front line, ordering the rest of the vehicles to return to our oil plant. As I entered the building I could see that there was a buzz of excitement. I spotted the Chief of Staff. Taking me by the arm, he led me to a large map. 'It looks like they've jacked in Basra, more precisely it looks like Chemical Ali has either been killed or done a runner; either way they seem to have given up.'

'I heard. Do we have any part in all of this?' I asked hopefully.

'Not yet,' he said, indicating the map. Using a pencil as a pointer, he explained that 7 Brigade had taken the airport and they had the Irish Guards on the bridges into Basra. The old town was still unknown territory and 16 Brigade had been asked to send 3 Para in to clear it.

'Bugger,' I said. 'Y'know, I was so close to the Iraqis today. I was tempted to walk over and say "take me to your leader". I hope they come across en masse when we finally meet. What sign is there of surrender so far? Wouldn't it be superb to get them to cross over to us?'

'They've just melted away. Could be a big trap, of course. But I think they have just given up and legged it. As for any "crossing over", I think that is now increasingly unpopular with Division. They have the blood up and want unconditional wins.'

The Brigade Commander arrived as we were talking and he indicated for me to follow him into a side room. Facing a map of Basra and with aerial photographs around the wall, he once more described what had happened that morning in Basra and what the 3 Para were off to do. Sipping tea, he turned to the area to the north of Basra and with a pencil outlined the likely positions of the enemy. To our east and running north was the Shatt al Arab, a wide river fed by the Tigris and Euphrates. The confluence of these mighty rivers was at the town of Al Qurnah and to the west was a place called Al Medina. This was spread along the banks of the Euphrates and comprised a series of villages with a small town served by government buildings and a hospital. We had been briefed that the Iraqi 25th Brigade was dug in there. We knew it had a high proportion of Sunnis and it had been expected to fight well. But how would it react to the collapsing situation around it? The Brigadier indicated where Basra province ended and the sparsely populated province of Maysan to the north began. Finally he outlined what he wanted 1 R Irish to do. We were to advance north on the available routes through the drained marsh and take Al Medina while covering Al Qurnah. Once we had Al Medina, we were to move forward and cover the crossing of the Euphrates into Al Qurnah, but we were not to cross the river at all unless told to do so. He emphasised this as there had been some strikes on our own vehicles by coalition aircraft and the only way to guarantee this did not happen was to stay south of the river until a controlled crossing could be arranged. I enquired when we would have to secure our objectives. The area was to be in our control by 0800 hours on 8 April.

The next day I had another detailed planning session, wrote orders in the afternoon and then called my orders group together for 2000 hours. In the main operations room, which was once the plant control room, the Intelligence Officer stood in front of the old electrical switch diagram, which was now covered in maps, and gave the general enemy picture. Then the Engineer CO gave the ground, along with the meteorological report. The Operations Officer was next up and he described the activities of friendly and flanking forces. I then took the floor.

I gave the mission: *Advance north within boundaries and seize the crossings across the Euphrates, then to swing left and secure the junction of the Tigris and Euphrates rivers with the Shatt al Arab, in order to set the conditions for allied crossings of the Euphrates.*

I described my intent: *Strike north with a minimum of bloodshed, with the aim of making contact with the Iraqi Brigade and Divisional HQ, with a view to incorporating them into our forces.*

For this task I had a new element in the Royal Irish battle group – the Iraqi Volunteers.

I had been in discussion for some days with the fledgling town council we had set up in Al Rumaylah. I was clear that we should incorporate Iraqis in our activities as quickly as possible. In Al Rumaylah 'VADGE' had spawned a town magistrates or local 'Bench' of sorts who ruled on property seized at road checkpoints. To establish ownership it asked questions such as 'You are a penniless nomad. How long have you owned a new fire engine and where did you buy it?' Most people seemed content to hand property to the Bench, whereas some resented handing over what they saw as Iraqi property to *ferengi*[99]. This had become an

---

[99] Foreigners.

interim town council and would become an elected body as soon as we could organise a poll. Remember we had been in the town only two weeks by then. I approached the elders and asked for assistance in the push north. I explained that I was going to seek to take the swamps, towns and fertile riverside strips to the north soon and, where possible, with the Iraqis joining our liberation and changing side in a bloodless advance. Initially they were not entirely with my reasoning. At first they offered 200 young men if I would supply uniforms and weapons – they were especially keen on our Irish caubeens – who would join as another rifle company. (They wanted Phil, who they called the Egyptian, to be their OC.) I explained through my new interpreter, whom we called Ali (he was a Kuwaiti whose name was actually Mansour, but he spoke English with an English accent and we told everyone that he was a British officer of Lebanese origin), that I had enough rifles and fire power – what I needed at this stage was advice, expertise and convincing legates who could act as my emissaries but who would act in partnership. There was a very long discussion. I had to leave before the end, but I was later delighted to receive a message from Abu Rifat, the town elder with whom I had worked since our arrival, saying that if they understood my intention correctly then I needed emissaries of equal standing with myself and that only he and Abu Bashir, the former Ba'athist, portrait painter and oil engineer who had been sent from Basra, had this authority.

The orders group broke up and I briefed the journalists that we would be leaving the next day to advance north. I warned them that they could follow but that it could get very ugly and not a little dangerous. To a man (and woman) they readily agreed to come. Having packed my kit, I sought to get some sleep. It was 2300 hours. I knew that the next day would be a long one. But the noise of a battle group of 1,225 men assembling is no small thing and I slept fitfully, waking up as each element arrived: A Company, B Company, L Company. The ANGLICOs were packing their gear and I could hear Stan giving orders. The Engineers recce arrived and I could hear Mick, their commander, wandering around, asking where I was. (We had been in the same SAS squadron.)

Awake now, I stayed in my sleeping bag, thinking about things. I had a great deal on my mind. I was going to take some serious risks. My plan was to seek an arrangement with the Iraqi Army to avoid bloodshed on both sides. I knew the Iraqis well enough to know that if cornered they could fight and might even surprise us with their resolution.

But I believed that this was a crumbling army that would welcome a way out.

I recalled the wisdom of Sun Tzu, sage of warriors from China in 500BC. He said, 'Generally in war the best policy is to take a state intact . . . For to win one hundred victories in one hundred battles is not the acme of skill. To subdue the enemy without fighting is the acme of skill.' And also, 'A victorious army wins its victories before seeking battle; an army destined to defeat fights in the hope of winning.'

I had briefed my ambassadors, Abu Rifat and Abu Bashir. They would, I hoped, bring me my victory in the form of an undertaking by the 25th Brigade not to fight. My calculation was that the Iraqi Army knew an attack was imminent and would be expecting us. If the village elders, as I suspected they would, had sent forward a request to parley, this would have the effect of either arranging a discussion, as it was planned, or ramping up the psychological pressure on the Iraqis as the hour of their destruction was announced. I recalled an old Second World War Navy veteran I had worked with as a student in Belfast one summer telling me that when you were going into a large action it was easier to be brave if it all happened by surprise than when you knew it was coming. My calculation was that, faced with the fear of our overwhelming force, the Iraqis would grasp any chance to avoid certain destruction. I wanted them to know the fateful hour was looming; there would be no surprise for them.

I would, however, be risking the lives of British servicemen in order to avoid spilling Iraqi blood. This was all on my head. Should I just blast my way forward? Who were these people, the Iraqis, to me anyway? But my heart told me that all would be well and that my duty was to avoid killing – at all costs. I would follow that still small voice of calm. But I would also have a great big stick and I got Stan to arrange a strike force of air power, which would avenge me instantly if it all went wrong. Once more Sun Tzu reminded me to 'use normal force to engage; use extraordinary force to win'.

I emerged at around 0300 hours on Tuesday 8 April and chucked my sleeping bag onto our trailer. Tea was being passed around and there was an air of excitement as we packed and mounted the vehicles, engines gunning and individuals preparing by the light of headlamps. One of our embedded journalists Alex Gardiner came over.

'I'm so proud,' he said in his jovial way. 'This is going to be a great thing – really.'

We chatted and as we parted, I climbed into the Comms Camel. 'Here we go, Herby,' I said.

'It will be fine, sir,' he said, sensing my apprehension. 'The men really believe in you – all of us, the Yanks, the Arabs, the lot.'

We set off, leading the now blacked-out convoy. Messages came up on the net as a group joined us or we heard a company column leaving to their particular task. The basic plan was that we would advance in two columns, a primary and secondary route. If we had to fight we would push forward where we could and I would reinforce success with my reserve, the Gurkhas.

C Company was behind the lead element on the main route of advance. Royal Engineers recce would lead with HCR, then came some strike vehicles from L Company with Sean at their head and then my tactical HQ, followed by C Company. We drove until I could see the armoured vehicles of the HCR and I stopped and walked forward to speak to Lettuce.

'It's as black as a witch's tit[100],' I said.

'The NVGs aren't even much cop tonight,' he said. 'We're using our thermal imagers.'

'Anything up front?' I asked.

'Plenty. It's crawling with them up there.'

We waited for the news that the other call signs were in place. It was 0430 hours. H-Hour was 0500. I was just wondering where the Iraqi Volunteers were, and whether they would even come, when I heard a vehicle approaching. Out of the gloomy darkness, a Southern Oil Company Toyota Land Cruiser emerged. It had coalition marking on both sides but it also had a large white flag. Rusty, my Intelligence Officer, stepped out and opened the back door. Out stepped Abu Rifat as I had never seen him before – in the full robes of a sheikh. Behind him stood the tall, impressive figure of Abu Bashir, in a blue shirt but with a shemagh wrapped around his head. I was so very glad to see these men.

'How do you think it will go?' I asked.

'It will be fine,' Abu Rifat said, '*inshallah*[101].'

'It is already fine,' Abu Bashir added confidently. 'We know many of the men ahead of you. They will listen to us. Already since your visit last night, messages have been sent. On my honour there will be no killing.

---

[100] 'Tit for tat' – rhyming slang for hat.
[101] God willing.

That –' he swung his hand into the air at the far distant throb of the giant rotors of the Cobra Venom gunships – 'will not be necessary.' The venerable Abu Rifat nodded in agreement.

We went back to our vehicles and waited for the appointed hour. The first rays of light were creeping into the eastern sky over the Shatt al Arab. The low hum of vehicle engines throbbed and the smell of diesel smoke was acute in the cool morning air. As I looked across the flat landscape the weird shapes that I had been struggling to make sense of began to become more than silhouettes, solidifying, separating and gaining a third dimension. I could see the fringes of the palm trees that lined the Shatt al Arab in the distance and light wisps of smoke that pointed earthwards to villages where the womenfolk were lighting the cooking fires as they had done for a thousand years, oblivious that a battle might be about to commence around them.

A shape that could have been an enemy tank emerged as a ragged piece of discarded metal, much closer than I thought. As the numerals on my Suunto showed 0500 hours I pressed the switch on my handset, 'All stations, this is Sunray, move now, call signs 10A and 30A acknowledge.' The replies, '10A acknowledged' and '30A moving now', came as we rolled forward.

The terrain was open, with only the raised road along which we travelled as a certain way forward. The drained marshes on either side were uneven, with a shallow wadi here and there and sparse thorn bushes. Low banks and piles of earth dotted the landscape, perfect cover for an enemy tank or anti-tank gun. A light dust marked the progress of the forward call signs.

We drove for about ten minutes until I heard '0A, this is 20A. Contact. Wait out.' The convoy halted. We waited for an eternity and then: '0A, this is 20A. Minefield to our front. Am investigating.'

I ordered the engineers in front of us to proceed. News came of a large crater in the road ahead of us. We halted. Then there were reports of enemy sighted through the thermal imagers. I drove forward and jumped out. 'What's the score?' I asked.

'It's a big hole – the engineers are looking into it,' Lettuce quipped, 'but there are bods up ahead beyond it.'

I trotted forward to speak to the engineers, rifle in my hand and pistol slapping at my hip. 'What's the form?'

'Looks clear,' said a staff sergeant huddled in a windproof smock. 'And there have been vehicles through lately. Could be they've opened it up for us and pretty recently too – in which case it could be a trap.'

I jogged back to the waiting vehicles and consulted with Abu Bashir and Abu Rifat. Abu Bashir stopped the conversation with 'Look, let's get on with this. Colonel, *sidi*, wait here.' They spoke hurriedly in Arabic, their faces close and Abu Bashir gesturing with his hands, palms flat upwards, fanning them towards the Iraqis' lines as if to shoo them off. Then they climbed back into their vehicle. It was almost light now and Abu Rifat shot me a reassuring smile as the Land Cruiser swept into the crater and out the far side and off into the distance. We waited. After ten minutes or so I could see the vehicle returning. As it negotiated the crater again, I walked forward to meet it.

'They are going,' Abu Bashir said.

'What happened?' I asked.

'It is just some ordinary jundies[102], but we spoke. We told them you would wish them to live and they were surprised. They thought they had to fight.'

'I told them to go in peace,' Abu Rifat said.

'Will they join us?' I asked.

'Is it not enough that they have left?' Abu Bashir replied.

'Let's go,' I said impatiently.

'Wait little, little time,' Abu Rifat said, catching my arm. I was now totally in the hands of these men. Either they had prearranged this and had taken themselves forward as proof of good will or they were two of the world's best poker players, about to lead us into a trap. I felt that I knew Abu Rifat well enough to know that I could trust him with my life. I had, after all, dealt with those who had issued him a death sentence – he owed me.

I waited for around ten very long minutes before I announced, 'I'll lead, the elders to follow next.'

As we descended into the crater the Comms Camel swayed left and right, then onto the road and off. When we emerged, to my amazement we passed tanks within 100m of where we had been standing. They were well dug in and had earth parapets hiding them as far as the turret hatches so that from the front only the muzzles of the 100mm guns were showing. Discarded radio headsets hung from the turrets by their flexes and AK-47s lay abandoned on the ground. We passed artillery positions with kit strewn around. In the open breeches I could see the massive

---

[102] Arab for common soldiers.

shell cases of 122mm rounds. An S-60 57mm anti-aircraft gun, pressed into the anti-tank role, had been dug in at the side of the road. From the front it was cleverly camouflaged and it faced straight down towards us. 'That would have shredded us,' Herby commented as we drove past. I realised that it would have been a bloody fight. I would have lost my recce force to these concealed weapons and would have had to send in infantry to clear these well-prepared positions in a bitter struggle. I recalled that these people had been at war for a very long time on and off: Iran–Iraq, the first war and now this. They knew what they were doing. Anyone who dismisses the Iraqis as poor fighters wants to go and mix it with them. They had run away, I agree, but that is because they had chosen to go – and at the bidding of their own elders, who they clearly respected.

This was not to be the end of the Iraqi Volunteers' day's work. Abu Rifat and Abu Bashir, with Rusty, the Intelligence Officer, went on to negotiate the surrender of several Iraqi positions, saving many lives on both sides.

We knew we were getting closer to the river as we could see date groves and more and more small canals. Palm trees grew at the side of the road now and through them we could see the low outline of hamlets, mud brick and flat roofed. Then road signs in Arabic and English announced that we were entering Al Medina and Saddam smiled down from a wall mural, wearing 1970s-style aviator sunglasses and Arabic dress. Mud walls on either side of the road concealed lush gardens and we could see the two-storey houses beyond them. As we drove into the town we spotted a large crowd. I stopped the convoy and had a translator go over with the elders to find out what was happening. The crowd sat impassively on rows of chairs under a tunnel-shaped tent about seven metres long, the floor strewn with carpets. It was clearly some sort of celebration. The elders returned and explained that an old man in the village had died and this was his funeral party. I asked them to find out what was happening with regard to the enemy forces. 'We already asked,' said Ali, the translator. 'They've gone.'

As we drove deeper into the town, it became more built up, the houses with walled gardens giving way to terraced houses with small gardens, then businesses with signs advertising their wares, here a mosque, there a petrol station, with drivers queuing patiently for their ration. How much do they get, I wondered. And who says so? I realised that I was the new authority in this town. As we proceeded, the crowds grew and began cheering spontaneously. Within a short time the crowds were very large, with men in a mixture of uniform and civilian clothes cheering at the side of the road. Beyond the crowd I could see life going on. At the baker's shop children and young girls queued for bread and a group of men stood at the door of a barber's shop, counting their worry beads. Here and there a man in military fatigues waved and cheered. At one halt I asked Abu Rifat to find out who the officer in charge was and to tell him to get his boys to make an effort to look like civilians or we would have to take them prisoner – and none of us wanted that.

We stopped our vehicles in the centre of the town and were mobbed by crowds. Some wanted to welcome us, some wanted to express their anger at the Ba'athists and others were eager to take us to arrest those they accused of being Saddam's men. In the midst of all of this I was told that there was some fighting at the hospital. I asked where it was and headed round, with my troops fanning out to cover the town. The hospital was a short drive away, in a suburb of larger houses surrounded by sand-coloured walls about 1.5m high with an ornate iron gate as access. On arrival we found surly crowds but no fighting. The hospital was a single-storey grey building that had seen better days. I went inside with my doctor in tow as my men kept the crowd back from the entrance.

Inside the door a delegation of two men and a woman in white coats came forward to greet us. The doctor in charge spoke good English and offered to show us around. He expressed himself with his hands as he indicated a dispensary here and treatment room there. The wards were clean and well kept (no MRSA here) but the facilities were basic and the doctor explained that drugs were in short supply. I asked my own doctor what she thought and she agreed the place was not half bad. We were shown into the room of a man who had lost a leg to an allied bombing. He was remarkably cheerful and blamed Saddam for the loss of his leg! I was amused to see a nurse running ahead of me taking down Saddam's pictures. I told her not to bother, and even took one as a souvenir. The picture was of Saddam dressed in the uniform of a field marshal, but what amused me was that his uniform was an exact copy of a British tropical service dress.

We left the hospital and I went in search of the Ba'ath party HQ. I stopped to ask a group of men where it was but instead they indicated a village outside town and told us that there was due to be a counterattack by the Ba'athist militia and that they were gathering in deserters from the Army. Back to my old adage of 'Do the last thing they would expect you to do.' I spoke to the Operations Officer in the back of the vehicle.

'Get C Company to cover the road. M Company are to stay put here and call forward the Gurkhas as a reinforcement.'

I then jumped into the front and told Herby to drive for the outskirts. There wasn't a moment to lose. It was my plan to seal off the village before these Ba'athists had got themselves organised, then send in C Company to control the area before I went and found the leaders. As we drove I called Brigade on the secure radio and asked for some air support. Some Lynx armed helicopters were sent forward and Stan brought two Cobras into play at the same time.

We drove back out of the town the way we had come and when we reached the outskirts I could see from the map that the men had directed me to the village I had spotted from the road earlier. As we drove towards it, past a good deal of abandoned equipment, it became clear that under the date palms the village was actually much larger than I had thought. It was at that point that I could see a crowd clearly in an agitated state. We halted to allow the supporting elements to catch up. I went to the back of my vehicle and spoke with the Operations Officer. 'Where is C Company?' I asked.

He looked sheepish. 'The Company Commander thought that he should go closer to the river and then—'

I stopped him there. 'It's not your fault but I am furious that OC C Company cannot be where I tell him to be. He has taken himself and his men off on a jaunt and left us with no reserve. Where are the Gurkhas?'

He looked concerned. 'An hour away.'

'Well, we're in the shit again,' I said. I looked at the village. Already, I could hear the helicopters approach. We didn't have an hour to wait for the Gurkhas or C Company to finish its sightseeing trip. The helicopters certainly didn't have an hour's worth of fuel and the time by which I was meant to have control of the crossings was getting closer. I walked around to the front of the vehicle and fished out my body armour, which I had taken off when we had gone into the hospital. 'Gather the blokes together,' I said gruffly to Magoo. I walked around to the space between my vehicle and the following one. We were very light on the ground. There was my Land-Rover, the BC, Richard and Stan. We did have an armoured car from the HCR and we had the Iraqi Volunteers. Just at that point two WMIKs arrived, one with the redoubtable Sean Lundy. 'Thank God for small mercies,' I said as he jumped down. 'We're about to take on the local Ba'ath party single-handed. Are you up for that?'

'No problem,' he said.

'Have you any call signs that can support us?'

'We're covering the river. I came as soon as I could.' He shrugged. 'This is it.'

'Right,' I said, turning to the group, 'here's the plan. The local Ba'ath party are about to have a go. But they're rattled and on the back foot. We should be sending a rifle company in to get them but the reserve has gone on a field trip with their OC. If we wait it could be too late. If we go in and they call our bluff we're dead men. They outnumber us hundreds to one. But if we keep our nerve we could disarm them. My plan is to brass-neck it, walk in and find their leader and put it to him straight: "Hand over the weapons." If it goes wrong, Stan, you'll have to get the helis to cover us out. You cavalry lads,' I said, turning to an HCR sergeant, 'will have to provide covering fire as we pull back. What do you think?'

There was an uneasy silence, then Stan Coeur spoke up. 'Well, you'll have four US Marines with you, so that evens the figures up a bit.'

'Right on,' Sergeant Aryolla said, nodding.

'And we got air,' Stan added as the two Cobras passed overhead, flying low.

'Wouldn't miss it for the world,' Sean said, and Herby gave me one of those 'you're fucking mad but whatever' looks.

'To be honest, fellas, I'm getting a bit old for this,' I said as I fastened my body armour. 'On my lead then,' I added as I made my SA 80 ready by cocking it. I turned to the Iraqi Volunteers. 'Wait here until we need you, then we'll call you forward. It could be pretty dangerous.'

'No, *sidi*,' Abu Bashir said, 'we're coming too. We can help.'

'I was hoping you would come,' I said, gripping his arm. I jumped into the front of the vehicle and as I did so Stan's Humvee pulled up alongside.

'Ready?' he said, cocking his AK-47[103].

We moved forward into the village. As we did so we went into the close cover of the date palms that surrounded the village as the helicopters

---

[103] Stan only had a pistol and we had organised an SA 80 for him but he preferred an AK-47 he had picked up off a dead Iraqi.

circled overhead. There were a few people around but they ran indoors as we passed. I was speaking to Shaggy, the Ops Officer, through the partition at the front of the driver's cab in the Comms Camel. He had direct communications with the Lynx above us.

'What can you see?' he asked them. They replied and he shouted over the din, 'He says there is a crowd about 100m in front. No weapons seen yet.'

We rounded a corner and crossed a small bridge over a muddy stream and then saw the crowd. I dismounted and walked towards them, with Ali and Abu Bashir running to catch me. 'Who is the Ba'ath party leader?' I asked. It was translated and the crowd remained silent, some pushing to get a better view. Suddenly Abu Bashir let rip with a long incoherent verbal blast.

'He's yelling at them to say they are women and to stand up and do something or tell us who is in charge,' Ali explained. Two or three men at once started talking to Abu Bashir, all waving their hands and gesturing, eyes bulging. It is sometimes strange to see Arabs doing this, as it is as close to fighting as you can get, yet when they finish they are as calm as can be.

Finally Abu Bashir turned to me in a matter-of-fact way and said, 'The boss is called Tariq.'

'Do Saddam's thugs all have to be called Tariq?'

'Different one,' Abu Bashir said. 'He's a wily old man. I know him but I didn't realise he was still in charge up here.'

'Where is he?' I asked.

'They say they don't know, but I know they do.'

Finally a man beckoned us to follow. We walked for about 100m with a crowd following. Our vehicles reversed and turned and nosed through the crowd to catch up. Some children had mounted the armoured car and were riding on it. At last the crowd spread out around an old man with a grey beard and a white dishdash and shemagh, standing in front of a large house.

'It is Tariq of Medina,' Abu Bashir whispered to me as he appeared at my side.

'Will you speak for me?'

Abu Bashir and Tariq spoke heatedly once more for some minutes. He then turned and took me by the arm. 'He says that he is no longer in charge but still has influence. He says that he will need time to gather in all the weapons.'

'So we just trust him?' I asked, almost incredulous.

'No. What I suggest is that he makes a pledge to you and then he will do as he says.'

I was suddenly exhausted. This constant round of pronouncements and verbal jousting was tiring. 'Whatever,' I said and sighed. 'Translate please, once again,' I said to Abu Bashir who had been joined now by Abu Rifat. 'I accept the surrender of the Ba'ath party of Medina,' I began. 'I do so with the authority of the Commander of 16 Air Assault Brigade in whose area this town now is. As a pledge of your good will you will surrender your weapon to me personally, Tariq, and I will pass it to the Commander and tell him you will gather the rest over the next few days.' This was translated with a great deal of added dialogue from Abu Rifat and Abu Bashir. All fell silent and the crowd looked at me. 'Well?' I asked.

As I did so a boy in his early teens emerged from the crowd to hand Tariq an AK-47 which was dripping wet and had clearly just been taken out of one of the water butts that stand outside houses in the region. Tariq handed it to me with both hands and as I took it he held on and said something. He then released the weapon and I passed it to one of my soldiers standing behind me. Abu Bashir translated.

'He says that the party is disbanded and that he will supervise the handing-in of weapons. He asks that he be left alone to do this and gives you his word that if it is left to him every weapon will be put out of use.'

'I accept and I really want to thank you both,' I said to Abu Rifat and Abu Bashir.

'He told him that you were mad,' Abu Rifat said, laughing, 'and that if he didn't want the same as Ayoub Younis Nasser in Al Rumaylah he had better do as you say.'

'They'd heard about that up here?' I asked, surprised.

'Oh yes, they thought you would have killed him by now.'

'No, the killing is over,' I said, smiling.

We walked back to the vehicles and loaded up. The helicopters flew low overhead. Shaggy spoke through to the front of the Comms Camel: 'The Lynxes have run low on fuel and have to go.'

'That's cool,' I said. 'Tell them thanks – they saved our skins.' We turned onto the metalled road and drove back towards the centre of the town. As we reached the junction with the main road back south I stopped and walked back to the Toyota. 'You have done much,' I said to Abu Bashir and Abu Rifat. 'I thank you. You have saved many lives.'

'You must come back soon to our town,' Abu Bashir said. 'You will come to my house and drink tea.'

'I would love to.' I smiled, gripping his large hand. Although I didn't know it at the time, I would never see him again. Over the last couple of weeks I had spent many hours with these guys, talking, discussing and learning. As they drove off I thought how lucky I had been to have them on hand.

# —15—

# CROSSING THE EUPHRATES

It was 8 April. Across the whole of Iraq coalition forces were advancing. 3 Para secured the centre of Basra without a shot being fired and 1 (UK) Division secured the area around it. In the north the Kurdish peshmerga fighters, reinforced by a parachute drop of US forces, advanced south, taking Kirkuk. The US forces rolled up through Najaf and Karbala and on to take Baghdad International Airport as the Iraqi information minister, Mohammed Saeed al-Sahaf, who had earned the nickname 'Comical Ali', was at the height of his denial of the scale of the allied advance. Saddam's regime had hours left to survive; nevertheless, elements of the Republican Guard were at their most deadly.

What I did not know was that while I was away doing my best to get my Headquarters wiped out, the RSM had had a bit of a moment too. As he waited outside the hospital for the doctor, an ambulance had driven up at speed. As it stopped a crowd descended and began to beat up the driver and to drag a wounded man out of the back. The RSM leapt in to pull them off but, making little progress, he struggled back, freed himself from the mêlée and cocked his rifle. He was ignored until he fired a shot into the air. When the crowd withdrew he grabbed two onlookers and indicated for them to pick up the wounded man. More soldiers ran to join him as he backed towards the hospital, the shot man being carried and the driver walking ahead of him, glancing nervously at the crowd. Once inside the hospital, nursing staff took over.

He asked the doctor what had happened and why they had attacked an injured man.

'They are two of the local Ba'ath officials,' he explained. 'They fled this morning when you came, in a stolen ambulance. They got shot at by the vigilantes. They thought that the safest thing was to turn back and surrender.'

There can be no doubt that RSM Beattie saved two lives. He was later awarded a Queen's Commendation for Bravery for his selfless actions.

It was 0730 hours when I arrived back at the town centre. Once again we were mobbed. I needed to find out where the various companies were and how we were getting on. C Company had been located and dispatched towards the bridge south of Al Qurnah. They reported themselves in position. I called Brigade and reported that we had the south bank of the Euphrates at the junction with the Shatt al Arab. I asked if we could cross. 'Absolutely not,' came the reply.

Standing on the river bank, the town to my back, I looked out across the Euphrates and could see men leaving Iraqi Army positions on the far side. Some walked away, others waved and some even crossed the massive bridge spanning that historic river to greet us. I was amazed that such a vital structure was still standing. Below me in the water I could see that a second military bridge had been prepared, submerged in about a metre of water, it was an easy wade for most vehicles. I took out my cigar tin and put a cigar between my lips, patting my pockets to look for a light, only to be almost crushed by ten or fifteen local men as they pressed in on me, offering theirs. I lit my cigar from about three lighters and blew a long puff of smoke to the delight of the crowd.

'Cigar, good, good, Churchill,' one man said.

Historic, I thought, the Euphrates. As I smoked, closely watched by the crowd of well-wishers, I recalled my images of that great waterway. Included in the area that 1 R Irish now controlled was a junction of rivers described in the Bible, in the Book of Genesis, chapter 2, verse 14, the Garden of Eden, where C Company now sat, 19km to the east. My daydreaming was interrupted by the crowd. An older man holding a bicycle came up to me with a group of men and in perfect English began to list the atrocities of the Ba'athists.

'See.' He indicated one man. 'They have branded him.' The man had a mark on his forehead. 'And this man, they cut off his ear.' The man had a small knot of skin where his ear had been. 'And this man has lost both ears.'

'I don't suppose he ever wears hats,' I observed. 'But why?' I asked.

'Back late from leave with the Army,' he explained.

I looked to Shaggy. 'I should try that on the next Commanding Officer's orders – absence would drop.' I asked what happened to those who didn't come back at all.

'They are shot,' the man said.

Another man held up a stump. 'Why do you think they do this?' he asked plaintively.

'Habitual wanking,' one of the rangers guessed.

Our study of Ba'athist punishments was interrupted by a call from M Company. They had found the Ba'ath party HQ. 'Mount up,' I said as I left the maimed men. There were clearly a few old scores to be settled there.

By the time we arrived the Ba'ath party HQ was wrecked and on fire. The boys from M Company had put out most of the fire. We discovered it had been an attempt to burn records. The Ba'athists needn't have bothered. Crowds had sacked the place anyway. I wondered if the destruction had been motivated by what they knew was recorded about them there. I had heard about such things before. It was always supposed that the destruction of the Gestapo HQ in Brussels had been no spontaneous mob action during the Second World War. It was perhaps matched only by the enthusiasm with which East German hordes had destroyed the Stasi HQs in their towns. In totalitarian societies, where informing on your neighbour is a way of life, much of the population would prefer that the records of what has gone on do not survive to spoil the image of oppressed people collectively fearing faceless tyrants. The reality in Iraq was that there was a single tyrant and that his henchmen were everyone else.

Once more there was a flurry of activity and messages as we walked through the Ba'ath party building. 'We've found the missing Phoenix drone[104],' one of the engineers from M Company said. He held up the remains of the wing of one of our pilotless reconnaissance drones, which had gone missing some days before. The unmistakable British roundel marking confirmed this. Other pieces were scattered about. They had clearly brought it back to the HQ to try to gain some intelligence from it.

---

[104] The Royal Artillery operated a remote pilotless vehicle, or drone, called a Phoenix. It could give real-time information to its controlling vehicle. A number were lost to enemy action and technical faults.

We brewed some tea in the midst of the wreckage. An agitated man ran into the compound, shouting. His pleas were translated and it seemed the crowd had cornered a Ba'athist officer in a nearby building. M Company sent some men to see if they could rescue him. Later I was drinking some tea on a low wall in the shade of a tree with my HQ team when I was called away by a sergeant from M Company.

'Well?' I asked. 'Did we get him?'

'He either got away or they've eaten him.'

'What?'

'We found a thumb and two fingers still attached and the sole of a human foot.'

'Probably wriggled free,' I suggested. I sat down beside Stan. 'You know Einstein said that as the circle of light grows the circumference of darkness around it increases. That was in the context of knowledge. I guess it runs true of liberation over evil too. There is a great deal of darkness being displaced here by our presence and we have no idea of its vastness or capacities.'

'That's a fact,' he said, sipping his tea.

We continued our inspection of the Ba'ath party HQ. It was on three floors and featured a large lecture hall and a series of offices. On the top, beneath the roof, there was a small room with hooks on the ceiling, an electrical set-up of various cables and an iron bedstead. Ali began to describe what each piece of torture apparatus was for. (Kuwaitis know these things. They have bitter experience, if not personally then from brothers and cousins. Ali had lost a number of his family in the first war. Some tortured, some killed, some just missing – taken to Iraq and never heard of again.) I really did not want the full tour so I headed off to admire the view. Below us in the courtyard an ammunition store had been found and reports came back that the school next door was also full of ammunition. Like schools elsewhere in Iraq it had been closed some two weeks before the war and used as a barracks and ammo store. It was remarkable, but as I looked around at the town of 50,000 people we had just taken and the detritus of the 10,000-strong Iraqi division which had melted away before our eyes, it was as if it was all a film set, as the population went about their normal lives again.

Wherever we went large crowds followed. I was asked if I would accompany one of the locals, who had put himself forward as a leader, to see the waterworks. I walked with him along the banks of the Euphrates as he described the rout of the 6th Division. As he spoke, children were playing on the abandoned artillery pieces and anti-aircraft guns that were dug in along the banks of the river. It was little wonder that the drone had been shot down over the bridge. It was very well defended.

I knew that a lot rested on the restoration of clean drinking water. My service across the world, especially in Africa, told me that without an assured potable water source, the locals would begin to drink whatever they could and, in their desperation and innocence, open the door to disease (and additionally increase our burden). We talked water for forty minutes. At the end I directed the men to produce washing water for the market and town centre. The taps were to be clearly marked and supervised so that it did not enter the food chain. I pledged to have drinking water paid for at a rate of 100 tons per twenty-four hours – enough to get by. The cost was 4,000ID per ton, so that would be 400,000ID a day or about £270. Cheap, even by Iraqi standards, if you had the money. They did not. Nor did we, but I would find it.

The next few hours were extremely busy. I found myself listening to petitions, touring utilities and issuing orders for the next move. Had the bridge been rigged for demolition? Could someone check? Where was the local police station? Could we get some police out on the streets? What was the situation at C Company's location? Where were the Gurkhas? Could we cross the river yet?

I drove with an escort to C Company's position. We looked at the scene from a vantage point high above the river. The bridge was intact but damaged. Another bridge to our left had been dropped by allied bombing and had been replaced by a pontoon. Sitting in a date plantation nearby, invisible from the air, was a convoy of bridging equipment, huge amphibious vehicles with floating spans, folded for the road move but ready on call to bridge the river had the allies destroyed the second bridge. Even as we watched, the civilians were crawling over the vehicles, stripping them. Within hours these vehicles would be wreckage.

Across the span we could see the crowds chanting and beckoning us. We drove as close as we dared without actually leaving the bridge. We waved back and then returned south. Strangely the market on the far side was in full swing and the traffic flowed. Back on the south bank OC C Company took me on a tour of the Iraqi positions. In broad daylight the thing that struck me most forcibly was the quality of the Iraqi equipment. They were older models, for sure. The majority of the tanks were T55s, but they were totally refurbished and in A1 condition. The engine compartments were clean and painted in silver with red highlights. They had been lovingly maintained and the equipment and spares were neatly packed, with each tank fully loaded with ammo. In one the radio was still on and we could hear the crackle of static. As I looked at these tanks, well sited and capable of having put up a good fight, I reflected that the money value that these represented was immense. Having seen the inside of the schools and the basic state of the hospitals, I was clear that this was a nation that could not afford to maintain such a mighty army. If nothing else, liberation would spell the end of this particular crippling drain on the resources of the Iraqi people imposed by Saddam Hussein.

As we examined the tank, the pulse of a massive explosion ripped through the air, a deafening crash striking us moments later. I looked to my left and a mushroom cloud of smoke rose into the air. I later discovered that this had been another T55 exploding about half a mile away. I was given to understand that locals reported that it was being looted when it went up. I suspect it was an accident, as we found no booby traps to my knowledge in the whole area. It was a timely reminder to my men about the risks of souvenir collecting.

I returned to Al Medina, driving along the raised road beside the Euphrates. It was a scene one could scarcely believe. The road was lined by a forest of date palms with hamlets of two-storey houses each kilometre or so, some constructed as they had been for the last thousand years. Small canals connected riverside villages and loaded canoes were taking produce between them. Every now and again we would pass a mosque. There were large numbers of worshippers; a reaction of liberated people the world over is no doubt to seek solace in a higher being. The crowds that lined the roads cheered whenever we passed and as we drove in our open vehicles the hot wind desiccated our faces and we grew tired of the constant waving. 'Now I know how the Queen feels,' I said to Ali.

Back in Al Medina I tried to speak to Brigade on the radio. I was impatient to cross and secure the far side of the rivers. My concern was that the enemy, having run away, might decide to return and make a stand. What was more likely was that some groupings or other would take advantage of the vacuum and strip the battlefield of abandoned weapons, seize control and then present us with a rival authority at best or an insurgency at worst. As I waited for a reply, we had another brew of tea and Alex Gardiner, in high spirits, took some memorable photographs. I spoke to a local man in his early thirties, who introduced himself in excellent English as Daoud. He was, he explained, an engineer and had come to welcome us. I sat and chatted for a good fifteen minutes with Daoud and I was impressed to find he spoke French and English as well as Persian. He actually had a PhD in engineering. He told me a lot about the events leading up to our arrival and was dismissive of the punishment meted out to the Ba'athists.

'It would not have happened if they had not deserved it,' he said. 'But now you must restore order because otherwise the poor people will destroy the things we need to live because they are ignorant and do not understand.'

'You are a remarkable man, Daoud,' I said. 'For someone so young, you have achieved so much.'

He paused and looked down for a while. Then he looked up at me with a mixture of anger and sadness. 'Have I achieved? You come to liberate us. How long have we prayed for this. Now you are here. Look at the quality of your clothes, your uniform. Those are what you work in. Your watch is worth more than everything I own. Look at the poor shoes and my clothes. They are my best. I have nothing.'

'Yes,' I said, 'your clothes are humble, but soon with hard work you will have these things too. That is why we have come, to allow you to benefit from your hard work.'

'I wish it will be so,' he said. We sat in silence.

I went for a walk along the perimeter that we had established, talking to the well-wishers pressing against the fence around the Ba'ath party HQ. As I chatted, a man carrying a small boy of about five handed the boy over the fence and explained to the interpreter that he was gravely ill. Once more our doctor came and examined the boy and quizzed the father through the interpreter. I asked what the score was.

'He's got liver cancer,' she explained. 'He's dying.'

I took the small bundle. He was naked and smaller than my daughter, who was four. I lifted him over the fence and placed him back in his father's arms. I asked Ali to translate. 'He has been called to God,' I explained. 'We cannot change that. I'm sorry.' As the man took the child he wept and pressed his face into the small child. The little boy was barely conscious and flies crawled around his mouth and eyes. I waved the flies away with my hand and we stood in silence until I got a call to come to the radio vehicle. 'I must go,' I said to the man. 'I'm sorry we cannot help.'

Back at the Comms Camel I was passed a handset. 'It's the Brigade Commander,' Reggie said.

'Right,' he said, 'you are clear to cross. You are to exploit north to the 36 northing and go firm.'

'Roger that,' I said as I gave back the handset. 'We leave in twenty minutes,' I said to Shaggy, the Ops Officer. 'Get the commanders in on me in five and I'll issue instructions.'

I had, of course, already outlined my plans for crossing earlier – L Company would lead in their WMIKS, with B Company providing the back-up. I would lead in a WMIK from the Recce. We had waited so long now that darkness was only an hour or so away and I wanted to get busy. It was 1800 hours as we reached the edge of the bridge. I gave a quick comms check and then we set off. A Recce WMIK was in the lead, with my vehicle second. As we rolled across the bridge there was a terrific roar of approval from the crowd. It was a remarkable experience. For the next forty minutes we drove along the road on the far bank in a scene that must have been like the liberation of France some sixty years before. Whole villages turned out to cheer as we drove by and to the left and right of the road I could see the farmers gently tilling their fields and the abandoned equipment of the Iraqi Army littering prepared positions.

'They must have left pretty recently,' my driver commented. 'They haven't started robbing yet.'

We drove into another village and the crowds mobbed us again. I was grabbed by the hand and led into a building that Ali explained was the Ba'ath party HQ. Sadly once more it was gutted. It didn't look like we were going to have another success like Al Rumaylah. I pushed my way back to my vehicle and we set off again. I was intent on getting to Al Qurnah in daylight. I passed orders for guides from C Company to meet us on the outskirts and to take us to the Ba'ath party HQ (I had ordered them to cross as we crossed to their west). When we got there, finding the Ba'ath party HQ could not have been easier, however. It was a massive building with an ornate façade, set in a compound with anti-aircraft positions on towers around it. We drove in and I was met by Colin Marks.

'She's been wrecked,' he said as I jumped down. The destruction was evident from the paper and ruined furniture scattered around outside.

'Any trouble?' I asked.

'Far from it; it is sheer joy. But they're pretty volatile too.'

'It kicked off in Al Medina at about this stage,' I said. 'I'm not certain we're in the business of mixing it with the locals to pull out any trapped Ba'athists tonight – too risky for our men. We'll wait until daylight.'

I went inside and the scene almost took my breath away. We were in a land where schoolchildren sat on the floor and the teachers wrote on the walls. But inside was a massive foyer with a chandelier that must have weighed a ton hanging in a vast cavernous dome. On the wall in front was the face of a hawk, rendered in plaster. It was around 3m high and 1m deep as it jutted from the wall. It was exquisitely detailed and must have cost a fortune. The ceiling was some 20m high and featured a dome of coloured glass, like a mosque, and around the second and third storeys were glass-fronted offices, all now ruined, facing onto the entrance hall. A sweeping staircase led up to the first floor, which was given over to large meeting rooms and a cinema.

'In case you're wondering, the cells are out the back,' Colin said, reminding me where I was.

'Empty?' I asked.

'Thankfully,' he replied.

We walked onto the first floor and as I looked out across the car park, now filling with our vehicles, I could see a large Chevrolet Suburban with the journalists pulling in. I waved to Alex and Sarah and then as I looked beyond them into the square outside the wall I could see a massive statue of Saddam.

'Look at that,' I said to Colin, as crowds milled round it.

'The locals say it's a memorial to the Iran–Iraq War. This was front-line territory, they tell me. He's pointing to Iran over there.'

'Not for long,' I said, before taking off and bounding down the stairs two at a time. 'Get an ATMP,' I shouted, 'Saddam is about to go on a short trip.'

We crossed the square, men from C Company and the ANGLICOs fanning out to cover us. I went forward and had a look at the statue. It stood around 10m high and was on a plinth that featured scenes from the Iran–Iraq War, with the Iraqis naturally winning. Crowds gathered.

'Get it down,' I called to Colin over the din.

A soldier climbed up the statue and fixed one of the towing cables we carried for recovering broken-down vehicles. We pushed the crowd back and then we scrambled clear.

'OK,' I shouted, 'go for it.'

The ATMP powered up and lurched forward. There was a crack, then the ATMP stopped for an instant before it pulled forward again and with a huge crash the statue fell to the ground. As it came down the arm smashed off and the legs separated from the feet, leaving the two massive poles that had supported the statue from within jutting into the sky. The crowd surged forward, some jumping onto the still-moving statue and others taking off their shoes to beat Saddam's face in what is supposed to be a grave insult. I looked at Ali and he was overcome with joy as the crowds milled over the now prostrate Saddam.

'You cannot understand what this means to me as a Kuwaiti.' He laughed. 'This man,' he said, kicking the massive bronze, 'killed my people and tried to steal my country.'

I hopped up on top of the statue with my close protection group to pose for a photo. As the light finally faded the crowds began to get wilder. There were large groups jumping up and down shouting and not a few weapons were brandished. I was becoming concerned that the jubilation was now a little too boisterous and might spill over to violence when a thump from an exploding grenade caused a sudden hush. Then the chanting started again.

'Get it into the compound,' I shouted to Colin over the deafening noise of the crowds.

The men of C Company pushed forward and reattached the cable, then towed the statue off towards the Ba'ath party HQ across the road. Others pushed the crowd back as they ran to get a strike in at the statue as it was dragged in a shower of sparks across the road and into the compound. Soldiers had to physically eject the Iraqis who had managed to get in with it, then the gates were closed and we had a chance to look at the figure more closely. Made of bronze, it must have weighed a couple of tons and showed Saddam in the uniform of a general with a pistol on his hip.

'Time to get back to Brigade,' I said as I jumped into my WMIK. This time with only a small escort I headed back to Al Medina. The town was in darkness now as the retreating Ba'athists had cut off the electricity and only the main routes had lights. I saw the Adjutant there. 'You have the town,' I said, 'I'm going to report to Brigade.' We set off south down the road we had travelled that morning. It seemed as if a lifetime had been squeezed into that single day. It was 2100 hours as I pulled up outside the Brigade HQ. I went in and found the Commander. We sat as I gave him a report and then I said, 'You may not be overly pleased but we've pulled down Saddam's statue in Al Qurnah.'

'The Americans are in Baghdad,' he replied. 'I doubt if the regime will protest. They're busy elsewhere!'

I then presented the rifle that Tariq of Al Medina had surrendered. 'I took your name in vain, I'm afraid,' I said.

'Be my guest,' he replied. 'One other thing,' he said. 'You have an important visitor. Air Marshal Burridge will visit tomorrow. He wants to see Al Rumaylah and then wherever you suggest on the Euphrates.'

'I know just the place,' I said. 'There is an abandoned Brigade HQ. He can see some Iraqi kit.'

We slept soundly that night, exhausted after a very long and momentous day. The next morning we packed our gear ready to leave for Al Qurnah. I left Shaggy with the Comms Camel. The idea was that I would host the visit by the Air Marshal and then join them up north when he'd flown back to Kuwait. I met the AM's helicopter at the HLS and drove with him to Al Rumaylah, pointing out some landmarks on the way. I knew it was probably my last glimpse of the town and I had become attached to the place and its people. How much has changed, I thought. We had arrived in an orgy of destruction and chaos and now it was the showpiece of the south. It was two weeks and one day from our arrival. The main purpose of the AM's visit was to see the school, which was gaining an increasing fame as a point of normality and a token of what we hoped to bring Iraq. The school had been warned of our visit and it was a great experience for me to see the progress that had been made in the last few days. We were greeted by Abu Nawfel dressed in a suit, with the unmistakable figure of Jari's wife Sabbah hovering in the background. I had briefed the AM that this guy had been the kingpin of the Ba'athists in the village and was now my faithful whelp. We were led inside and Abu Nawfel showed the AM to the headmaster's seat. Air Marshal Burridge gave a short speech and the teachers listened attentively. He finished with a cheery 'Are you happy with these chaps?', pointing to me. 'Oh yes,' said Nasser with an obsequious smile. (I was waiting for him to reach up and touch his head as a reminder of our close working relationship.)

We visited the CIMIC house and showed the AM the old cells and the new information centre that we had set up and then we drove back to his Puma and flew north. We passed over the area where Operation Fury would have been and I could see that there was a great deal of abandoned equipment. I noted where we had watched the Iraqis on our recce for Operation fury and was surprised to see some trenches only a hundred metres from where we had been and a couple of abandoned tanks beyond that.

I had given the pilot a grid for our next stop and as we circled I could see that the lads had laid out an HLS and a soldier was standing ready to marshal us in. From the air we could see the Iraqi position we had selected was quite extensive and had a number of armoured vehicles of the T55 and MTLB type (an armoured command centre). After we landed we walked around and I drew the AM's attention to the quality of the vehicles (although by this time they were not looking so neat, having had the attention of looters during the night). Naturally a large crowd had gathered and we had to push them back to allow the Puma helicopter to take off with the AM on board. We all, Brigade Commander included, helped push the crowds back as the rotors whirled above us, blasting sand and grit, shouting '*Yallu shebab*[105]' as the crowd joined in the fun and we shooed each other off the HLS.

I bade farewell to Jacko and drove to visit C Company. They were settling in very well and sorting out their equipment. I spoke to a deserter who had taken refuge with them. He was extremely nervous and begged us to send him back to our POW cage and safety. He explained that he was a member of the Republican Guard and had been left behind in hospital when the others pulled out. He had no desire to be left in Al Qurnah. I wondered why he was so concerned. What had he done to attract such attention? Then I remembered the men in Al Medina with the mutilated ears. 'Are you responsible for crimes against these people?' I asked. He looked to the translator and as he heard the question in Arabic his face shot around to look at me, protesting '*Lah, lah, sidi, lah*[106].' I knew what I needed to know and turned and walked out. '*Lah, sidi, lah,*' he called after me.

My HQ needed some new lodgings so we set off to explore. We found a perfect place. In Al Qurnah one of the things to see was 'Adam's Tree'. Set in the garden of a hotel was an ancient (dead) tree. The locals claimed it had been the apple tree from which Adam and Eve had eaten the forbidden fruit. In any case the hotel, closed off for many years, sat exactly at the confluence of the River Tigris, flowing on the left, the River Euphrates, on the right, and where they joined, the Shatt al Arab. The hotel itself was a single-storey affair, which had definitely seen better days. Two brothers (who tried to raise an objection when I announced that I would be moving in) supposedly owned it. The hotel had a terrace which overlooked the whole scene and all in all it was very pleasant. An added bonus was that the room I took had a working toilet (Arab style), although I made the ANGLICOs dig one in the garden for their use, as they had never come to terms with Arab plumbing and insisted on stuffing toilet roll into all of the working toilets, which rendered them stinking and blocked. Somehow that bit of culture (foreign to the Brits too, but they adjusted) just did not cross 'the Pond'.

---

[105] Let's go, boys.

[106] No, no, sir, no.

It was a beautiful place indeed. The one big drawback was that it had a pretty bad blast from mosquitoes at night, so you had to wear full protection at biting time. In the early evening the sun would go down over the Shatt al Arab and turn the sky a deep red before the patio behind the hotel was plunged into darkness with only the stars on a velvet blue sky to light us. We felt very content. Morale was high and the local Iraqis were extremely welcoming and friendly. There were occasional shots at night but these were mostly people shooting weapons to test them or celebrations at weddings and parties. My men were on strict instructions not to shoot unless they were certain there was a threat but not to take any chances. As it turned out, that is just what they did.

We settled into the hotel in the Garden of Eden on Wednesday 9 April and on the Thursday morning I went shopping. The company commanders were busy liaising with the locals and each had their area to look after. We took the view that many of these places really needed no garrison. I decided to see the place and took off my pistol belt and body armour and went out with Ali. We exchanged some dollars for Iraqi dinar at a street trader's stall. We then went to a shop and bought some flatbreads and vegetables from the market and a big fish from the fish market. As I walked, children would caper about shouting 'Hello mister', probably their only English, surrounding me and asking Ali about Britain and pointing at me. As I bought something, small hands would reach out and take my purchases and I would walk with an army of little bearers. Many of the adults, very welcoming to me, would scold the children, saying 'let them shop', or 'leave them alone' and 'they are guests in our country'. When we walked back to our temporary HQ, they would jostle forward to hand over the shopping and I would marvel at the rubbish I had bought, rewarding each little hand with some dinar.

The whole idea, of course, was to get out and talk to the Iraqis, hear their views and listen to their hopes and fears. I learned a great deal from these welcoming and cheerful people. Even in their poverty and difficult situation they were generous and hospitable beyond belief. We talked about the war, the Iran–Iraq War, Palestine and so on. One older man claimed that he once worked as a guard at a British base up north near Fallujah, which was just outside Baghdad. He explained that there was an RAF base near Fallujah in the 1950s and that the RAF families lived in the town. I asked him what it was like. He explained that he didn't come from Fallujah and that the people there were very Sunni and disliked strangers, although they got on well with the British families. He was, he explained, a Shia.

'How do you know who is who?' I asked.

'We just do,' they explained.

Then Ali laughed. 'They said I should know.'

'So they know you are Sunni?'

'Of course,' he laughed. 'That's what they're saying.'

'Is this thing a big deal, you know, the Shia/Sunni thing?' I asked Ali as we strolled back.

'A BIG deal,' he said. As we walked I told him about the Holy Cross in Ardoyne. 'Yeah,' he said. 'I saw it on the TV.'

# —16—

# INSIDE 'INTELLIGENCE HQ'

By the afternoon of Wednesday 9 April US forces had taken Baghdad. The Ba'athist regime had crept away. The symbolic climax was the pulling-down of Saddam's statue in the centre of al Fardus Square, outside the Sheraton hotel where most of the journalists had stayed. Resistance was now confined to Saddam's home town of Tikrit. On 10 April Kirkuk in the north fell, as did Mosul. Then on 11 April Tikrit fell. The allied commander, General Tommy Franks, declared, 'This is an ex-regime.'

On the Thursday evening we decided to have some supper under the stars and barbecued the fish on the terrace, with a couple of the men gathered round. It was getting late for us (about 2200 hours) when a series of shots rang out from the direction of the main river, only a couple of hundred metres from where we sat. I went across to C Company's HQ to find out what was going on and there was a report that C Company had shot a man at a road checkpoint. The patrol had believed he had had a hand grenade. When they found him it had turned out to be a tomato.

C Company reported to me that it had put a vehicle checkpoint on the bridge just before last light to control the movement of weapons and stolen goods across the river. As the light fell they could see someone watching them furtively from some bushes and this was reported to the patrol commander, who told them to keep an eye on the man. We were well used to this sort of observation in Northern Ireland – what we called 'dicking'. The 'dicker' moved closer and could be seen waiting and watching and then disappeared, until just as the light faded he stepped out, shouted in Arabic and brandished a round object which looked like a grenade. Convinced that their lives and the lives of the Iraqis who were at the checkpoint were in danger, they fired. There was no time, they explained, to shout a warning. The man fell. He was recovered immediately and given first aid. He had taken three rounds in the legs[107]. An interpreter was sent for and the wounded man was treated and given morphine. As the morphine took effect he immediately perked up, becoming talkative and even inviting the patrol around to his house for some tea.

When interviewed later, his version of the incident was slightly different. He had gone to the market in Al Qurnah to get the late bargains, he explained – they sell off the fruit cheaply at the end of the night. He had bought a bag of various fruits and vegetables and was heading back over the bridge when he saw the patrol. He had no papers and no idea what you would need to cross the checkpoint, so he waited and watched to see what they were looking for and whether they seemed friendly. He tried to get closer but at the same time not to be seen by the patrol, and then as it got dark he decided to be bold, so he stepped out and took out a tomato. He held it above his head so that they could see it and shouted 'tomato' in Arabic as loud as he could. He then only remembered waking up in a heap and feeling pain where he had been shot.

This tale illustrated the difficulty of policing a region where cultures are different and the language barrier extreme. I closed the case, as there had been no malicious behaviour on either side. It was an unfortunate accident in a dangerous and tense situation. We knew Saddam loyalists were out there somewhere and there were any amount of weapons in the hands of opportunists and roving bandits. Reports of attacks elsewhere in the British sector had put us on our guard. Frankly we were expecting to be attacked at some stage soon. I was also concerned that sixty shots had been fired and the man had only been hit three times. I told Colin to get the men to check the zero[108] on their nightsights as soon as possible.

---

[107] I had briefed the men to shoot low at night, as the tendency of most shooters is to aim high in poor light. This was no humanitarian step – just good drills I had learned in my special forces days. It meant the enemy fell into your shots.

[108] To 'zero' a rifle is to make sure it is shooting straight.

The following day I was called once more to Brigade HQ and given a delicate task. Task Force Tarawa, a US Marine organisation, had arrived just outside the town of Al Amarah. There was the strong possibility that the 10th Iraqi Division, which was supposed to be there, had deserted en masse or was getting ready to do so. The collapse could have been from the approach of the Leathernecks[109], but it could have been that there was pressure from local anti-Saddam resistance groups. This was a region that was perilously close to Iran and there was a well-established tradition of resistance from a variety of groups, most notably the Kurds and pro-Iranian Shi'ite militias. A reconnaissance from 16 Air Assault Brigade was due to fly there the next day but I was asked to go forward by the Brigade Commander to see what was happening on the ground and to make contact if possible with the Iraqi resistance. I was to meet with a forward Recce team from Task Force Tarawa at the airfield in Al Amarah.

It was just first light when we set off north towards Al Amarah early the next morning. As we drove in the Comms Camel with an escort from L Company in WMIKS we knew that we were travelling on a road onto which allied troops had so far not ventured. There were some fascinating sights. Buses painted in Iraqi Army colours were sitting at the side of the road, the victims of air strikes. Armoured vehicles of various types and from a number of foreign origins, French, Chinese, Brazilian, Russian, had been abandoned. The former occupants had probably not gone long, for they had not yet been looted and some had signs of very recent activity. We passed a battery of Roland anti-aircraft missiles. This was pretty modern equipment and I was surprised to see it in Iraqi hands. At the town of Al Majarr al Kabir I saw a man running across the road with an AK-47. I stopped the vehicle and called him over. Frightened villagers watched from doorways as I spoke to him through Ali. 'What was he up to?' I asked. He replied that he was looking for his brother. I confiscated his rifle and sent him on his way.

We continued towards Al Amarah. When we reached the outskirts I could see smoke and as we drove into the town there were very few people and I could sense a surly atmosphere. We drove on to the airfield and, sure enough, Task Force Tarawa was there in strength. They had been there overnight. I spoke to some of our Special Forces people and members of our Pathfinders platoon from 16 Air Assault Brigade.

---

[109] US Marines.

They introduced me to 'Jimmy', a CIA operative and what you would imagine little Jimmy Osmond (of 'Long-haired Lover From Liverpool' fame) looks like now. He was standing at the back of a Chevrolet Suburban and was wearing a mixture of civilian dress and combat gear with a great deal of sophisticated equipment littered around. They had an Arab translator who was resting in a sleeping bag at the side of the road. Jimmy introduced me to Jeff, another of these Special Forces types, who had heard that I was coming and had arranged a meeting with a local sheikh, Sheikh Mohammed al Badi, who was supposed to have a control over the resistance. He had already been to a meeting with him and had got the impression that the sheikh was very well organised and knew how to broker power. He described the meeting at the sheikh's home and how all the major players in the utilities and town police had been present. He also mentioned a local resistance fighter known as Abu Hatim, who appeared to have some popular appeal among the masses in the region but with whom there had been no contact yet. I asked him to set up some meetings and he said he would try. Meanwhile I resolved to find out more about Abu Hatim.

I was asked to go into town to see the CO of the battalion that was responsible for the area. He had been looking for two US Marines reconnaissance vehicles that had been left behind after an aborted mission. 'Oh,' I said, 'I know exactly where they are. They're burned out and at the main traffic junction in town.' (We had passed them on the way in.) We set off to find them and before long a large crowd indicated that there was some sort of a commotion going on. I could see some armoured Cougar personnel carriers and I knew these must be Tarawa vehicles. I dismounted from my Land-Rover and went forward with Ali to see what was happening, only to find a large crowd inside a building, which was described as the Intelligence HQ. Al Amarah was the base for Chemical Ali, and he had overseen the suppression of the 1991 rebellion from there. The main street had been built since then and it was believed that special underground cells had been constructed for political prisoners.

By the time I'd found the CO of the battalion, Lee Miller, the crowd were becoming increasingly frantic. 'We got a shit storm here,' he explained over the shouting. 'They figure that there's a lot of Kuwaiti prisoners down below us in cells.'

I went and looked for someone in charge and found an imam. I took him to one side and was soon joined by a sheikh. (In Southern Iraq Shia clergy wear hats according to their rank. A sheikh will wear black robes and a white hat and a sa'id, the next highest rank, roughly equivalent to a bishop, wears a black hat.) Lee and I talked to them through Ali. I could see Ali was becoming uncomfortable. The locals could tell he was a Sunni and I knew that he was upset because it was claimed there were other Kuwaitis under the floor. The negotiations carried on for a while. I needed them to help us get the crowd back out onto the street. We tried on several occasions to clear the compound, blocking the gateway with armoured vehicles, so that we could have a chance of finding the entrance to the underground complex, but to no avail. The crowd came through every crack and opening like water. I asked if we could find anyone who might know the entrance. In the excitement everyone claimed to know something. With the help of the clergy we got one of these chaps into a room inside the building. Ten or twelve 'supporters' pushed their way in, too.

'Do you know where the entrance is?' I asked the first man.

'Yes,' said the man with a gasp, as if to say, 'At last.'

'Good,' I asked. 'Where is it?' A sudden cacophony of voices answered the question, each pointing in a different direction. 'SHUT UP!' I yelled. 'You.' I pointed to the man. 'Where is the entrance?'

'Well,' he began, 'my aunt used to work at the prison in Basra and when she was there they released the prisoners in 1991.'

'Yeah, yeah,' I said impatiently. 'And . . .'

'Well, in Basra they always—'

'Stop,' I said, frustrated. 'Do you know where the entrance is *here*?'

'Not exactly, but—'

'Get him out,' I said. We went through a total of seven of these informants, all of whom declared they knew where the entrance was, only to ante up some crap like 'My dad used to live in Baghdad . . .' or 'When Chemical Ali was a boy he was in the same class as my father and he said . . .'

I had almost given up hope when two men were hustled into the office. 'What have we here, Ali – clairvoyants?'

'No, sir, Ba'athist secret policemen.'

At last we had someone who might know. The men explained that they had not worked in this particular HQ but knew lots of people who did. They were at pains to point out that they were under the protection of the clergy, who had guaranteed their safety. I assured them that they would be safe with me. I cut straight to the chase. Were there Kuwaitis under the floor? The taller man, in his fifties with a hawkish face and a trimmed moustache, shook his head. No. He was sure there were not. So what has got everyone excited? I wondered. After a silence, one of the sheikhs explained that voices had been heard calling up through the pipes. I made my way through the shouting crowd to see for myself. I listened at the pipe and as I did the clergy managed to shut the crowd up long enough for me to hear a distorted call from far underground of '*Shwei, shwei*[110]' and '*Khallas*[111]!'. Sadly, I realised that they had been hearing themselves shouting. The vibration was being picked up from the ground and transmitted back through the pipes.

This was useless, I realised. We tried to hustle the secret policemen out but the crowd saw them and went mad. Now the clergy took the front rank, holding the angry men back while Lee Miller and I were having to drop those who got through with our fists. Eventually we managed to get the Ba'athists back to Lee's armoured vehicles.

'I reckon we're beaten here, Lee,' I said.

'Sadly, I agree,' he replied.

That morning was a testing time and we had come close to being attacked ourselves as we ushered the Ba'athist policemen along. Ali, normally mild-mannered, came to the fore as a man of significant courage as he put himself between the crowd and the men and defended with his fists the representatives of his country's sworn enemies, the Ba'athist secret police. I returned to the building and apologised to the sheikh, explaining we could do no more. The sheikh said that he felt we had done all that we could and that he was sorry for his people. He then asked me if it would be permitted to have a Shia parade in the town that day. I looked to Lee.

'You're in charge,' Lee said.

I turned to the sheikh and said, 'I am happy to grant this wish on the provision that no weapons are carried.' He agreed.

Months later it was revealed where all the political prisoners were. As it turned out, they *were* actually underground and in Al Amarah, in mass graves nearby.

Back at the airfield, I met up with Lee and agreed that 1 R Irish would take over full responsibility for Al Amarah the next day.

I drove off to look around the town. My first stop was the sports

[110] Little, little.
[111] Enough!

stadium on the edge of town that I had noticed going to and from the airfield. I had decided that we might occupy the stadium as our base. It was conveniently situated with clear fields of view all around it and a sturdy fence some 2.5m high. It was also one of the few places in town that could accommodate my entire battle group. Built by an Indian company, it was a magnificent structure with a capacity of around 25,000 and a large car park. The football pitch at its centre was still green and well tended and it was surrounded by a running track. But as I walked in, it was teeming with looters who were now smashing the place to pieces.

I tried to remonstrate with them for a short while, but when I asked why it was being destroyed one looter simply said, 'We hate it because it was his,' meaning Saddam's.

'It's yours now,' I explained.

'I know,' the looter replied. 'So we're getting our bit.'

I quickly tired of this and put a magazine of pistol shots into the air, whereupon hundreds of looters scrambled out of every crack and ran off. After looking around, we crossed back into the main town, where we were met by another noisy demonstration. We halted as this apparent protest came towards us, thousands of people chanting and waving flags and pictures. As they drew closer we could see that the flags were the black and red flags of Shia and the pictures were of the bearded Baqir al-Sadr, murdered in 1980 by Saddam and symbol of Shia to many, and of course pictures of Husayn bin Ali, grandson of the Prophet Mohammed.

'What the fuck is goin' on here?' Herby said as we watched the procession pass by.

The crowd was all men, mostly young, moving at a jog-trot beside a vehicle in which a sheikh was whipping up a frenzy by calling out a cadence, which the men would repeat. As they did so, they beat themselves and some even whipped their backs with chains. They passed us as if they could not see us, lost in a trance.

'It's Juma, their Sabbath,' I explained, 'and these are the Shia, followers of Husayn, who was killed by a rival Islamic sect in the early years of Islam. The Shi'ites punish themselves at Ashura for not defending Husayn. Just sit still until they've gone. They mean us no harm but there is ample scope for a large misunderstanding here.'

When they had safely passed, I returned the 70km south to the Brigade HQ and reported to the Brigade Commander, as the staff packed up the

HQ around us. 16 Air Assault HQ was also on the move. We sat and talked as the other COs arrived. The Brigade Commander then gave us our orders.

# —17—

# AL AMARAH

It was 11 April 2003 and it looked as if operations were winding up across the country. Two days before, a day after we had toppled the statue in Al Qurnah, the US forces had pulled down another in Baghdad and symbolically the capital of Saddam's regime had fallen. We were entering stage four of the operation, 'nation building' as the US called it. The whole brigade was to move to Maysan province. 1 Para was to take over Al Qurnah and 1 R Irish had responsibility for Al Amarah, a city of 300,000 people, not much smaller than Belfast. It had been the scene of a battle during the First World War when Townshend's force had marched north.

What no one anticipated before the invasion was the degree of wanton destruction and looting that would occur as decades of repression was unleashed in a maelstrom of violence. As the Iraqi forces left, it was spreading like a Biblical plague. The vacuum left by Saddam's regime, for which the allies had no apparent plan, was being filled by spontaneous destruction. The Iraqi Army were routed and dissolving or being deliberately dismissed by the victorious allies. The civil authorities and police stayed at home to await the call to whatever order would replace the regime. Weapons abandoned on the battlefield were disappearing into unregulated hands. At some point in the future they would re-emerge aimed at us, unless we could establish a peace where rifles had no place. That could not be achieved by force alone but through a mutual understanding with the Iraqis founded on trust. The Iraqis, after the upheaval, needed security to underpin the peace. This would have to be built up and quickly. For Al Amarah my mission was to repeat our success in Al Rumaylah by making contact with the powerbrokers and establishing my bona fides as someone who was on their side but who would brook no disorder. I would try to deliver the services in Al Amarah as I had in Rumaylah, by harnessing the Ba'athist infrastructure and then allowing it to find its own level with the guidance of the elders. This would be my biggest test yet.

Back in Al Qurnah I got together the senior commanders in the orders group, or O Group. I could see fractures and fissures caused by the pace and strain of the preceding days. Some of the senior officers were not doing well. For some fatigue had taken its toll. Others were just out of their depth. I would need to provide strong leadership to bolster them. It was early evening and we had gathered in what had been the bar of the hotel. I gave orders for the move north, explaining the situation in Al Amarah as best I could. At the end there were very few questions. I could see that there was an uneasiness born of the sheer size of our new role, but it was one in which I knew we could not afford to fail.

This would be different from anything we had seen so far. We had to occupy a town which had liberated itself – or at least believed it had done so. It had been the southern bastion of Chemical Ali and no doubt we would encounter those with whom he had had close dealings – for good and for ill. There was also the matter of a whole division's worth of weapons missing up there, so if it did go wrong we would need to brace ourselves for extreme violence. However, I explained to my officers, we would go forward, our hands extended, and seek to work with these people. Where there had to be retribution, it would be swift and we would tolerate no challenge to our authority. At the same time we would establish a new order based on the Iraqi people and back it by whatever means necessary in order to lead them to their future of freedom and prosperity.

Outside Ali waited for me with a little surprise. I had asked him to find something in the market for us to have as barbecue on the terrace. As I walked out he stood there with a goat.

'Supper,' he said with a smile.

'Not exactly to go,' I said.

A fire had already been built and we took the goat across to the edge of the terrace that looked over the confluence of the three great rivers and there, with the sun setting, I took out my Fairburn Sykes knife. 'This is like Abraham and Isaac,' I said to Ali as he held the goat, and with that I dispatched the animal to the hereafter with a single cut to the throat. We bled it and then some of the Royal Engineers hung it up to strip off the meat – or as much as we needed – before giving the rest to some locals who were watching. It was bloody tough meat.

We arrived in Al Amarah the next day, 12 April. Sitting in the centre of the city, between the River Tigris and the Chahaila Canal, is the old town. It dates back millennia and would have been known to the Children of Israel in their time of slavery in Babylon. The Chahaila Canal feeds a tributary called the Maqharrah which winds off to the east and towards the town of Chahaila and beyond that Iran. This was where, for centuries, an important river port stood and it is still the main hub of the town. Townshend's force landed here on 3 June 1916. South of this is the Al Awwashah neighbourhood, with quiet streets and large houses, home to the middle classes, predominantly former Ba'athists, although oddly the resistance leaders had villas there too. The Ba'athist hospital is there. Across the river, the Hayy Al Muallmin district is a relatively affluent area but gives way to the south to less salubrious housing. As one stood at the southern entrance to the town and looked north the left bank of the river was new-build government offices and the like, including a hospital; the right bank was the old town, cafés and the market (souk). This had been a military cantonment when the British were there. The sports stadium was on the left bank and on the edge of the Hayy al Muallmin district, but set apart. Facing the hospital on the south bank and shaded by date palms was Chemical Ali's old house, which was previously the old British Officers' Club. The older parts of town are mud-brick houses, some with exposed brick and some rendered. Large waste areas dot the poorer part of town while in the centre there is a public park with a children's playground. Al Amarah once basked in the shade of thousands of ancient palm trees but even as we arrived they were being felled for fuel.

1 R Irish set up home in the stadium. We allocated the companies space in the stands and soon 1,225 men and women had disappeared into the fabric, finding their own little spots. Toilets were dug in the surrounding waste ground and also in the stadium, boys on the long jump pit and the girls on the high jump pit (we had around fifteen girls in total). I set up home in an office in the foyer facing onto the track.

The stadium concealed a long-range Al-Samoud missile, an Iraqi-made

Scud, which was parked under the stadium. It was mounted on a massive vehicle called a transporter-erector-launcher (TEL) and the missile was 12m long and 1.5m wide. The Al Samoud had a longer ranger than the SS1-B Scud missile (250 miles compared to 175 miles) which was so prominent in the First Gulf War. Our main concern was that it was designed to carry a conventional, nuclear, biological or chemical warhead. None of these would be good but somehow the thought of sitting beside a chemical or biological weapon seemed more worrying, for fear of any leaks. By the time we arrived it had lost its wheel to looters and one chappie was having a go at taking bits of metal off it with a hammer.

I turned to Ali. 'Go and explain that if he hits the wrong bit he'll be the first Iraqi to walk in space.'

'And surrounded by angry Paddies,' Shaggy added.

The man sitting astride the missile was banging away, oblivious to us. He clearly thought he had got a real prize here. He had stripped away some panels to reveal a tangle of wires and pipes around the body of the missile. I recalled from my briefings during the First Gulf War that one of the components used to make Scuds fly was fuming sulphuric acid. I didn't fancy getting any of that on my overalls. Ali spoke to him and the man replied, shaking his hand in an irritated manner. I gather Ali then told him that the thing was live and could go off at any moment. Ali patiently explained that it was a missile that could fly miles and explode. As he listened, the man's jaw dropped further with every sentence. When Ali finished, the man let it sink in for a second, then in a single movement slid to the ground and, gathering his dishdash in one hand and hammer in the other, he headed off with a quick step that became a run and then a sprint as he ran for his life out of the stadium, shouting to fellow looters. We stood watching him in amazement and then all fell about laughing. I thought everyone in the world knew what a big missile was. Ali explained that the bloke could hear fluid in it and had thought it was a tanker for petrol, which he had been trying to tap off[112].

My room in the stadium was simply set up with a table, camp cot, a mosquito net, some camp chairs and my boxes with various goodies like coffee and cigars. I even had some Iraqi apple whisky. (Doctors believe that I'm over the worst of the liver damage it caused.) I had set up my

---

[112] We had it removed and destroyed by the Royal Engineers. When it went off, at 15km distance, it broke windows in Al Amarah.

bunk and was writing some instructions for the companies at a makeshift table when a guard emerged into my room from behind the poncho that acted as my door with a visitor, Sheikh Mohammed al Badi. This was the man that Jimmy from the CIA had talked about. The visitor had arrived with Jeff, the Special Forces guy. I was delighted to meet the sheikh as I believed he was potentially an ally. Sheikh Mohammed was in his early thirties, tall and slim with a black beard. He was dressed in the black robes of a sheikh with a white turban. He was fragrant with an unusual perfume in contrast to my sweaty hum. He wore sandals on his feet and I noticed his fine hands with long fingers that had never laboured. The sheikh was extremely polite and explained that while he spoke English he would prefer to address me in Arabic. Ali was called and we sat down to talk, Sheikh Mohammed arranging his robes as he sat upright in his chair with a noble air about him. Magoo and Corporal Stevens brought some tea in the small glasses we had for such occasions. We had bought them in Al Rumaylah as all discussions in Arabia are best begun with a little hospitality. He accepted a cigarette.

The sheikh began a long soliloquy about how he had been actively assisting resistance from Iran and now he had returned to help his people. He spoke in a low and resonant voice and as he spoke he would look thoughtfully into space as if repeating it by heart. During our discussion, he emphasised that though they wanted little from us, he did need us to endorse his candidates for the running of the town and to provide some security, as he feared there would be a power struggle. He warned me that the Ba'athists were strong and would seek to re-establish their power. I told him I was pleased to see him and that I would enjoy working with him but that he should understand that power was not mine to give away as such and that I intended to call a meeting to which all factions would be invited and to which he would be most welcome. He was not overly pleased but agreed to come. I asked if he knew of a venue in which we could hold such a meeting but he said he did not, adding that everywhere was destroyed. With that he stood up and we parted on what I felt were good terms.

As he left he told me in English that he was pleased to be working with the British. We exchanged telephone numbers. I had an Iridium satellite telephone that worked, on and off. Sheikh Mohammed had an extremely sophisticated Thuryah satellite telephone like the one the journalist Sarah Oliver had.

Afterwards I spoke to Jeff and thanked him for his efforts. He was an asset in his own right and had already done a great deal to get to know the politics of the town. Later I sat down to reflect on my meeting with the sheikh and smoked in silence.

As I stood up at last to make my way out to speak to Brigade in order to give the Commander a feel for what had been said, I was met in the foyer by a small delegation of new Arabs, led by a tall man with flowing robes and a traditional shemagh. He was a striking fellow in his early forties, slim but wiry, with a strong lean face and large thoughtful eyes. He had the hooked nose of a Bedouin and a well-trimmed beard, shaved underneath in the style of the Howeitat Bedouin tribe. His teeth were prominent and when he was listening they rested on his bottom lip, giving him a half grin, but when he smiled he beamed. This was the famous resistance fighter Abu Hatim[113], the 'Robin Hood' or 'Prince' of the marshes. Originally a builder, Abu Hatim had opposed Saddam from his initial bid for power. The Iraqi Secret Police, the Mukhabarat, came for him but he had fled to the marshes and for the next twenty-five years led a resistance against Saddam's regime, sometimes from Iran. Revered in the marketplace and with huge local support, it had been Abu Hatim who struck the fateful blow against the regime in the area and caused them to flee rather than face his marsh warriors.

Abu Hatim introduced me to Yasim, his sidekick. Small and shifty, he always seemed impatient and he spoke in a high-pitched voice. Yasim struck me, from the first instant I met him, as a bit of a chancer. He was wearing a combat jacket and was concerned that my guards had relieved him of his pistol, a Czech CZ 9mm, when he was searched before meeting me. They did not ever search any visitors in robes on my instructions. The other supporter was a man with a distinctly Persian look. Skinny and bearded, he wore jeans and a checked shirt with working boots and carried a notebook. The fourth man was introduced as 'the Brigadier', the former head of police in the town, a big fierce-looking man with grey hair and a grey moustache. He stood well over six feet tall and was built like a bouncer. I could tell that he was once used to getting his way but was now in fear for his life and totally

---

[113] It is usual for Arab men to be named after their oldest child, hence Abu Rifat – father of Rifat – and Abu Nawfel – father of Nawfel. Abu Hatim, however, was single and childless. I immediately realised that the name was in fact a *nom de guerre* referring to one of Islam's greatest victories over the crusaders at the battle of Hattin in 1187 and won by one of Iraq's greatest warriors Sa'aladin. In this case, the name means 'father of the victory of Islam'.

obsequious to Abu Hatim. He was dressed in a grey double-breasted suit.

I invited them in and asked the boys to find some more chairs. I asked Corporal Stevens and Signalman Cascarino to make some more tea and we all stepped into my room. I apologised for the humble surroundings and Abu Hatim apologised for the destruction.

'I was too busy to stop it. You will understand, I'm sure,' he said. 'They tell me you did not tolerate it for long either. You seem to know how to deal with my poor people.'

We laughed and I tapped my pistol, which was lying on a box beside my bed. 'It speaks a language we all understand.'

We sat and exchanged pleasantries over tea and then got down to business. Abu Hatim explained that he had heard that I had had a meeting with Sheikh Mohammed al Badi. I said that this was so and he had only recently left. I explained to him about my hopes for a town council and asked if he was prepared to participate. He was eager to have power passed to him completely and once more I had to explain that while I could not pass up my military authority over the town, I was eager to work in partnership with the locals. Abu Hatim then explained that Sheikh Mohammed had returned from Iran very recently and was indeed a man of some standing. But he went on to say that he, Abu Hatim, had spent the last twenty-five years resisting Saddam and his regime, operating from the marshes, and he had the groundswell of support from the people of the town. I asked once more if he would come to a meeting and if he could suggest a venue. He suggested the hospital and said that the meeting should be at 1000 hours the next day.

'Who should be there?' I asked.

He reeled off a list of potential people and I asked him to arrange for the most important pair in my view to come, Sa'id al Jaber, who I had already established through Sheikh Mohammed was the most influential cleric in town, and the senior non-Ba'athist doctor, Dr Yassim Aboud Yassim (no relation to Abu Hatim's assistant), who I knew, as an educated man and a non-Ba'athist, would add some reason to the debate. Jeff had briefed me that these two were crucial to winning the confidence of the people. He told me that the most senior doctor in town had been a Ba'athist. I explained that I would like him to come too.

'You had better ask him,' Abu Hatim laughed, gesturing to Yasim who looked like he would have merrily killed the doctor. He gave me a telephone number, producing another extremely swish satellite telephone.

As Abu Hatim left he asked me to make a visit early the next morning to an important place in town, which he emphasised I must see. He explained that it was the British war cemetery. 'You will see how we hold you in respect and look after your dead.'

The next day I had a few calls to make. I had intended to see both the town hospital and the Ba'ath party hospital. I also wanted to visit the old city and to see the Town Hall, which was in the centre of town. We set off in a convoy, as I wanted my Royal Military Police detachment to accompany us and get a feel for the town. Our journalists came along too and I now had Phil Ballard back with me as the translator. The first stop was to be the cemetery. We drove the long way through town and close to the old souk. As we passed the old town barracks, formerly the British barracks in the 1930s, I saw an old Army of India pack howitzer standing outside the gate[114]. Amazingly the whole town had been looted, as had the barracks, but this fine piece of history, albeit in a slightly down-at-heel state, remained. I stopped to get a closer look. Sure enough it was a mountain field gun, a two-pounder and built so that it could be dismantled and put on mules to be taken over the mountains, bearing the markings of 'Birmingham 1916'.

'We must recover this and bring it home where it belongs,' I said to Phil and Herby as we stood and looked. We did recover it and the plan was for it to be returned to the UK to be refurbished and placed in the mess as a souvenir of Operation Telic. The restoration would have been expensive, we realised, but worth it given its distinguished history. We needn't have worried about the cost, however, as the Army had it seized and destroyed in Kuwait, something that the Ottoman Empire, the Ba'athists, looters and the allied invasion had failed to achieve.

Just then a shot cracked over my head and I turned to see a man with an AK-47 standing at the side of a building about 50m away. He was looking open-mouthed at the RSM, who had fixed him with a steely glare. Some of the soldiers on the escort got ready to shoot, but the RSM raised his hand to stop them, looked at the man and told him to 'Fuck off!' The gunman seemed to understand and ran off into the

---

[114] It had stood, Abu Hatim later explained, outside the British Officers' Club until 1958, when the club was given over as a private residence and the gun was moved to outside the barracks. The club was most recently home to Chemical Ali but was now occupied by squatters. The compulsion that the Iraqi Army had for painting things (which they had inherited from the British) had actually preserved the piece extremely well.

market. I assume he was a released prisoner and had seen an opportunity to settle his debt to the Fedayeen. Weeks earlier we would have shot him dead. Now we thought it was funny. We continued in our vehicles across the President's Bridge over the Chahaila Canal and on to the cemetery.

The British Commonwealth War Graves Commission cemetery is near the centre of Al Amarah, in the park beside the Chahaila Canal. Set in a shady grove of date palms, it has a sturdy iron fence around it and is split into three sections: the Islamic cemetery, which is now used as a football pitch; the Hindi cemetery, which has been defaced but is still there, with a crumbling monument; and the Christian and others cemetery, which is intact and very well preserved. We entered through the gatehouse where the caretaker lived. It was a bit like entering the 'Secret Garden'.

The first remarkable thing was the fact that while we were normally surrounded by crowds wherever we went in Al Amarah, when we walked through the gates of the cemetery they peeled off, as if an invisible force field prevented them from coming in. They left my side and raced off to grab a place on the fence to look in. Soon the fence was lined with faces staring in at us. Inside the 'Chowkidar[115]' or caretaker, Mosun Ali, stepped forward. A small man with a welcoming expression, he was overjoyed to see us and ran in front to show me the way to the cemetery proper. It opened before me like an oasis. I recall it was at a time when we had just received reports that vandals had been desecrating our war graves in France and here was such a stark contrast, to stand in a recently liberated land among the graves of men who had lifted the yoke of Ottoman oppression from the people of a fledgling Iraq ninety years before and who were still accorded such respect and dignity.

The graves as such were unmarked and lay under a hand-cut lawn the size of around three football pitches. The gravestones had been removed in 1930 because acidic elements in the soil were eating the stone. Instead, at one end of the cemetery was a long stone monument 90m long and 2m high in slate grey stone and reminiscent of the Vietnam memorial in Washington, with the names of the dead recorded on the wall in alphabetical order, by rank and regiment, with regiments arranged by seniority, each under their cap badge. The cemetery contained the remains of over 3,000 British and Commonwealth servicemen, including two Victoria Cross holders, a Royal Navy

---

[115] A Hindi word.

lieutenant and a lieutenant colonel from the North Staffordshires. At one section were the cap badges of the Connaught Rangers, Royal Irish Fusiliers and Royal Irish Rifles. As I read the names of these fallen Paddies, the majority from the wild west coast of Ireland in County Mayo, I could see names of men whose namesakes were serving in the battalion today. One of my sergeants from County Longford actually had a great-uncle buried in the cemetery. Flowers and shrubs grew in neat rows where the graves were divided into sections and date palms shaded the cool lawn. In the centre was a Portland stone monument of a cross with a sword embedded in it. Our small party moved around and looked in wonder at the tranquil surroundings, as birds sang and soft winds ruffled the palms of the date trees that shaded the precincts. Mosun Ali and his sons watched, their chest swollen with pride as we admired their work and diligence.

As I stood there taking in the beauty of this peaceful garden and reading the names on the wall, Mosun Ali approached me with a large bundle. 'Please, *sidi*,' he said, 'this for you.' I took the bundle, which contained a book showing the layout of the cemetery and details of all the men who were buried there. It described each man, where he came from and even his parents and occupation. The VCs had their citations added, as did the holders of the DSO. It was a sad reflection of history that when I looked at the section with the Irish names, while the Ulstermen from the Fusiliers and Rifles had full accounts of themselves, many of the Mayo men had very few details beyond their dates of birth and death and service numbers. Many, I noted, were regular Army but the vast majority of the men of Connaught were wartime volunteers. One of the soldiers who was reading the book with me enquired as to why there were so few details of the Southern Irish casualties. Ironically the scant details were the result of a fear of terrorism, even in 1922. I explained that the book was compiled in 1921/22 when Ireland was in the grip of a civil war. To live in the west of Ireland and to admit to having a relative, even a son or husband, killed in the service of the Crown would have brought the IRA murder gangs to your door the same day. It is only very recently, the last few years, that Ireland has allowed itself to recognise this momentous sacrifice to freedom in the World Wars. In the De Valera era it was airbrushed out of history. A Southern Irish soldier suggested that maybe the people didn't think it was important. I explained that Ireland lost 49,000 men dead in the First World War. Its casualty rates across the Irish regiments were eighty-five per cent. Against the population of Ireland at the time it was a huge loss.

Compared to the modern US population today (currently at around 240 million) it would be the equivalent of losing 3.5 million US servicemen – indeed the population of modern Ireland. It was important.

'Where is the VC winner buried?' I asked Mosun Ali.

'Two.' He held up two fingers and ran to one spot and pointed down and then to another spot near the wall about 50m away and pointed again. I had no idea how he knew that these shallow depressions held Victoria Cross holders but he seemed to.

'So you know every grave by heart?' I asked.

He came to my side and with me still holding the book he leafed through to the page showing the first VC citation. He pointed to the grave number, Plot XVI, 14 L. He then turned to a diagram of the cemetery and pointed to the Portland stone cross, just to our rear, marked on it and noted XVI. He then indicated 'J, K, L' pointing to the row at our feet then he pointed to the diagram where the graves on these rows began at 20 and counted, '19, 18, 17, 16, 15,' and stepped back, pointing at his feet, '14.'

'That's amazing,' I said.

'We have cared for this place for three generations. We know every man here. I am glad to give you the book. We do not need it. We know it. It brought us much trouble too.'

'Trouble?' I asked.

'Yes, *sidi*, the Ba'athists used to come when they were drunk and ask for the book. They beat us up – all of us, even the children – but we did not tell. The whole town has looked after this book. It has been moved around for its safety. I'm sorry, but no cover now. But it is safe and now we give it you.'

This took me aback. 'You got beaten up for this book? I'm so sorry that you suffered for this. But we are grateful. I only hope the poor pay we give you in some way compensates for what you have suffered.'

'Pay? We get no pay. Not for fifteen years. The last visit we had was the Australian Consul, who came in 1994 but he did not come back. Iraq was a dangerous place.'

'So if you did not get paid, how did you live?' I asked.

'I am a civil engineer and my son is engineer too. We do this in our . . .' He hesitated. 'Free . . .' He corrected himself. 'Spare time. Whole family helps.'

'But why do you do this thing for us if we give you no pay and never come to visit?'

'Because we knew you come back to save us one day. We – the whole town – know. It was a comfort. We wanted you to be pleased to see how we have kept this place for your people.'

I was choked with emotion. As I looked around I noted that the ordinarily garrulous crowd were silent too, watching me as I surveyed the scene. I now knew why Abu Hatim wanted me to see this place. I turned to the caretaker. 'We have come back and I want you now to accept the grateful thanks of all the many nationalities who lie here. Tonight have a party. Here is thirty dollars. Celebrate we are back.'

At first he did not want to take the money. I insisted. The most touching thing to me was that they had not been warned that we were coming; they couldn't have known, as I had only decided that morning to go there. Yet the garden was freshly cut, the borders and lawn mature and carefully weeded, the hedges immaculate. I turned to a young soldier standing beside me.

'Look at this place,' I said.

'It like Roselawn[116], so it is,' he noted.

'But that's the point,' I emphasised. 'When we came – it could have been any day in the last eighteen years – they were ready. That's dedication.'

Then the ranger noted rather profoundly, 'It's like the day of judgement – you never know when you'll be called. They were ready, all right.'

We went to the Chowkidar's house and we sat and had some tea. We chatted with the family about their life, the power cuts and water (the key issues). As we emerged from his house and walked out of the precincts of the cemetery, the crowd parted and Mosun Ali, walking beside me, was as proud a man as you could ever meet. We left the book there. It is where it belongs. We must never let these people down again, I thought to myself. I hope we don't.

We made our way to the Ba'athist hospital. I had arranged to meet the chief doctor. He was a short, squat man in his fifties with a broad face and a trimmed moustache and thinning hair. When he spoke he did so with great passion and his eyes bulged. We were invited into his office in the hospital and the doctor bade us sit down. I was there with Phil and Sarah. At the doctor's desk, totally ignoring us, was a Shia cleric who was watching Iranian TV and frequently using the doctor's telephone. I went to introduce myself but he spun round in his chair to present his back to me. I decided not to slap the back of his head – just yet. I sat down.

---

[116] Belfast's main cemetery.

The doctor began loudly, no doubt for the benefit of the cleric: 'I am indebted to the religious men, they have protected me since the Army went.' He smiled in an obsequious manner towards the young clergyman, who ignored him and carried on chatting on the phone. I asked how things were for him now. 'Not good.' He sighed. 'They blame us for everything. I can say that Saddam was bad now, but then we had to live. It is much worse now. They came to my house and took my car. The clergy protected this place or they would have taken everything. We are so grateful to them.' He smiled once more, nodding towards the arrogant young Shi'ite. 'You, when you came, all fell apart.' He stabbed towards me with his finger. 'You know, I believe it was part of the plan of the Americans and British to make all chaos and destruction,' he said, wagging the sausage-like finger at me.

Tea had arrived and I took one of the tiny cups as the waiter tipped a large spoon of sugar in. As I stirred my tea I explained that we had sought to liberate Iraq and I too was distraught at the looting. I assured him nobody on the allied side had foreseen such destruction.

'How could you not foresee this?' he said, raising his hand. 'All is destruction. All goes over the border to Iran to be sold. What you do?' he asked, eyebrows raised and hand suspended in mid air, shoulders shrugged.

When we finished talking we stood up and I glanced at the cleric, who once more spun round in the chair to face away from me. I loudly continued, 'Did you know I'm meeting Sa'id al Jaber now – I believe he is the senior Shia cleric in town? Yes, at the hospital. I have promised to tell him of the things I need and anything that upsets me.'

As if propelled by a spring the bad-mannered young Shi'ite leapt up and gave a slight bow towards me before sitting to pretend to be busying himself in paperwork.

So the bastard speaks English, I thought to myself.

We drove north towards the bridge that would take us to the town hospital but via the Town Hall in the centre of the old town, where the old buildings with ornate windows executed in marquetry reflected the former wealth of the busy river port. The Town Hall itself was a splendid building, with pink tiles and a palm grove in front. My six-vehicle convoy rolled into the entrance driveway only to discover there was a swarm of looters moving around inside, carting away furniture. We tried to shoo them off but they ignored us. The massive entrance hall was filled with the wreckage of furniture and we were ankle deep in paper. A filing cabinet crashed onto the ground behind me from the first floor. I looked up to see some looters dart away. Phil was running about shouting but to no avail. I drew my pistol and, aiming out of the window at a high wall to my front, fired a single round. Once again this had the desired effect and the looters emerged from everywhere to run out of the building. We looked around and found that the place was not actually too badly damaged structurally. It would need to be totally refurbished inside but the fabric of the building was intact. We set off again for the meeting in the hospital.

When we arrived I was greeted by one of our patrols. We had a platoon permanently stationed there now to protect this vital town asset and its equipment. Crowds milled around and I went to find Dr Yassim. He was a small man with a beard and was working at his desk as I was shown in. We chatted and then, noting it was five to ten, Dr Yassim led the way through a bustling reception area to their lecture room, the venue for the conference. It was arranged with rows of seats facing a raised stage, which had a double blackboard. Written on the board in neat copperplate English were some medical instructions for the antenatal care of pregnant women. There was a dais for a speaker but the staff had set a chair in the centre of the low stage with a table to one side for me to address the meeting. A bowl of plastic flowers had been placed on the table. Sheikh Mohammed was there and so was Sa'id al Jaber, the Shia cleric of whom I had heard so much and who was treated with great deference by the others in the room. We were introduced. Sa'id al Jaber was in his late fifties or early sixties and looked not unlike Sean Connery. He was clearly a very placid man but had an air of authority about him. Sa'id al Jaber introduced his assistant, a mad-looking bastard with goggle eyes under thick glasses. He wore the robes of a cleric and had the sudden jerky movements of a tightly wound spring.

I invited Sa'id al Jaber to sit with me but he declined and urged Sheikh Mohammed to sit with me instead. More chairs were brought and I had one placed for my translator – Ali and Phil were to take it in turns – and a seat for Abu Hatim. We waited as the hall filled. Some staff from Brigade came, along with the heads of the utilities – power, sewage, water. Some representatives came from the schools and we settled down as I looked for Abu Hatim. I could see that some of those at the meeting were not a bit pleased to see the Ba'athists there.

Eventually I went into the foyer to look for Abu Hatim, only to discover him clearly upset about something and about to leave with his delegation. I spoke quickly to one of Abu Hatim's aides as he stared ahead, his face a mask of fury. They had been told that I was sitting at the front with Sheikh Mohammed surrounded by former Ba'athists. It was, they feared, a calculated slight on him. Did we not know who had liberated the town? Abu Hatim was dressed in the robes of a tribal elder and had a set of white calfskin leather military Sam Browne belt equipment with silver G3 rifle magazines and (empty) pouches for grenades. His robes were snow-white and his equipment was finished in silver and gold thread. Yasim hovered at his side in the same combat jacket he always wore. He looked like thunder. I realised that this meeting was for them their Luneberg Heath. They had come to accept the surrender of the Ba'athists and, I suspect, they had envisaged a more adroitly stage-managed scene. I explained that I could see that there had been a misunderstanding, and then added that if Abu Hatim left there could be no meeting or indeed council, as he was the leader of the men who liberated Al Amarah. This was translated and he visibly relaxed. I asked if we could talk. He agreed and Abu Hatim and I went off into a quiet room. Phil translated.

'Look,' I said, 'I need you. We need each other. I don't know what Sheikh Mohammed has done to upset you but I need to find out what help he can give me.'

'Help? He has no men and nothing to give,' Abu Hatim said. 'He has spent the war [sic] sitting in Iran. *I* fought Saddam and *I* drove them out, not him, not you.'

'I accept that, Abu Hatim,' I began. 'I thought we would be allies. We still can be. I need your help. I need your patronage. We both need the Ba'athists. You have your policeman, the Brigadier, and I have my doctor and power man and water man. It's this simple. We can do away with them right now and sit and hate them in the dark or we can put them to work and make it very clear that either they do as we say, in which case we might even keep them – who knows, or we might have to deal with them early on. What do you say?'

Abu Hatim looked at me, his eyes fixing mine. There was a long, uncomfortable silence. Then he beamed and laughed. 'OK, OK, we go,' he said in English. He grabbed my hand as we stood up and we walked hand in hand into the meeting.

There was a shocked silence in the room. The locals and Brigade staff were obviously amazed, while the Arabs were wondering if they were seeing a new alliance, as Sa'id al Jaber watched with hands folded in his lap and a contented look, like the bride's mother. I was happy that the man who commanded the best organised faction on the streets publicly endorsed me. Sheikh Mohammed glanced at a book on his lap and underlined a word nonchalantly, ignoring this grand entrance. I took my seat, registering the nuances.

I asked Sa'id al Jaber to begin the meeting but he deferred to a very old man who had arrived since I had left and who was dressed in the robes of a tribal elder and sheikh. This, it transpired, was Sheikh Ishmail, senior of the tribal leaders in the marshes[117]. Tall and noble, he was very frail as he was helped to come forward. He sat in a chair that was brought for him and Ali sat on one side while a supporter sat on the other, both sitting forward with their ears close to him and reporting, Ali in English and the other man in Arabic, what Sheikh Ishmail said in his faltering high-pitched voice.

'They have been before,' he wheezed. 'We had good times and bad times but they gave us Iraq. They made Iraq. Look around, we are from many places but we are Iraq. They did this. In the bad time we talked about how good it would be if they came back. They are here now. Let us not make the same mistakes. Hear what they have to say.' Then turning to me, he held out a piece of paper in a hand that shook as he extended it, parchment-like skin stretched over long bony fingers. It had some names in shaky Arabic script. 'These are my friends in London. They know me. Ask them to visit.'

I took the list and glanced at it. I could not read Arabic but realised that they would all be dead these many years. Sheikh Ishmail, I was later to discover, was over 100. As he finished he raised an arm to show he had said his piece and attendants rushed to help him to his feet. He bowed slightly to Sa'id al Jaber and then to me. I sprang to my feet and nodded my head and touched my chest with my right hand. Sheikh Ishmail shuffled out of the meeting leaning on a stick as all present rose to join me standing in deference to this clearly respected elder until the door closed again behind him and his followers.

I sat down and looked over to Sa'id al Jaber, who nodded and smiled. I began to set out our position. I made it clear that we, the allies, had come once more to liberate the people of Iraq, not from a foreign oppressor this time but from their own kind. For too long Iraq, I asserted, which should be among the wealthiest and the most powerful in the region, had suffered and had bent under the weight of a dictator. He had now gone. I urged them to look with pride in Al Amarah at the

---

[117] When the British had come in the 1920s and after the Iraqi uprising, they handed power to the tribal elders. This was unpopular with the townsfolk but played to the strengths of the pro-British Hashemite King and the desert tribes.

liberation and to remember that they did it for themselves. It was the rifles of the tribes under Abu Hatim who had routed the Ba'athists, but the coalition allies had come to their aid, first the US Marines then the Royal Irish. Now, I emphasised, the fighting was over. Now we all had to work to rebuild the province. I pointed to the Ba'athists.

'We need these men,' I explained. 'They must be made to work. They have the skills, they have the knowledge. Make them pay back through work.'

Abu Hatim nodded in agreement while many in the room looked on with astonishment. I turned to the plans to form some sort of a council. I suggested it be nominated straight away. I then listed the other needs, to get the power running and the water going. We had to deal with the sewage and open the schools. Above all, we had to stop the looting. I wanted to push home the message from General Brims: make it clear, looting was theft. And the theft was of *their property*. It no longer belonged to Saddam. Finally I addressed the issue of guns. There were too many guns around. There was too much shooting and we needed to deal with the criminal gangs. As I spoke, I looked at a little fat man with a thick moustache and a couple of days' growth who was standing at the side with a Tariq pistol pushed into his waistband. I finished on that note and handed the floor to Abu Hatim.

He spoke up in agreement with me but emphasised the need to use the Ba'athists and the need to get the utilities working and the schools open. Finally he told them that he would be vigilant over the matter of weapons. One voice of dissent objected to the Ba'athists and more joined. I glanced at the little fat doctor who had lectured me on how I had caused all of the upheaval, but he was listening intently to the argument, mopping his brow with a large hanky and glancing at Abu Hatim.

Finally Abu Hatim raised a hand and said, 'If I can live with them then so can you.'

As Ali translated this I looked up to see a now silent audience, some glancing at their feet, others studying notes. There was a brief pause and then the whole room began talking at once. Eventually we decided that Sa'id al Jaber would nominate the council. He put Abu Hatim in charge. Sheikh Mohammed would be in charge of procedure. He nominated the Ba'athists to look after their own utilities and Dr Yassim would handle all medical matters. The schoolteachers had hidden the school supplies at home and the head teacher of the primary school could not be at the meeting because he had barricaded himself into the high school with both schools' furniture, such as it was. The momentum that had begun gathered pace and within hours there would be police on the streets directing traffic and firemen parading outside their station at the beginning of their watch, exactly as they had been taught to do by the British firemen who had trained them many years before.

After the meeting I spoke to Abu Hatim. 'Who,' I asked, 'was the man with the gun at my meeting?'

'Nothing to do with me,' Abu Hatim said. 'He's a gangster and wants to be recognised as a resistance fighter. He has shot people in the town for their possessions. I would have dealt with him but you said there was an end to the fighting.'

'I see,' I said. 'I do not like people coming to my meetings with guns. It shows a total lack of respect to my forces and me. I don't like people who shoot others so they can rob them either. There is little I can do now but I don't want to see him armed at my meetings again.'

Abu Hatim laughed. 'You will not need to worry about him.'

# —18—

# JOINT PATROLS

On the way back to the stadium I felt hopeful that some form of normality would descend on our lives. The policemen on the streets were directing traffic in their blue shirts and Iraqi flags were beginning to appear on buildings, which I regarded as a sign of growing confidence. In the old town, shops were operating normally. I called Brigade with an account of the meeting to supplement the version their staff had brought back.

That night there was a great deal of firing of weapons, not at anybody in particular, but by way of celebration. This was part of the wallpaper as far as my men were concerned. Instructions were passed to all patrols not to react unless they were actually shot at, but they were to confiscate any weapons seen. I was in talks with Abu Hatim and his representatives at the time about mounting joint patrols with the RMP and his men. I looked forward to sharing the burden of securing this town. We were getting reports from the locals that relations in the town of Kut, to our north, between the US forces and the locals were poor and there was sporadic fighting most days. I did not want that to spread to my area. My excellent RMP commander, Gyn Parry-Jones, a little Welsh chap, was a no-nonsense policeman who brought experience of policing nascent societies in Afghanistan and Macedonia. He was negotiating with Yasim about formalising the resistance into a gendarmerie to assist the old Ba'athist police. The production of badges was the subject that most fixated Yasim, as well as weapon licences. (I let Yasim have his pistol back as he had been a good boy for the last day or so.)

One of the big problems we had at the stadium was with the crowds of children who gathered at the fence to shout to the men or try to barter for sweets and food. Often they would offer old bayonets or the like in exchange for rations, money or magazines like *FHM* or *Maxim*. I forbade any trading of this nature. Firstly it was undisciplined and secondly I was not sure they were ready for western decadence. Many of the town's young men would also flock to stare at my few females and Sarah, with her long red hair, in particular. Sometimes mischievous lads would throw stones at the soldiers – as in so many places, out of boredom and to see if they could get a reaction. On one occasion a little chap of around eleven brought a 12.7mm bullet he had found. Holding it against a railing to steady it, he was hitting the striker cap with a rock, no doubt to launch the bullet at our vehicles. Why he wanted to do this, who knows, but he succeeded in setting the round off. What he did not realise was that rifle barrels are specially constructed to withstand the thousands of pounds of pressure a detonating bullet generates. His hand was not. He was carried into us at the stadium and we evacuated him to the hospital but he lost his hand nevertheless.

I enquired of one of the men I was drinking tea with at a riverside café one afternoon why the children stoned us, albeit rarely.

'They see it on TV,' he explained.

I was intrigued. 'Yeah, when they see pictures of the West Bank in Palestine and Gaza, the kids are stoning the Army vehicles. Yours look just like them. It's a sort of game. Take no offence,' he said.

'Sure, we used to stone the Brits after school when I was growin' up,' said one of my sergeants who was standing nearby. 'Them or the peelers or the Huns[118] at the bottom of our road. We loved it.'

The stoning took a strange turn when one of my sergeants, Sergeant McLaughlin, was riding his motorbike into town and a young lad threw some stones at him. He chased the lad and was suddenly surrounded by a large crowd. He indicated that the lad had been stoning him and, after a pause, the crowd set about the boy. Sergeant McLaughlin ended up having to extract the lad and help him escape on his motor bike.

Little by little joint patrolling became the norm and joint checkpoints were established. One of the hazards of the checkpoint at the southern gate of Al Amarah was a dead cow. The smell was disgusting and the local dogs were gathering from miles around. We got the engineers to bury it. I always wondered why the poor thing was killed in the first place. I had

---

[118] Irish Catholic slang for Protestants.

seen that sort of thing before in Bosnia when the Croats pulled back after the 1995 Dayton Peace Accord: they slaughtered all the livestock in the areas they left. The bloated cow at the gates of Al Amarah reminded me that the Ba'athists who had retreated from that town were as hostile to the populace as the Croats were to the Serbs.

16 Air Assault Brigade set up home just outside the town in an old military cantonment. I went to visit and I was a little surprised to see that one of the abandoned tanks in the barracks was an old British Chieftain. I recalled that the Shah of Iran had a fleet of these and this was no doubt booty from the Iran–Iraq War. The new Brigade HQ was set up, with the boys from the Royal Irish Rangers having created a new 'Camp Killaloo'. It was good to see the lads again and I asked them to come down to see us at the stadium.

The platoon sergeant of the TA lads was Sergeant Wilson. He was an athletic man with fair hair and a scar on his cheek that ran to his chin. He was mild-mannered but a real motivator. He had been the Pipe Major of the battalion before he retired from the Army. He was an old friend and colleague. His uncle, 'Hippy' Wilson, had been the Pipe Major of the 2nd Battalion the Royal Irish Rangers when we had been in Dover and Cyprus with the UN. His grandfather had been a Pipe Major too and had piped at my wedding back in 1986. This Sergeant Wilson had once paid me the great honour of piping my father to his grave and as well as being an old friend I owed him a debt of kindness. He was in rare form when we met.

'How are the lads?' I asked.

'Stickin' out[119],' he replied.

I watched some of the men, stripped to the waist, filling sandbags for a gate sangar they had built.

'They love it. Still, it's gettin' a bit hot,' he said.

I told him how proud we were of the way the TA lads had performed. 'Are you surprised?' he said. 'Sure, as you said yourself, when you are called up you are not TA any more, you're just part of the Army.'

'And that's a fact,' I said, slapping his back.

They might have been mechanics, insurance salesmen or carpenters, but when they put on their uniforms they were like any other man in the battalion. I believe it is one of the great strengths of the nation that our soldier citizens will come when called – all volunteers – and perform

---

[119] A Belfast expression meaning 'outstanding'.

as these have done. That was the strength of the British regimental system. It is the spirit that animated these men's forefathers in the Second World War and the First World War before that. It was certainly alive in these men as I watched them working, laughing then sipping from their water bottles against the immense heat and the strain of their exertions.

I went to see the Brigade Commander, who told me I would be getting a visit from some of the General's political advisers the next day. 'They want to see how you're getting on in the town,' he explained. The main purpose of the meeting I had come for was to coordinate the brigade's activities across the Province of Maysan. 1 Para had the southern sector and 3 Para patrolled the border with Iran. 3 Regiment Army Air Corps had the area to the north and 1 R Irish had the city of Al Amarah, which was the capital. Each of the commanders was asked to give a resumé of the local conditions and any concerns. When it came to me I had three main points.

'The locals are concerned that a lot of stolen goods are being smuggled out to Iran. We'll need to show we are doing something about this, although the problem is a big one. Secondly, there are joint patrols in Al Amarah and that means irregular militia, supervised by my companies and by Major Parry-Jones, so if you need to come into the town, please check with us to avoid any misunderstandings. Lastly, the marching season starts on Friday. It is Juma, or their Sabbath. This is the season of Ashura when the Shia remember the death of Husayn bin Ali, grandson of the Prophet Mohammed, at Karbala. The Shias parade through the town between 1200 and 1400 hours. They work themselves up quite a bit and it's a good place to avoid during those hours. We don't want any misunderstandings.'

That night was particularly noisy and there was a lot of shooting into the air. I had a company of the Light Infantry attached to my battle group now, mounted in their Warrior armoured vehicles, as well as a troop of Challenger 2 tanks from the second Royal Tank Regiment. At around 2100 hours I sent a message to Yasim, who was supposed to be the head of the local militia, to tell people that the firing had to stop or someone would get injured. Not long afterwards I had a report of a clash between two rival groups. It could well have been Yasim leading his militia against those who were firing their weapons, but for me enough was quite enough. I decided to show my hand. I called Shaggy, the Operations Officer, and told him to mount our own demonstration. He briefed the

Company Commander and the Light Infantry Company led the tanks on a drive around the town at 0200 hours.

I saw Yasim the next day. 'Sleep well?' I enquired.

'No,' he replied. 'The buildings were shaking and my wives were up all night with the noise of your tanks.'

'Exactly,' I said. 'We'll do that every night until the shooting stops.'

We all had a very peaceful night the next night, although the Brigade Commander told me not to have tanks in the town any more as it was upsetting the locals. I couldn't be bothered to explain.

The political advisers arrived and I took them on a visit to the town, including the Town Hall and the market. We stopped for tea at a café on the riverside and a large crowd soon mobbed us. The café was like any you would find across the Mediterranean, except the tables and chairs had seen much better days. Notwithstanding this, the waiter showed us to a table and, flicking the ancient chair with a napkin to make sure there was no dust, he held it for me as we sat and with a flourish presented the menu (then pointed to tea as the only thing they had). Luckily that was all we wanted.

I decided it was time to have our own version of the BBC's *Question Time*. We sat in the outdoor café and answered questions from the audience. The crowd loved it and questions ranged from the rights and wrongs of the war to when would the utilities be up and running, when were we going to sort out Palestine and would Manchester United come to play the local team? I had a chance to quiz the crowd, too, and took a straw poll as to who was the most respected local leader. Abu Hatim won a landslide victory in this little survey, but I also got a strong show of respect for Sheikh Mohammed. It was clear that Sa'id al Jaber was significant but seen as a figurehead rather than a leader as such.

At one point a wizened old boy was pushed to the front and, coming smartly to attention, he threw up a snappy salute and rattled off his regimental number in English. He then announced that he was a veteran of Glub Pasha's Arab Legion and had served with the British Army in the 1940s. I shook his gnarled hand and asked how he was. He replied in Arabic, even though I tried to explain that I didn't understand. He stopped and looked a little amazed[120], but before we could continue the demands of the crowd drew me into another panel discussion.

---

[120] Of course in days of Empire, British officers serving with Imperial units would have been expected to speak to their men in their native tongue, as often few spoke any English. In the same way Marcus and his English officers in the Gurkha company always spoke to the Gurkhas in Nepali.

The owner of the café was delighted with this audience and served endless sweet tea, which was passed to us over the heads of the crowd by tens of careful hands until each small tea glass was gently placed in front of us to a *shukran* (thanks) to which they would reply *afwan* (pleasure). At last we dragged ourselves away from the audience and to our vehicles, mobbed by the crowds. Before I left, I waved to the café owner for a bill but he smiled and waved his hand to decline, indicating the now-bustling café, with every table packed and waiters rushing around with trays of tea.

We still needed to get some sort of solid order to the town and to do this we had to get as many unregulated weapons handed in as possible. We had made it clear that we appreciated the feeling of unease that existed in the town and were prepared to tolerate a licensed weapons system if we could get it into place. I had made it clear that I drew the line at small arms, however, and anyone caught with an RPG or the like was in serious trouble. I made this the responsibility of my RMP Company Commander, Bryn Parry-Jones. He patiently negotiated with Yasim about the design of firearm permits and accounting methods. I knew that there were thousands of weapons out there and that regulation was a fig leaf. As in Al Rumaylah, I was more focused on producing a society where guns had little or no part. This was not just the pipe dream of some do-gooder. I was well aware that we were in a honeymoon period and that if we failed to control events through the locals then events would begin to control us. That was in the Ba'athist plan. The Iraqi Deputy Prime Minister, Tariq Aziz, had spelt this out, saying: 'People say to me, you are not the Vietnamese; you have no jungles and swamps to hide in. I reply, let the cities be our swamps and our buildings be our jungles.'

While talking to Yasim and his helpers, I had discovered that there were a number of large ammunition stores around the town and we knew that these were being looted, but a shortage of manpower meant that we could only be in so many places at once and we would have to rely on help from the irregulars to secure them. I visited one of the sites outside town and found Abu Hatim's man who was guarding it surrounded by a mob and about to get a beating. To my relief he had managed to keep them at bay so far. I took the lead and grabbed two of the crowd who looked to me as if they were ringleaders. I took down their names and addresses and then explained that they were now responsible for the security of the ammunition and the safety of the lone guard. If there was a problem I or Abu Hatim would be coming looking for them. They looked suitably torn and confused. While I actually thought they would see straight through that one, we had no further trouble there. At another massive compound, I saw that we had arrived too late and the ammunition bunkers were smashed open. The looters had abandoned the shells and taken the boxes. 155mm shells were strewn everywhere. We simply did not have the men or resources to deal with this. (Many of the recent attacks in Iraq have featured shells looted from ammo dumps such as these. If they are Russian shells the insurgents break them open and use the explosive, which looks just like the hard core used on railway tracks at a glance, or if they are UK and US shells they string them together with detonation cord to create what are euphemistically called 'Daisy Chains'. These are detonated by command wire when coalition vehicles are alongside. Even armoured vehicles are not impervious to these blasts.)

There was also increasing pressure on the stadium from the sheer weight of numbers of those who would travel out just to stand and stare. At one point it was particularly dangerous when crowds tried to surge in through the front gate each time it was opened. Looking at the tempting boxes of rations and the like through the fence must have become too much for some. At one such scuffle at the gate, the RSM had become embroiled and had grabbed the ringleader. He dragged the struggling man into the base. The man looked at him in terror now. Separated from his mates, his courage deserted him. He tried probably the only English he knew: 'I love you.' The RSM saw the funny side and let him go.

It got so bad that, not wanting this harmless jostling to become a confrontation, I asked Yasim and his men to help. When they had not appeared after an hour I supposed they had forgotten, until a convoy of vehicles turned up full of burly men and, in a flurry of beatings with rods and boots and gunshots in the air, the crowd disappeared in about thirty seconds flat. It didn't last though, and the crowd drifted back, but from then on their behaviour was more subdued.

While on the one hand I was keen to control the crowds who flocked to stare at us, isolation in the stadium from the ordinary townsfolk was also a worry and I knew that this could become an issue, as it had with security forces bases in Ireland and Bosnia. However, allowing routine access to civilians in an insurgency is an invitation for an attack. For this purpose we moved a CIMIC team into an abandoned villa in the centre of town to act as the first point of contact with the populace. Initially the mortar platoon under Captain Jamie Rea and 'Aunty' Billy McKenna secured it, but as relations with the locals strengthened we reduced the guard there to a section of eight men. From this base, which had a good vantage point across the town, we also began to set up a network of observation posts and we soon had line of sight between the stadium, the hospital, where we had a small garrison, and the CIMIC house. Now if anything happened in town we would be able to get a report fairly quickly and also be able to forward mount troops if we suspected there was a need.

One evening after the visit of the political advisers, who had returned to Divisional Headquarters now, I was sitting in my room when I had an unexpected visit from Yasim. He wanted an issue of captured weapons for some new recruits he had secured. I was explaining that this was not Woolworths and he couldn't just turn up and get some weapons without prior arrangement between his boss and myself, when into my room walked a group of other men. Immediately I could tell there was serious tension between the two groups and I asked the newcomers to go outside to wait while I finished with Yasim. When I returned to the room Yasim did not hang about and was clearly anxious to get back to Abu Hatim. After he'd left, I asked the other men to have a seat, ordered yet more tea and excused myself as I went to speak to the guard.

'Someone needs to think about what they are doing,' I said. 'I've just had a stand-off in my room between two groups. People need to at least let me know I have visitors.'

Andrew the 2IC appeared and apologised but pointed out that we were now so stretched that the guards were in fact the cooks and everybody was deployed either on guard or on the ground on patrol. It was like Dungannon on the night of the Dissident attack against the traffic police. There were simply no spare men to stand guard. I went back to speak to the new delegation. As they were introduced I realised why there had been tension. This was a delegation from the PUK. The Kurds.

The Kurds, who were themselves split into various factions, had enjoyed a high degree of UK and US assistance with their struggle with Saddam prior to the invasion. I can only suppose that they assumed that once the allies came they would be elevated into the position of power in Iraq, despite their only representing around nineteen per cent of the population. I had a long chat with the delegation, during which time they outlined what they described as 'their demands'. It was clear that they thought that we, the allies, would roll over and give them whatever they wanted – because that was what they were used to. Among these demands was a requirement for $40,000 and some weapons. They gave me a handwritten list. Then they wanted to know how we would set about handing power over to them. As calmly as I could, I made it clear that they were getting nothing. They could, I explained, come to my next town council meeting if they liked, which was due in two days' time, and the issue of power could be solved with all the other players. They didn't look too pleased and quickly left, leaving telephone numbers in case I had a change of heart. They did not come to my council meeting and I later learned that they had visited Brigade HQ with the same demands as soon as they left me.

I called the officers together to tell them that everyone needed to work a little harder in coordinating our activities. There was a delicate political game being played out against the backdrop of military operations. There was no textbook and we had to learn as we went along. As I spoke a bucket of water was thrown over me from above. I looked up and a head appeared, laughed and then disappeared. I went straight up to find out who exactly it was. To my complete amazement I discovered it was an RMP corporal, who proceeded to make it clear to me that I should be a bit careful where I stood and that he was busy cleaning his room. What particular duty was he on, I enquired. None, he reiterated. He was cleaning his room.

'Good,' I said, 'we have a guard for my room then.'

He was put on duty to make sure that we did not have a repetition of the debacle with the PUK. What I was not to know was that the RMP are run on different lines. The corporal could not see what right the CO of an infantry regiment had to put him on duty, even though he was attached to that battle group. Did I not realise he was a corporal in the RMP? Later he reported the fact that he had been put on duty during his time off to his RMP superiors who took this very seriously and a full-scale inquiry was launched.

While this juvenile incident was being played out and distracting me from my responsibilities to a now 1,500-strong battle group and a town of 300,000, I was called off to talk to one of Abu Hatim's henchmen. 'We have the address of someone you may wish to talk to,' he explained. It turned out to be the address of an individual who was reported to be none other than Chemical Ali's driver.

We had been briefed that on the evening of 9 April, British forces had struck at the home of the infamous arch henchman of Saddam Hussein and architect of the genocidal Anfal campaign, which had resulted in the murder and disappearance of 100,000 Kurds. After the raid, British officials admitted that they had killed two of his bodyguards. They later announced that the raid was a complete success. Chemical Ali was, they claimed, dead. But that was not what we were now hearing from the locals and I knew that if the Kurds in our area got a sniff of this target they would strike. I have no idea how long the man had been around but once again I detected a crumb being fed into my cage by Abu Hatim to remind me who had the power among the locals, no doubt as a direct result of the unfortunate encounter in my room. I had B Company mount an arrest operation and within the hour a man was brought into the stadium in handcuffs. I went to speak to him with Phil. Immediately he began the whole 'I know nothing' routine until I stopped him.

'Tell him I know exactly who he is and what he's done. Make it clear that he is going to jail in any case. If he cooperates I can help him.' This was explained. The man looked at me with large, frightened eyes. 'All I want to know,' I said, 'is did you drive Chemical Ali out of Basra on the night of 8 April and is he alive?'

'*Nam*,' (Yes) he said. This I understood.

'*Nam* . . . and what?' I said, agitated.

Phil spoke again, shouting and making it clear we were not up for fun and games. The man, looking pathetic in sandals and a sky-blue dishdash, rambled on. Finally Phil turned to me and smiled. 'Says he met a convoy coming out of Basra. They changed vehicles and Chemical Ali got into his. He took him to Baghdad. Says he has just come back. Chemical Ali is in Baghdad.'

I slapped my hands together. 'Book 'im, Danno[121].' He was taken directly to Divisional HQ the same night. When I returned to my room my new sentry had gone.

The following day the Brigade Commander visited Al Amarah and I elected to take him on a walk around the town. He had warned me 1 R Irish would be returning to the UK shortly as we were to begin our planned move to Inverness in Scotland, which had been delayed by the war. Tom Beckett, CO 1 Para, joined us on this walkabout as he was going to take over the town.

We visited various sites, including the gold souk. Most of the traders here were from Iraq's small Jewish community. We walked through the old town and went to have tea with the caretaker of the town's Christian church. There were in fact two churches in Al Amarah, decked out

---

[121] A famous catchphrase form the 1970s TV show *Hawaii Five-O*.

specially because it also happened to be Holy Week. The churches were surprisingly well kept and the small Christian community turned out to see us. They had been under a certain amount of pressure since the liberation and one Christian-owned alcohol shop had already been burned in what could have been the herald of a fracture in this multi-faith town. (I had had words with Abu Hatim about this but I had not taken any direct action, as I was wary of drawing too much attention to the Christians and their shops.) As we left, some of the local children ran to mob the Brigadier. We started to chase them off but he was quite comfortable. His bodyguard was less sure. We finished by walking back to the Town Hall, where some agitated youths ran up to us. Their leader spoke good English. He could not have been more than twenty or so.

'You must come quickly; there is a serious problem. This could cause a fire which you will never put out,' he explained. 'Your men are doing a very bad thing.'

The Brigadier bade us go and returned to his vehicle while Tom Beckett and I went to see what the problem was. In a building across the road from the Town Hall there were a number of my troops who were acting as escort to an RMP patrol. Inside the building the RMP had three men in robes up against the wall, with a pile of belongings beside them.

'What's happening?' I asked.

The RMP corporal in charge looked up from where he was noting down the property he had confiscated. He seemed slightly flushed with his success and began excitedly, 'We were passing and we saw an armed man in here. We came in and caught these guys.' He indicated over his shoulder with his pencil the three men, who I could now see had the robes of tribal elders. Sheikh Ismail, more than 100 years old and champion of our cause in the town, looked round at me.

'OK,' I said to the corporal. 'You've done nothing wrong. But I want you to leave now. Just leave everything and please go.'

'But . . .' he protested.

'Please,' I said, trying to stay calm, 'just go. Now.'

They left. I recall saying to Tom Beckett, 'This was a near miss.' I do not recall who was translating but I was profoundly apologetic to the sheikhs. They explained that they had been meeting to discuss whether Jeff and the US Special Forces team could have the house they were in as a base in town. It was an old Ba'ath residence and the council had agreed that the tribal elders should decide. The RMP had spotted the sheikh's bodyguard at the gate. This was explained to Sheikh Ishmail, who listened open-mouthed, as some very old people do, and then smiled and turned to me.

'OK, OK,' he said, putting his gnarled hand on my shoulder, smiling and patting me like a small child who has forgotten his manners. '*Taman*[122].'

It was getting dark as we returned to base. We had a town council meeting the next day. I was looking forward to some lively debate.

Turnout at the meeting was disappointing. I had a message from Abu Hatim to say he could not come and nor could any of the tribal elders. Sa'id al Jaber didn't appear either but unfortunately his mad sidekick did. We discussed the progress so far and I asked the heads of the town's utilities to report their progress. Electricity was intermittent and the water ran twice a day, with washing water available all the time at fixed locations. Dr Yassim Aboud Yassim pointed out that normally there was an annual spraying of the marshes for mosquitoes and if there was no spraying this year there would be a long-term danger of a return of malaria. I noted this and promised to investigate a spraying regime. Sewage was under control but there was a need for specialised assistance. I could see that the mad cleric was bursting to talk so I finally gave him the floor.

He launched into a complaint that we had been corrupting the young men of the town by giving them pornography. (He was referring to the magazines *FHM* and *Maxim* and the like.) He also complained that the women were being provocative. He flicked his head as if he had a great mane in imitation of them and added, 'They are doing *this* with their hair.' (No doubt they had been watching Sarah or one of the RMP girls wash their hair, albeit from quite a distance. The only female in the battalion itself, Corporal Boyson, a South African lass, had short hair.)

I said that the women would go soon as the base was due to move again to the airfield outside town and I regretted that he would have an even longer walk to go and see women '*do this*' with their hair, as I flicked my head like him. Everyone at the meeting roared with laughter and he sat down. He was furious and accused me of taking the mick, which in itself drew a gale of laughter from the rest of the meeting. He looked around with a face like he had sat on an anthill.

Other than that it was all very positive and the news was upbeat. Tom Beckett was present taking notes because it looked like he would host

---

[122] It's fine.

the next meeting. The town was a very different place from the one I had driven into six days previously. There was water and light. Outside the traffic flowed and the schools were back. We were not out of the woods yet, but we were on the way. I could not have been putting Al Amarah in better hands than those of 1 Para and Tom in particular. They would expand their responsibility to cover most of the province of Maysan, about the size of Northern Ireland.

As I finished the meeting and we all mingled in the committee room, I thought to myself that I would miss this place. We were saying goodbye, shaking hands, with me promising to come back one day, when the little Ba'athist doctor came over. I was expecting to hear another farewell but he embarked on a rant about how his other car had been confiscated now and he had to walk to work. He wagged his little fat finger in my face again.

'The looting,' he scolded, 'was all your fault and if I only –'

'I'll stop you right there,' I said, suddenly angry. 'You are alive. You have a job. And it's all thanks to me. Would you like me to have a word with a few people on your behalf about your car, your house, your life? Shall I put it in their hands? What will they do, I wonder?'

His face was a picture. 'I really just meant to thank you for all you've done,' he said, shaking my hand and then shuffling away.

Now that we knew our time in theatre was drawing to a close, it became the cause of some excitement. We had a photograph of the whole battle group drawn up in the stadium. The Gurkhas held a party in the afternoon. They had bought up every chicken for miles around and made cages for them, before chopping them up and putting them in an enormous bhart. I joined them for some bhart with some cold drink we got from the local market. (It was not unusual for our interpreters to send out for carryouts from town. Delicious meals of fried rice or birianis were produced with wonderful bread.)

The next day was Juma and once more we adopted a low profile. I had a rather pleasant surprise, however. Among the mail I was handed was a letter of particular quality. I opened it and read it. In shock I read it again. It was dated 6 April:

Dear Colonel Collins,

The other day my attention was drawn to the address you made to your Battalion before the conflict to unseat Saddam Hussein began and I asked to see as much of the transcript as possible. For what it is worth, I just wanted you to know how <u>profoundly</u> moved I was – and I know many others were too – by your extraordinarily stirring, civilized and humane words. What you said somehow encapsulated, in a brilliantly inspired way, everything that we have come to expect of our Armed Forces and demonstrated why, quite simply, they are the best in the world. But what was so moving, and so deeply heartening, if I may say so, was that you totally understood the nature of Iraq and her people and the need, above all, for respect if the peace is to be won.

I do hope you will forgive me for writing in this way, but it made me so proud to read what you said. It was in the highest traditions of military leadership and I simply <u>had</u> to express my admiration.

I hope my brother, your Colonel-in-Chief, will also forgive me for interfering in his Regiment, but as you have a reinforcement company of one of my Regiments – the 2nd Battalion Royal Gurkha Rifles – I felt there may be <u>some</u> justification! Whatever the case, this brings you and all your people my heartfelt good wishes and constant thoughts as you carry out your difficult duties in Iraq. May God go with you all.

Yours most sincerely,

Charles

I wasn't certain that it was Prince Charles, because it was signed in fountain pen. But when I showed it to Sarah, the journalist, she confirmed that it was indeed his signature, which she had seen before for some reason. I was delighted, of course, and called together as many of the men as possible to announce that 'Today the Prince of Wales has sent you his heartfelt good wishes and constant thoughts.' The letter was passed around and much read.

# —19—

# FRIENDLY FIRE

The GOC had asked to visit and he flew onto our sports pitch that morning. I knew that my time was limited as we really needed to be gone by midday before the Shia parade. While there was no threat specifically, it was only common sense to avoid this passionate event. The GOC seemed to enjoy his visit and we took him to see the British cemetery and then into the heart of the old city, where he received a rapturous welcome that I had arranged. I had said to Abu Hatim that the more friendly the town was, the more I would be trusted by my superiors to help. I explained that my boss was coming for a visit and that I needed a warm welcome and a guarantee of security for him. He gave his word. He was more than equal to it, even if on occasions his cover men, who he had put in to ensure security, were a little obvious. The GOC didn't notice a thing and was cheered from one end of the town to the other. The GOC seemed agitated, however, and we did not linger, although it would have been perfectly safe so long as we were clear by around noon when the Shia went to mosque.

As the GOC returned to our sports pitch to meet his helicopter, I went off for a final sweep around town and, to my horror, just outside the British cemetery and beside the mosque was a US Civil Affairs unit setting up shop to distribute a new coalition newspaper. There was no harm in the paper itself (except, possibly, for the full-page advertisement on the back page of a girl in a bikini with a mobile telephone) but it was the wrong time and the wrong place. I stopped and asked them to pack up, explaining it was Juma and about to be fairly lively. I also pointed out that their chosen spot was beside the British cemetery, which had been respected for the last ninety years, and we did not want to draw the wrong sort of attention to it. They reluctantly moved on.

Shortly after they left an explosion rocked the town on the northern edge and a pall of smoke rose into the sky. The fire brigade reacted, as did my operations (contingency) company. When they arrived at the scene of the explosion they found it was a roadside bomb but thankfully no one had been injured. It was explained that a representative of a pro-Iranian Cleric, Ayatollah Mohammed Baqir al-Hakim, was the target[123]. He had been due to visit to preach in the mosque for Juma. The local police asked for assistance in examining the blast from a forensic viewpoint. It was the first indication I'd had of growing undercurrents of tension and rivalry, which were to boil to the surface and ultimately result in the assassination of Ayatollah Baqir al-Hakim in Najaf a year later. In any case, it was increasingly obvious it was not a good day to be hanging around the town.

I went to visit some Bedouin who were camped out on the marshes outside town and as I sat and drank tea with them they explained that they had no real idea of the events that had gone on over the war but they had been told by their tribal chief to cooperate with the British (they actually referred to us all as 'English'). During our chat the senior man explained that there was a serious problem with sore stomachs, sore throats and vomiting. It sounded like the food or water. I asked where they got their water. To my horror he indicated the brackish ditch near to the campsite.

'I hope you boil it well before drinking it. I recommend a rolling boil for ten minutes,' I explained.

He simply had no idea what I was talking about. When I probed this, he explained that before we came the Bedouin had depended on the Ba'athists to give them water and since that had stopped they just took water where they could find it. I realised that it had been clever of the Ba'athists to manipulate the Bedouin in this way, as they had a sure method of controlling them and to interface with them on a regular basis. Yet another insight into the world of Saddam Hussein. Now this dependency had eroded the care the Bedouin would traditionally have

---

[123] With hindsight, it was almost certainly the work of followers of Muqtada al-Sadr, a rogue Shia cleric, as he moved to take power from the pro-western and moderate clerics. During the following year Al Amarah would see an upsurge of violence from his 'Mahdi Army' that would claim the lives of eight British soldiers and hundreds of his followers.

taken when getting and preparing water and left these nomadic people without an essential life skill, exposing them to risk from disease.

I drove to Brigade HQ to brief the Brigadier about the bomb and to make a plea for a Field Health Team to go and visit the Bedouin. I believed they needed some practical help. But when I arrived Jacko asked me to come into the garden near his HQ as there was something he wanted to talk about. I anticipated that it was to ask me to break the news to the men of the Royal Irish Rangers, who were acting as the guard to the Brigade HQ, that when we left they would have to remain to guard the HQ. They would possibly have thought that when we went they would go too.

We sat down and he cut straight to the point. 'Tim, there's been a complaint lodged against you by the Americans. It has come from the office of General Conway himself and, I can't put this any more easily, they're accusing you of war crimes.'

I was completely numbed and could hardly take in what he had said.

'General Brims has ordered the CO of the SIB to come to theatre and to do an investigation and to have a report on his desk in ten days' time, 30 April at the latest. Be careful what you say and do from now on.'

'War crimes? I can't believe what I'm hearing,' I said. Was this a bad dream – war crimes?

I left his headquarters to go and speak to the men from the Royal Irish Rangers about our imminent departure and the fact that they would be staying. They were understandably disappointed that they weren't coming back with the 1st Battalion. I was unable to give them a steer for how long they would have to stay and could not be much comfort to them. (I must admit I was not on top form. I still could not believe it. War crimes?)

Back at base, I called the Adjutant and the 2IC together. I broke the news to them.

'It must not distract us from our last few days here in Iraq,' I declared. 'In any case, as far as I'm aware the allegations are against me and not the battle group.'

As I returned to my room I glanced again at the letter from Prince Charles. If there is one thing for certain, I thought, the British Army will defend me and in ten days this nonsense will be over. I decided not to worry about it. The US would be experts on war crimes, no doubt. So long as I had not exceeded the treatment they mete out at Guantanamo Bay in Cuba, I should be in the clear, I mused. Above all General Brims, who had accepted my hospitality and had visited the town under my protection that very morning, would not let me down.

That night we prepared the plan to hand Al Amarah and the surrounding countryside over to 1 Para. At around 2100 hours Colour Sergeant Chris MacDonald came up the stairs to the area we had set aside for briefing. As he came in I looked up.

'Burning the midnight oil, eh?' he joked. 'I've a couple of visitors here. Will I tell 'em yer busy?'

'No, send 'em up and could you get Herby to organise some tea, please?'

'Sure, I'll do it meself,' he said with a smile. 'I'm bored down there.'

I watched him leave, humming cheerfully, and marvelled at the apparent ease with which he carried his own worries on his shoulders – he was recently divorced and separated from a five-year-old son whom he worshipped – while refreshing everyone else with his good cheer and optimism.

Shortly two men, one a former Iraqi Army officer, were shown in. They were, they explained, representatives of Ayatollah Mohammed Baqir al-Hakim, leader of the Supreme Council for the Islamic Revolution in Iraq (SCIRI), a major anti-Saddam opposition group, head of the 12,000-strong Badr Corps resistance movement and arguably Iraq's most respected cleric (and the target of the attack that morning). They said they had heard about me from the people in Al Amarah and the sheikh had sent them to ask for my help.

'There will be a war,' they warned, 'and we can stop it but only if the sheikh [meaning Ayatollah al-Hakim] has the British sympathies with him when he moves to take the power away from those who would seek to kill.'

I wondered who they meant. Their pitch was not unlike the Kurdish demands of the previous week and would have been difficult to comply with. They wanted to be elevated to a position of total control over the allied interface with the Iraqis. We talked for more than two hours and the subjects ranged from looting to the Israeli–Palestine question. This topic clearly fascinated them. I told them I believed that in exchange for its help in securing Iraq the British would use their influence with the US to settle the Palestine question and persuade the Israelis to honour the spirit of the Oslo Peace Accords. We finished with them outlining their aspirations for a relationship with the British and I promised to pass on their message to my superiors, but I explained that I personally could be of no help and said I could not explain why.

As they got up to leave, the Iraqi Army officer who had been translating turned to me and said, 'You know I saw you coming to Al Medina.'

'Me?'

'Yes you, Colonel Collins. I was a staff officer with the brigade when your men came, those felah[124], I watched you come.'

I was intrigued. 'What was the reaction?'

'Well, we knew something was going to happen because we got a message to say a delegation would come the next day under a white flag and we should not shoot. We thought they wanted us to surrender. When they explained we could just go, leaving our weapons and equipment, or we could join the allies, we went. We felt that we had all had enough fighting and we wanted to go home. Some wanted to stay but when they saw us all going they left too. But when we left it all went wrong and some were attacked by the locals. I got captured. They gave me the choice of working with them. They treat me well and I am one of them now. I wished I had come over to you but now I like where I am.'

He then added that there was a strong respect for the British Army. He explained that many of the old Iraqi Army's ways were based on British ways of doing things and some officers had been on courses in England. He asked if I had anything he could read about the British Army. I did not have much except a copy of the magazine *Soldier* and the *Sandy Times*, the 1 (UK) Division news sheet. I pointed out that the edition of *Soldier* had my now-infamous pre-battle speech.

'If your bosses want to know why the British have come,' I said, 'tell them to read that.'

The next morning, I had a message from Abu Hatim to say he wanted to come to see me. We arranged a meeting for around 1600 hours that afternoon.

Preparation for our departure went ahead with the only exception being a brief observance of Easter. We had a church service for Easter Sunday in the stadium. Things were still fragile. The padre held the service with us sitting on the terraces as we took communion from a gold communion set that we had had in the battalion since the First World War and palm crosses were passed. I hoped that this Easter the message of rebirth and salvation would be a good omen for Iraq and Al Amarah in particular.

---

[124] Farmer or marsh dweller. A pejorative term in this context.

Abu Hatim arrived at the appointed hour, for once. He was dressed in flowing robes and a snow-white dishdash. It was perfectly pressed and he had a light perfume on. I was filthy in comparison, in the same combat suit I had worn throughout the war. Jeff had come along too, as had Yasim, also in tribal robes for this special occasion. He was even unarmed. We talked about the progress we had made and our hopes for the future. I had grown fond of these guys over the past week. It's important to understand that when each day has so much packed into it and death is only a heartbeat away days seem like weeks and weeks like months. We had a photograph taken and then he shook my hand and embraced me.

'Come back one day,' he said. 'Tomorrow I will send you a medal, a small memento of your time. I took it from a Ba'athist general and there is no one else in the world he would less like to have it than you!'

We rose with the dawn the next morning and packed our equipment. I looked around my little room in the stadium for the last time and then threw my bag onto the trailer of the Comms Camel. I had been told that Mark Hartigan, who would replace me as commanding officer on return from the Gulf, was eager to visit and he arrived by helicopter as we finished handing the stadium over to 1 Para. Around the stadium there was great excitement from the crowd, the usual mixture of greetings, attempts to get some barter going and pushing to try to get access to the stadium and whatever delights they imagined we had concealed there. As I chatted with Mark Hartigan, some shots rang out from across the waste ground behind the stadium. He looked quite shocked.

'They are just showing off,' I reassured him. 'It's nothing personal.'

As we drove out of the busy bustling town it was back to normal functioning (or as normal as Al Amarah gets) and the sun was shining.

# —20—

# RETURNING HOME

We were to drive to a Brigade concentration area at an abandoned airfield called Qualat Salih, where we handed over the ammunition and stores that had been issued for the war. The place was a sea of organised chaos as vehicles were stripped and ammunition accounted for. We cooked some lunch and watched as dark storm clouds gathered. The airfield itself had received a great deal of attention from coalition air power over the last twelve years and much of the infrastructure was in ruins. Battle debris littered the surrounding area and stray dogs circled, no doubt hoping for scraps. We had been warned to stay on the hard standing as there was a considerable amount of unexploded ordnance lying around[125].

A planning team had to head for Kuwait to arrange the return of the battalion to the UK, so I set off in the Comms Camel with the replacement CO in tow, along with the RSM and Adjutant, to return to Fort Blair Mayne, almost one month to the day since we had left. Our journey south took us along the main route, skirting Basra, and via Al Zubayr and other landmarks that had been places of wonder the previous month, now scenes of desolation, ravaged by war and the attentions of looters.

---

[125] The following day, a detonation of one of these unexploded bombs tragically took the life of Lance Corporal James McCue, 27, from Paisley, Renfrewshire, from the 7th Air Assault REME battalion. Struck in the back by a fragment of a shell, probably set off by a stray dog, he was yet another tragic casualty of the war.

As we passed close to Al Qurnah we were directed away from the town and I was both shocked and saddened to see why. Ill-disciplined troops who had thrown sweets, rations and sometimes rubbish to crowds of children had generated a form of disorder that had become a hindrance to movement through the town's streets. Hostile crowds of Iraqis, eager hands proffering trinkets and snatching anything that was not securely attached, had replaced the cheering crowds of the last time we were in the town, only a week before. Some ran along waving old bayonets or Iraqi dinar with Saddam's face on them. (We had found these by the hundreds of thousand on the battlefield but they had now become worth many times their value to the administrative elements who were flooding into the country and were eager to get a souvenir that might suggest that they had been there at the leading edge of liberation.) These once-welcoming people were now reduced to begging and barter and dodging among the wheels of the lorries to do so. Gone were the good-natured smiling faces; a hungry desperate mass now raced along beside our vehicles, corrupted by just the sort of behaviour that I had tried so hard to prevent. I could see that as I left Iraq it was on the precipice of a slide to anarchy born of ill discipline and ignorance. My heart went out to the Iraqi people, orphans in their own country and now being treated like refugees.

The further south we went, the worse the crowds at the side of the road in towns became, with the border town of Safwan sealed off altogether. As we drove through some places I noted that there were piles of junk outside the mosques. I recalled that a cleric in Al Amarah had told me that on the previous Friday the clerics had called for a return of looted stores. It looked like all the junk in the world had been dumped at their door instead.

My final impression of Iraq was of a land truly invaded by aliens. The look on the faces of the people was despondent, lost and angry. The heat was rising and, as the vigilante in Al Rumaylah had said, in more ways than one.

We crossed back into Kuwait and arrived late at night in Fort Blair Mayne, which was now looking shabby and unkempt. Gone were the guards and the passwords, the smart painted signs and the rows of carefully laden vehicles. I felt like a ghost returning to a long-abandoned home. When we had driven out it was sharp and business-like. Now the ravages of the desert wind had collapsed several tents and the hessian fabric covers for the makeshift washing area flapped in the breeze,

The British cemetery
in Al Amarah

The Ba'athist doctor looks
delighted to see me again

Home at last. Henry joins
in the spirit with some
camouflage trousers

(MARK LARGE/DAILY MAIL)

My last day in uniform

# SWORN STATEMENT

I, MAJ Re' Biastre, 096-528163, having been duly sworn, do hereby depose and state:

I am assigned to the 402nd Civil Affairs Battalion, Buffalo, New York. I am the team leader of Direct Support Team 4 (DST4). The battalion was mobilized in December 2002 and deployed to Kuwait in early January 2003. My team was one of five direct support teams that were assigned to support the British division (1 UK) during military operations in theater. My team was assigned to support the 16 Air Assault Brigade (16 AA), one of the brigades assigned to 1UK.

In late February 2003, I began to perceive a high level of anti-American sentiment among the British officers. I first noticed this sentiment among the British officers when BG John H. Kern, commander of the 352nd Civil Affairs Command failed to make an appointment with the commanding general of the 1 UK. Many British officers commented to me that BG Kern's failure to make the meeting was typical of the arrogance of American officers. After hostilities commenced, many British officers began to express their resentment of Americans more openly. They questioned the need for Britain to be in the war and they characterized President Bush as a "cowboy." They complained that British Prime Minister Tony Blair was acting as a "puppet" of President Bush. They often claimed that the majority of the British public did not support Britain's participation in the war. The feelings of resentment among British officers were particularly intense after "friendly fire" incidents where American forces inflicted casualties on British forces. I first noticed this occurring after an American Patriot missile shot down a British Tornado fighter-bomber.

On March 27, 2003, at approximately 1200 hours, MAJ Nader Ramishni, the G-5 for 16 AA, tasked my team to take a photographer to the headquarters of the Royal Irish battalion (1RI) in ar Rumaylah and provide armed escort for a British non-tactical vehicle (NTV) to 3 Army Air Corps (3AAC). We arrived at 1RI headquarters at approximately 1300 and dropped the photographer off. Captain Dye Jones, the officer whom we were escorting to 3 AAC, went inside the headquarters to talk to his counterparts in the 1RI CIMIC. While my team waited outside, members of the 1RI CIMIC team were telling us about the area and that they had given out candy earlier in the day. At this time there was a British truck with British soldiers giving out what the CIMIC team said was candy. Color Sergeant Slater, a team sergeant for the 1RI CIMIC, asked if I had anything to give the kids who were in the area. There were approximately 30 children and I had over 100 lollipops, so I told the Color Sergeant that we had candy for the children. Color Sergeant Slater asked me to distribute the candy. I had my team sergeant, SSG Dale Spencer, line the boys and girls up separately. I went over to the girls and gave each a lollipop. I then went over to assist SSG Spencer in passing out the candy to the boys. CPT Brian Stoll, my assistant team leader, took photographs of me passing out the lollipops.

`Not **more** friendly fire!'

Biastre – a man of many uniforms – strikes
a pose, delighted with the press attention

Ayoub Younis Nasser,
aka Abu Nawfel

My escort deliver
me to the Sheraton

A view over Baghdad
towards Sadr city from
the US observation post

The Reuters compound with a nervous guard. Not familiar with wide-angled lenses, he thought he was out of shot

My high-risk drive through Baghdad. The favourite western shampoo was a brand called 'and shoulders'

shredded by the heat and winds, flapping like long-forgotten prayer flags on a Buddhist shrine.

It was eerily quiet as we walked into the mess tent. Once bustling and alive, it was now empty, dusty and shabby. The duty chef had some stew waiting for us. After eating in silence, we unloaded our trucks and I set up my bed in the tent where I had planned our enterprise. As I lay awake in the dark, I wondered how much good we had done the Iraqi people by this offensive. Even now, the good will and optimism of the previous month somehow seemed sullied by the chaos and the absence of any tangible benefit for the people we had gone to liberate and not to conquer.

I had once wondered if I would survive the coming war. Now I had returned, grateful for the good fortune at having survived, along with all of my men, but soiled by the knowledge of the allegations that had been levelled against me. At the back of my mind was the certainty that senior RMP investigators were already quizzing my men for any flaw, however tiny, that they could exploit against me. My mind searched my own mental record of events to identify my vulnerabilities as I drifted into an uneasy sleep. I still had no idea of what the charges were.

Morning brought a desert storm and the stark scene of the crumbling, abandoned camp. I spoke on the radio to Brigade to try to get them to release the battalion to travel back to Kuwait, as I'd learned they were having a rough time. Shortly after I had left the airfield, the storm that had been threatening had burst onto 1 R Irish with a biblical vengeance. It had lashed men and vehicles with icy fingers, reaching into every tent and sleeping bag. The suffering had been compounded when the communal lavatories had filled and overflowed in the torrential rain, and for the first time in our war large numbers of men were suffering from stomach complaints and were laid low by vomiting and diarrhoea. Morale was fragile as the men waited, not knowing when they would be drawn, no longer buoyed against adversity by a sense of purpose and beginning to feel the cold and suffering with aches and fevers. After much persuasion, permission was granted for the sodden battle group to make its way to Kuwait. Our business north was finished but it was with no sense of triumphalism or swagger that my men rumbled south in their vehicles under a leaden sky, now lounging where they had once been alert and guarded, impassive and sullen where they had been cheerful and optimistic.

I met the battle group as it arrived in camp. At least I had brought them all back safely. As I stood at the gate I was glad to see the many faces I knew and loved so well jumping down from their vehicles to begin to unpack kit, stretch sleeping bags out to dry and set about restoring our once-crisp camp. As the sun came out and men and clothing dried, the humour slowly returned.

I was summoned back to Al Amarah for a final office call with the Brigadier. As I flew north in a Gazelle helicopter, below me the evidence of the movement of a large army was written on the landscape in thousands of wheel tracks and hundreds of shell scrapes. Convoys of reinforcements, British and American, were streaming north. We refuelled at Basra Airport and then continued north across the date palm-lined canals beside the Tigris towards Al Amarah, before turning inland. As we flew away from the river and towards the north-east, two features struck me.

The first was the vast area of drained swamp, in which evidence of now-perished communities could be made out among the dusty wastes where the swamp reeds had become rotten stumps and oases had dried and crumbled into dead heaps of ancient palms. Abandoned boats sat almost inexplicably in the middle of the desert. Saddam had been as thorough as he had been ruthless in his destruction of the marshes, its people and its ancient way of life.

The other feature was the number of deserted military positions surrounded by abandoned equipment, millions of dollars' worth of hardware dumped and never used, an expensive testament to one man's vanity and the greed of the sanctions busters who had profited by supplying this hardware. The humble villages and mean houses around these positions screamed offence at the waste.

My helicopter landed at Camp Killaloo and I went straight to the Brigade Commander's office. After we'd discussed the past weeks I enquired after my war crimes investigation. The Brigadier was equally in the dark. I left him and went to visit the Royal Irish Rangers. They were a lot more cheerful than I had seen them on my last visit and they were once again improving their positions, joking and playing sport.

On return to Kuwait, I took the opportunity to visit Kuwait City accompanied by my Kuwaiti translators. We made an odd sight as we drove into the city in our sand-coloured Land Cruiser, which was looking fairly battered by now, sitting alongside gleaming BMWs and Mercedes at the traffic lights. The obvious wealth of this tiny country with its bright lights and well-stocked shops was all the more shocking after being so close to the poverty of its neighbour. I had lunch with Khalifa, a good friend, in his father's restaurant. As ever, there was far too much food and their generosity was boundless. We went to the kitchens to see the flatbread being baked. The dough was patted flat and stuck to the side of large clay ovens, then peeled off and served immediately, hot and delicious.

I wanted to get some souvenirs for the children and some jewellery for Caroline but ended up with all sorts of coffees and dates and spices that Khalifa insisted I would not be able to get anywhere else. I was delighted with the tangle of streets that made up the central souk. Mostly covered, it was divided into the gold market, the fruit and vegetable market and an astonishing fish market that featured the day's catch and was as much an aquatic zoo as a market, with whole sharks on display beside colourful fish and squid. Even the traders were a curiosity, with Iranians rubbing shoulders with Arabs and Asian traders.

As I strolled through the souk, an American hailed Mike Murdoch, who had long since replaced Mike McGovern as OC B Company, across the crowded market, who then introduced the man as the commander of the US unit that had replaced B Company in the oilfields.

He turned to me and said, 'Are you Colonel Collins? You were looking for a little burned girl, weren't you?'

My pulse raced. 'Yes, yes – have we got her?' I tried to contain my delight. It was, of course, the girl from Al Rumaylah whose whereabouts had become a high priority in the whole division.

'Yeah, we found her,' he said.

'At last! Where is she? Is she OK?'

'She died the same day she got burned. They buried her at the side of the road, but I heard they dug her up and have her in storage now. You sure caused a stink over that – we were looking . . .'

He went on, but in my grief for her father, I didn't hear another word.

In camp, tent flaps were tied up and boxes were thrown open as men in shorts and T-shirts scrubbed, cleaned and sorted the tangle of gear that had supported us in war. Vehicles were stripped and cleaned. The men's chat was subdued as they worked, a mixture of looking forward and reflection on what they had just experienced. Gone was the youthful optimism of two months before. Somehow the battalion had lost its innocence and lightness and now the talk was more adult, practical and serious.

The commanding officer isn't much use when men are packing kit and so, between putting my own kit into boxes and taking them to the Quartermaster's department to be plundered by the RAF police, I often found myself in Kuwait City and the company of Khalifa. I also wanted to stay out of the camp as I was aware that people kept disappearing off and it became clear that the RMP were in-country, though I didn't see them. While I had been assured that they were investigating only the allegations that had been levelled by a mysterious US source, I had enough experience of them to know they would be trying to find a chink of light through which they could attack me. I cannot tell you how frustrating it is to know that your men are being interviewed about your conduct and invited to betray you. I knew that I had to stay calm until I could get to the UK to get a lawyer to counter anything that the SIB might accuse me of and that the investigation might take many months. In any case, I reflected, what could they allege? Nothing had happened that could possibly have constituted a war crime.

On one afternoon the RSM was called away. I realised immediately that he was being taken off by the RMP. I was certain that here was someone who would put everything into perspective. In the meantime the whole battle group sat in our dust-blown camp pretending that we didn't know what was going on.

I busied myself in organising the battalion's return to the UK. If the trip back was as chaotic as the trip out I knew it would require close attention and vigilance. The battalion was needed back in the UK as it was due to move to Inverness in Scotland to change role, leaving the Air Assault Brigade and coming under the operational command of HQ Northern Ireland. But my inquiries into the arrangements for the return of the battalion drew a blank. One ray of light was the news that Virgin Atlantic Airways, in a flush of patriotism, had offered to fly 1 R Irish home. Their plan was to land in the newly prepared Basra Airport as a symbol of UK friendship with the people of the emerging free Iraq. It would have been a high-profile event – the first troops returning home. Excitement ran through the camp at the prospect of going home and seeing families again. There was great disappointment at the news a day later that it had been shelved because it was officially seen as unfair to British Airways. My anxiety increased when senior staff at the Headquarters of 1 (UK) Division told me that the cancellation was partially because I would have been on the flight. I was told that the direction from the top was that neither 1 R Irish nor I were to be made celebrities by the media under any circumstances. It was clear that senior officers had other plans for me. The flight was cancelled and 1 R Irish was stranded in the desert. I was saddened and amazed at the whole episode.

I decided to have myself sent back to the UK as cargo on a C-117 Globemaster. The flight was arranged at very short notice and I had an hour to get to the airport. We flew back via Cyprus and I arrived in the UK in the back of the hold along with eighteen tonnes of freight and a noxious sample for the Chemical Research Establishment in Porton Down. (The UK was at this point desperately seeking to find some, any, evidence of weapons of mass destruction to back up the Prime Minister's claim that the Iraqi Army could deploy such weapons in forty-five minutes – which at the time we all believed.) When we landed and the cargo door finally opened, I could see the first green leaves of spring.

# —21—

# PREPARING FOR THE ONSLAUGHT

As I waited for my driver in the impersonal arrivals lounge at RAF Brize Norton, I received an important message to call the Director of Corporate Communications (Army), or DCCA in MOD speak, Brigadier Matthew Sykes. I called from an untidy side office. He was hugely animated by the news of the investigation. I explained that I wasn't even supposed to know that it was happening and that I could tell him very little. He was very keen to hear what he described as 'my side of the story', explaining that he would not sit in judgement. I repeated that I did not even know what I had been accused of. Brigadier Sykes then gave me an unguarded rundown of what I had been accused of. Some of the charges – starving captives, beating prisoners, controlling the towns that I had liberated by fear and so on – were so preposterous that I could only think that he had been mis-briefed. (As it turned out, he was, in fact, spot on.) He warned me not to talk to the press.

After leading one of the nation's regiments in a highly successful operation, the two-hour drive to my family in Canterbury, through a hazy spring morning, should have been a joyful one. But for me it was a sombre and reflective time, with questions to which I had no answers crashing around in my head. Principal among these was simply 'Why?'

The camp had been bustling with activity when I left on a snowy evening in February. Now as I arrived back the skies had cleared and birds were singing in the trees, but the camp was deserted. Caroline was waiting at the gate of Quebec House. For a short while the burden that

I carried was lifted as I greeted her and my sleeping baby son. The older children were at school. It should have been a happy return to a home that I had often wondered whether I would ever see again, but my predicament allowed me little peace.

After a short spell at Quebec House, I went to the office to deal with the backlog of work that had built up during my absence at war and to check on the progress of the return of the rest of the battalion. This at least was good news. As if my departure had removed a log jam, the men were to be flown back the next day. Ironically the media were soon all over the camp and the arrival of the main body of troops was feted in the TV and printed media.

The news of the investigation had spread through camp and the atmosphere was extremely downcast on the day of my departure. By now, the RMP SIB had taken over my office and I was warned to stay away from Battalion HQ as there was a danger that I could 'influence' witnesses. I was also told, in confidence, from the Royal Irish Regimental Headquarters, that the further Board of Inquiry, which I had found out about in theatre, into the death by suicide of Ranger Cochrane, which I had been told was ordered by a regional commander (General Officer Commanding 4th Division) had in fact its origins in HQ Land. It seemed I was being closely watched from on high.

The greatest relief was being able to speak to Lewis Cherry, a lawyer who agreed to take up my case and if necessary defend me in court. Lewis was an old acquaintance from his service with the Army. He was late of the King's Regiment but was now the undisputed champion of the soldier on the court martial circuit in Northern Ireland[126]. He advised me to keep a diary of events and any contacts I had. It was his view that there was a more complex tale behind the allegations and he wanted to have all of the background recorded just in case. Lewis warned me at this time that, whatever the outcome of the investigation, I was going to be disappointed by the reaction of the Army hierarchy and I could expect little support.

I arranged a short holiday to Paris for Caroline and me the following week. She needed a break as much as anyone, but try as I might the spectre of this whole thing hung over me like a pall. During that time I sat her down and explained the situation. As ever, she was extremely optimistic and convinced that those who I had served so faithfully, as well

---

[126] I must qualify this by saying few of his cases ever reach the court martial stage.

as the many friends I had in the Army's senior echelons, would deal with this as quickly as possible. She could see no reason to worry. I was less sanguine. I told her that I was convinced that there was a sinister element behind it. When pressed, I couldn't explain why – I didn't know myself – but the whole affair was gathering pace and spiralling out of control.

On return from France, I was still waiting for someone to tell me what was happening when I had a call on the evening of Tuesday 20 May 2003. It was Brigadier Matthew Sykes and he simply said, 'It's out.'

'What's out?' I asked.

'Come on, you know perfectly well. The thing we discussed is out. The press know and the *Sun* are running a story tomorrow.'

'How did "it" get out?' I asked. 'I haven't even been told officially.'

'Well, it is,' he said and rung off.

I spoke to Lewis Cherry. It was good to speak to such a wise head. I told him about the conversation I had had with Sykes. 'Put it in the diary,' he said in his jocular way. 'The Army have a number of problems that I cannot tell you about,' he explained, 'and I can't tell you how I know. I suspect they want an officer to go down to balance the books. It looks very much like you're him.'

He warned me not to talk to anyone about the case. I was numb. 'But I need to find out who has leaked this,' I explained.

'That you will never really know,' he said.

I asked about talking to my friend, former embedded journalist Sarah Oliver, to find out if this was common knowledge on Fleet Street.

'You can ask questions and you can take advice,' he warned, 'but you cannot brief anyone, on or off the record. Those are the rules. I very much doubt if you will get any help from DCCA; in fact they will be waiting to nail you if you so much as nod to the media, so be careful you do not inadvertently add to your burden.'

'That is all very clear,' I said solemnly.

I called Sarah Oliver. 'I'm amazed,' she said when I outlined the events as they had unfolded. 'We've heard nothing. What exactly are you supposed to have done?' she asked.

'I'll be honest here, Sarah,' I said. 'I won't know until I read the *Sun* tomorrow. No one has told me officially. I only have it "off the record" or from second-hand briefings which I am not supposed to be getting.' I added, 'You know I cannot give you an interview, on or off the record.'

'I know,' she replied. 'But you were there to guide me through your world on the battlefield. I would like to be there to guide you through the battlefield of Fleet Street. I'll be down tomorrow on a private visit, if that's OK. And you are right about press briefing, they'll use anything they can get – even one word – so don't talk to anyone.'

I was relieved to talk to someone who knew the business. And I knew I could trust her never to break a confidence.

# —22—

# ACCUSED

The next day, Wednesday 21 May, I read the *Sun*. The banner headline on the front page screamed:

COL TIM PROBED ON WAR CRIMES

Inside it carried on:

> ACCUSED
> Collins 'Kicked and punched POWs'.
> He 'shot at feet of Iraqi civilians'.
> Local chief was 'pistol whipped'.

The *Sun* was very well informed indeed. The actual allegations were in fact much more extensive than I had been warned about by Sykes and the piece contained some lurid detail. It was so accurate that it had to have come from within the MOD as no one else outside of HQ Land was aware of this degree of detail.

By the time Sarah Oliver appeared, it had been featured on the television and radio news. Because I was prevented from speaking to the media I was loath to answer the phone. In any case I had no definite idea what the allegations were; I still had only had Brigadier Sykes's briefing and the *Sun* to go on. Sarah was not in the least bit disappointed when I explained that I would still be unable to help with an interview. She pointed out that she had been with the battle group when the events in question happened. Indeed, her dispatches at the time were full of the stories that were now under investigation. She would dearly have liked Caroline to give her story in an interview, but we agreed that we felt that would be letting the Army down. She understood that my first loyalty was to the Army and we left it at that. But I now had a better understanding of the pitfalls of the media game and a better feel for what to expect. I was certainly better equipped to deal with media approaches. I wondered why the Army didn't have a department who could offer this type of advice and guidance to their employees. One would have thought it was vital in the twenty-four-hour news world we live in.

I was still half-expecting the telephone to ring, with some senior army officer offering help or advice. But no one from the Army called. When the phone did ring it was mostly journalists looking for scoops. I knew they were only doing their job, but the tactics used by some of these journalists to woo me were most amusing. I even listened to some for a while, enjoying their approach: Would I like to come out and play golf? What about lunch? There is no doubt that some of the guys and girls are a real loss to Special Branch and would be ace players at recruiting sources. But I was clear: duty prevented me from speaking to the media and if nothing else I would do my duty and obey orders.

My civilian friends called to offer support, as, of course, did my family. I was delighted that after a while some good friends and peers from the Army were not afraid to call to give me their support. I urged them all to keep a low profile with regard to contact with me and explained that as there had been no senior military contact setting out the Army's position on the situation they should be careful not to get soiled by association with me.

Then at eight o'clock at night I finally had a call from a senior officer, Matthew Sykes, but it wasn't a call of support, quite the contrary. He accused me of giving interviews to the media. When I protested that this couldn't be so, he pointed out that I had told Tom Newton Dunn from the *Mirror* that I couldn't make any comment, and that this in itself constituted an interview. His logic baffled me.

In the evening, I had a call from the brigade commander of the 2nd Infantry Brigade based in Kent, Brigadier David Santa-Olalla, a distinguished officer who held both the MC and the DSO, to say that he had been put in charge of me and would act as my 'commanding officer' in the case. In Army terms this meant that he would be the first judge of any evidence put against me. At last. For once I was greatly relieved. I had a point of contact and he was a real soldier. I didn't want some operational virgin, the sort of Cold War warrior who filled the high command of the Army, judging my case, as they could have no idea what soldiers really did in the field. I travelled to Dover Castle, where Brigadier Santa-Olalla was based. He told me he did not at that time know what I was being had up for and he explained how things might pan out. His feeling was that the investigation would take another ten days to two weeks and then I would be interviewed.

The following day all the papers carried the story, but the tenor was at least cautious if not supportive. I had a call from a journalist from a popular daily paper who tipped me off that an individual within the MOD, hugely frustrated by the apparent support the media were throwing behind me, had changed tactics and was now briefing another 'scandal' involving me. The pitch from this journalist was 'I know that you are being investigated about the death of a young soldier. Do you want to give me your side of the story? If you do then my paper will portray it to balance the story but if you don't, well, you will have to live with what the MOD say.' I was furious. I suspected that the informer (the word we used in Ireland was 'tout') within the MOD who was leaking this stuff was hoping I would trip myself by speaking to the media. Much as I would have liked to put over my side of the story, it could have been a trap. I hung up without replying. He had his answer.

The following day was a bombardment from the press. Three papers yelled: COLLINS PROBED IN NEW INQUIRY. The tout, badly briefed as ever, had given the papers a couple of pointers in the direction of two sources: Evans, the vicar who had left the battalion under the cloud of various stunts including failing to turn up for his own church services, and Paul Cochrane's father, Billy. Evans claimed that I had been 'grilled by the RMP' over physically assaulting him and had yelled obscenities in his face. Two papers published this libel. All I knew about Evans since he had been removed was that he had given evidence under oath to an earlier Board of Inquiry and they had dismissed his evidence as 'disingenuous and implausible'.

Once again I took the decision to stop answering the telephone after nine in the morning. Sarah Oliver called each morning at around eight o'clock to give me an overview of the day's papers. On the first couple of days she felt that there was a fairly strong gut instinct across Fleet Street that I was the victim of a smear campaign by people within the Army who were jealous. She told me that some of the broadsheets were heading for Iraq to do some digging. I was delighted. I was sure that even though the Army was loath to support me, surely there would be no shortage of Iraqis who would leap to my defence.

By the following day the media had discovered that the real story behind the whole thing were the allegations levelled by the US Army Reservist, Re Biastre, the little fat chap who had blundered into Al Rumaylah and who had wept in my office. It transpired that he was brought to book after his fall-out with me. He sought to protect himself by levelling accusations of war crimes at me. What I didn't realise was that his original allegations had been contained in a rant against the British forces in general and that his original statement ran to over 3,000 words. An investigation by the *Mail on Sunday* had established that the US Army had edited the version they sent to the MOD down to 2,395 words, for reasons only they know.

The pressure from the media became even more intense. I bought another mobile phone and only gave the number to my immediate family and Brigadier Matthew Sykes. Meanwhile I was becoming curious as to what the Army wanted to do with me. Was I on permanent gardening leave, for instance? I called the Army's personnel centre in Glasgow to find out if there was a plan to give me a job. I spoke to a staff officer in charge of colonels' jobs, who wasn't very helpful. What he did say was that while I was already selected for promotion to colonel I could just as easily be deselected and that if my circumstances changed, I would be deselected. I pointed out I hadn't been convicted of anything yet and I didn't think I would be and wasn't this was all very premature? I then asked him if my guilt had already been decided. He did not want to take it any further.

I called Brigadier David Santa-Olalla and he said that he would speak to Glasgow. He called back within a day or so to say that he'd secured a job and that I would be given a temporary role for six months setting up a Peace Support Academy in Sarajevo as an acting colonel. The fact that it was a temporary job meant that I would not be receiving the pay of colonel or the seniority. I found this very odd as the only reason I wasn't already a colonel was that I had agreed to lead my battalion in the recently completed war. Now I was to be held back for a further six months, which meant that in terms of pay, seniority and pension I was a full year behind. He said he was sorry but it was the best he could do. I spoke to Lewis Cherry, and explained the situation. He laughed. He wondered what on earth I had expected!

The next day, Friday, I was awakened early by a phone call from Sarah Oliver. Her assessment of press attitudes was that the quality newspapers were firmly on my side, right across the spectrum of political views, from the *Guardian* through *The Times* to the *Telegraph*, as well as the tabloids. To her amusement, even the *Sun*, who launched the initial story, had received such an adverse postbag that they had done a volte-face and were now firmly on my side. She was very optimistic and pointed out that while the Army had obviously abandoned me I had the support of the British people and many in Ireland. An increasingly large postbag and calls of support brought this home to me.

Two of the quality broadsheets had been to Al Rumaylah and what they had found out was revealing. It was through these papers that I was to learn a little more about Ayoub Younis Nasser (Abu Nawfel), the headmaster, Ba'ath party official and leader of the death squad whose home I had raided on the night of their planned murders. Reporters from *The Times* and the *Daily Telegraph* revealed a number of lurid tales of his involvement in Ba'ath party activities prior to the war and after. Anthony Browne from *The Times* revealed that a villager, Mawood Jaber (the medical student), said of Abu Nawfel:

He is a hated figure here. We know him as 'The Thief Ayoub' because he stole from the schoolchildren.

*The Times* also revealed that Abu Nawfel had recently been sacked as a part of the nationwide purge of Ba'athists. In an interview, the timid Ahmed (the English-speaking oil engineer) told *The Times* that:

The books and pens were given free by the Ministry for Education, but he still took money for them . . . The British soldiers gave a bicycle to the school for the children but Mr Nasser locked it away, planning to sell it.

This would have been a bicycle that the British CIMIC team gave the school at around the time that I had taken Air Marshal Burridge to the school. The mystery of who was behind terrifying the Imam was cleared up in a passage from *The Times*:

'He [Nasser] met with other members of the Ba'ath party and wrote secret reports. Many people went to jail because of what he wrote,' said one middle-aged man who did not want to be named. 'One man went to prison for six months for being heard to criticise the Ba'ath party, while another was jailed for unacceptable religious practices.'

325

If you met Ayoub Younis Nasser, you would never believe he could be involved in such skulduggery. Both Channel 4 and the BBC carried footage of him reconstructing for the papers and TV the scene where he was attacked by me, claiming in the film that it had all happened outside his house in full view of the townsfolk. The locals begged to differ. Abu Mohamed, leader of the village council I had established, said if it happened at all then:

> No one else in the village saw it. There were no other incidents with the British.

During this time I was grateful for the vigorous support of the local community in Kent and Canterbury in particular. Julian Brazier, the local MP, was most vocal in my support and wrote several times to the Armed Forces Minister, Adam Ingram, deploring the whole matter. The Chief Constable of Kent, Sir David Philips, was retiring and the Kent Police invited me as their guest of honour to their mess dinner to see him off. It was a welcome break and a good chance to see the senior policemen whom I had got to know during our time in Canterbury, including Chief Superintendent Gary Beautridge and Superintendent Paul Brandon. I must say that among my many firm friends and supporters in the crisis they were able to offer some of the most relevant advice. As I described what I was going through to a group of senior policemen, they smiled and nodded knowingly. Yes, they faced the same sort of mud-slinging all the time. One astute officer pointed out that there were those, in their naivety, who would like wars to be conducted within the rules of civil society and that I would be judged on those standards. With the experience of someone who dealt with criminals on a daily basis, he said that I could expect to face any amount of unsubstantiated accusations. 'You are,' he explained, 'a sitting target now.' He warned me not to rise to any bait and to let my solicitor deal methodically with each and every charge. Their advice and support was most welcome and left me feeling very much better. Here were men who served the community and they treated the allegations as just one of the downsides to public service. I did wonder, however, why the Army wasn't doing more.

Later that day I had a call from the Commander of the Field Army General Cedric Delves, who'd been my commanding officer in the SAS. Apart from giving me a morale-boosting pep talk, he also warned me of the need to keep my own counsel. That evening I received another enigmatic phone call from a well-heeled small-format newspaper to say that they had been contacted by an anonymous benefactor who was prepared to fund my legal defence and that I should consider taking up the offer.

The following day, a Saturday, I had a call from two prominent members of the House of Lords, who offered me their support as well-wishers. One of them said that I needn't worry as there was a groundswell of support across parties in the Commons and in the Lords.

In the media, the campaign against me was in complete disarray and Biastre was centre stage. It was revealed that he was not actually a member-badged operator in the US Special Forces, but a Civil Affairs officer (although in theory within Special Forces Command). His assertion, as he stood weeping in my office in Rumaylah, that he was a New York cop was also found to be slightly disingenuous. He was a part-time traffic policeman in upstate New York in a small town called Angola, near the border with Canada, a long way from New York City. A reporter, Sharon Churcher, had drawn a pen picture of Biastre based on interviews with Biastre's wife Debbie and some people from his home town. The article described Biastre thus:

> To his critics, he is a man without direction. He joined the Army reserve at the age of 17 but never fulfilled his ambition of becoming a full-time soldier. After eleven years with the police force, he is still a part-time patrolman. He had also hoped to become a psychologist.

His real employment was in a school. And no, he was not a teacher. He was a career guidance councillor. In many respects, I reflected, the statement Biastre had made to the US Army against me was a commentary on other aspects of his life. Sad, confused, heavily edited, filled with unfulfilled longings and worthy of considerable pity.

Matthew Sykes called at around teatime on Saturday 24 May. I briefed him on the offer of legal support and he appeared nonplussed. Strangely he asked me if there was anything else that had gone on Iraq that I hadn't told him about. I thought this odd and asked him to clarify what sort of things he had in mind, but he became quite irritated and said, 'You know very well what I mean.' I protested that I didn't and that ended the conversation.

Later that evening I had a further call from Sarah Oliver, who told me that the *Sunday Express* were preparing a splash but she knew no further details except that they were very excited about it, and it was something pretty big. I called Sykes back to tell him what I had heard and asked if that was why he had been quizzing me. He admitted it was and said that an allegation been made that was a significant departure from the previous accusations. He would not elaborate. As you can imagine, I was dumbstruck by this news, and wondered what I had been accused of now. Sykes refused to tell me and I simply had to wait for the newspaper to come out the next day.

I went to church the following morning and bought the papers on the way back. We had left in a hurry as it was Olivia's birthday and there were excited preparations for her party. Spreading my collection of newspapers out across the coffee table, I could see that Biastre had featured on the front pages of most papers. All bar two were pursuing Biastre as the source of the whole tale and most papers carried portraits of the man and details of his unfulfilled aspirations. One colleague from the local police force was not surprised to hear that Biastre had filed a report complaining about a superior, as he had done the same thing in his role as a part-time traffic warden.

I then turned to the two papers that had taken an editorial decision to go in a different direction. The *Sunday Express* accused me of murdering an Iraqi Ba'ath party member whom I had asked my soldiers to douse in petrol and set alight. I had then allegedly shot him. According to this tale I was now under arrest in the officers' mess in Canterbury. It also repeated a libel that I had 'bullied and struck' the unit's chaplain, Nick Evans, when he challenged my authority.

The *Sunday Mirror* screamed: COL TIM REGT. IN 9 GRAVES 'PROBE'. It was another invented story: that my men, with my knowledge, had shot dead nine Iraqi prisoners of war outside Basra. (Never mind that we had never been to Basra.) I was numbed. My anger and confusion was added to by one line in the *Mirror*. It read: 'A senior Ministry of Defence spokesman said last night, "We have spoken to SIB in Basra and can find no information on a search for bodies or shallow graves."' This was cagey, in my view. But the next line floored me. It was the final straw. It caveated the rebuttal with 'I cannot be 100 per cent sure'. This was an indictment of me, for sure.

Whoever the 'senior Ministry of Defence spokesman' was who made those comments, he had clearly confused the *Mirror* and the public as to the integrity of both me and the whole Royal Irish Regiment. He could as easily have said, 'It's simply not true and we know for certain that neither Collins nor any of his men have ever been to Basra.' For me it was a declaration of war. Biastre *had* made allegations, there *was* another Board of Inquiry into Cochrane, but these latest allegations were simply *untrue*. The Army knew that better than I did. Why did the Army let it pass? Malice? Incompetence? Attack me and I will bide my time; attack my men and I will give battle. I called Sykes. He was cheerfully dismissive and when I asked him what he intended to do about the matter he said quite simply, 'Nothing. Be more thick skinned.'

This latest news prompted a call of support from the Colonel of the Royal Irish Regiment, General Sir Philip Trousdell. I missed the call (we were still not answering the phone) but the message he left was very welcome. One of the broadsheets called and this time I did answer the phone. They were most sympathetic. When I was asked how I was dealing with the flurry of calls I admitted it was not going well. Off the record they offered to send someone round to help deal with enquiries. I was grateful but declined. I would only be accused of dealing with the media by the DCCA (I am still unclear as to what this department's official role actually was) and in any case surely that was the job of my employer, the Army.

It was extremely disappointing that the Army had simply stood by, not lifting a finger to help. On the contrary, the Army, in the form of DCCA, verbally attacked me if there was the least hint that I was talking to the media, which I had never been guilty of. It all supported my view that any honour within the Army and any vestige of a duty of care as an employer to me and my family no longer existed. It came as a disappointment, but sadly not as a surprise by this time.

In the Army's book *Serve to Lead*, which is given to every officer as he arrives at the Royal Military Academy Sandhurst, there is a quotation that encapsulates what is required of Army commanders. It reads:

> There is one trait in the character of a leader that above all things really counts . . . Being straight. Once those under him find out that a commander is absolutely straight in all his dealings with them, and free from the slightest trace of self interest, they will love him as their leader, trust him, work for him, follow him – and, should occasion arise, die for him.

In the service guide to behaviour, entitled *The Values and Standards of the British Army – Commander's Edition*, paragraph 33 states:

Commanders must also recognise and respect the fact that adherence to the values and standards of the Army demands from their soldiers a degree of commitment and self-sacrifice which goes beyond that normally expected from other citizens. For that reason it is particularly important that commanders discharge in full their responsibilities to those under their command. It is a function of leadership to communicate with, and to respect and protect the rights and interests of subordinates.

In other words servicemen enter into a covenant with the nation when they volunteer for service. They will endure hardship and suffering and fight the nation's enemies, prepared at an instant to lay down their very lives in the defence of their country. All ranks accept that they should abide by certain rules, including having no contact with the media unless it is directed by the MOD. In exchange they expect and require that when they are attacked in the media, either individually or collectively, the Army takes appropriate steps to defend their good name and reputation, where reasonable and where the facts are at hand. Since they have taken the individual's liberty to do so and right to self-defence in common law, this is only fair and worthy. To fail to act when they are able, and all the evidence of an individual's good name is available, is a breach of trust and dishonourable. I believe that the Army's failure to support me was without principle. It flew in the face of its own guidance. It was hypocritical. Its failure to counter the slur against the men of the 1st Battalion Royal Irish Regiment was without honour. I commend *The Values and Standards of the British Army – Commander's Edition* to the British Army's high command as a crucial text to read and digest.

I packed the family into our car and we headed for Brighton to stay with my sisters. Once there I met some old friends and considered my position over a drink. Finally I called Lewis. His advice was clear: sue. He wanted to publish a letter to the media on my behalf as he felt it was time to bring the public's attention to the disgraceful behaviour of the Army. The Army had unwittingly made me the British Dreyfus[127] and was

---

[127] Alfred Dreyfus was a Jewish French officer wrongly accused of spying and framed by elements in the French Army at the end of the 19th century. He was convicted of treason and sent to Devil's Island. When the extent of the French Army's involvement in subverting the case was revealed by Emile Zola's famous newspaper article titled *J'accuse*, Dreyfus was pardoned and the by now totally discredited French High Command reformed.

attacking me with anonymous briefings against me. It was disgraceful and cowardly behaviour and would not stand up to public examination. I was wary of this approach, however. I could not at that time believe it was a deliberate stunt. I just thought that the MOD were inept, not malicious. In any case, at that time I did not want to alienate my employer, the Army.

The following day I was the subject of a discussion on the Jeremy Vine show on BBC Radio 2 featuring Sarah Oliver and Colonel Bob Stewart. I had not been not aware that it would be on the radio and I was driving along in our car, heading for some friends' house for lunch, when I heard it begin. I glanced at Caroline and without a word we agreed that it was time for the children to hear the full debate. It was a most uncomfortable thirty minutes for me. I was relieved that when I arrived at our friends' house (he is German and she is Iranian) they were dismissive of the whole affair and intent on distracting me with their kind hospitality.

Over the next couple of days, I corresponded with my new libel solicitor, Ernie Telford. A senior partner in the law firm McCartan, Turkington, Breen, Ernie was an expert in his field and meticulous in his approach. I went over the offending libels carefully. The *Mirror* had carried an article about Cochrane and was based on an interview with Billy and Lynn Cochrane. They published and mocked a letter that I had written to them on the night of Paul's death. We counted seventeen inaccuracies in the piece and three major libels. Taken with other articles written about Cochrane, there were firm grounds to proceed, but Ernie and I agreed that the Cochranes had suffered enough in losing their son and to sue them would be to ruin a family who had very little.

A different tack was taken against the charges of murder and a detailed rebuttal of each and every point was prepared in a detailed counter to the *Sunday Express* and *Sunday Mirror*, sweeping up the accusations attributed to the padre, Nick Evans. We took the decision not to pursue him for his libels. A clergyman who is prepared to level false accusations and allow them to be repeated in a national paper is beneath contempt. We would sue the *Sunday Express* and the *Sunday Mirror* for their libels, however.

I was now defending myself against allegations of war crimes, being investigated by the SIB. I was central to the investigation of a charge of fostering a regime of bullying being investigated by a Board of Inquiry. I was engaged with two national papers in a major libel action. But why? Where was all this coming from?

Some light was shed on the matter on Friday 30 May. The *Sun* published an article concerning photographs showing the abuse of Iraqi prisoners by men of the 1st Battalion the Royal Regiment of Fusiliers, including sexual assaults. The photographs had emerged in a chemist's shop where the photographs had been sent to be processed. I wondered if these were the 'other issues' Lewis had mentioned. These were indeed serious and had real substance. This time the Army did have questions to answer. For once the media spotlight swung off me and I was left in peace.

I visited the General Officer Commanding Northern Ireland and the Colonel of my Regiment, General Sir Philip Trousdell, at his headquarters in Lisburn. I had known him since I was a newly joined lieutenant and he was a company commander. I had received several calls of support from him over the preceding weeks. He assured me that there was a great deal of work being done behind the scenes by the Regiment to help. I was appreciative but explained that I now wanted the entire thing fully examined so that there could never be any stain left after the matter was concluded. He agreed that that would be best for all concerned.

My luck with obtaining any support whatsoever from the Army continued to run badly. I applied for a new Army quarter so that I could move my family when I took on the new job, which was based in Wiltshire, but was told that there were no houses available. I explained that the house I was in was the house for the commanding officer of the battalion at Canterbury and that it would be unfair on the incoming commanding officer for me to stay there. It made no difference, I was told, there was no house for me. Because of my time with Special Forces I held the highest clearance security vetting. My vetting was due to be renewed in June of that year. The vetting officer called at my home to say that my vetting was now delayed until the autumn but would not elaborate as to why. At that point it occurred to me that, with a temporary job, temporary rank, no additional pay for my new rank, delayed vetting and no house to move to, it looked very much as if the Army system had already decided I was guilty.

# —23—

# CLEARED

June 2003 was a frustrating time. Media interest had thankfully abated, but I was still no further forward in my knowledge of what I was supposed to have done or when the SIB would interview me. I was busy filling out appraisal reports for those who had served with me in the Gulf. I am a firm believer that in the Army, people are our greatest asset and aside from actual operations looking after our people was the most important thing we did. Not everyone in the Army shares that view, but I was content to work as long as needed to ensure that my men had the best chance possible.

In early June I went to Sarajevo to visit my new job. It was a most refreshing break for me to be actually doing something again and in such a beautiful place. After arriving home late the previous night, I had left again at 0430, tiptoeing out of the house and picking up the mail that had been left beside my briefcase, before leaving in a taxi that took me to Heathrow and onward to Sarajevo via Vienna, where I had to sprint to catch the connection. We stayed at the Hotel Marsal near one of the ski resorts that had featured in the Winter Olympics in the hills above Sarajevo. The ski resort was still in ruins after the war but the hotel had been refurbished.

On arrival, I only had time to drop my bags in my room, as the first conference began immediately. At the end of a long day I sought some solace and relaxation by climbing the mountain outside the hotel. I climbed for an hour, wading through alpine meadows heavily scented with summer flowers and humming with insects laden with pollen. The sun was warm as I found my way up the steep slope. At the top I surveyed the scene across the Hercegovina Mountains, peaceful and tranquil, and reflected on the many lights, seasons and scenarios in which I had seen that same landscape.

Below I could see the city of Sarajevo. I had served there during the siege when death was commonplace and the desperation of the population was tangible. It looked peaceful now, from my mountain-top perch. Across the hills in the distance I could see the Muslim enclave of Gorazde. I had planned contingency after contingency for the relief of the British battle group stuck there in 1995 and besieged by the Serbs. I had been in Bosnia for the uneasy peace that sprang from the Dayton Accord. I recalled Christmas Eve 1995 in Kiseljak, far below me now, where the Irish serving with the British SAS and the Irish serving with the French Foreign Legion had got together in the abandoned brick factory that snowy evening to talk of home. I had travelled to Bosnia frequently in 1999/2000 in my role with the Director Special Forces staff, when a Person Indicted For War Crimes (PIFWIC) had been detected for arrest on behalf of the International War Crime Commission. The UK had taken many of these killers unawares, at home, in the street, at market, to hand them onto The Hague. Before being dispatched to Sarajevo I would read the indictments. I could never believe the horror these people were responsible for, and will never relate the lengths we went to in order to detain them. Now, here I was, no longer one of the good guys, a hunter, but a war crimes suspect myself, the hunted. While I didn't know the exact charges levelled at me, I was sure I would be pretty small fry in my cage in The Hague alongside Slobodan Milosevic, Madame Plavsic and General Galic, not to mention the other creatures with vowel-hungry names who had once been the prey, and on whose capture I had often briefed the Supreme Commander of NATO, General Wes Clarke.

As a war crimes suspect, I wondered what sort of attention I was attracting. Would the British Secret Intelligence Service (SIS) and General Communication Headquarters (GCHQ) be monitoring my phones? I doubted it. Would someone close to me be meeting strangers to discuss my movements, mood and intentions? Would muscular men be studying my photograph or taking the opportunity to sit near me in a pub or restaurant so they could identify me when the order was given to floor me and handcuff me. Would I be stripped and put in a white forensic suit, inside a container, before finally being asked to formally identify myself to the War Crimes Indictment representatives?

My mind then strayed to other operations when I had watched the sunset with no expectation of seeing the dawn. I recalled coming across the dead in Africa, discarded without dignity, and realising that I too could end up like that. As I looked back over my service in both Gulf Wars, Africa, the Middle East, Far East, Colombia and Central America, I realised that the dream was over. The bond of trust was broken – and not by me. I would never again willingly volunteer to put my life in danger for my country. In future I would join the common herd, fighting only if my family and hearth depended on it and taking, consuming and enjoying freedom. I had given enough, indeed all that I could give, and was now betrayed.

I jogged back down the mountain to shower before supper. I then remembered that I hadn't opened the mail in my briefcase. There was the usual stuff, letters of support, invitations to address meetings and dinners, and then a note from a journalist that brought me up sharp. It simply said that a daily paper had the telephone number of my new mobile and that it was being monitored. Transcripts of my conversations existed and were being held in a safe. It warned that I should be very careful what I said. In an instant my Special Forces instincts took over and, leaning out of the window, I burned the note and the envelope. (Love 'em or hate 'em, the British look after the sources first and foremost.) I later regretted burning the note. It was evidence of malicious intent somewhere along the line. It seemed it was not the SIS who were watching my movements but Fleet Street. But where had they got the number? Caroline would not have passed it on, nor would my mother or my son. Apart from DCCA, they were the only people who had it and I could not believe it was passed from within the MOD. It wasn't even a month old. I would never know who had betrayed me or how.

Brigadier David Santa-Olalla had predicted that I would be interviewed around the beginning of June. By mid-June the RMP were no closer to bringing me in for interview. I was also curious as to how this new Board of Inquiry, which had been announced with such fanfare weeks before, was progressing. Once again mysterious visitors had been tramping through the camp and I was not supposed to notice. I called Brigadier Santa-Olalla and outlined my concern at the time it was taking. I also mentioned my difficulty in finding somewhere to live. The following day brought a plethora of results: I was given a date for my interview with the SIB, 25 June; a senior officer, Brigadier Donald Wilson (in whose area we had been during the firemen's strike), was to be the head of the Board of Inquiry into Ranger Cochrane's death; and the Defence Housing Executive called to say that they could offer me a house in mid-September.

I continued with the paperwork that was brought to my door on a regular basis and waited for my chance to speak up. The day before my SIB interview I had a call from General Delves, who wanted to wish me luck. I set off early the next morning to pick up Lewis from Southampton Airport. We were to meet the SIB in their Headquarters in Bulford. As I travelled down I listened in horror as the details of the slaughter of six members of the RMP the previous afternoon in Iraq were reported on the radio. The men were from 156 Provost Company, attached to the 1 Para battle group led by Tom Beckett. It was reported that the incident happened at Al Majarr al Kabir, the town where I had seen the man running across the road with the AK-47 and had disarmed him. (There was no doubt they were a dangerous bunch there, but to execute six RMP? That was a serious departure from the norm.)

I met Lewis off the flight. We chatted as we drove to Bulford. He was curious, in the light of what had happened to the RMP the previous day, to find out about the area in Iraq where we had worked. I explained that things had moved on since we had left and there had been a series of shooting incidents in Al Amarah and a number of locals killed.

We then turned to my case in detail and went over a script that I had prepared giving him some background to our time in Iraq so that he could help me put the whole thing into perspective when we met the RMP. Then he sat back and explained the rules of the game. I was to say nothing. He knew I was eager to clear my name but I would not help myself if I was anything but cautious with the RMP.

'They are not on your side,' he emphasised. 'The SIB will get no thanks from those who are pursuing this matter if you walk out of there a free man, so watch what you say.'

I protested that I had nothing to hide.

'You would be amazed at what can be made from nothing. The procedure is, we listen to what is said in the disclosure brief and we adjourn and you brief me on anything not in your notes and then I give them a written answer for use in the interview.'

We arrived at HQ SIB in Bulford. Inside it was long and narrow with offices down each side of a corridor that ran the length of the building. The bottom half of the building had three or four 'interview suites'. We arrived and Lewis went off to meet the Commander of the SIB,

Lieutenant Colonel Green. I took a seat in the waiting area and read the well-thumbed magazines and literature from various firms of solicitors. After about forty minutes Lewis returned and we went down to the interview suite. We met the sergeant who would take notes, a small Liverpudlian with gelled hair, and at last Lieutenant Colonel Green himself. I was expecting some emaciated, dour individual with a pallid complexion and a personality void but he was quite the opposite. He struck me instantly as an affable sort of guy. The sergeant and Green left us to discuss the accusations that he had put to Lewis in my absence.

There were essentially six: firing my weapon at the tyres of the looters; shooting into the ground during the struggle at the back of the gunmen's pick-up; striking a man who had assaulted me when I had stopped them stealing the oil from the tank behind the Ba'ath party HQ; beating up Abu Nawfel; striking the man who had grabbed my weapon during the prisoner breakout; placing Biastre under illegal custody and abusing him by making him stand in the sun for forty-five minutes; and, potentially the most serious charge, mistreating the RMP corporal who I had placed on duty outside my room on the night of the visit by the Kurds.

There were, of course, supplementary accusations. These were quickly dealt with. One was that I had been too zealous in closing the back of my Land-Rover when we took over some prisoners that CO 3 Para had captured near the Hammar Bridge. All I could recall of the incident was that we did take some prisoners back to my HQ when we handed the Hammar Bridge to 3 Para. The men were dressed in civilian clothes, but each had an AK-47. My recollection of that meeting was that there was shelling going on and I didn't think it was a good idea for the commanders of two battle groups to be loitering where they could be targeted. The other accusation was that I had illegally used the money that Abu Nawfel had been arrested with by ordering it to be spent on the repairs to the school. Under Army law it should have been sent back to Division to be incinerated. Lewis later pointed out to Lieutenant Colonel Green that I had not at any time actually had the money – I'd seen a bag and I was told there was money in it, but I hadn't *seen* the money – and so that was hearsay. They quickly dropped both of these charges. Once the interview began again, Colonel Green asked me why I seemed to be present at all the incidents concerning 1 R Irish.

'That's simple,' I explained, 'I'm the only one in 1 R Irish, indeed 16 Air Assault Brigade, being investigated.'

'But I know that some senior officers are wondering why you were constantly bumping into crowds, prisoners and the like,' he continued. 'Why were you always at the front line?'

'Because that is what modern battlefields are like. There often is no front line. This was not an exercise. Those losers have never been to war. I'm not in the least bit surprised that they have no idea what it is like. The incidents you are investigating me for must have happened a thousand times across the battlefield. If you were there you would see such incidents.'

Then we got down to the six main charges. We left the room, I briefed Lewis on each and he took notes. We then went back in for further interrogation. Over the space of the next six hours my statements were examined. Lewis would elaborate where necessary. I was fortunate that I had been accompanied in Iraq by the media, because what they had reported at the time coupled with eye-witness accounts, mainly from the attached arms and the US Marine ANGLICOs, tallied closely, whereas the statements from those who had accused me were mainly hearsay, or completely different from what everyone else had said. We spent some time on each statement and I would sit and listen as Lewis verbally jousted with the RMP. I tried not to intervene but could not resist the odd sarcastic comment when the RMP found themselves down a particular rabbit hole, such as the incident where I captured the 100-strong group of escaping prisoners.

'So,' I enquired, 'what is the correct drill for arresting groups of 100 or more when you are alone?'

They let that one pass. By late afternoon many of the cases had been demolished.

Returning to the remaining allegations, we dealt with Biastre first. His claims were wildly over the top and his statements contradicted themselves. (So it had only taken three months and the interest of the international press to sort that schoolboy incident out.) The next question was did I shoot the hole in the floor with my pistol or with one I had taken from the battlefield? (This was something the SIB had chipped in themselves and was quickly dismissed, as Abu Nawfel had agreed with me that it was my Browning I had used. We would know, we were there and both of us had had a great deal to do with pistols during our lives.) The RMP then put an allegation to me that I had an Iraqi pistol and an AK-47 during my time in Iraq. At that point I could not contain myself any longer and despite Lewis's protestations I took violent exception to this charge.

'That's a damn lie to say I had an AK-47!' I shouted at the two startled SIB men. 'At no time did I have less than three AK-47s. Because the fucking SA 80s don't work and the AKs do. It was a war, you know.' The issue was set aside. The RMP wanted to know what I had done with the weapons at the end of the war. They seemed quite surprised when I informed them that they had been handed in to be decommissioned for the regimental museum.

The struggle in which Abu Nawfel was injured was discussed. Unhelpfully I admitted that I had no idea how his head got split but accepted that I could have been to blame as we struggled in the darkness of his house. He claimed I had clubbed him to the ground outside his door with my pistol and his wife had claimed that I had hit him over the head with her mirror in the hallway (no doubt in hope of compensation for a new mirror). At that point the RMP sought to present their surprise piece of evidence. A video they had of Abu Nawfel reconstructing his beating for the camera. Before the sergeant could get it to play, Lewis casually enquired, 'Is it the BBC or Channel 4 version, or one you made yourselves?'

'You mean there are other films of him describing the events?' an irritated Colonel Green asked.

'Oh yes,' Lewis replied, 'several.'

We dispensed with that one as the SIB admitted they weren't aware that Abu Nawfel had been so industrious in his reconstructions. We were then left with the mock execution, dropping the captured weapons onto him as he sat in the street outside his house and kicking him up the arse. It was quickly accepted that the mock execution story was rubbish. Corporal Magowan had cleared the rifle Abu Nawfel had been hiding, as Abu Nawfel had placed a round in the breech. It was accepted that this was a normal and necessary safety precaution. This was discarded at this point. As for dropping the weapons on him, I conceded that when I was handed the bag of weapons, which he had constantly denied knowledge of, I emptied the bag out in front of Abu Nawfel as a way of demonstrating his lies. I accepted that one may have fallen onto him. The SIB accepted that that might not have been deliberate. Finally we had differing allegations as regards the kick. I explained that I had put Abu Nawfel into the approved kneeling restraint position, using my foot to sweep away his legs because he would not cooperate. Abu Nawfel claims he was kicked in the back. My second in command, in a statement, insisted that I kicked him up the arse. I conceded that while I meant to take his legs away to get him down (I was holding him in one hand and my rifle in the other), it was possible that either case might be true. How anyone could be sure in the pitch darkness, I don't know.

That ended the interview, except I repeated that as far as I was concerned at least three lives were saved that night and the next day 130 weapons handed in that could have taken many more allied and Iraqi lives had they been left to the insurgents. If what I had done was wrong all I had to say was I would have done it again, lives were saved and so much for the rules.

We then focused on the RMP corporal who had had his night off spoiled. I drew the SIB team's attention to the fact that when he was put on duty the sky outside was ablaze with gunfire and every other member of the battalion was stood to that night.

'So you would say it was dangerous?' Colonel Green helpfully inquired.

'You had six men from the RMP shot dead there yesterday – what do you think?'

The interview over, I was shocked to discover that the SIB then wanted to fingerprint me and take a DNA swab. I had returned from a war and now here I was being fingerprinted like a common criminal. It was agreed that we would leave it until the next time. The SIB reminded me that the charges against me were so serious that they could arrest me if I did not show up for future interviews. I said that I was aware of this and would come whenever called.

I drove Lewis back to the airport and asked him how he thought it went.

'Well', he said, 'you think your asides are funny – and they are, mostly – but they really do not help and you are playing into their hands. Next time no drifting off the script.'

Monday 30 June was the date set for the second Board of Inquiry into the Cochrane affair and I was invited to attend to give evidence to Brigadier Donald Wilson. The hearing began with the surprise news that the Army had conceded that it was unjust not to grant me substantive rank of colonel and from that point I was a colonel and would receive the pay and seniority of a colonel. (It was an extremely odd place to discover that I had been promoted – usually someone writes to you – but the Army was in such disarray at that stage with regard to me – and everything else – it had become the norm. At least I didn't find out about it in the papers or on the radio or TV.)

The hearing itself was brief. The main thrust of the inquiry centred on my leadership style. Brigadier Wilson asked if I was perhaps too forceful a leader.

I presumed that we were talking about the company commander I had sacked before the Northern Ireland tour of duty and the failing company commander who I closely supervised throughout his chaotic tour of duty. I asked the Board to clarify this.

'Do you tend to drive men rather than teach them?' Brigadier Wilson went on. 'Shouldn't company commanders be allowed to make mistakes and then learn by them?'

My answer was simple. Where the lives of the young men whose welfare their parents have entrusted to me are concerned, there can be no latitude. I had sufficient good leaders in my battalion to allow me to dispense with or restrict the weak, in order to ensure the safety of our people. That was foremost, and our performance as a result was proven to be of the highest standards. To me that was all that mattered. As evidence I cited letters I had received from the General Officer Commanding Northern Ireland at the time of our 2001 tour, General Sir Alistair Irwin, and our senior policeman, Chief Superintendent Davy Pickering, congratulating me on a superb tour of duty, Davy Pickering describing it as the best battalion he had seen on duty during his time. My two-star General officer, an RAF Air Vice Marshal much respected across the three services, who commanded the organisation to which 16 Air Assault Brigade belonged, wrote after I had been awarded the Queen's Commendation for Valuable Service for that tour of duty, saying of the deployment, 'Your own performance – and indeed that of the battalion – has been nothing short of the best we have seen in Northern Ireland over three decades.'

The chairman of the Board conceded that the assessment of my performance and that of 1 R Irish in the most recent Gulf War by the commanders there was markedly similar. I thanked him for that and told him that was my answer: 'I brought all my men home safely from all my tours of duty. The only exception was a man who died at his own hand while talking to his father on the telephone, for reasons I still do not understand. I could not have prevented that. And surely that is why we are here today?'

I finished by pointing out that I had turned around a battalion that was at approximately half strength when I took command, handing it over just short of full strength. I had also dealt with a serious attempt by organised drug gangs to penetrate my battalion, as well as the consequences of a suicide, a rape and the death of a teenager in a training accident. I had received absolutely no help or support in any of those endeavours (much less encouragement) from the Army's high command, who now belatedly wanted to review this period. At the same time I had successfully led the battle group on three operations. In my view there were institutional flaws and they were all in the Army's chain of command. That concluded my evidence. I passed the Board a written submission detailing my approach to command.

My second appearance with the SIB was in Catterick in North Yorkshire. I met Lewis at Darlington station and this time he drove me to the interview. By now we were back to the utter nonsense of who said the word 'arrest' first with regard to Biastre and why did I fire here or use my pistol there. This trend of questioning, which seemed to be comparing the events in Iraq to a scuffle in Margate, struck me as indicative of the reason I was sitting there. It was one thing for the general behind this whole nonsense whoever he was and who no doubt had never seen action, to imagine how wars should be; it was quite another thing to be in the middle of one.

The questioning then focused on such technicalities as 'Did you invade Major Biastre's personal space?' and 'What word did you use here?' At that point I went off script again and became rather angry. At the time of the incident Biastre mattered to me not one jot, I explained. I could remember only a certain amount about the incident, because I had a company under attack on the Hammar Bridge, I had three of the people whom it was my duty to protect under a death sentence and I had the potential of a local insurrection to contend with. I could only recall dismissing some Walter Mitty character because through his incompetence and clowning he was threatening to kick off the fighting before we were ready. I could not make it any clearer.

We then got back to their desire to fingerprint me and take a DNA swab. This discussion revealed another interesting fact with regard to what was and was not said between Sykes and the Sunday papers on the evening before the *Sunday Express* and the *Sunday Mirror* published their libels. It had been alleged, by one of the papers, that a pistol had been recovered from a grave outside Basra, with my fingerprints on it. Lieutenant Colonel Jeremy Green stated that he had made it clear that Saturday evening that it was not true, they were not investigating a murder and that in any case they did not have my fingerprints to compare. (Why, I wondered, did a 'senior Ministry of Defence spokesman', whoever that was, not make this clear to the papers?)

This interview concluded with Lieutenant Colonel Green stating that he would be sending a file to my commanding officer reporting me for a number of offences. I returned to London and Lewis to Northern Ireland.

I now focused my attention on the libel. The papers were standing by their story and were prepared neither to apologise nor admit it was untrue. While they had elected to avoid portraying the stories as *true*, they were now holding to the Reynolds Judgment. This was based on a case five years previously in a libel trial concerning the former Irish Taoiseach, Albert Reynolds, who had brought and lost a libel action in the High Court. This judgement appeared to show that papers don't have to *prove* that a published allegation is true; they simply have to demonstrate that it is in the public's interest in publishing it and that they have acted *responsibly* and *in good faith* in doing so. The papers in my case contended that I was a public figure, that I was of media interest and that allegations had to be published in the public interest. But the Reynolds Judgment also requires the papers to act responsibly and in good faith. But they did proceed, however, on the implication by the 'Senior Ministry of Defence Spokesman' that he couldn't be 100 per cent sure. They believed that they had acted in good faith because of this woolly reply. The fact that I was never in Basra, no one had my fingerprints, there were no bodies and the assurances Brigadier Matthew Sykes had said he had given them, should have been enough to make them pull the story. But they were confident enough on the basis of the briefing by their source to ignore what Brigadier Sykes had said. To win the case, the source would become a central figure. It certainly looked like the original source of both of these libels was one and the same person.

We elected to take the case to the High Court in Belfast. It was my home ground. While putting any case in front of a jury carries human risk I was confident of enough support from across the communities in Northern Ireland, from Loyalist through Unionist to Nationalist to most Republicans, to feel that I would get a fair hearing. The risk was that there might be a jury comprising Loyalist drug runners or Republican Dissidents. Then I was probably for it. I was prepared to take the chance.

I took over my new job based in the Combined Services Command and Staff College in Shrivenham, setting up the Peace Support Training

Academy in Sarajevo. This was to be a multinational arrangement aimed at bringing together officers from the armies of the former warring factions to study and, we hoped, achieve a mutual understanding. It was a fascinating job and I had an interesting time working with the New Bosnian Herzegovina Army, as well as partners from contributing nations led by Brigadier Larsen from Denmark, a superb leader and able diplomat. My work took me to New York to the United Nations, Vienna and frequently to Sarajevo. Around this time it was announced that I would be posted for three years to become the Deputy to the Assistant Chief of Staff responsible for training at Headquarters Land Command at Wilton in December. This job would see me responsible for training the Field Army. I immediately cancelled the house I had been allocated in Shrivenham and applied for one in Wilton instead. I was assured that I would be given a house in December which I naturally took at face value.

I took my family on holiday to Germany and we travelled south to Bavaria. Between swimming, climbing mountains and identifying each cow in the fields by name for Olivia, my five-year-old daughter, I wondered what my fate would be. Would I be returning to face charges or would the whole thing have blown over? The matter weighed heavily on me. After three weeks we were driving home through the vineyards and schlosses of the Rhineland when my mobile phone went. It was Brigadier David Santa-Olalla. He said, over a crackly line, that he had now reviewed the evidence that had been sent to him by the SIB. He had considered it carefully and had decided that there was no case to answer. It was over. I could barely believe my ears.

# —24—

# GETTING OUT

I returned home relieved, to be sure, but still confused as to why it had all happened. Who had gained? While the MOD put a spokeswoman up to announce the end of the inquiry, saying that 'there was no stain or blemish on my character', there were no telephone calls of congratulations from those who had tried so hard to nail me. Brigadier Sykes did call, of course, just to make sure that although I had got away with the case, I was not to speak to the press. I was very clear on that. Not surprisingly I did get lots of calls from the press because the story had already been 'leaked' from within MOD. My wife Caroline, however, was not in the Army and she gave an interview to the *Mail on Sunday* expressing her relief at the end of the whole attack on me.

I visited General Sir Cedric Delves. He confirmed that the matter was over but cautioned me that I had stuck my neck out and had been too closely identified with some of the more robust actions that had gone on in the war. He cautioned me to be very careful in future, for next time I might not be so lucky. However, he finished by saying, 'Don't ever change.' The Army needed me just as I was. From a famous SAS leader and much-decorated war hero this was a boost indeed. I knew very well I had to be careful in future. I would make my enemies no gifts of an unguarded flank. But, noble and upright men like Brigadier Santa-Olalla, and General Sir Cedric Delves aside, it was clear that my enemies, eaten by envy and motivated by professional jealousies, were many and powerful. I realised that the prospect of advancement in the Army was limited.

I carried on working between Shrivenham, London and Sarajevo, with my posting to HQ Land looming in December. I still wondered how the Army actually saw me. I was sent a two-fold message to answer that on 31 October 2003. I was staying with my sister in Woking when my brother-in-law woke me up at 0630 to say that he had just heard on the BBC's Radio 4 *Today* programme that I had been awarded the decoration of Officer of the Order of the British Empire (OBE).

'Don't believe everything you hear on the radio,' I called back and went back to sleep.

I caught the train to London later that morning and there on the news stand was the announcement: COLLINS GETS OBE. I bought a paper and there I was on the front cover. In London I went to my office and checked with the official announcements on the MOD website, and sure enough I had indeed been awarded an OBE. To say that it was unusual for someone in the Army, indeed any organisation, to find out about such an award after the rest of the nation via the media was an understatement.

Apparently there had been a press jamboree the previous day in MOD to announce all of the many awards on the Operational Honours List arising from Operation Telic, the British contribution to the invasion of Iraq. It appeared that no one had seen it fitting or appropriate to tell me while the news was leaked to the media. The message was clear: 'We didn't get you, you did OK, here's your medal, now piss off[128].'

I received a call later that morning from the Commandant of the Joint Services Command and Staff College where I worked, General McColl generously phoned me personally to say that there had been a cock-up, he was sorry I hadn't been told and, yes, I was to be awarded an OBE.

In December 2003 I moved to HQ Land Command near Wilton, a picturesque town close to Salisbury. My job was to oversee the training of the Field Army and this meant coordinating the resources for the two divisions – 1 (UK) Armoured Division, based in Germany, and 3 (UK) Division, based in the UK – and a virtual division called 'Theatre Troops', a collection of logistic, signals and intelligence brigades. Training is the cornerstone of the UK's military capability. The modern British Army has developed its success by a mixture of intuitive learning, operational experience and deductive learning processes. Where

---

[128] In mid-November 2004, long after I had retired, they even gave me a campaign medal. There again, no one could deny I was there!

possible this is all conducted within an All Arms Collective training environment. The spectrum of this learning reflects the range of tasks faced by the Army and is satisfied by the training opportunities, expensively bought in the training grounds of Canada, Germany and Kenya and beyond. Overseas training in the complex and harsh terrains of the desert, the jungle and the Arctic enhances it. It sets the British Army aside from most other armies and puts it in the same league in terms of ability, if not size, as the US Army. It was my job to coordinate these activities.

The experience gained on such training yields improves the British Army's ability to adapt quickly to new environments while suffering low levels of environmental diseases and injuries. It also gives the British Army a considerable edge when they have to engage with local populations and seek to maintain, enforce or restore peace. This crucial interaction and acceptance of local conditions has paid dividends in both blood and treasure on operations, most notably in Iraq. It has also attracted the admiration of our allies and the respect of the indigenous populations with whom we have come into contact. It is all very expensive, however.

When I arrived in Wilton, rather than getting to know this vast organisation, spread out across the world as it was, I found myself immediately thrust into the defence of our training regime. The treasury wanted to find billions of pounds in savings, no doubt to fund Gordon Brown's social service and world debt agenda and the Armed Forces, not a vote winner and led by those who would never stand up to central Government, was an easy hit. In any case, recent history has shown that the defence sector can be battered with swingeing cuts and yet still be one of the few public services to deliver the goods. This combination of dedication, ingenuity in the face of resource starvation and weak leadership made it an ideal target for savings. The measures being considered to find these savings were set to cripple the training system. Once attacked, it was very possible that the training regime might never recover, in which case the Army would become much less effective. The Army was already massively overextended. Some 12,000 troops had been allocated to supporting the police in Northern Ireland. With the insurgency in Iraq, Afghanistan, the Balkans and a major undertaking to convert the Army to a 'digitised force[129]', operational commitments took

---

[129] Making all radios and navigational aides interoperable and giving the UK's army a capability to work alongside the US Army.

up all that was left. In fact, by the Government's so-called 'Harmony Guidelines', which allowed time between operational deployments of twenty-four months, the Army was 17,500 men short. Against any future contingency there is nothing. The overstretch in Field Army units meant that a lot of the training had to be cancelled anyway. The Army was doing too much with too few resources. It was quite frankly depressing.

There was a Dunkirk spirit in the headquarters, however, and the leaders saw to it that everyone approached these intractable problems with a cheery smile and made the best of it all. I must admit I was too cynical by this time and no longer had the sort of ambition that drives senior army officers to make do with less in order to please a civil servant. I was more inclined to do an Oliver Twist and insist we wanted some more. But I was at Wilton barely a week when I realised that asking for more was not in our culture, we just did with less. I spent two weeks there watching the preparations to reduce our already stretched training budget before going home to Canterbury for Christmas. (Naturally the promise in July of an Army house in Wilton was hollow. The Government had sold off so many 'surplus' Army houses that there weren't enough to go round now.)

I returned to work in Wilton on 5 January 2004 and handed in my resignation. It was no longer the Army I had joined. From a massive force stationed across the world and ready to meet the unexpected when I had signed up in 1981, the British Army is now largely based at home and on operations across the world, barely able to meet its commitments and debilitated by the budgetary constraints. Undermanned, the regiments cannot fill their ranks under the current rules. The training regime has been largely civilianised, which brings the attendant problems of bullying and misbehaviour. (At night the trainees are left with a ratio of the order of one adult Army instructor to 250 trainees. Bearing in mind these are teenagers, some as young as sixteen, this is a scandal. If a school were run like this it would be closed down.) Additionally, the actual training places become available very slowly, and as a result a young person who turns up at a recruiting office is often invited to come back in six months or more. So much happens in a teenager's life in six months we rarely see them again.

This is no way to man an army and the figures show it does not work. This has come about because of the success of the civil service in gaining power over the controls of the Armed Services and their attempts to run it as a business. Coupled with this we have simply had some bad leaders. Those who I call the 'Neithers'. These are the self-publicists who are neither soldiers (most have never been in a fight of any kind, even in the playground at school) nor businessmen, though some like to flatter themselves that they 'run' multi-million-pound businesses. They enjoy business talk and like to pretend that they are up with the latest business thinking. These staff pigeons have even developed their own language, an argot that charts the Byzantine budgetary structure and cripples innovative thinking. It is in fact a mechanism for combing the thinning hairs of the Army's once proud mane to cover the parchment-thin skin of this formerly world-class service. There can be no doubt whatsoever that real businessmen would do a much better job running the Army. We, as a nation, have long since discovered that the in-house entrepreneurs in the public sector are low grade. The private sector has the cream and a business like the Army – if it is to be run as a business – needs this sort of talent. They would need military advice for sure, and that is where the men with proven leadership and field experience come in. Alternatively generals could run it as an army. But that seems to be outmoded.

I left the forces convinced that there was a burgeoning need for a merciless cull at the highest levels to cut out the destructive dead wood that was stifling initiative, pandering to the civil service assaults and failing above all to give any leadership whatsoever to the services. As I write, young servicemen face civil court for actions that have occurred on active service. With the military justice system having failed on operations, it must be time to re-examine the reason it exists. Ultimately it is a failure at the highest levels of command and if it were to happen in the health service or police resignations would be demanded. Only the Army and the established Church seem to be above accountability. The crisis is so real that it is an obvious, imminent threat to the security of our nation. The failure of the system, when it comes, will be catastrophic and irreversible. The senior military officers who have allowed and in some cases conspired in this failure are culpable and must be held to account. Better still, the nation could retire the whole generation of failing senior officers and avoid the looming disaster.

I predict dark and difficult days ahead for the British Army and fear that the rot will only be stopped when there is a radical change at the top of the Army, with the introduction of some fighters who will deliver the country's defence needs and demand the resources to do so.

When I resigned there was not the least surprise within the Army. I felt relieved of a great burden. It took the media a week to catch on and when they did there was the inevitable flurry of excitement. Naturally the Army suspected that I had orchestrated the media response, but I pointed out that if I had wanted to orchestrate the event I would have had a splash the day it happened, not a week later. In the twenty-four-hour news world, they worked considerably in arrears; surely I must do as well. In HQ Land Command, Brigadier John Cooper, my boss, accepted this as probably about right and I was left alone from then on. In my preparations to leave the Army, I was meticulous at keeping records of everything that I did and claimed in way of entitlement and in keeping John apprised of where I was and what I was doing and above all who I was meeting. I did not want any repetition of the spiteful campaign of the previous year. I made sure that after twenty-two years I got every entitlement owing to me and left no vulnerable flank from which I could be attacked.

The libel actions were reaching their climax and I asked in December 2004 if the Army and Brigadier Matthew Sykes in particular would be ready to give an account of what had or had not been said on the evening of 24 May 2003 when the *Sunday Express* and the *Sunday Mirror* had written the libels. I expected that, as my employer, they would be happy to account for their actions voluntarily. I had passed all my solicitor's documents to the Commander Legal at HQ Land. During an interview with Commander Legal at Land, he warned me to be careful of what I said about the matter. He confided that the news of my being cleared in August had been leaked three weeks ahead of me being told.

Early spring brought the welcome news that both the *Sunday Express* and the *Sunday Mirror* had conceded the libels including Evans's allegations and the matter would be settled without a hearing. What was disappointing was that the Army refused to meet with my solicitors and hid behind the MOD solicitors when pressed for help. Ernie, my solicitor, was amazed by this evasive behaviour but pointed out that it was not actually a problem because on the day the court would have simply ordered them to attend. I cannot imagine why the Army had been so reluctant to give evidence if they were honest in what they said and told the truth.

Two days prior to settlement of the case in the High Court in Belfast, Ernie called and asked if I would like to issue a statement to the media. I explained that I was unable to as I was still a serving Army officer and that there was no way that the Army would have the willingness or even competence to issue one on my behalf. He offered to issue one for me. I asked that we work on it together, which was agreed, but it would be his statement. The statement said in effect that I was sad that, having fought the Army's battles for twenty-two years, they had dishonourably abandoned me over the libels and that it seemed that the concept of honour was dead in the Army. I took a copy across to the media desk at HQ Land and passed it to the civilian that worked there to pass to DCCA. I then set off for the Director of Infantry's Dinner at Warminster in Wiltshire.

This was a black tie event that attracted the commanding officers of all the infantry battalions as well as the staff who dealt with infantry matters. I knew many of those there and we had a good evening catching up. When we sat down for dinner I was taken aback by another incident that made me realise how far the Army and I had grown apart. The Director of Infantry, a brigadier, leapt to his feet and announced that the leader of the Drumcree protest in Northern Ireland, Harold Gracey, had died – raising a glass as he made the announcement. I thought this action was totally without decorum. Even more extraordinarily, the general who was speaking at the dinner rose to address the company took up this theme, talking about how many of our enemies had been vanquished: 'Slobodan Milosevic is in The Hague, Saddam Hussein is in a jail we know not where, and Harold Gracey is dead.'

I looked across at the Royal Irish colonel sitting beside me. He raised his eyebrows. Neither he nor I had any admiration for Harold Gracey – the other colonel was a Southern Irish Catholic – but we immediately thought the same thing: surely the British Army exists to defend the right to free speech and peaceful protest? Harold Gracey was an old boy who sat in a caravan on the bridge on the Garvaghy Road, protesting. Surely we were fighting in Iraq for exactly those rights?

The next day I travelled to London to attend a meeting before flying over for the settlement in Belfast the following day. I was in London at around eight in the evening. My mobile phone rang and it was no less a person than the Chief of the General Staff. He asked what I was doing putting out the statement I had worked on with Ernie and told me that it had been intercepted by DCCA. 'No,' I explained, 'I gave it to the media operations at their desk in Wilton.'

'But,' he continued, 'you've won your victory over those wretched allegations from the Yank and you've settled the Cochrane affair – why are you doing this?' He reminded me that we had been drinking together until two o'clock that morning. 'You said then that the whole affair was over.'

I agreed. He was quite right about Biastre and the Cochrane affair. They were ancient history. I had indeed seen both off. I then explained that these libels were nothing to do with Biastre or Cochrane, they were about totally untrue stories in the media that accused me, and more importantly the men of 1 R Irish, of murder. I told him that it had been in the Army's power to kill the stories before they had even been published. He was silent, then admitted he had not been briefed on that. He then suggested that surely the DCCA organisation had been helpful. I begged to differ and pointed out that they had been – on this issue alone – evasive, unhelpful and frankly difficult.

He changed tack and suggested that the tone of what I was saying was potentially harmful. He finished by saying, 'If you think I'm one of the good guys and am trying to make things better, then I'm asking you not to put this statement out. If you think I'm part of the problem, then you must do what you like.'

When it was put in those terms, of course I agreed to withdraw the statement. I had a lot of respect for General Jackson. He was a leader who had been in operations. We needed more like him. I called Ernie at home and asked him to pull it. Ernie was a little taken aback. 'What,' he asked, 'have those people ever done for you?'

'Nothing,' I agreed, 'but Mike Jackson is not part of the problem and I'm pulling the statement because he asked me to.'

Having arranged my resettlement course in Cadiz learning Spanish, I handed over my responsibilities at HQ Land and cleared my desk. My boss had been away for a meeting on the afternoon of 6 April 2004 and I had been holding the fort. On his return he stuck his head around the door to say he was back.

'You'll want to get going,' he said.

'I do,' I replied and I grabbed my briefcase. I went downstairs and climbed into my well-packed car and drove out of the Army after twenty-two years and six months, my final act in the Army.

The following day was my last day in uniform. I went to Buckingham Palace and was presented with the OBE by HRH Prince Charles. I had first worn an Army uniform in the Combined Cadet Force at my school in 1971. I had joined the Territorial Army at seventeen on 22 May 1977. In the presence of our future King, thirty-three years later, I wore my uniform for the last time.

# —25—

# ALL FOR THE GOOD?

It was strange to be running on a beach in April with the temperature in the 30s and the spray blowing off the sea into my face and beading on my beard. I was used to the gloomier climes of Wiltshire. Exile was pleasant but I could not help but wonder what forces had placed me there. My Spanish course lasted sixteen days and I returned via Gibraltar at the end of April.

Before my return to Canterbury I travelled to Dublin to accept the honorary patronage of the Trinity College Philosophical Society. In doing so I was invited to address the society. My talk was general but in light of the meeting of the EU heads of state that was happening at the same time I touched on a reappraisal of Ireland's role in the modern world. I posed the question 'Is Ireland's traditional neutrality valid in modern times?' I explained that it was my belief that we in the West were at war with an enemy who resented all that we stood for culturally and religiously. For complex reasons, which I contended were better understood in Ireland than in the US, the faceless enemy, global terrorism, had gone to war to address a feeling of injustice and to fight what they collectively perceived as an oppressor. These were actors out with any nation state and therefore had no truck with diplomacy. They spoke the language of violence, but meeting this with violence was no answer in itself. That said, I suggested that all nations had a duty to become engaged in the war against terrorism, if only to show solidarity and to assure their citizens of some form of security – and that included Ireland. The faceless enemy could only be brought to the negotiating table if its violence was stifled by a blanket of security, as we had seen on the island of Ireland itself after thirty-five years of terrorism.

The enemy, I explained, did not recognise Ireland's neutrality, nor did they understand it. Seeing the St Patrick's Day celebrations in the US, they would recognise that Ireland had a special relationship with the US and to them their enemy's friend was also their enemy. Thus they would never accept that Ireland was neutral. Ireland, I urged them, must add its modest defence forces in order to claim a voice in the debate on world affairs, using its influence to moderate the US outlook on the world and in turn help to moderate the old-world attitudes to the US. If that were successful, then Ireland, along with the UK, could act as an interlocutor for more productive, cordial and progressive ties between the US and the EU, so damaged by recent events.

My final point was that as long as men treated each other as less than men, then fear would lead to violence, which would lead to conflict and thus more fear. The way to break the cycle was to insist on the highest standards of treatment and justice for all and I urged this influential university to continue to demand those standards in all the actions of nations and to lead the way as they had always done.

What surprised me was that this controversial address was well received. While they were not directly involved in the conflict – indeed Irish opinion was overwhelmingly anti-war – I was touched by the pride that many in Ireland took in the achievements of the Royal Irish. We had an interesting question-and-answer session in which I was asked if killing Muqtada al-Sadr (leader of the Mahdi Army at that time engaged in battle with US forces) would stop the insurgency in Shia areas? I reminded the meeting that not a mile from the spot on which I stood, General Maxwell[130] had decided to shoot fourteen leaders of the 1916 Easter Rising, having already suppressed the rising. That single action, I contended, was an excess that turned the actions of fanatics into the will of a nation. I explained that I for one would urge the US not to repeat that mistake. Iraq had to be won through the will of the people of Iraq and not through the use of force, fear and coercion.

I awakened the next morning to receive a call from Sarah Oliver. She asked if I had seen the papers. I hadn't and she urged me to get hold of some English papers to see some photos. I walked out onto Dublin's

---

[130] Afterwards I discovered that in the room listening to my talk, was one of General Maxwell's descendants. He heartily agreed with the call for restraint.

O'Connell Street and as I walked to a newsagent's shop I recalled it was a year to the day that I had left the war zone of Iraq. What would this anniversary bring?

Turning into a tobacconist's shop, I was stopped in my tracks as I was confronted by the shocking images of Iraqi prisoners being tortured in the most degrading and inhumane way in pictures on the front of all of the papers. I bought a copy of a daily paper and read the appalling revelations that had emerged from Abu Ghraib prison near Baghdad, which amounted to systematic torture. How could the coalition forces come to such a lowly state of behaviour, indeed conduct worthy of Nazis? It was clear that something in the command and control system had failed. The leering US reservists in the photographs who were clearly enjoying torturing the prisoners evidently did not regard the Iraqis as valid humans. Catching a taxi to the airport, I reflected on the fact that this latest revelation was surely fuel to the already brimming cauldron of hatred that was tearing Iraq apart. It was exactly the opposite of what I had been preaching the previous evening.

It was, I firmly believe, the result of a misunderstanding and not of any direct policy. Since the end of the war, attempts to impose security had brought coalition and especially US troops into confrontation with the Iraqis. There were many and complex reasons for this. The US had certainly got the worst patch to look after. The 'Sunni Triangle', an area around the centre of Iraq and predominantly Sunni, had been Saddam's power base. It only needed a spark to set off the rising and a few ill-considered actions by elements of the US forces provided that spark. The Sunni Triangle was now living up to even the worst expectations. The Shia south, controlled by the British, was relatively calm by comparison. The Iraqis, on the other hand, tormented by shortages of basic amenities such as clean water and energy to provide some air conditioning in the soaring temperatures, were driven to protest. This was a nationwide phenomenon but it was controlled in the British sector by well-honed public order operations. Encounters in the US sector were of a more violent nature, possibly because there was a more ill-disposed population, but it also became very clear that in the US military there was no culture of engagement with the local population.

Most senior US military commanders eschewed the more conciliatory UK approach as being 'soft' and 'over-cautious'. In the US regions there was a temptation to control the locals by fear and the threat of force. In reaction to the robust US forces' handling of protests there were outbreaks of open violence. This played into the hands of the Ba'athists, who orchestrated opportunist attacks and violent dissent and drew the populace into the cycle of bloodshed, to which US forces in turn reacted with increasing ferocity. Additionally, as they were notoriously suspicious of any Iranian influence, the US military was not instinctively well disposed to the anti-Saddam resistance (albeit they had been heavily sponsored by US and UK intelligence agencies), whom they might have more effectively harnessed. This was especially true of the Supreme Council for the Islamic Revolution in Iraq (SCRI) – the main Shia anti-Ba'athist grouping, who had opposed Saddam from exile in Iran.

My own analysis was that this intuitive mistrust of all things Islamic among many (but by no means all) American servicemen was a direct result of the atrocities of the 11 September 2001 terrorist attacks on the US. This was not helped by the tardiness of some figures in the US administration to acknowledge the lack of evidence for any links between the al-Qaida attacks and Saddam Hussein's Ba'athist regime. In every case this destructive cycle played into the hands of the anti-coalition elements. Both Shia extremists and Ba'athist loyalists benefited greatly. Sunni-inspired foreign fighters – many genuine al-Qaida – isolated and unable to inspire the Iraqis by their own efforts, reacted with glee when overreaction by coalition forces drove eager young men into their arms. Sadly it was not a new phenomenon. The shooting dead in Londonderry, Northern Ireland, of fourteen innocent civilians on Bloody Sunday in January 1972 had exactly the same reinvigorating effect on the flagging Provisional IRA's recruiting.

What I found particularly ironic in modern Iraq was that the young fighters on both sides were motivated to a large extent by identical outrage – unprovoked assault on their homeland and the loss of innocent life. Both the insurgents in the streets of Iraq and many of the GIs fought out of a need for vengeance, the cycle of retaliation gathering pace with every fresh killing. It was a pattern, familiar from the streets of Derry to the Ardoyne to the hamlets of Bosnia, which like a pestilence had found the right conditions for an epidemic in post-Saddam Iraq. The most obvious symptom of this disease is the mutual tendency to relegate members of the opposing faction to a subhuman species in the mind of the antagonists. These scenes from Abu Ghraib that I was looking at in the paper were the most graphic images of the manifestation of this hatred in Iraq so far. By the summer they would be more than matched (and to some degree as a consequence) by the burned corpses of US contractors hanging from a bridge in Fallujah.

I returned home to Canterbury on Friday and received a call the following day from a contact in the media asking if I had seen the photographs in the *Daily Mirror*. I assumed that he was talking about the same Abu Ghraib images, but in fact the photos in question purported to show British soldiers torturing prisoners in the back of a lorry and urinating over them. The thrust of the question from my contact was 'Are they genuine?' It was too late to get a paper – they had all sold out – so I opened the *Mirror* page on the internet and looked at the images. Immediately they seemed wrong, even viewed on a monitor screen. If you have lived in Iraq for any time you know the essence of the place. It is very dusty and very hot. The soldiers and captive in the photograph were spotless and they were in the back of a green four-ton lorry – of which there were very few in Iraq. It too was spotless – which in the dusty conditions was impossible. Other major flaws included the type of rifle and the fact that it had no sling attached – mandatory in operational theatres. After looking at the images I was able to go back to my contact and tell him, off the record, that the photos were very transparent fakes. The following day I listened in utter disbelief as the Chief of the General Staff, General Mike Jackson, apologised to the world for this behaviour. Surely somewhere within the MOD there was the capability of making a proper assessment of the photos? They could simply have called any one of the thousands of troops who had served there – even myself – to ask. Another instant assumption of guilt. This had to stop or the nation, indeed the world, would lose faith in the British Army as a force for good. The Arab world reacted with fury and in Gaza, British war graves were desecrated – an action that had hitherto been unknown in the region.

I had been asked to visit the Headquarters of the French Army in Lille on the following Tuesday, 4 May, to give a presentation to the French High Command on Operation Telic. The French Commander, his staff and the divisional and brigade commanders, greeted me. I delivered my talk in English, by invitation of the General. I was deeply impressed by the response and the extremely perceptive and relevant questions I was asked afterwards and by their unanimous support as soldiers for their American and British colleagues. The French Army has a background not dissimilar to the British Army's in terms of the influence of Empire. The General asked me, in light of the successes I had described of my Iraqi Volunteers, if there was a policy of utilising locals to enhance our understanding in Iraq – 'auxiliaries' he called them. I had to concede that there was no official policy. He then turned to more topical matters and asked me what I thought of the photos apparently showing British soldiers abusing Iraqis. I was able to confidently assure him they were fakes and published in a paper that took a consistent anti-war line. I explained to him that I was at that time bringing a legal action against that newspaper group for a similar accusation against myself.

'Why then,' he asked, 'did your Chief of the General Staff prostrate himself so and apologise, if they were such blatant forgeries? We would never do that in the French Army.'

I replied, 'Sir, I have no idea.'

I did reflect privately, however, in light of the obvious incompetence shown over the torture pictures, that it was possible that much of the shameful treatment doled out to me had similar origins – sheer incompetence. My confidence in that belief was heightened more than a week later, long after the incident had any news interest, when the MOD announced with a fanfare that the RMP had been carrying out an investigation and could now say that the lorry in the alleged abuse photographs was never in Iraq and that further investigations into the activities shown continued. Did it occur to them that if they could prove that the lorry wasn't in Iraq then the people in it . . . ?

Looking back over the Iraq war and the tumultuous effect it has had on Iraq, our nation and indeed myself, I wondered where it was all for the good. It is clear to me now that it was a great thing that was done, but that it was marred by a series of blunders, misunderstandings, occasional stretches of the truth and some lies. These have led to untold and often needless casualties both in Iraq and on the home front. The deaths of Dr David Kelly, the MOD scientist caught up in the 'Iraq Dossier[131]' scandal, and TV journalist James Forlong[132] were a direct result of stretching the facts. There can be no doubt, however, that the world is a better place without Saddam Hussein. Iraq was living in slavery to his every whim and excess and the Middle East needs the influence of a stable Iraq in

---

[131] A BBC journalist, Andrew Gilligan claimed that the Government had deliberately 'sexed up' the Iraq Dossier claiming Saddam's forces could deploy chemical weapons in forty-five minutes to mislead the nation as to the need for war in spring 2003. It was revealed that Kelly was the source of the leak which Gilligan had exposed. Kelly took his own life under suspicious circumstances.

[132] James Forlong filed a TV news report showing footage claiming that the submarine he was on had fired a cruise missile during the report. It was later shown to be false. The boat did fire cruise missiles; just not at that time. In any case, on board a modern submarine, I'm told, the sensation of the launch of a missile is slightly less dramatic than a toilet flushing. He was later found hanged in his home.

order to prosper. To say otherwise is arrogant and outrageous; we would never have tolerated such a regime in Europe – why should the Iraqis suffer? But if the end was right, I was left wondering why then. What was the actual imperative to go to war in Iraq at that time? Why did the Bush administration settle on the invasion of Iraq without the full backing of the international community?

There exist a number of possibilities: The first was that Iraq posed a clear and present danger to the world and it was believed that there was every possibility that they had the means, motive and intention of using weapons of mass destruction imminently (Tony Blair's forty-five-minute claim). This logic dictates that there was no alternative but to go to war and that it was an altruistic war waged to protect mankind from an extraordinary threat. That case is now widely discredited and it will be for history to judge to what extent President George Bush and his allies, including Tony Blair, actually believed that, or used it as a flag of convenience to prosecute the war, or indeed deliberately misled the public to achieve their own ends.

This leads to the second possibility, that this was a war made in Washington. It could have been for a range of reasons. Was George Bush haunted by the war that his father called a halt to? Was it a war that was waged as an outlet for angst over the attacks of 9/11? Was it a war waged to remove a threat to regional allies? In any case, even taken together, these do not add up to a legitimate reason to invade without the extensive backing of the international community. It may be argued in some right-wing corners that a war that removed a brutal dictator was legitimate in that the ends justify the means. Saddam's crimes are starker than ever, now that after the invasion we can see the evidence of his mass murder. But our western culture is built on democracy and democracies are founded on law. The unwritten code is that all, people and government, adhere to the law. That means that the law must be respected, upheld and defended and that governments must act scrupulously within the law or become as unscrupulous as those they would seek to remove.

The final possibility was that the war was waged as a cynical raid to mug the Iraqis for their oil wealth to satisfy an insatiable western need for fuel in order to feed our self-indulgent and decadent lifestyle. The conspiracy theory. I give this little credence: it falls down on many counts, not least on the fact of the expense that the war has generated. Professional armies do not fight for tyrants and the sense of moral righteousness that is at the core of both the British Army and the

American forces would not tolerate this. Such a motive could never be concealed from or accepted by the military. Were it ever suggested, the professionals would – certainly in the US Army – simply refuse to act on the basis of morality.

If the war was for the greater good of the Middle East and the wider world, then it follows that there must have been some plan to help a new stable and democratic Iraq emerge from the war. Evidence of this is scant. There simply appears to be no plan within the coalition to reoccupy Iraq or fill the vacuum that was bound to be left after Saddam (although it is argued that there was a detailed plan constructed by the US State Department and that it was ignored by the Pentagon). In any case, there was no evidence of any plan on the ground when I led my battle group forward in March and April 2003. As Saddam's forces retreated a vacuum was created. If one ignores a vacuum one has to live with whatever fills it and the consequences that follow. In this case it was the Ba'athist-coordinated insurgency and the foreign fighters. There can be no doubt that the Ba'athist regime had laid in the resources for it to begin. As Tito had prepared Yugoslavia for a guerrilla war, recognising that conventional forces would probably defeat his Field Army, so Saddam, learning from Tito, prepared Iraq. Once more I recall Tariq Aziz's words: 'People say to me, you are not the Vietnamese; you have no jungles and swamps to hide in. I reply, let the cities be our swamps and our buildings be our jungles.'

In Yugoslavia the concealed arms dumps fed a bitter civil war for almost a decade. In Iraq, with external assistance the insurgency could last even longer. The twist in the tale for the Ba'athists, who ran a secular state, was that it was Islamic fundamentalist who took up their sword when the regime was defeated and Saddam was captured. And they are a more terrible enemy. Indeed, they were presented with a unique opportunity by the fall of Saddam and were driven by the belief that the infidel's reliance on conventional power and a civilisation rooted in the idea that material gain was the goal of mankind was the infidel's most vulnerable flank. They belong to a belief system that deplores materialism and curbs individual choice, preferring instead to submit to the will of Allah as interpreted by the Mullahs. The very act of dying in conflict with the invader had the double effect of terrorising the unbelievers' war machine and home population while assuring the martyr a fast track to Heaven. Insurgency cannot be defeated by force alone and Iraq, nor indeed any Middle Eastern country, cannot have a western democracy imposed on it. We need a middle way.

Currently the US-led coalition is engaged in 'nation building'. The US notion of nation building is worthy of examination. Stanley Karnow in his *Vietnam, a History* sought to describe this approach as a form of 'missionary zeal . . . to reform their [Vietnamese] institutions, reminiscent of French imperialism'. By this he meant the export of the American ideal, as the 19th-century French crusaded the ideal of 'la France'. He tells us they used the term 'nation building' in the belief that the Vietnamese might adapt to western institutions and methods imposed on them, not realising that they were unable to easily follow such a western cadence, which made no sense to their ears. It could be seen as arrogant, he goes on to say, were it not pursued with an utter conviction and sincerity, which were equally naive. Norman Mailer echoed this when he suggested that America's one true religion is America. However, Maximilien Robespierre, the French revolutionary, cautioned, 'No one welcomes armed missionaries.' In the absence of the influence of the wider international community there is the danger that the mistakes of Vietnam will be repeated in Iraq, with the attendant risks to the wider region. (Equally, were one to substitute the Fundamentalist Islam of today for the Communism of the 1960s, the dangers of a repeat of 'The Domino Effect' are significant).

In contrast, the traditional British approach to peace-enforcement operations is based on sixty years of experience since the Second World War and the application of the sound principles espoused during the Malayan emergency by Sir Robert Thompson. These include the setting of a time frame for political progress, separating the insurgent from the population, acting scrupulously within the rule of law (in this instance international law and conventions), the strengthening of the local economy and basing operations on sound intelligence in order not to alienate the population.

I do not advocate one system over the other, however. I simply deplore the current state of affairs and wonder what incompetence or neglect has brought us to this point. The technical expertise and resources existed to fill the vacuum left by Saddam. But that expertise was ignored and the people of Iraq were relegated to extras in the drama that was to unfold within their own country. The blunder of disbanding the army and the police force threw the very people who could control the looming chaos, looting and crime out onto the street. They spoke the language and understood their people and were extremely loyal to whoever was giving them orders (as I found to my advantage). This mistake was compounded by the crass approach to the changeover of the currency.

This above all, I believe, gave life to the insurgency. By the time the policy had been reversed it was too late.

Finally the Ba'ath party was ignored. Anyone with any understanding of sinister organisations like paramilitaries – and I class the Ba'athist in this bracket – would realise that it is crucial to swiftly gain the confidence and cooperation of the population in order to isolate the thugs and then deal with them, or else accept that they will return. This was clearly understood in Nazi Germany, where carefully directed Allied efforts, coupled with the sheer war-weariness of the population, rendered the stay-behind 'Werewolf' organisation ineffective; certainly the spontaneous risings envisaged in post-war Germany did not materialise. Unfortunately, there were no such concentrated or coordinated efforts in Iraq. Yet we still have access to the knowledge and experience of those who so effectively oversaw the de-Nazification of Europe, people who could have helped to understand and then dismantle the Ba'athist machine. I recently met a British officer who had taken part in this process in 1945/46 and the similarities that he described between the problems of dealing with Nazis, anti-Nazis and displaced persons back then had remarkable parallels with 2003/04. These parallels are all the more apparent when the extent to which the Ba'athists modelled themselves on the Nazis is revealed.

Alongside the Ba'athist insurgency, the extremists from both the Sunni and Shia traditions took advantage of the situation and exploited the violence to their political advantage. Notably a Shia cleric, Muqtada al-Sadr, spawned the so-called Mahdi Army, or 'Army of the Chosen One', which carried out attacks across Iraq and brought significant violence for the first time to the British-controlled southern Iraq. Taking over a sect that represented the majority of Iraqis by murdering its leaders, Muqtada al-Sadr projected himself into a position of power from which only the Shia leaders could remove him. They were impotent, caught between a rock and a hard place. With a proven distaste for becoming involved in politics (they failed to give leadership to the 1991 Shia rising) the moderate and pro-US and coalition clerics Ayatollah Abdul Majid al-Khoei and Ayatollah Mohammed Baqir al-Hakim (leader of SCIRI) were murdered, al-Khoei stabbed by thugs and al-Hakim blown up along with over 100 other innocents at Friday prayers. Al-Hakim's uncle, Grand Ayatollah Sayyed Mohammed al-Hakim, was lucky to escape a similar attempt to kill him. These acts effectively neutered the Shia clerics and handed the power over the youth on the streets to al-Sadr. A spiralling cycle of violence, costing the lives of US servicemen and innocent Iraqis, threatened to undermine the whole mission in Iraq. This spiral is set to continue. The Shia violence was only dampened when Iraq's most senior cleric, Grand Ayatollah Ali al-Sistani, was brought back from the West where he was receiving medical treatment to broker a ceasefire. But the trend was set and Iraq had taken another step towards anarchy, civil war and dismemberment.

A contractual bonanza has developed in Iraq, which is seeing some classic mistakes repeated in its post-war struggle to get onto its feet and generate an economic infrastructure and democratic political system. Though Iraq has the funding and shortly will have the oil revenue to fund its own security forces, having dismantled the nation's own armed forces, the coalition has found it is proving near impossible to rebuild or replace them – at any price. (Those on the Army Board dismantling the British infantry take note.) The firms that are rebuilding the infrastructure are foreign and the contractors that provide them with security are private, foreign firms. They are in a race to provide a basis from which economic benefits might make the towns and cities of Iraq more pleasant places to live and thus take the sting out of insurgency. But they have also become the prime target of the insurgents' attacks and kidnap has become a money spinner for criminals, a source of leverage for terrorists, as well as a common hazard for those who work in Iraq, from charity volunteers like the late Margaret Hassan (some say Iraq's Mother Teresa) to those like British worker Ken Bigley, who follow their fortune to Iraq. The private military sector has become significant in Iraq now with the equivalent of an army division's strength of contractors working there for premium wages. An emerging brand leader in the private military sector and a British company, Aegis Defence Services, won a massive contract, the largest private military contract ever, to coordinate intelligence for the coalition in Iraq and the activities of the private military sector. It has recruited some of the most able and experienced operators and has furnished its operation with vehicles and equipment of the highest specification that would be the envy of any army. Ironically it appears that they are enjoying more success in their pursuit of security than the military and may even offer a suitable template for future operations. The dangers of the theatre are all too real, as I was to have illustrated to me in March. Colour Sergeant Chris MacDonald, formerly one of my soldiers and on leave from the Army (he was the mild-mannered watchkeeper who I had last seen in Al Amarah during the visit of Ayatollah al-Hakim's men), was involved in an incident while working for a private company in Mosul, northern Iraq. I was given to understand he was in an unarmoured car when he and a Canadian colleague fought off a terrorist attack on his convoy, ensuring that the man they were paid to protect got to safety, while accounting for a significant number of the enemy. Sadly both of them died of their wounds as a result.

Iraq must stand on its own feet one day. That means it must be given the chance to rise from its years under Ba'athism and to do so it must be in the hands of the educated classes. It is, however, crucial that these educated Iraqis have both the incentive, in the form of unhindered control of their country, and the freedom from the fear of being murdered, if they are to succeed. For that reason, regardless of the rights and wrongs of the war, the whole international community must fall in behind the US and her allies to ensure Iraq achieves that independence and self-confidence. But in doing so we in the West must accept Iraqi solutions to their problems, and that means not interfering too much in their process if the democratic elections of January 2005 are to produce a lasting peace. The coalition forces cannot leave Iraq anytime soon. The cost has been terrible already, in the lives of Iraqis and the lives of young American and British troops. When Iraq does rejoin the international order and by doing so brings some stability to that benighted region, then it will all have been worthwhile and a source of pride for those who wished Iraq well, especially the families of those who fell to make that progress possible.

On 19 March 2003 I told the Royal Irish battle group that we should leave Iraq a better place for us having been there. History must judge us as to whether we did or not. The world must not fail in this endeavour or it will be a much less safe place to live. As I look back over the events of the last two years I see startling parallels between the good will and optimism of the men who gathered in the deserts of Kuwait to go to liberate Iraq at the beginning of the 21st century and the generation that marched off to the First World War at the beginning of the 20th century. It was, we felt, a great endeavour and would be an act that would strike a blow for freedom and free a nation while helping to end the scourge of global terrorism. For my grandfather's generation, who left the plenty and optimism of the Edwardian era and the *belle époque* in France to march, cheering, to a war to end all wars, they too were optimistic. The First World War was sparked by a gunshot in Sarajevo in 1914 fired by a fanatic, the anarchist Princip. A colossus reacted. It was supposed to be over by Christmas. Arguably its consequences did not end until the fall of the Berlin wall in 1989. Might 9/11 have been our Sarajevo of the 21st century? A religious anarchist, Bin Laden, orchestrated that event. A colossus reacted. When and how will it end? Comfortable and well resourced, did the West move too quickly to vent its spleen on a tangible enemy in Afghanistan and Iraq as a result of a wound caused by an intangible foe, Bin Laden and al-Qaida? Will the consequences of the invasion of Iraq end with peace and stability, or will this spiral of violence continue to blight this century and distort and compound with competition for resources and fuel and water? History will judge the actions of this generation. It is still not too late. To get it right we must study history so that we do not repeat its mistakes.

# EPILOGUE

'**R**oyal Jordanian are pleased to announce that RJ 0816 to Baghdad is ready for boarding. Would all passengers proceed to Gate 6 . . .'

'Baghdad, OK, OK, sit down,' said the Jordanian police sergeant, trying to prevent a rush, but it was the signal for rows of burly men to don sunglasses and head for the departure gate. The private security consultants, as they are known, shrugged on their fleeces and daysacks and began queuing to be searched once more. Brits with shaven heads and tattoos joked with tanned South Africans in safari shirts whilst New Zealanders, mostly distinguished by the Maori amulets around their necks, lounged and listened. The majority of the Americans were defence contractors, obviously tradesmen and older than the others, sporting goatee beards, substantial midriffs and dyed hair under carefully shaped baseball caps. They tried to look fierce as they mixed with the younger US security consultants, who mostly kept their own counsel.

I listened to a conversation about the relative merits of 6.8mm ammunition over 5.56mm. One American was explaining that he carried a spare barrel for his M16 that he could change with a torque wrench and two bolts. 'In case we ever get into anything so stupid that I run out of 5.56mm. I jus' need to quickly zero then I'm back in business,' he explained nonchalantly. Nearby a hefty Brit mouthed words while he read a copy of *Viz* and his youthful colleague nodded, his eyes darting around the lounge nervously. His chum leaned back in his chair and added that he also had a spare trigger that cost him $350, which he could 'drop in and push in two pins and you're good to go'. (After twenty-two years in the Army, I can tell you that anyone planning a major overhaul of their weapon in contact with the enemy has never seen active service. Why didn't he just carry more ammo?) The big Brit either didn't hear or couldn't care less as he pored over his comic.

Behind us, separated by a smoked-glass window, the incoming passengers climbed the stairs to the arrivals lounge, many of them with an extremely relieved look on their faces.

It was two years almost to the day since I had arrived in Kuwait in command of 1 R Irish. Now I was a jobbing journalist working for the *Mail on Sunday* and about to return to Iraq to report on the elections that were finally about to take place. The faces of the security consultants who were leaving Iraq revealed a lot about pre-election Iraq and Baghdad in particular. An unholy alliance of the Ba'athist Fedayeen and Sunni fighters from a wide range of terrorist groups, including al-Qaida, had made it the most dangerous place on earth. But as one who had helped overthrow the old regime, I was curious to see if there was any prospect that we might leave Iraq a better place, as I had appealed to my men to do at the outbreak of the war.

After being bussed to the waiting aircraft, an unmarked white Fokker 28, we were greeted by the Royal Jordanian crew as they relieved the passengers of their heavier luggage before letting them up the steps onto the aircraft. The crew were all ex-South African Air Force and joked among themselves in Afrikaans between greeting the passengers in perfect English. The only Jordanians were the rather obvious 'sky marshals'. With black leather jackets and standardised moustaches, they each cradled a briefcase, no doubt containing the tool of their particular trade, as well as a couple of spare magazines.

The plane doors were closed and a man behind me nervously whistled as the smell of sweat filled the cabin. The pilot introduced himself as Francie and rolled his 'Rs' as he assured us all that the businesslike Richard, who was our cabin steward, would attend to our every need. As the plane taxied for take-off he urged us to keep our seatbelts fastened loosely during the trip and tightly fastened as we began our approach to Baghdad.

An hour later we found out why. To the accompaniment of more nervous whistling, Francie tipped the plane on its nose to begin a steep spiral descent into Baghdad, dropping rapidly from 24,000 feet to confuse any surface-to-air missiles that might be seeking a constant heat source from the engines, fired by one of the estimated 200,000 insurgents somewhere below us. With a final sweep onto the runway and a fast taxi to the stand we were down. 'Welcome to Baghdad,' Francie announced. 'I hope you have a safe return.' It said it all about the place. No worries about connecting flights or car hire here. This was the final destination – literally for some.

Outside the arrivals lounge, I met a Private Security Detail (PSD) from a company owned by a good friend. I was to get a lift with them to the centre of the city and my accommodation at the Sheraton Hotel (I chose this hotel as the last time I had been in Baghdad, in August, it was a hive of journalists). The commander of the escort, a South African, greeted me with 'Welcome to the most dangerous place on the planet,' before handing me a bulletproof vest and settling me into the back of an armoured Land Cruiser. Jonny, the driver, an old acquaintance of mine and late of the Swedish Army's elite Frogman Unit, explained the emergency drills to me as they loaded their rifles and pistols. 'We call it "Bangdad",' one of the team said. I had a good idea why.

As we headed out of the airport compound a sign announced the dress state for military personnel. It could be summarised as 'every bit of armour you have and then some.' The airport road looked like a battlefield. The date palms that once lined the central reservation were now blackened stumps and tank tracks crisscrossed the mud, clogging the road with thick sods that bumped under our wheels. We reached the other armoured vehicles in our convoy as they waited just beyond the barrier, making us four in total. The tailgate of the rear vehicle was open, carrying a sign in Arabic reading 'Stay at least 50m back or deadly force will be used'. A rear gunner looked out over the sights of his rifle from behind an armoured screen. They were not kidding.

The drive to Baghdad was measured and fraught. Moving at a steady pace with power in reserve, the PSD communicated by radio, spotting threats and issuing instructions. As we drove the men briefed me on the latest situation. Intelligence estimates said that the insurgents had up to two hundred and fifty suicide bombers ready to go, with in excess of one hundred and fifty vehicles prepared as bombs.[133]

---

[133] I wondered how they could be so certain. It later transpired that al-Zarqawi's right-hand man and technical bomb maker had been captured two days earlier and had confessed to the new Iraqi authorities. He had also confessed to thirty-two attacks, including the bomb that killed Ayatollah Mohammed Baqir al-Hakim.

As we neared Baghdad Jonny pointed to a motorway flyover. 'This is the most dangerous road in the city and up there is the most dangerous spot,' he explained.

This is what is known as the wrong place, I thought, the most dangerous spot on the most dangerous road in the most dangerous city of the most dangerous country ... I counted five ragged holes where suicide bombs had blasted through the bridge, the edges of the two-metre-wide scars marked by fingers of steel reinforcement cables. We passed a spot where a bomb had created the biggest hole yet, flattening the crash barriers on either side of the road and on the central reservation.

'This is where the Kroll team got hit – lost all their men and the principal[134]. The bomber drove straight into them head-on. They didn't stand a chance,' Jonny said. (One of the men killed was a Para, Corporal Dollman, who had been with 1 Para when we invaded Iraq. After retirement he, like Chris MacDonald and hundreds of others, had sought to take advantage of the bonanza, only to discover that it came at a price.)

'Kroll are a big company and always like to point out that they have people in every theatre. The joke here is that they now even have people on the Moon,' noted one of the boys. The black humour that is common to soldiers everywhere was just as keen here.

We soon approached the Green Zone, the former administrative capital of Saddam's regime that was off limits to ordinary Iraqis and now home to the coalition forces, private military companies and the British and US embassies. It was also where the Interim Prime Minister, Dr Allawi, had his offices. The approach to the Green Zone was guarded by cheery Iraqis in their new desert fatigues waving us through as we held up our badges for inspection, passing us onto a grim-looking GI, most of whose face was covered by a helmet and wraparound sunglasses. He was backed by an M1 Abrams main battle tank, its barrel pointing straight at us. Looking intently at each badge and then at the bearer's face, he pointed at each one then, satisfied, motioned us on with a flick of his wrist.

Travel inside the Green Zone was slow and measured along the broad tree-lined dual carriageways. Armoured civilian vehicles drove respectfully around the numerous Humvee patrols scanning with their machine guns. 'There's no doubt they would shoot if you got too

---

[134] The guy they were paid to protect.

close,' my South African bodyguard said over his shoulder. The buildings of the Green Zone were on a grand scale and many were familiar from TV footage. The Triumphal Route consisted of a mile marked at each end by massive hands crossing scimitars over the road, the hands allegedly modelled on Saddam's own. From the wrists hung baskets containing thousands of Iranian helmets which spilt out and were concreted in across the road so that the tanks and troops who processed up the route would do so walking on the heads of the hated Iranians. Naturally the route had been constructed to celebrate the Iraqi 'victory' over the Iranians in 1989. Nearby was the Tomb of the Unknown Soldier. Palm trees shaded all the buildings in the Green Zone but Saddam's palace sat in particularly splendid gardens, the lawns now crossed by numerous tank tracks. We passed out of the Green Zone through the aptly named 'Assassin's Gate'. To my right were the shattered ruins of the Secret Police Building, the notorious Mukhabarat HQ. Passing checkpoints in reverse order, GIs then Iraqis, we were waved off into the Baghdad traffic, a jumble of ramshackle cars with origins in France, Germany and Japan driving in a fashion which appeared to be utter chaos.

Crossing the Tigris into Baghdad proper, I could see that the city still bore the scars of war. It was more subdued than when I visited in the summer and election posters hastily pasted onto any flat surface fluttered in the breeze, adding an edge to the already scruffy look of the place. We passed two cars moving suspiciously slowly, one close behind the other, which alerted my escorts. They exchanged a commentary over the radio and prepared to take evasive action. As we drew level the reason for the slowness became apparent: a man was sitting on the bonnet of the rear car, a rather new BMW, and was pushing the front car, an older Mercedes, with his feet.

'You could make a fortune introducing the tow rope into Iraq,' Jonny said with some relief.

Jokes aside, the team were coiled to greet any wrong move by such a vehicle with a hail of lead and smoke grenades as they made their escape. The current modus operandi of the suicide bomber was to swerve into the middle of the all too obvious private security convoys in heavy traffic before detonating their bombs. Armour was no protection. A car packed with five or more 155mm artillery rounds, each weighing up to 40kg, would kill even the crew of a tank.

'I suppose you've just got to watch for the ones that look really nervous and are praying,' I ventured.

'That doesn't help much,' Jonny responded nonchalantly. 'Most drivers in Baghdad look terrified and pray a lot and it's little to do with bombs. Most of these cars don't have brakes, just a horn.'

After taking a side street we were suddenly on the banks of the Tigris. On one side were battered three-storey houses and on the other a riverside park and cafés and restaurants that had seen better days, with names like 'Top Fish' and 'Tigris Catch'. We then had to negotiate a series of barriers manned by Iraqi security guards from the 'Babylon Eagles' sitting on plastic chairs with AK-47s across their laps. At the final barrier we stopped while the vehicles were searched. It was here that I had to part with my PSD. They wanted to walk me to the door of the hotel but they weren't able to come with their weapons, so I bade them farewell. Instead I was escorted the rest of the way by two National Guardsmen from Oregon. Tired and subdued, they looked more like *Star Wars* stormtroopers than humans in their armour, helmets and goggles. They wished me well as they handed me over to two Saddam lookalikes with AK-47s in the lobby.

'Good luck,' said the sergeant in charge. 'You'll need it. You're a brave man,' he added.

'Brave?' I was surprised. 'But this place is full of western journalists,' I explained.

'No it is not,' he said as they shook their heads. 'You're it. You have a good day now.' He smiled as he set off.

Seventeen storeys high and with 700 rooms at one point (it now had only twenty working rooms), the hotel was *a* Sheraton and not *the* Sheraton. When relations between Saddam's regime and the West cooled the well-known chain pulled out but the regime kept the name and badge and everything else. It struck me as just like the Holiday Inn Sarajevo where I had stayed during the siege in 1994: same worn-out 1970s furniture, same rotting carpets and the same vast lobby with rooms around balconies for the first five floors. I just hoped the déjà vu would not extend too far, as my room in the Holiday Inn had taken a direct hit. Luckily I was out (and I didn't get a reduction on the £100-a-night rate either).

I didn't have a reservation but bluffed it out at the front desk. The clerk rather sportingly looked through a large but clearly empty booking folder before 'finding' my booking. I would, the man at the desk explained, have to pay in US dollars at the cash desk further along the lobby. I walked past jaded brass signs and some very Middle Eastern abstract art and found the desk deserted. I rang the bell for attention –

and the same man appeared from under the desk. 'May I help you?' he asked. It was like a *Two Ronnies* sketch. Having parted with around $300, I went off to the lift with two hastily dressing 'bellboys', both in their late fifties, hurrying behind.

In my room the men fiddled with a light switch and changed a bulb while one indicated with a flourish an array of old toothbrushes, toothpaste tubes and razors laid out carefully beside the sink. I was not certain if he was showing me the room's amenities or the lost property department but I thanked him with a '*shukran*' and a Jordanian dinar as he turned the tap on and off, smiling and looking at me to see if I had understood how to operate it. As the door closed behind the men I looked around the room – at least as shabby as the Holiday Inn during the siege but not as cold – before opening the shutters and stepping onto the balcony. My room overlooked al Fardus Square where Saddam's statue had been pulled down two years before. The plinth now had a new sculpture, by the look of it the work of a primary school art class, and was ringed by banners touting candidates for the election.

As I walked around the hotel, deserted for the most part, I headed for the roof to get a view of the city. After pulling at the chain of the door that led onto the roof, I found myself in a rooftop observation post with two West Virginia National Guardsmen, a land surveyor in his late fifties and a nineteen-year-old student. With their Southern accents and ruffled demeanour they reminded me of two characters in *Gone With the Wind* during the fall of the Confederacy. The men politely explained that I should not be up there but since I was a Brit I could have a look. I asked if I could take some photos and they agreed, but explained they could not be in the photos. With ten days left of a year-long rotation, they had seen the worst of it and were now looking forward to going home. 'I jus' hope we don' get 'stendud,' said the older sergeant, his eyes searching some far horizon. 'We're real tired now.' My heart went out to them. I hope they got home safely.

I was keen to meet some of the smaller players in the 111-candidate list that the election had thrown up and to hear their stories. As luck would have it I was sitting in the lobby when a man approached me. Speaking in Oxford English, he explained that he believed he knew who I was. I stood up and offered my card. He read it and said, 'I thought so. I admired your speech. I was glad that you were cleared of those ridiculous charges.'

He introduced himself as Dr Kamal Field al-Basri. In his fifties, with a placid and intelligent look, he reminded me of President Musharaff of Pakistan. Dr Kamal, with a PhD from Strathclyde University, was economic adviser to the Ministry of Provisional Affairs and headed the Iraq Institute for Economic Reform, an Interim Government thinktank. But it was his role as candidate for the Faily Kurds, a Shia minority from central Iraq, that I was most interested in. While not a Kurd himself[135], Dr Kamal empathised with the plight of this ancient people whose history stretched back 6,000 years and who had suffered persecution under the Ba'athist regime. I was introduced to the leader of the Faily Kurds, Mr Thair Feely, an energetic and personable man. Thair Feely, or Abu Dan, had led the Faily Kurds out of the United Iraqi Alliance, a coalition formed under the guidance of Ayatollah Ali al-Sistani, Iraq's top Shi'ite cleric, and the party tipped to top Sunday's poll. Three crucial issues had led to this split: full citizenship for all Iraqis, including Faily Kurds; a settlement that would allow all deportees to return to their country; and justice for the crimes they had suffered, including compensation for homes and property lost. Before leaving them I asked if I could come with them to the elections hustings which were to be held the next day in the Baghdad Convention Centre. We arranged to meet in the lobby the next morning.

Taking supper alone in the Palestine Hotel across the road, I listened as the waiters eagerly discussed the elections. From the little I could gather – my Arabic is almost nonexistent – I could detect that the men were Sunnis. When I spoke to them they all spoke good English. Two of the waiters were apparently for the election and against the insurgency. Dismissive of the 'jihadis', or foreign fighters, they assured me that the atrocities that were being committed were most un-Iraqi. I believed them. The third had a hankering for the old regime. He was older and he explained that under Saddam it was safe and whilst they didn't have much they had all that they needed. It was the first time I had spoken to anyone who wanted the old regime back. Later, standing in the darkness of the empty hotel – there had been a power cut – and listening to the sporadic shooting outside, I felt a little uneasy about the great crusade we had undertaken to remove Saddam. Had we done the right thing?

---

[135] Dr Kamal was in fact the son of a Welsh soldier who had come to Iraq during the Second World War, settled and married. Embracing Islam, when his father died he was buried in Najaf, near the Iman Ali and holy of holies for the Shia.

I met up with an acquaintance who was guarding a team from the Canadian Broadcasting Company, CBC, who were staying in the Palestine Hotel. Apart from a sense of relief that there were some other Westerners outside the Green Zone, albeit only six of us, it was good to talk. We had a beer in their room whilst we discussed the state of affairs. My contact, ex-military, described how he had worked on the UN weapons inspection programme in Iraq back in 1997 and 1998. His description of Baghdad back then was fascinating. Vibrant and secular, it had cheap cafés of a good standard and crime was nonexistent. He recalled he had heard of only a single mugging of Westerners, but even they were only robbed of their Iraqi dinars. They were allowed to keep their western currency. Then the muggers returned two hundred and fifty dinars each so that their victims could at least get a taxi home. This chimed with what Dr Kamal had told me and with my own experience. Crime was a rarity in Iraq. It was true that I had witnessed looting on a massive scale, but I now saw it more as grabbing what one could in an uncertain time, a visceral reaction, rather than common theft. But the image of a peaceful country was tempered by his description of the ever-present Mukhabarat watchers and the knowledge of what these people were up to behind the façade of decency and order.

I spent an uneasy night back in the Sheraton Hotel. The guards in the lobby were transfixed by a game on their mobile phone and had hardly noticed me walk by. As I looked out over the city from my room, only the flickering of a campfire on a nearby balcony (because of the power cuts cooking, once more like Sarajevo, was done on open fires) or an occasional shot in the night punctuated the stillness created by a self-imposed curfew.

Monday 24 January was a cloudy day in Baghdad. A sandstorm filled the air with a fine, cloying dust. The mortar threat was high and flights from the outside world were suspended. I waited in the lobby for Dr Kamal, smoking a Montecristo No 2 and drinking Turkish coffee as increasingly agitated GIs rushed in and out, until one finally approached me to enquire if I had seen one of their number who had gone missing. I hadn't but suggested he may have gone into one of the hundreds of empty rooms for a sleep. 'Soldiers do strange things when they are tired,' I explained.

A man sitting nearby watched me relight my cigar and as I blew some smoke he smiled. 'Montecristo No 2?'

'Quite right,' I said. 'Would you care for one?'

'No, thank you,' the man said. 'I do not smoke them but Saddam did.'

I enquired as to how he knew this and he said that he had worked at the palace. Fascinated, I began to chat with him. 'So how impressive was Saddam?' I asked. 'To meet, was he so scary after all?'

'It was not what he did, it was what he was capable of,' the man replied. He thought for a moment and laughed to himself and then said, 'I will tell you what he was like – but this is not a true story, I think. During the last years he was convinced that there were spies. Also when things went badly he liked to give blame. On one occasion as he was sitting at his Revolutionary Council meeting and yelling at the ministers: "You are useless! You think you know better! Well, I tell you the next one who does not do exactly what I say when I say," – he slams his fist, *Bang!* – "I will show them." Just then a messenger comes into the room and hands Saddam a note. He reads it and then he shouts, "Shit!" and bangs the table once more, still reading the note. The ministers look at each other and, unsure if it is an expression of disgust or an executive order, fifteen compliant arses strain to his command. The smell is terrible and Saddam storms off. In the silence that follows, the elderly Taha Maruf, the Vice President, turns to Tariq Aziz and, motioning towards the eighteen-stone General Sultan Ahmad, Minister of Defence, beside him says, "I'm just glad it was 'shit', because if he had said 'fuck' then I really don't think I would have survived." '

Just then the lobby flooded with GIs. 'Search the whole place,' a major ordered. As this was happening Dr Kamal appeared and we set off. As I walked with Dr Kamal to meet Dr Timimi, adviser to Barham Saleh, the Kurdish Deputy Prime Minister, with whom we were going to travel to an elections hustings, I enquired about an explosion I had heard earlier.

'It was the offices of Dr Allawi's party,' Dr Kamal explained. 'Suicide bomb.'

As we walked the hundred metres to the security barriers I counted a further five explosions. I drew my Arabic shemagh around my face to disguise my European features as we left the compound and went to Dr Kamal's car. 'You don't look like one of them,' shouted Specialist Kirk from the Oregon National Guard helpfully.

I shrugged and stepped into a small Peugeot 309, cramming myself into the back seat with Dr Timimi and Dr Kamal as Mohammed our driver and Achmed loaded their pistols. As we swept into the Baghdad traffic I knew I was one of very few Westerners in the whole city not behind armour or concrete. I was aware of the risks and had heard all the jokes about the favourite shampoo for Westerners in Baghdad being a brand called 'And Shoulders', but in many ways I was safer: I was with men who knew the city and who were on their own ground. Plus nobody would mess with Mohammed and Achmed lightly. 'I have known their parents since 1963,' Dr Kamal explained.

The election meeting was at the Baghdad Conference Centre in the supposedly secure Green Zone. Built by Saddam for a meeting of the Arab League, it was an impressive structure and to me faintly reminiscent of the NATO HQ in Brussels. The meeting was not well attended. Dr Kamal pointed out that we had passed through ten security checkpoints to reach the meeting and that the United Iraqi Alliance had called a meeting to coincide with the Faily Kurds' press conference only that morning. But for the twenty-five or so who did attend, Abu Dan (Thair Feely) spoke in a statesman-like manner and Dr Kamal delivered a coherent and imaginative outline of their economic plans. Both spoke in Arabic and then perfect English. Their policies were straightforward and to me sheer common sense. Abu Dan emphasised the need to outlaw racism, restore the rights of all Iraqis and enshrine equal citizenship in the constitution. Dr Kamal called for reform of the oil industry and what he described as 'strategic industries', including agriculture, infrastructure projects to generate employment and the privatisation of transport and tourism.

Dr Kamal took me to meet Dr Allawi, the Interim Prime Minister, at his smart office complex. Set in the Green Zone, the offices were in a squat building richly decorated inside. English workers from the John Smith Institute in London – appointed to assist the Interim Government – rushed about ignoring us as bodyguards lounged around, eating and sipping soft drinks.

We waited in Dr Allawi's outer office, but it was soon clear that our planned meeting had coincided with a visit from US Ambassador Negroponte. Instead we met Dr Sawsan al-Sharifi, Minister for Agriculture, a former Ba'athist and an elegant woman in her forties, with a doctorate in economics. She explained that the problems facing Iraqi agriculture, like most sectors, were immense. In agriculture 70 per cent of land was government-owned. Only 30 per cent of usable land was cultivated and that was only working at 32.95 per cent of its potential. She was optimistic about the future, however, and confident that there would be progress.

We left to visit the British Embassy, which was guarded by ex-Gurkhas.

As I entered I was delighted to meet my old RMP warrant officer and Bryn Parry-Jones's second in command, now guarding the Ambassador and in his final year of Army service. We met Dr Kamal's contact, a First Secretary who gave us a useful brief before he and Dr Kamal got down to the discussion of economic matters. It was clear that Dr Kamal's enthusiasm and optimism were infectious and the outlook was once more positive.

That night we watched the Iraqi TV coverage back at the hotel as we ate fresh fish that had been cooked over an open fire in a riverside café then delivered to the hotel by Mohammed and Achmed. Abu Dan was rightly pleased with the news report. He was already quite well known. Dr Kamal looked slightly more forlorn. He sensed my curiosity at this and nodded at the screen showing his briefing. 'Now I cannot leave the compound in safety again.' It was the reality of life in post-war Iraq.

Night-time in Baghdad was a quiet and lonely time for the only Westerner in the area. A dog howled in pain somewhere in the darkened city. Shots were fired deep within the gloom and in the deserted street below my room the National Guards had abandoned their vehicles, loaded machine guns hanging limply on their mountings. They were sleeping nearby no doubt and no one would dare to touch their vehicles. Why would they?

The following morning, the picture I got of post-war Iraq was one of confusion and fear mixed with optimism. I sought out some contrasting viewpoints on the state of Iraq and the forthcoming poll. Nathal, a Christian lady who ran a shop in the Palestine Hotel, was fearful. 'They [Christians] all go. Very, very dangerous for Christians now,' she explained. I asked about the elections. She was set to vote Allawi. The Sunni who ran an antique stall in the Sheraton was saddened about the crisis facing Iraq. He too thought that under Saddam, while not perfect, things were better. 'It is not safe. The foreigners must leave now. We have a tradition to resist foreigners and invaders. It is so strong. It cannot be beaten.' I asked what he thought should happen to Saddam, who was being held only five miles away in Camp Victory, a massive coalition base. He shrugged his shoulders. I then asked who he would vote for. He was also set to vote Allawi. 'He's the only one I've heard of,' he explained.

This was part of the problem. The list was big and the major players overshadowed the smaller groups. Some groups like the

Royalist Sherif Ali bin Hussein had effective poster campaigns but enjoyed little sympathy for their list. I did detect that the secular tradition in Iraq was still significant and my straw poll showed a stronger support for the secular parties than was being widely reported at the time. My own guess was that Allawi would do better than generally expected. But then I remembered something that Dr Kamal had said. No one really knew how many Iraqis there actually were. There had been no census and the only figures were those returned by Saddam's regime during the UN 'Oil for Food' programme. Dr Kamal pointed out that no one trusted Saddam's figures and the Iraqis had a generally very low regard for the UN. Any result is just an indication of the true feelings of Iraq but not an accurate return. Some are prevented from voting, some don't want to and some cannot because they are not recognised people within Iraq enjoying full citizenship and voting rights. Why, I wondered, was there such a resentment of the UN? Dr Kamal explained that they were perceived by many to be corrupt and naive.

Walking alone outside the compound to visit the BBC and Reuters in their secure compound nearby, I stopped to talk to some ordinary Iraqis. I encountered two small boys with a sheep on a lead. One was called Quais and the other Abdul. 'What is the sheep called?' I asked pointing to it. 'Kebab' was the reply. They grow up quickly in Iraq. Nearby some workers in orange overalls were restoring a park on the banks of the Tigris. The foreman spoke a little English but was intent on keeping his men at work. A bribe caught his attention for a few minutes. I asked about the elections, and once more his vote was for Allawi. I noticed they had a football with them and I tried to get them to pose in three rows for a team photo.

'I want to tell people back home that I am the manager of Abu Ghraib Felons FC,' I explained.

'Too, too busy,' the foreman said, waving off the suggestions and urging the men to start work again.

'Be careful you don't get a set of these,' said one of the young men in perfect English as he pulled gently at his orange overalls.

'Good point,' I agreed and left to find the BBC compound.

Heavily guarded behind blast barriers, the BBC and Reuters had their own private army of minders who searched me as I arrived. They stayed pretty close to home, they explained, and rarely ventured outside now. It was just so dangerous. I walked back to the Sheraton compound, attracting stares from the Iraqis as they worked in the park or strolled near the river. Suddenly I was much more self-conscious. I was not the head of a battle group or a security consultant surrounded by a well-paid security detail, but an individual, alone and easy prey.

I visited the Faily Kurds' offices in the Sheraton. Here Dr Kamal and Abu Dan had their desks in a bright room with the latest computers, laptops and mobile phones, along with well-produced election material. But it was 'Bangdad', of course, and even though guards patrolled the lobby with AK-47s there was a 9mm pistol on Abu Dan's desk. I listened as Abu Dan and Dr Kamal recounted the events that had led to the oppression of Iraq's two million Faily Kurds. It was estimated that one million Faily Kurds had perished under the Ba'athists, most during the twenty-five years of Saddam's leadership. Because they were identified as Iraqis of Iranian origin after the break-up of the Ottoman Empire by the British in 1924, this association with Iran had been enough to make them only half citizens of Iraq and figures of sectarian hatred. Abu Dan had personal experience of the oppression. Arrested in 1979, Abu Dan had been sentenced to death along with fifty-two other men in a trial that lasted less than thirty minutes. With fifty-six men in the dock, the 'judge' asked the fifty-second man to raise his arm. At this fifty-three and fifty-four received a sentence of fifteen years in prison and fifty-five and fifty-six were sentenced to ten years each. Everyone else would be executed, including Abu Dan. He had been among the last four awaiting execution when he was released in an amnesty when Saddam came to power (and after his father had paid bail of $10,000). He fled the country immediately, as did two others (one of them was Sa'id Samir Nadir al Mousawi, an influential Shia clergyman living in Iran). The fourth man, who stayed, was rearrested five days after his release and immediately put to death.

Abu Dan described his experiences in prison. This included an incident at Abu Ghraib where he and sixteen others were chained to gas cylinders and blindfolded as one of their number had his wife and six-month-old baby daughter tortured to death in front of them. The cries were terrible, he explained, and if you moved, the cylinder would ring on the concrete and thus attract a savage beating. So they listened motionless, helpless. But it was only when I asked about his family that he allowed any emotion to show. He had lost sixty-two members of his close family, including all his brothers-in-law and one sister, in a single year between 1980 and 1981.

'When I see their houses and I remember how we played as children and . . .' He stopped and I sat embarrassed that I had raised the subject.

He tried to begin again but stopped once more to gather himself. I apologised for prying, but he waved his hand. 'No, you must hear. People *need* to know.' One thing was clear. The people of Iraq needed closure on the issue of the crimes, including murder and rape, that were common, systematic and well organised in Saddam's Iraq. 'We must have justice,' Abu Dan stressed, 'or there can be no rest. Why should the Yugoslavs have justice and we don't?' It was a fair point and for me, as somebody who had taken part in the hunt for Persons Indicted for War Crimes in the former Yugoslavia, none of the indictments I had seen there came close to the horrors Abu Dan and Dr Kamal had described.

It was my last day in Baghdad and I needed to arrange my trip home. After leaving the Faily Kurds I tried to get a lift to the airport with a security detail. I had been having difficulty getting through to anyone on my satellite telephone. When I did get through there was a major problem. The situation was so tense that the PSDs were not going out. It was at times like this you realised that Baghdad, indeed Iraq, was really a series of islands where the coalition forces and the new Iraqi authorities held sway behind blastproof barriers and sentry towers. The rest is the sea, and *here be monsters*. The simple reality is that the insurgents hold sway outside the compounds and travel in their ocean is hazardous. I was stuck. I had no escort to deliver me to the airport. I turned to the Faily Kurds to see if they could smuggle me to safety. Dr Kamal immediately agreed. 'You will have it,' he said. I insisted I should pay but he flatly refused to take any money. 'To us it would be an insult,' he explained. I then changed tack. The money, I explained, would be from the *Mail on Sunday*, a large paper, and they would not expect the Faily Kurds to carry one of their people around for free. He relented and agreed that the driver Mohammed could accept some money but the Faily Kurds, as a group, could not. I gave Dr Kamal $200 and he passed it to Mohammed, who understandably looked pleased but nervous. I realised that this was no milk run. We would be taking a serious risk. If I was discovered I would be beheaded after being 'exploited' by the insurgents and probably tortured. Mohammed would be killed on the spot. He was a very courageous young man. I could see he would have preferred not to do the run, money or not. But unwittingly I had put the noble Faily Kurds in an impossible situation. Having been asked for help, they would never refuse. But they were more aware of the risk than I could ever be. They lived with it every day. With Mohammed's help I once more donned my disguise. Shemagh wrapped tightly around my head, I put on sunglasses to cover my face totally. 'Keep them down,' motioned Mohammed at my white hands.

As I walked to the car Specialist Kirk, back at his guardpost at the exit of the compound, called over, 'You still don't look like one of them!'

This time I called back. 'Well, I am one of them.'

At the gates the guards laughed at my appearance then joined in adjusting my dress. 'Now,' they announced as the stepped back, 'you Iraqi.' Mohammed loaded his pistol.

The drive to the airport was about as dangerous a thing as I have done for a while. We left the compound and headed for the bridge over the Tigris towards the Green Zone, but to our horror a barricade blocked the road and we had to pull up. Men suddenly emerged from houses to our left and right and then the car was shunted from behind by an Opel Senator estate with five or more men in it. I looked at Mohammed. We were in deep shit. I realised that as there were no guns in evidence the men were probably opportunists, but they had unwittingly struck gold because I would be worth thousands of dollars as a hostage. They were bound to see through my disguise – which was more than I could do as my sunglasses were steaming up under my scarf. Then the car shot forward and just as suddenly reversed in a smooth curve. Slamming it back into first gear, Mohammed sped off, sending the men scurrying left and right like chickens in a farmyard as I was pressed back into my seat by the acceleration. I caught sight of two or three startled faces looking down at me as we drove past. We swerved onto the road and then off into a back street. Swearing and praying intermittently, Mohammed deftly executed another J-turn when we found that road barred as well. Eventually we found ourselves in heavy traffic in central Baghdad among ancient taxis, battered lorries and street hawkers walking among the traffic at significant risk of being knocked down. Weaving in and out, to a cacophony of car horns, we made our way towards the bridge. It was a high-risk strategy. I had been told that the insurgents were setting up road checks in the back streets dressed in police uniform and wearing balaclavas – which was not in itself unusual. If we hit one of these, with only a single 9mm Browning Hi Power between us, we were in big trouble. But before long we were passing over the bridge and joining the queue into the Green Zone and safety.

As we rolled up to the Iraqi Army post the guard smiled and pointed at me: 'You Iraqi.' He laughed and his mates darted over to join in. I laughed too, the laughter of a much-relieved madman. The GIs at their checkpoint simply stared in disbelief as I flashed my badge and we rolled into the Green Zone.

After passing through the Green Zone we emerged once more out into the 'ocean' and the road to the airport, the road that Jonny had warned was so dangerous. I reclined my seat right back and wrapped my shemagh more closely around my head as Mohammed inserted a tape of noisy Arab music into the tape deck. I saw little of that part of the journey, except when we slowed down behind a convoy of Humvees. In our small red Peugeot we were a very suspicious item and I knew the GIs would reduce us to wreckage at the least wrong move. The Hummers turned off and we sped once more towards the airport. Finally the car halted and a man with blue eyes and a ginger moustache looked down into the car at me. I sat up and removed my scarf.

'Colonel Collins?' he said in disbelief. As fate would have it he was ex-1st battalion Royal Irish Rangers and ex-2 Para, a County Kerry man now working in a private company that had the contract to guard the airport. 'I'll not even ask what the fock you are up to.' He laughed. 'I wish you luck.'

His colleague was an ex-Indian Army Gurkha. 'Which regiment?' I enquired.

'8th Gurkhas.'

'Simoor Rifles?' I ventured.

His face lit up. 'How do you know?'

'Did you serve in Sierra Leone?' I asked. He did. 'That's how I know.'

Mohammed and I parted at the Baghdad International Terminal. 'Goodbye, Naqeed. Don't come back soon,' he called, waving. I can't blame him, it was quite a trip.

Back in Amman the talk in the souks and coffee shops was optimistic. I was curious to gauge how the Jordanians felt about the situation in Iraq and the war in general. The Jordanians share the same origins as the Iraqis after the Ottoman Empire and are their most sympathetic neighbour. I asked about the election and the likelihood that there would be a low turnout of Sunnis because of intimidation. Strangely they were not so concerned about the possibility of a Shia-majority parliament. 'We have 75 per cent of this country Palestinian. It is no problem,' one man said. 'People just want to live, that is all. Not all Iraqis are Islamic. Not all Muslims are Shia. Not all Shia are religious. Iraq is a strong country and her people are good at heart. It will be fine.'

Overall the Jordanians were optimistic about the future and took a more positive view of Iraq than I had encountered hitherto. Later, in the souk I spoke to a young Palestinian. He was less optimistic but more focused on the fate of his own people. I told him what the Jordanians had said. 'They will say whatever their king says,' he explained. 'They do not think for themselves here.' I'm not certain that is true. The number of Iraqis I met in Jordan and the evidence of good will, including large numbers of election posters urging Iraqis to vote in the January elections, told me of the optimism of those who had a clear view of the realities and were close enough to judge.

Two thoughts were foremost in my mind as I finally left for London. First that among the very many good reasons for liberating Iraq, lifting the twenty-five-year death sentence on people like Abu Dan was one of the most important. Secondly, the international view of what was needed and what was actually happening were still at odds. The UN's main contribution to the whole election was to insist on one in three of the candidates being women. Iraq was secular under Saddam and women had played a full part in the administration, but even so all the parties were finding it hard to recruit enough female candidates. Such a progressive idea was all very well in New York, and I have no issue with it in principle, but I did leave Iraq feeling that they had a way to go yet before they were ready for the PC lobby. Equal citizens' rights for all and an end to racism, as well as full citizenship for an oppressed people within Iraq who are as many as the population of Ireland – the Faily Kurds – should ideally be addressed first.

Back in the UK I reflected on the possible effects on the election of two unfortunately timed events. A court martial for alleged war crimes by a group of men from the Fusiliers battle group, part of 7 Brigade in the invasion, was now under way in Germany, and the inquest into the loss of the six RMP in Al Majarr al Kabir was published, to the anguish of the families. I realised that timing was just another cock-up. I knew that there was not enough political acumen within the British High Command to understand that, having delayed the trials and inquiries for so long (fifteen months in the case of the Fusiliers), it would have been sensible to delay for another month in order to let the elections happen. I was equally aware that in the Middle East people expected that sort of thing when you encountered armies. They certainly expected it of their own armies, though they were understandably disappointed by the British and US Armies, whose Abu Ghraib trials had just ended. So overall no real lasting harm was done by this unhappy coincidence.

There were rays of light too. To my delight I discovered Abu Hatim was standing as a candidate in Al Amarah. Now married at the age of forty-six and with a new son he was, for me, representative of the brave new Iraq. I felt that despite the chaos there was hope of a better future. It also appeared that the regular GIs and Marines from the US military had been transformed. Individual initiative was abroad for the first time in many years and they were learning quickly. I could see that an already competent military had attained new heights of self-confidence and ability. The British Army, still doing an excellent job on minimal resources, was sadly going the other way and looking to me like a dying star. The final cut, the destruction of the regimental system for financial savings, coupled with the rudderless self-destruction of the inept investigations that were still covering the military body like a plague of sores, pointed to a failure of leadership and a need for a revolution in the command structure of the British Army.

Those whom I had interviewed in Iraq, from the interim administration to the man in the street, agreed there had been some terrible mistakes made in the immediate aftermath of the war. Amongst the most serious were not appreciating what effect the war would have internally in Iraq and failing to see the danger of the Ba'athist regime's final challenge, the well-planned insurgency. The disbandment of the Iraqi Army and the police coupled with the inability to understand and harness the old regime's various security apparatuses compounded the mistake. The failure to provide power and light and commerce coupled with some heavyhandedness allowed the insurgency to flourish.

In our own country the military's failure to look after its people, swinging budgetary cuts and inept media handling exacerbated by incoherent outbursts and excessive commitments had reduced internal morale in the armed forces to rubble and had harmed the nation's perception of the effectiveness of our defences. The political controversy over the war itself was one that the Prime Minister would be lucky to survive politically. But it had also harmed our alliances and world standing.

Knowing both the British Army's plight and Iraq so well, I think that both need to get a lot worse before they get better. For both the key is competent, uncompromising leadership to guide them out of this slough of despond. I will watch both with great sympathy and my very best hopes for better days to come.

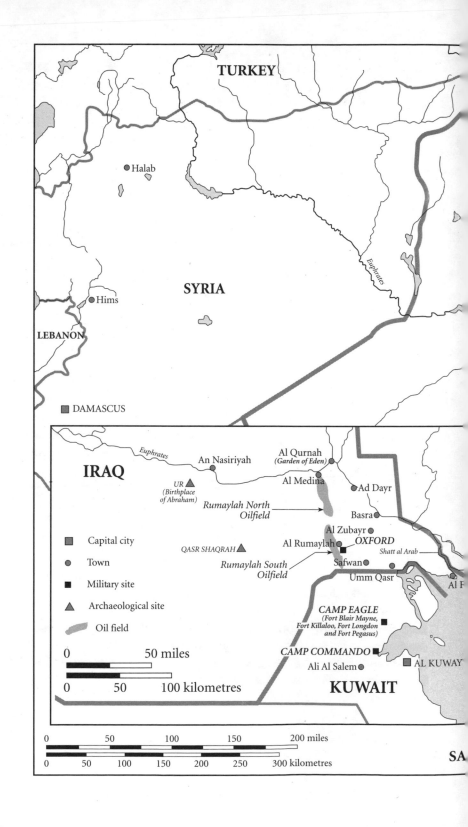

TURKEY

● Halab

SYRIA

● Hims

LEBANON

■ DAMASCUS

*Euphrates*

IRAQ

*Euphrates*

● An Nasiriyah

Al Qurnah
*(Garden of Eden)* ●

UR ▲
*(Birthplace
of Abraham)*

Al Medina ●

● Ad Dayr

*Rumaylah North
Oilfield*

Basra ●

Al Zubayr ●

QASR SHAQRAH ▲

Al Rumaylah ● *OXFORD* ■

*Shatt al Arab*

*Rumaylah South
Oilfield*

Safwan ●

Umm Qasr ●

Al F

■ Capital city

● Town

■ Military site

▲ Archaeological site

Oil field

*CAMP EAGLE
(Fort Blair Mayne,
Fort Killaloo, Fort Longdon
and Fort Pegasus)* ■

0          50 miles

0      50      100 kilometres

*CAMP COMMANDO* ■

Ali Al Salem ●

■ AL KUWAY

KUWAIT

0      50      100      150      200 miles

0    50   100   150   200   250   300 kilometres

SA

# GLOSSARY

| | |
|---|---|
| 1 Para | 1st Battalion of the Parachute Regiment |
| 1 R Irish | 1st Battalion the Royal Irish Regiment |
| ANGLICO | Air Naval Gun Fire Coordinators |
| ATMP | All Terrain Mobility Platform |
| ATO | Ammunition Technical Officer |
| Battalion | A unit of infantry usually around 700 men |
| BC | Battery Commander |
| Brigade | Three or more battalions |
| C-130 | A four-engined heavy-lift aircraft sometimes known as a Hercules |
| CDS | Chief of the Defence Staff |
| CDT | Compulsory Drugs Testing |
| CIMIC | Civil Military Cooperation |
| CMC | Crisis Management Centre |
| COBRA | Cabinet Office Briefing Room |
| Comms Camel | A hard-topped Land Rover with an array of radios |
| CS | Combat Support |
| CSS | Combat Service Support |
| CSM | Company Sergeant Major |
| DCCA | Director of Corporate Communications Army |
| DFID | Department for International Development |
| Division | Three brigades |
| DShK | 12.7mm heavy machine gun |
| DSO | Distinguished Service Order |

| | |
|---|---|
| ECM | Electromagnetic Countermeasures |
| ECOMOG | Economic Community of West African States Ceasefire Monitoring Group |
| EO | Executive Outcomes |
| FTX | Field Training Exercise |
| GCHQ | General Communications Headquarters |
| GOC | General Officer Commanding |
| GOSP | Gas/oil Separation Plants |
| GPMG | General Purpose Machine Gun |
| HCR | Household Cavalry Regiment |
| HF | High Frequency (radio type) |
| HLS | Helicopter Landing Site |
| Kukri | A Gurkha knife usually around 12" long with a curved blade |
| LAW | Light Anti-armour Weapon |
| MC | Military Cross |
| MILAN | 115mm wire-guided, semi-automatic, command-to-line-of-sight, anti-tank rocket system |
| MO | Method of Operation/Medical Officer |
| MOD | Ministry of Defence |
| MRE | Meal Ready to Eat |
| NCO | Non-commissioned Officer |
| OC | Officer Commanding |
| PIFWC | Person Indicted for War Crimes |
| POW | Prisoner of War |
| PSD | Private Security Detail |
| PUK | A Kurdish separatist organisation |
| QM | Quartermaster |
| RCT | Regimental Combat Team |
| REME | Royal Electrical & Mechanical Engineers |
| RMP | Royal Military Police |
| Royal Irish Rangers | Irish Territorial Army regiment |
| RPG | Rocket-propelled Grenade |
| RSM | Regimental Sergeant Major |
| RUC | Royal Ulster Constabulary |
| RUF | Revolutionary United Front |
| SA 80 | A British 5.56mm rifle |
| SAW | Squad Automatic Weapon |
| SCIRI | Supreme Council for the Islamic Revolution in Iraq |

| | |
|---|---|
| SF | Special Forces (SAS or Special Boat Service [SBS]) |
| SIB | Special Investigation Branch of the RMP |
| SIS | Secret Intelligence Service |
| SLA | Sierra Leonean Army |
| SSO | Special Security Organisation (Iraqi) |
| SSO | State Security Organisation |
| T55 | Soviet-era medium tank with a rifled 100mm gun |
| TA | Territorial Army |
| TALO | Tactical Landing Operation |
| TAOR | Tactical Area of Responsibility |
| TEL | Transporter-Erector-Launcher |
| TLT | Tactical Leadership Training |
| Tokarev | A Soviet semi-automatic pistol |
| UDR | Ulster Defence Regiment |
| UNAMSIL | United Nations Mission in Sierra Leone |
| USAF | United States Air Force |
| UVF | Ulster Volunteer Force |
| VC | Victoria Cross |
| VHF | Very High Frequency (radio type) |
| WMD | Weapons of Mass Destruction |
| WMIK | Weapons Mount Installation Kit |
| WSB | West Side Boys |

Some of the Iraqis who feature in this book include:

Oxford
Colonel Atiff – commander of the Iraqi Oil protection group
Lieutenant Colonel Kasim – staff officer of the Iraqi 148th Brigade
Lieutenant Colonel Rait – commander of an Iraqi battalion captured in Oxford

Al Rumaylah
Abu Bashir – counsellor, advisor and friend
Abu Rifat – wise town elder and friend
Ahmed – a young oil engineer and advisor
Ayoub Younis Nasser (aka Abu Nawfel) – Ba'athist school headmaster, arrested in connection with attempted murders
Jamil – Ba'athist foot soldier arrested in connection with attempted murders

Jari – a senior Ba'athist
Mawood Jaber – medical student, advisor and friend
Nawfel Nasser – son of Ayoub
Sabbah – Jari's wife
Tariq – town executioner and head of the Ba'athist resistance in Al Rumaylah

Al Medina
Daoud – a young man with much potential
Tariq – a Ba'athist leader

Al Alamarah
Abu Hatim – 'Prince of the Marshes' ally and leader of his people
Mosun Ali – caretaker at the British cemetery
Sa'id al Jaber – senior Muslim cleric
Sheikh Ishmail – tribal leader
Sheikh Mohammed al Badi – cleric and anti-Ba'athist
Yassim Aboud Yassim – doctor
Yasim – assistant to Abu Hatim

Baghdad
Achmed – trusted bodyguard
Dr Kamal Field al-Basri – friend, advisor and Economic Advisor to the Iraqi Interim Administration
Mohammed – trusted bodyguard
Thair Feely (aka Abu Dan) – politician and leader of the Faily Kurds

# APPENDIX

## Structure of
## 1 (UK) Armoured Division

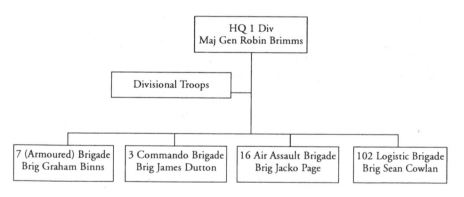

HQ 1 Div
Maj Gen Robin Brimms

Divisional Troops

7 (Armoured) Brigade
Brig Graham Binns

3 Commando Brigade
Brig James Dutton

16 Air Assault Brigade
Brig Jacko Page

102 Logistic Brigade
Brig Sean Cowlan

# 16 Air Assault Brigade

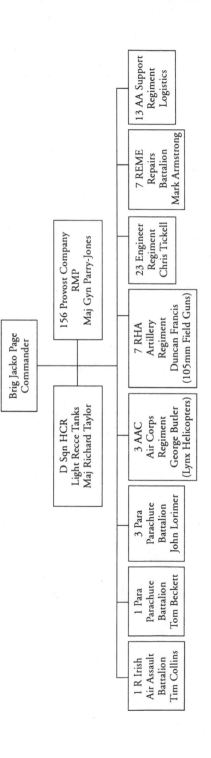

**Brig Jacko Page**
Commander

**156 Provost Company**
RMP
Maj Gyn Parry-Jones

**D Sqn HCR**
Light Recce Tanks
Maj Richard Taylor

**1 R Irish**
Air Assault
Battalion
Tim Collins

**1 Para**
Parachute
Battalion
Tom Beckett

**3 Para**
Parachute
Battalion
John Lorimer

**3 AAC**
Air Corps
Regiment
George Butler
(Lynx Helicopters)

**7 RHA**
Artillery
Regiment
Duncan Francis
(105mm Field Guns)

**23 Engineer**
Regiment
Chris Tickell

**7 REME**
Repairs
Battalion
Mark Armstrong

**13 AA Support**
Regiment
Logistics

# 1 Royal Irish (1,225 strong Battlegroup)

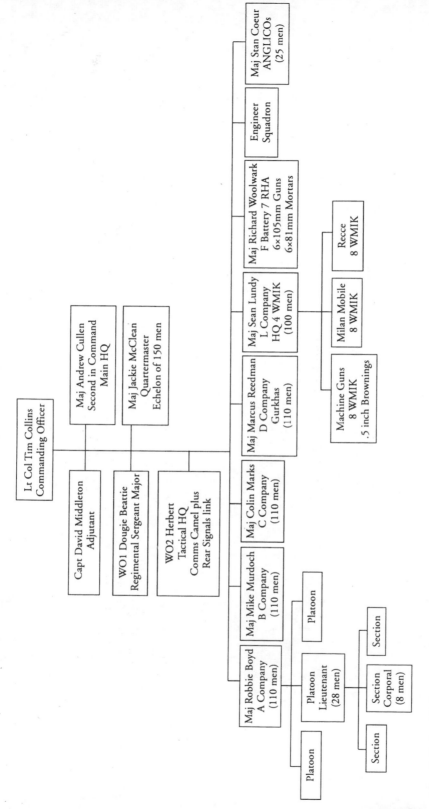

Lt Col Tim Collins
Commanding Officer

Maj Andrew Cullen
Second in Command
Main HQ

Maj Jackie McClean
Quartermaster
Echelon of 150 men

Capt David Middleton
Adjutant

WO1 Dougie Beattie
Regimental Sergeant Major

WO2 Herbert
Tactical HQ
Comms Camel plus
Rear Signals link

Maj Robbie Boyd
A Company
(110 men)

Maj Mike Murdoch
B Company
(110 men)

Maj Colin Marks
C Company
(110 men)

Maj Marcus Reedman
D Company
Gurkhas
(110 men)

Maj Sean Lundy
L Company
HQ 4 WMIK
(100 men)

Maj Richard Woolwark
F Battery 7 RHA
6×105mm Guns
6×81mm Mortars

Engineer
Squadron

Maj Stan Coeur
ANGLICOs
(25 men)

Platoon

Platoon

Platoon
Lieutenant
(28 men)

Section

Section
Corporal
(8 men)

Section

Machine Guns
8 WMIK
.5 inch Brownings

Milan Mobile
8 WMIK

Recce
8 WMIK

Note: A, B, C and D Company each have three platoons with three sections in each.

# INDEX

Figures following the letter 'n' after a page reference relate to the footnotes

recruitment in Ireland 35–7
self-confidence 24, 29
sniping 32–4
Territorial Army reserves 100, 291–2
First Gulf War 121, 192
Footer, Simon 29
Forlong, James 358n132
Fort Blair Mayne 128, 309–12
Fort Campbell 83–4
Fort Killalo 128
Fort Longdon 128
Fort Pegasus 128
Franks, Tommy 92, 263

Gardiner, Alex 149–51, 180, 237–8, 254, 257
Garvaghy Road 44n19
gas-oil separation plants 117–18
Gberi Bana 15–16
George Cross, Chris Finney 223–5
Gibraltar 85
Gilligan, Andrew 358n131
Girdwood incidents 57–65
glossary 386–9
Good Friday Agreement 52
Gorazde 334
Gornji Vakuf 32
Gracey, Harold 351
Grattan, Henry 47
Green Goddess 85–6, 89
Green Zone 370–1
Green, Jeremy 337–40, 342–3
Gurkha Security Guards 5–6
Guthrie, Sir Charles 9

Hammar Bridge 155, 164, 169, 190, 208
Hanna, William 52
'Harmony Guidelines' 348
Harrison, Andy 7, 9
Hartigan, Mark 308
Hassan, Maragret 363
Heal, Sid 113
Heaney, Stewart 54
hearts and minds operations
East Tyrone 75–6
Sierra Leone 6

Herbert, 'Herby' 127, 178, 189, 230, 241, 244
hexamine solid fuel 166
'Highway of Death' 111
Holy Cross and girls' school 53, 58, 65, 262
Hoon, Geoff 9, 88–9, 114
Hughes, Francis 48
Hussein, Saddam
seizure of power 120–1
singular power 145
stories about 376

Indian Army Grenadiers 9
Ingram, Adam 326
Inniskilling Fusiliers 24–5
inoculations 96–7
**Iraq**
background to state 120
ethnic make-up 122
future 364–5
Iran war 121
people 121–2
post-war 378–85
religious make-up 122
**Iraq war**
demilitarised zone 112
displaced persons 220
effective end of war 263
fighting nears end 249
four fronts 115–17
initial planning 91–5
insurgency warnings 215
international divide 105, 115
invasion plans 127–9
journalists 124–5
liberation emphasis 130–3
looting and destruction 271–2
motivation same on both sides 356
movement to Kuwait 103–5
poor kit 97
possible reasons for 359–60
preparations in Kuwait 107–35
reviewed in retrospect 358–65
sandstorm 169
smell 143